The Risk of Interpretation

On Being Faithful to the Christian Tradition in a Non-Christian Age

Claude Geffré

Translated by David Smith

PAULIST PRESS
New York / Mahwah

Thanks to Professor William Loewe for his contribution on the footnotes.

Geffré, Claude
    The risk of interpretation.

    Translation of: Le christianisme au risque de l' interprétation.
    Bibliography: p.
    1. Theology—Methodology.   2. Hermeneutics—Religious aspects—Christianity.   3. Theology—20th century.   I. Title
BR118.G4213   1986   230'.01   86-25464
ISBN 0-8091-2861-6 (pbk.)

Published by Paulist Press
997 Macarthur Boulevard
Mahwah, New Jersey 07430

Printed and bound in the United States of America

CONTENTS

INTRODUCTION 1

Part I
THEOLOGY AS HERMENEUTICS

I. FROM KNOWLEDGE TO INTERPRETATION 11
  1. The Reasons for the Present Change in Theology 11
  2. The Consequences for Theological Practice of the
     Hermeneutical Orientation of Theology 15

II. HERMENEUTICS ON TRIAL. 21
  1. The Crisis in Hermeneutics 23
  2. The Present Change of Emphasis in Hermeneutics. 32
  3. The Theological Implications of the Present Change
     in Hermeneutics. 39
  Conclusion 45

III. DOGMATICS OR HERMENEUTICS?. 46
  1. The Movement from the Dogmatic to the
     Hermeneutical Model 47
  2. The Historical and Theological Aspects of the
     Disappearance of the Dogmatic Model 51
  3. The Truth of Theology as an Interpretative Language. 59

IV. THE THEOLOGIAN'S HERMENEUTICAL FREEDOM 65
  1. The Special Function of Theology 66
  2. The Meaning of a Rule of Faith in the Church 69

iii

Part II
THE INTERPRETATIVE TESTIMONY TO FAITH

V. THE RESURRECTION OF CHRIST AS AN
   INTERPRETATIVE TESTIMONY.........................79
   1. At the Origin of the Word "Witness"....................80
   2. Experience and Language in the Testimony of the
      Resurrection 84
   3. The Testimony of Believers Today......................91

VI. THE ATHEISTIC HERMENEUTICS OF THE TITLE
    "THE SON OF MAN" IN ERNST BLOCH 95
    1. The Investing of Yahweh by Jesus or the Exodus Theme 97
    2. The Coming of the Kingdom of God as an Earthly
       Kingdom 100
    3. The Dialectical Overthrowing of the Cultic Title
       "The Son of God" by the Eschatological Title
       "The Son of Man".....................................104
    4. The Value of Exegesis of the Title "The Son of Man"
       According to Bloch...................................106
    Conclusion 108

VII. FROM THE GOD OF THEISM TO THE CRUCIFIED
     GOD 111
     1. The Situation of the Discourse About God Today 112
     2. In Search of the Proper Name of God 118
     3. God as Good News for Man Today......................124

VIII. "FATHER" AS THE PROPER NAME OF GOD...........129
      1. The Biblical Revelation of God the Father 130
      2. From Attribution to Invocation.........................133
      3. God the Father or the "Differentiated Life" of God 135
      Conclusion 138

IX. THE BREAKDOWN OF HISTORY AND THE LORDSHIP
    OF CHRIST...140
    1. The Present Context of a Christian Reflection About
       History..140
    2. The Oneness of Christ and the Oneness of History 147
    Conclusion 154

Contents   v

Part III
THE PRACTICE OF CHRISTIANS REINTERPRETS CHRISTIANITY

X.   THE TESTIMONY OF FAITH IN A NON-CHRISTIAN
     CULTURE 159
     1. A Faith Subjected to Critical Theory 160
     2. The Encounter Between Christianity and the Diversity
        of Cultures 167
     3. The Conditions of a Prophetic Testimony 173

XI. THE IDEOLOGICAL FUNCTION OF
     SECULARIZATION 181
     1. The Vocabulary of Secularization and the Function
        of Ideology 182
     2. Secularization as the Historical Product of Christian
        Faith 186
     3. The Ideological Function of Secularization 193
     4. Secularization and the Future of Christianity 197

XII. CHRISTIANITY AS A WAY 201
     1. Christianity as the Religion of the Exodus 202
     2. Christ as the Way and the Imitation of Christ 206
     3. Christianity as Orthopraxis 212
     Conclusion 214

XIII. TOWARD A CHRISTIAN INTERPRETATION OF HUMAN
     RIGHTS 216
     1. An Ambiguous History 217
     2. The Charter of Human Rights and Biblical Revelation 224

XIV. REINTERPRETING THE CHURCH'S MISSION 231
     1. The Vocabulary of Mission and Evangelization 231
     2. Mission as the Vocation of the Whole Church 233
     3. Inculturation as a Demand of Evangelization 236
     4. The Evangelization of the Poor as the Criterion of
        Authenticity of the Church's Mission 242
     5. Promoting Human Rights as the Demand Made
        by the Gospel 245
     Conclusion 248

Epilogue. THE SILENCE AND PROMISES OF FRENCH
     THEOLOGY 250

Contents

1. French Theology Yesterday and Today 251
2. Contemporary Orientations in French Theology 260

ABBREVIATIONS 269
NOTES 270
BIBLIOGRAPHICAL NOTE 297

INTRODUCTION

> What interests me is the "interpretation," in that it ddves the
> word a life that goes beyond the time and the place at which it
> was spoken or written. "Interpretative" language gathers all
> these shades of meaning together in itself.
>
> George Steiner (*Après Babel*, p. 27)

About twelve years ago, when my book *Un nouvel âge de la théologie*
appeared, one of my critics concluded his review by renaming it "A New
Age of Apologetics." This struck me as ironical, since I had taken pains to
show how certain forms of apologetics had reached a dead-end either because they were too firmly rooted in rational arguments that lay outside
the sphere of faith or because they followed an existential approach based
on an analysis of the implications of human subjectivity. After all, I really
have nothing against apologetics, and in the course of its long history
Christian theology has never ceased to defend itself. But why should the
theologian be suspected of apologetics in the pejorative sense of the word
every time he is only trying to show how pertinent the Christian mystery
is to modern man in his attempts to understand and live in the world? If
he is to avoid making a caricature of his theological work, he should perhaps measure the distance separating apologetics in the classical sense of
the term from fundamental theology, which I defined in my book as "hermeneutics of the Word of God and human existence."

Ten years later, I am still unashamedly continuing in this direction.
The first request I must make of the reader is that he should be alert to
the title that I have given to this collection of essays in theological hermeneutics: *The Risk of Interpretation*. The word "risk" is ambivalent. In
speaking of the risk of interpretation, the reader should not forget that I
am also speaking of the risk of distortion and error. In the case of Christianity, there is an even greater risk—that of faith itself. My intention in
this book is to enable the reader to have a better understanding of faith—
to recognize that faith is not faithful to its own thrust and to what is given

1

to it to believe unless it leads to a creative interpretation of Christianity. The risk of simply handing on a dead past because of a failure to be both bold and lucid is no less serious than that of error.

I am not unaware of the fact that hermeneutics have been on trial in recent years, especially in the French cultural context (see Chapter II). I do not want to make hermeneutics the Trojan horse of theology which will overturn all the obstacles in the path of theological understanding, but I would insist that theology is from beginning to end a hermeneutical task. It is not just a question of affirming that, since the beginning, the Church's theologians have never ceased to reinterpret the Old Testament in the light of the New and that they have never failed to reinterpret the Christian message in the light of the successive changes that have taken place in society and culture. (Henri de Lubac's historical works should convince us of that!) No, it is also a question of taking hermeneutics seriously as an intrinsic aspect of contemporary knowledge and of drawing every possible conclusion from it for theology as an understanding of faith.

Since the emergence in the nineteenth century of a new "historical consciousness," we have had a better appreciation of the fact that every act of knowledge must be an act of interpretation. We are also, thanks to the analytical method and the criticism of ideologies, aware of the illusions and prejudices inherent in each act of knowledge that claims to be objective. It is true to say that we nowadays accept the definition of scientific knowledge as interpretative knowledge and agree that the classical distinction made, for example, by Dilthey, between the natural sciences in the perspective of explanation and the human sciences in that of understanding is no longer so relevant. This means that the argument, conducted in the name of structuralism against hermeneutics as a method of reading texts and made on the pretext that it is congenitally imprisoned in a metaphysical understanding of the relationship between the sign and the signified, now seems to me to be of minor importance in view of what is at stake in the new paradigm that theology seen as hermeneutics represents. What is more, the possibility that Scripture can be read structurally as Christian tradition would also seem to confirm the firmly hermeneutical destiny of contemporary theology.

Together with such theologians as Edward Schillebeeckx and David Tracy, who are also friends and colleagues, I have come to see the present task of theology more and more as a critical and mutual correlation between the interpretation of the Christian tradition and that of our contemporary human experience.[1] However diverse the subjects that I discuss in the present work may be, I have always presupposed this hermeneutical method, even though I have not made it explicit in every case.

I cannot reread the whole of Christian tradition by abstracting from what I would call man's contemporary states of consciousness, nor can I interpret our present world of experience with all its ambiguity without being inhabited by the world of Christian experience. We belong to a way of speaking far more than we possess it, and in the same way we belong to history far more than we master it. How can the theologian decode contemporary human experience unless he is informed by the conscious or unconscious effects of centuries of the Judaeo-Christian tradition?

This process of mutual interaction, in which I am unable to dissociate my interpretation of traditional texts from my present experience, is bound to lead to the risk of a creative interpretation of the Christian message. I am aware that the misuse of the word "creative" can hide our powerlessness to explore the riches of the past. But when I speak of creative interpretation, I am not thinking of the misuse of an interpretation claiming to come from nothing. I am thinking more of a resumption without repetition of the Christian message, which is only faithful to itself insofar as it produces new historical figures in the form of writings or original practices. If we are to recognize the creative character of every interpretation, we have to demystify the illusion of a meaning that is believed to be concealed behind every text (in the mind of its author, in the reconstitution of its socio-historical context or in its initial reception) or even within the text itself. We should rather look for the meaning in that "forward point" that is to be found where the sphere of the text and that of our own understanding meet.

This interaction between the text and its interpreter takes us back to the classical image of hermeneutics that began with Gadamer—the image of conversation. Even though Gadamer opposed the claim made during the Enlightenment that pure objectivity could be achieved, and insisted on the importance of the tradition within which every interpreter was included, the conversation model can still give rise to the illusion of translucence between the text and its interpreter. That hermeneutical ideal has now to be replaced by a hermeneutic of suspicion that can be critically questioned with regard to the conscious or unconscious presuppositions both of our pre-understanding and of the conditions under which the text that we have to interpret was produced. In the case of the conversation model, it is above all characteristic of the analytical method that it reveals the latent, inhibited and paradoxical meanings of the discourse that come between the analyzed and the analyst. And what is certainly true of every interpersonal relationship is even more true of social communication. I have suggested that theological hermeneutics are a rereading of earlier texts with a better understanding of the Christian identity in mind. In this task, the need for an ascetic lucidity cannot be overlooked. All the contemporary critical theories insist on that, whether they are based on psy-

choanalysis, the Marxist criticism of ideology or the genealogical method
in its various forms, following either Nietzsche or Michel Foucault. (See
Chapter III.)

It is worth adding at this juncture that, while agreeing with Gadamer
that the whole process of interpretation is followed with understanding in
mind, I also recognize the great merit of Paul Ricoeur's emphasis on the
importance of the text, its objective structure, its internal organization and
the conditions under which it was produced. A correct interpretation will
result from an interaction with the interpreter's world of understanding,
but this will always take place in the projection of the matter of the text
and subject to explanatory procedures of the most rigorous kind based on
literary or structural analysis. That is why, far from concluding that hermeneutics have reached a dead-end as an exercise in understanding, it is
right to affirm that explanation has become the true path of understanding.
(See Chapter II for the change of emphasis in hermeneutics under the im-
petus of structuralism.) The theologian who practices hermeneutics would
undoubtedly benefit by accepting the asceticism that results from the objectivity of the text. Rightly anxious to stress the contemporary value of
the Christian message for the world of today, he is often tempted, we
know, to take "messages" from his text when in fact the text does not permit it.

These prefatory remarks must suffice to reassure those who may object to my insistence on the value of hermeneutics because, in my plea for
risking a creative interpretation, I am holding the Church's tradition
cheap. On the contrary, it is rather because we are preceded by a tradition
that is resistant to us that we shall never come to the end of our search for
new meanings in it and our attempts to distinguish what is accidental from
what is essential and unique. Creativity and lucidity are in no way opposed
to each other. On the contrary, they are the best of allies in the complex
process of reinterpreting Christianity. It is only the historical distance that
allows us to mark off successive layers that may cover the original meaning
of the message to be handed on. It is also only a methodical suspicion that
can help us to discern the relationship between the sphere of the imagination that is peculiar to faith and the infantile sickness of desire or a secret
will to dominate. The great spiritual writers were always prompt to discern
the spirits!

I do not deny that a need to find a creative interpretation exposes us
to the risk of a wrong interpretation. But is it also true that an insistence
on lucidity also exposes us to the risk of reductionism? I am very familiar
with this kind of aporia. How are we to know whether what is available to
be believed at one period has not already become the norm of what has to
be believed? It is obviously more reassuring to rely on the common good

shared by all believers and to appeal to the "scandal of the weak." Nonetheless, it is clear from the history of Christian thought that fear is always a bad counselor and a refusal to look the indisputable results of criticism in the face is a sure way to a bitter future.

If we are convinced of the eternal youth of the Gospel, why should we pretend not to know about contemporary man's new states of consciousness? Further on in this book (Chapter X), I shall have something to say about the historical situation of believing and the fact that it simply does not allow us to retain a naive faith. Or should we rather speak of the "second naiveté" of a faith that has passed the test of criticism? And, in the circle of "believing" and "understanding" that continues to revolve, I am personally convinced that a critical lucidity does not in any way compromise the God-orientated spontaneity of faith. What is more, I think that I am being quite faithful in this conviction to the man who taught me how to read Thomas Aquinas—Marie-Dominique Chenu. Faith, he told me again and again, does not do away with the order of the human spirit.

I have no need to comment at length on the plan of the present work. It did not take me long to work it out, and I hope that it will at once be clear to all my readers. Part I is more methodological and is based on fundamental theology or what is now known as theological epistemology. I have tried to resituate the hermeneutical process of theology historically and to draw the consequences of this in order to redistribute the theological task. For more than a century now, the hermeneutical problem has arisen again and again, each time in different terms. The responsible theologian has to go beyond the successive modes of French structuralism and cannot remain in blissful ignorance of the fact that a profound change of emphasis has been brought about in modern hermeneutics by new methods of reading texts. These were initially very disturbing, but they have had beneficial effects. In Chapter III I have tried to describe the hermeneutical model of theological writing and to show how it differs from the classical dogmatic model of theology. I even dare to hope that it will be clear that, by putting a certain type of dogmatic theology on trial, I am not disputing the rights and the lasting validity of dogmatic theology as such. In the final chapter of Part I (Chapter IV), I discuss the basic vocation of the theologian, which is, I believe, to "mediate" between the teaching of the magisterium and the living experience of the Christian people.

A common criticism of contemporary thought is that it is always getting bogged down in methodological debates about preliminaries, but this danger of formalism is, of course, ever present in theology as a whole. Theology, however, is concerned from beginning to end with the matter of the text or with the world to which we are sent back by the Judaeo-Christian

Scriptures, that is, by the astonishing breaking into man's life of the gratuitous love of God. That is why I have not hesitated to bring together in
Part II of this book a number of easier essays concerned with all the most
fundamental realities of the Christian revelation. From the earliest days of
Church's life, the language of faith has always been an interpretative language. In Chapter V, the first chapter of Part II, I demonstrate this fact in
relation to what constitutes the heart of the apostolic preaching, that is,
the resurrection of Christ. In Chapter VI, I discuss the work of Ernst Bloch
in the field of contemporary atheistic hermeneutics of Christianity. In contrast with this, I go on in Chapters VII and VIII to ask a number of questions about the conditions governing a reinterpretation of the discourse on
the God of Jesus which will take seriously the fundamental aporias of traditional theism in the contemporary order of the spirit. Finally, our acute
consciousness of the lack of a need for God in a history handed over to itself
impels me to reinterpret in new terms the meaning of the Lordship of
Christ over history. In that chapter, I point to a few landmarks among the
many tendencies in the theology of history.

Theological hermeneutics, in its anxiety to give a contemporary relevance to the Word of God, cannot rest content with the production of new
commentaries. Because he is dealing with texts that bear witness to the
active Word of God, the theologian has a special and very demanding vocation to exercise it, in other words, to suggest meaningful practices for
the Church. But that is still a considerable understatement. The practice
of Christians is a theological locus that prompts the theologian to think
when he is creatively reinterpreting the Church's two centuries of faith.
The whole of the Christian community is competent to interpret the "signs
of the times" and to enable various historical figures to live from the un-
fathomable fullness of the mystery of Christ. This competence comes from
the Spirit who is never absent from that community.

All the themes discussed in Part III of my book have to do with the
practice of the churches confronted with new historical, social and cultural
conditions. It would be true to say that we have still not drawn every possible conclusion from our examination of certain theological arguments
worked out during different ages of faith. I can say with certainty, however, that it is the practice of Christians themselves that is reinterpreting
Christianity today. That is true of the handing on of faith either in an atheistic culture or in a society with a great non-Christian religion (Chapter X).
It is also true of the non-religious attempts to reinterpret Christianity in a
secular world (Chapter XI). It is equally true of the revival of the classical
theme of the imitation of Christ in the light of our new understanding of
the relationship between orthodoxy and orthopraxis (Chapter XII). It is
even true of painful struggle undertaken both outside and inside the

Church for religious freedom (Chapter XIII). Finally, it is true of the Church's new understanding of mission in dialogue with the great non-Christian religions and in playing a part in promoting human rights (Chapter XIV). In each of these instances discussed in Part III, I have questioned Christian identity in confrontation with ethical and political or sacralizing reinterpretations of Christianity.

I have already defined the theologian's work as finding a critical correlation between the Christian tradition and contemporary human experience. In considering this very complex experience, I have always insisted on man's new "historical consciousness" and all the critical demands that accompany this. My readers ought, however, to know that taking the risk of interpreting Christianity means reinterpreting again and again the good news of salvation in the light of this counter-experience of the great and world-wide suffering of contemporary mankind. I am saying this here to forestall a criticism that my approach is hypercritically intellectual.

Most of the texts collected in this volume have been previously published elsewhere over the past ten or so years.[2] Several of them have been revised or corrected and some have even been completely rewritten. I do not hesitate to say publicly that I have often been prompted to theological reflection not only by my work of teaching theology, but also by occasional and very varied stimuli. Very few of these stimuli have been purely fortuitous. For example, after being obliged to take into account various forms of western atheism, I was led to think more and more about the co-existence of Christianity and the great non-Christian religions and about the re-emergence of neo-paganism. At the end of the second millennium, Christian thinkers have to do more than simply deal with the challenge of religious indifferentism. They have also to go beyond the alternative of theism and atheism and give their attention to the lasting phenomenon of what some have greeted as the "genius of paganism."

Part I

Theology as Hermeneutics

Chapter I

FROM KNOWLEDGE TO INTERPRETATION

My reason for choosing this title was because I wanted to describe the change that has taken place in theology during the past twenty or so years. In that time, it has ceased to be treated as constituted knowledge and has become pluralistic interpretation. To express this in another way, it has moved as a study from dogmatic theology to hermeneutical theology. I know, of course, that for many theologians the word "interpretation" has become taboo and that, if we are to speak of the change that has occurred in theology today, we must speak of a much more radical change that has been brought about by the crisis in hermeneutics. I shall, in the course of the following chapters, be examining whether the new ways of reading Scripture and the dogma of the Church have in fact rendered null and void the hermeneutical function of theology as a means of giving a contemporary interpretation to the meaning of the Christian message.

1. THE REASONS FOR THE PRESENT CHANGE IN THEOLOGY

In order to understand the change that is still taking place in theology, we must above all take into account the greater depths of meaning given to the notion of revelation and the recent history of the hermeneutical problem. I would like to begin by making three statements about revelation.[1]

(1) We are more acutely aware nowadays of the fact that the Word of God cannot be literally identified either with Scripture or with dogmatic pronouncements. Scripture and dogma both bear partial witness to the fullness of the Gospel, which belongs to the eschatological order.

(2) Revelation is not a communication from on high of knowledge that has been settled once and for all time. It points both to God's action in history and to the experience in faith of the people of God which is conveyed in an interpretative expression of that activity. To put this in a dif-

11

ferent way, what we call Scripture is already an interpretation and the response of faith also forms part of the content of revelation.

(3) Revelation only reaches its fulfillment and becomes fully significant and contemporary in the faith that receives it. That is why, as the Word of God given in a human word or in a trace of God in human history, it does not depend on a scientific method based on historical criticism. In its cognitive aspect, faith is always an interpretative knowledge that is marked by the historical conditions of a particular period. Similarly, as an interpretative discourse, theology is not just a different expression of a permanently identical content of faith that lies outside the effects of history. It is an interpretation that makes the content of faith accessible to us today.

On the basis of these three brief statements, then, we may say that we must take the historical nature of all truth, including revealed truth, and that of man himself as the interpreting subject, seriously if we are to understand theology as hermeneutics. Modern thinkers do not wish to obliterate the contingent character of truth as earlier metaphysicians tended to do. On the contrary, they would claim that historicity is above all the condition governing the restoration of meaning. Modern theologians are trying to draw every possible conclusion from this re-evaluation of historicity.

I believe therefore that, as our insight into revelation becomes more lucid, we shall recognize that theology is always an exercise in hermeneutics. In this context, I see hermeneutics as an interpretation of the contemporary meaning of the event of Jesus Christ based on the various languages of faith that it has brought into being and I would insist that none of those languages, not even that of the New Testament, should be given an absolute value in this process of interpretation. Jesus is the master of all periods of history and we have the task of re-expressing what was manifested in him in relation to our own experience of man and the world.

The change in theology brought about by this movement from knowledge to interpretation has also, as I noted at the beginning of this section, to do with the recent history of the hermeneutical problem. I do not intend to trace this history back to Dilthey and Gadamer in this chapter,[2] but will simply point to two aspects of the question that are directly concerned with the present changes in theology. These are, first, the protest against historical knowledge and, second, the protest against speculative knowledge.

The Protest Against Historical Knowledge

I have already referred to the impact that the historical method has had on theology. Leaving aside the modernist crisis, we are bound to admit that, initially at least, the introduction of historical methods liberated theology from a scholasticism that was completely cut off from the historical sources of faith. Later, however, scientific exegesis and a scientific investigation of the history of the origins of Christianity helped to bridge the gulf between history and dogma, the gulf between exegetical and theological truth.[3]

Exegetes came implicitly to presuppose that the truth of Christianity was to be found in the text of the Bible and that this could be restored by scientific methods. In this way, exegesis became the way that had to be followed in order to reach that truth, which was identified with the content of an earlier text. This led to some misunderstanding of the contemporary experience of the Christian community and the strictly theological meaning of the scriptural texts for today being examined less rigorously.

It is the great achievement of philosophical hermeneutics since Dilthey that the claims of historical knowledge in the sense of positivism have been called into question and that it has been shown that it is not possible to restore the past without the help of a living interpretation conditioned by the present situation.

Since Karl Barth, theology has been a hermeneutical exercise in which an attempt is made to make the Word of God speak to man today. Bultmann criticized Barth for having held the critical study of the texts too cheap, but he himself also reacted against the positivists' conception of history in their claim that an exact knowledge of the past could be reached using the methods of the exact sciences. Existential knowledge, that is, an interpretative knowledge that is inseparable from the self-interpretation of the subject himself, is, unlike the objectivizing knowledge of historicism, the only authentic historical knowledge.[4]

Since the appearance of the work of Gadamer[5] and Pannenberg[6] we have come to recognize that the protest by the representatives of existential hermeneutics against historicism is itself held captive by the Kantian problem, according to which the order of facts (the object of the experiential sciences) is kept separate from that of meaning or value (the object of ethics or metaphysics). In order to escape from the damage done by historicism, Protestant theologians have gone beyond the supernatural authority of the Word of God without having recourse to the criticism of history. The result has been that a disastrous distinction has been made between the task of the exegete and historian and that of the hermeneutist and theologian. The first seeks the meaning of the event in the light of its historical context, while the second tries to give a contemporary interpretation to the meaning of that past event for us today. As distinct from psychological hermeneutics, according to which the text is understood as an expression of the author's subjective existence, the new form of hermeneutics looks for the meaning of the text while respecting its historical otherness.

The Protest Against Speculative Knowledge

The protest against historical knowledge in the sense of historicism, then, has shaken the confidence of those fundamentalist theologians who claimed to be close to the truth of the Word of God when they were reading the words of Scripture literally. Generally speaking, however, it is not possible to speak of a movement from knowledge to interpretation or of disturbance of dogmatic security unless we also include the protest that has been made against the speculative knowledge of contemporary philosophy.

(1) The earlier onto-theology which provided theology with its conceptual basis was dismantled by the new ontology of Heidegger, who tried to restore thinking about being. This earlier metaphysical theology may well have been exceptionally successful in its time, but we can no longer with equal impunity do theology on the basis of metaphysical thought. Nor can we innocently continue to identify the theology that comes from the God of Jesus Christ with the theology whose nature and level are purely ontological. What is more, philosophy has also abandoned its claim to "absolute knowledge." This means that theology has certain consequences to draw from this for its own reasoning about everything that separates a philosophy of knowledge from a hermeneutical philosophy.

(2) In the second place, the claim of theology to be a perfect and universal systematization of the Christian message has come into direct confrontation with the contemporary criticism of ideology and especially with the latter's vow of non-dialectical totalization, its rejection of historical complexity and its stubborn resistance to what is real. All of us are, after all, marked by a Nietzschean suspicion of truth.[7] Truth is not "perspectivist," but we have to admit that it can only be reached within a certain perspective. All discourse is therefore provisional and relative. There is no knowledge—only a language of interpretation that is relative to the perspective of the one who speaks it. The truth is pluriform to the extent that reality itself is also pluriform. This sharpened consciousness does not necessarily lead to the destruction of a dogmatic faith in the Christian sense of the word, but it does make us view more cautiously a certain kind of dogmatic theology that is offered to us as the only authentic way of interpreting the Christian message. Insofar as theologians are conscious of the fact that their science is always in a hermeneutical situation, they will be more modest and more questioning.

(3) Finally, I have to point out that the change in theology from knowledge to interpretation is the result of a change in credibility structures in the life of contemporary man. By this I mean that the historical conditions of faith and therefore those governing theological discourse have changed radically. What was already latent during the modernist crisis at the turn of the century has now broken through. It can be described as a conflict between the authority of faith and that of reason in the debate between men. Many Church discourses have become unimportant for many of our contemporaries, not only because of religious indifference and looser social practices, but also because of a much more lively awareness of the division between Christian faith and man's new states of consciousness.

Autonomy of consciousness is an inescapable datum of modern life and it goes together with a rejection of the claim, made in the name of the authority of God or of the Church's magisterium, that theological knowledge is infallible. The content of truth of theological teaching is not accepted on the strength of the authority that offers it, but only on the strength of its credibility. "Authoritarian" theologies such as those of the Word of God in the Barthian sense or Catholic theologies like those of the Roman school are no longer in accordance with the contemporary order of the Spirit.[8] But, as in other periods of its history, theology cannot abandon its task of mediating between reason and faith and perhaps this task can best be fulfilled by a hermeneutical theology like that of Pannenberg, who tries in his work to react against the supernaturalism of the theologies of the Word of God and base the credibility of the Christian message on the events of its foundation.

2. THE CONSEQUENCES FOR THEOLOGICAL PRACTICE
OF THE HERMENEUTICAL ORIENTATION OF THEOLOGY

In this section, I would like to point to a number of changes that have taken place within theological practice itself. All these changes are very closely connected with each other, but it is possible to place them under four different headings. These are, first, a new treatment of the traditional places of theology, that is, Scripture and tradition, second, a new articulation of Scripture and dogma, third, a change in the theological act, and, finally, the emergence of new places, changing the function of the traditional places of theology.

A New Treatment of the Traditional Theological Places

The attitude of theologians toward the traditional places of theology, namely Scripture and tradition, has changed. They are, in other words, treated less as "authorities" than as textual objects in the sense of a reference. Scripture is not regarded first and foremost as a datum in the sense of a content of truth that has simply to be appropriated. It is seen rather as a testimony taking us back to historical events.

This approach to Scripture therefore calls for an interpretation that is made in faith and is historical, which means that it must be relative. In a structural perspective, it could be said that there is no truth as such in the text, but that reading produces various meanings. The theologian, however, receives the text from a community. Because that community, which is the Church, is in a state of continuity with the early community of the Church which produced the text in the first place, it cannot do anything that it likes with the text. That continuity is the condition that makes tradition possible. Reading Scripture in faith, then, is always hermeneutical in the sense that we interpret the text now within the same tradition as the one in which it was written. It is therefore possible to speak of a certain continuity of meaning linked to a historical continuity, even though the event of Jesus Christ always gives rise, on the basis of our own historical situation, to a different interpretation and a different expression. Reference to the origin of the meaning, that of the founding event, is, of course, essential, but the message cannot be handed on simply by repeating knowledge that has been constituted once and for all time. It can only be passed on by presenting what was manifested in Jesus Christ each time in a new and contemporary way. That is why a living theology is always a hermeneutical undertaking.

A New Articulation of Scripture and Dogma

Regarding theology as a hermeneutical undertaking always involves calling seriously into question the distinction between the datum and the construct employed in traditional theology. It also necessitates going beyond the antithesis between a positive and a speculative theology, which has for more than three hundred years been an obstacle to unity in theological knowledge.[9]

This distinction in fact brought about the division between reason and history in theological thinking and led to the triumph of a form of scholasticism that was cut off from its biblical roots. Historical positivism and theological rationalism both have the same origin, that is, a misunderstanding of the past based on a lack of hermeneutical insight. I believe that misunderstanding to be inherited from Kant, who distinguished between knowledge of the facts and the search for meaning. Positive theology limited itself to recording the documents of the past. Speculative theology was then able to take up its work of theoretical construction, as though it were possible to be satisfied with a naive distinction between a datum, the meaning of which could be read by putting contemporary understanding between brackets, and a construct only very distantly related to the datum. We know too that a list of the sources of faith cannot be made unless we also abandon ourselves completely to the task of interpretation.

Going beyond the distinction between the datum and the construct inevitably led to a change in the functions of theology. We no longer accept the tripartite division of dogmatic theology that originated with the Counter-Reformation, that is, an exposition of the Church's teaching, the provision of proof of that teaching on the basis of Scripture and tradition, and finally reflection at a deeper speculative level.[10] Theologians no longer appeal to Scripture simply in order to justify or confirm the teaching of the magisterium, as they did in Catholic circles until the Second Vatican Council. What happens now is that our reading of Scripture leads us to a reinterpretation of the Church's dogmatic pronouncements, while taking into account the situation of question and answer that prevailed when they were originally made. The language of dogma expresses the Church's consciousness of what it was experiencing at a given time. Just as it is not possible to say that the Church and the kingdom of God are identical, so too is it impossible to speak of an identity between faith and the Word of God. We should not try to identify either Scripture or dogma with the Word of God if we really want to see them as complementing each other in the Church's gradual appropriation of the riches of the mystery of Christ. In the concrete, the hermeneutical function of theology can be measured by the mutual articulation of dogmatic confessions of faith and Scripture. We read Scripture with that sphere that is constituted by the Church's tradition as our point of departure. That has for a long time been the method used by Catholic dogmatic theologians, but a different procedure has also to be put into practice. We have, in other words, to reread Scripture with our own sphere of history as our point of departure, in order to understand what a given dogmatic definition had in view and what can be traced back to the spontaneous expressions and the attitude of the period in question. (See below, Chapter IV.)

The Change in the Theological Act *as* Intellectus Fidei

It should be clear that the changes described above are bound to lead to a change in the theological act as *intellectus fidei*. We can, in other words, no longer identify the *intellectus fidei* with an act of speculative reason moving according to the pattern of the subject and the object and trying to explain what we are given to understand in revelation on the basis of a number of metaphysical reasons. The *intellectus fidei* can be assimilated with a "hermeneutical understanding," which is not a simple act of understanding, but a mode of being in which an understanding of the past is inseparable from an interpretation of self.[11]

This seems to me to be very important, so long as it is not confined to a psychological form of existential hermeneutics. Gadamer has shown that understanding is never a merely subjective attitude toward a given "object": "Understanding itself must be regarded less as an action of subjectivity than as an inclusion in the process of transmission in which the past and the present are constantly mediated."[12]

It is therefore possible to say that the immediate object of theology is not an "object" in the sense of a complex whole of propositions which I am trying to understand, but rather a complex whole of texts included within the hermeneutical territory exposed by revelation. I try to let the new being of the Bible and its readings and rereadings made by the Church be unfolded on the basis of my living relationship with Christ, the Lord of history. If this new being of the text is to be revealing for me, I have to overcome the cultural distance separating me from the text that I have re-situated in the historical context within which it was produced. At the same time, however, I have to take care not to do away with the otherness of the text, since it is above all that distance that contains so many new possible meanings with regard to my present situation as the one reading the text. Theology is therefore an endless movement of interpretation in which there is always a risk that unforeseen answers will be given to the new questions that are put to the text.

The Emergence of New Places

The concepts of scholastic philosophy were not used as a medium by the theologians of Vatican II. They employed either the relational concepts of existentialist philosophy or the vocabulary and results of sociology, psychology and the other humane sciences. Despite this, however, they still had a secret desire to reconstitute a totalizing discourse on the world and man within the framework of Christian symbolism. With our present knowledge, we recognize now that this task can no longer be accomplished by simply putting these new places, the humane sciences (which is in any case a vague concept), in the place of Christian philosophy, without completely changing our way of doing theology. These places are not so much new places as new modes of rationality or different approaches to the individual and collective reality.[13]

As hermeneutics, theology must take into account in its interpretation of the Christian message, whether it is evangelical or dogmatic, the critical analysis of the conditions of production of all language. Before integrating new themes, it has therefore to question itself about its attitude toward its own language. It cannot be satisfied with being a purely spontaneous discourse that simply affirms itself. On the basis of a socio-political analysis, it has first to understand the ideological function that its own discourse may exercise. Second, it has also to abandon itself to a sociological reading of the various ecclesial messages, while taking into account a rigorous analysis of the structures of communication and production of messages in society. In the third place, it may also want to question itself about the symbolic function of the language of the Bible or of dogma in the light of recent psychoanalytical techniques. Finally, it is compelled by structural analysis never to reflect about pronouncements by abstracting from their act of making pronouncements.

All this goes to show that an epistemological debate is always presupposed in the much publicized dialogue between theology and the humane sciences. [14] Theology must also make use of every possible means to reach a better understanding of Christian belief. It must take care to safeguard its irreducible originality, but at the same time remember that it can never constitute a totalizing knowledge divorced from new scientific approaches to reality that are not so much totalizing discourses as attempts to verify and produce rationality.

Finally, I would like to point out that the movement from theology as knowledge to theology as interpretation is inseparable from the emergence of a new place, namely Christian praxis, which is both a place of production of the meaning of the Christian message and a place of verification of that message. Theology can therefore be defined as hermeneutics giving a contemporary interpretation to the Word of God. There cannot, however, be a theoretical interpretation of Scripture that at the same time abstracts from the contemporary experience of Christians. Theology is not knowledge constituted before the praxis of faith and the living charity of Christians. The latter is the place and the instrument of the interpretation of Scripture. The praxis of the Church is not a simple reconditioning of a message that is always the same. It plays a part in structuring the elaboration of the message.

The importance attached to praxis as a theological place is more than a mere change of emphasis in theology. It is a veritable transformation, and we have not yet taken all its consequences fully into account, above all in the insuperable modern question of theological pluralism. As a theology of praxis, theology cannot simply continue to interpret the Christian message differently. It is bound to create new possibilities of existence. There is also a dialectical relationship between Scripture and signifying praxis. If it were possible for Scripture to justify any Christian practice, it would not be signifying. The theology of praxis takes the risk of anticipating the future. It does not simply provide a contemporary interpretation of what has preceded it in history. It is also the practice of hope whose place is the non-place and not past being.

I have tried in this chapter to describe the change in theology as a movement from knowledge to interpretation and to define contemporary theology as hermeneutics providing a contemporary interpretation of the Word of God. Although the recent theories of reading have been very successful, I still think that a hermeneutical reading of those texts that bear the Christian message should also be possible. Many modern exegetes recognize that it is necessary to appeal to the complementarity of the structural and the historical methods. I do not see why it should not be possible to appeal in dogmatic theology to several different types of reading. We do, however, tend to attach more importance to the ideologies that go together with these different types of reading than to the ways in which these different methods may help theology as an understanding of faith. As such, theology is at the service of the Church and therefore responsible for a message. The study of the self-functioning of the texts that are entrusted to theology must consequently be at the service of the comunication of that message. I know, of course, that some scholars believe that the hermeneutical reading of a text is indissolubly associated with a metaphysical way of thinking and that that way of thinking belongs to the past. They should perhaps define more precisely the form of "metaphysics" of which they are speaking.

As we shall see in the following chapter, I do not think that it is possible to keep to a purely structural approach to the language of the Bible in order to postulate the theological problem of revelation in and through human words. If we do, we risk remaining enclosed within the texts and not being able to deal with the conditions governing the possibility of a revelation, that is, of a meaning that is given and not simply reconstructed. Language is more than just a system of signs. It is the event of a word. I am therefore bound to question myself about the signifying intentionality that is at the origin of language. That goes back to a phenomenological approach to language. Meaning only exists in an encounter between consciousness and reality. That approach to language, however, is not enough. The necessary presupposition for revelation and a theology of the Word of God is a recognition of the ontological level of language as onto-phany, that is, as a manifestation of being.

Chapter II

HERMENEUTICS ON TRIAL

For more than ten years now it has become commonplace to regard theology as hermeneutics of the Word of God. Attempts have been made to describe in this way the movement of theology from "dogmatic" in the sense of "authoritarian" to "interpretative" in the sense of being conscious of the historical nature of all truth, including revealed truth, and all knowledge, including theological knowledge. This transition from a constituted knowledge that is sure of itself to a pluriform interpretation is the response on the part of theologians to the claims made by philosophers protesting against historical knowledge in the sense of historicism and against the absolute nature of speculative knowledge. Some theologians, both Catholic and Protestant, have tried to draw conclusions from Heidegger's hermeneutical phenomenology and in particular from the latter's insistence that all knowledge of being—and therefore of God—can only be understood through an elucidation of that being who postulates the question of being, in other words, man himself. Theology, then, has come to be seen as hermeneutics of the Word of God and as hermeneutics of human existence. Theology has become, in other words, hermeneutics insofar as it understands that there can be no statement about God that does not at the same time imply a statement about man.

To express this in a different way, the theologian cannot simply continue to look for the intelligibility in themselves of scriptural or dogmatic pronouncements. He must try to bring out their meaning for today. That above all points to the distance between speculative and hermeneutical understanding.

This hermeneutical form of theology is, however, increasingly challenged today. I am not so much thinking in this context of those who advocate and have developed a theology of history or a political theology and have consequently denounced hermeneutical theology as a pure theology of the word that simply puts forward a new theoretical interpretation of Christianity. These theologians rightly stress the historical praxis of mankind—and therefore the historical praxis of the Church—and insist that this praxis must be included as a constitutive element in any hermeneutics that claim to give a contemporary interpretation to Christianity. It would, however, be relatively simple to show that a hermeneutical theology that is correctly understood can never do without praxis, both as an element that determines hermeneutical understanding and as the final aim of the movement of interpretation. The Judaeo-Christian revelation is above all an historical event, and for this reason it is necessary to overcome a mistaken antithesis between a theology of the word and a theology of history.

When I say that theology as hermeneutics is challenged, what I have in mind is something much more radical than what I have described in the preceding paragraph. The hermeneutical method of reading texts is itself on trial. In the first place, there is the particular debate in the sphere of exegesis between the hermeneutical approach and the structural approach to Scripture. In the second place, there is the more general and perhaps more radical challenge to the distinctively hermeneutical way of thinking that is found at the beginning of all theological understanding even when the theology in question is not explicitly hermeneutical. That is the movement back to a permanent intelligible factor beneath the superficial reflection of what can be perceived by the senses or beyond the contingency of historical events. It is ultimately always a question of rediscovering the intelligibility of being beneath what can be sensually perceived or of restoring a continuity of meaning beyond a cultural or historical distance. In this, hermeneutics have continued to be congenitally linked to a metaphysical way of thinking and have therefore been rejected by all those who have criticized logocentrism and have tried to deconstruct metaphysics. Hermeneutics have to give way to what the most radical thinker in the movement of cultural change, Jacques Derrida, has called grammatology.

It is fashionable in France today, even in theological circles, to speak of the crisis in hermeneutics. I am personally of the opinion that, if we go to the ultimate point of this radical questioning of all hermeneutics, it will become impossible to do theology at all. I am bound to confess that I remain unconvinced by the theological attempts to keep hermeneutics at a distance and adopt a structural approach to theology, not only as a method of reading texts, but also as a mode of thought.

I would like, then, to begin by discussing the most important aspects of the present crisis in hermeneutics. I will then go on to ask what change in hermeneutics will be brought about if these new methods of reading texts are taken seriously. I will follow this by an attempt to define some of the consequences of the calling into question of hermeneutics by the contemporary movement that is characterized by its rejection of logocentrism for the practice of theology. The reader will not be surprised if I continue to defend hermeneutical theology as a real possibility, especially in view of the fact that I believe that many of its present critics are opposed to it because they have not understood the way in which it is developing now.

1. THE CRISIS IN HERMENEUTICS

It would be quite impossible to provide a complete and balanced account of the present crisis in hermeneutics. What can, however, be said straightaway is that it coincides with the general crisis in Western thought. I shall in this section be mainly concerned with the situation in France and shall be dealing above all with the criticism of hermeneutics as a method of reading texts and with the radical challenge to hermeneutics as an expression of metaphysical thought. Before I do this, however, I should like to make a rapid survey of the challenge to hermeneutics made by the German criticism of ideologies.[1]

Hermeneutics and the Criticism of Ideologies

Gadamer's philosophy of hermeneutics aims to be more than a methodology of the science of interpretation. It has more than a merely epistemological dimension and does more than simply tell us what we have to do in order to understand. It in fact has an ontological dimension and has the task of stating the conditions governing the possibility of an effective understanding.[2]

Following Heidegger, Gadamer tried to elaborate a theory of hermeneutical understanding that was truly philosophical as a structure of our being-in-the-world and not as the origin of knowledge in the epistemological sense. With this aim in mind, he rehabilitated the concept of tradition that had been completely discredited by the Enlightenment, claiming that there was no effective understanding without consenting to a tradition that constitutes us. It is precisely against this aspect of Gadamer's hermeneutical philosophy that Habermas has protested. It is the lasting achievement of the Enlightenment to have made us aware of the demands made by critical reflection as correlative with modern man's autonomy and emancipation, but Gadamer has, according to Habermas, driven that critical authority out of the field of hermeneutics, with the consequence that his work is suspect insofar as it results in an imperialism that is not critical of tradition.

Habermas has himself outlined a general theory of intersubjective communication in which the concept of a "criticism of ideologies" is central. He makes use of this concept in particular to show that we have to abandon once and for all time the false ideal of disinterested knowledge. It is no longer possible, as it may have been during Marx' time, simply to denounce ideology as a metaphysical and religious superstructure, since science itself has now become the dominant ideology.

At first sight, this criticism of ideologies would appear to have the same function as hermeneutics in its denunciation of the false absolute value of science and its illusory claim to disinterested knowledge. But Habermas believes that, despite appearance, Gadamer's theory of hermeneutics still retains, because of its blind trust in tradition, an idealistic conception of human knowledge. In his opinion, it regards interhuman relationships as translucent and fails to expose the relationships of power and even violence that form an integral part of the tradition that sustains us and therefore form an obstacle to all human communication. Despite its claim to universality, Gadamer's hermeneutics fail to provide a criterion that will distinguish between false and authentic consciousness. It must therefore be superseded by a criticism of ideologies that is able to put all types of human dialogue to the test in the light of the demand for universal communication that will be free of constraint and violence.

Reading as Opposed to Interpretation

A fundamental presupposition made in every hermeneutical approach to a text is that it will be possible to discover an original meaning hidden beneath the letter of that text. The new theories of reading as opposed to interpreting texts, however, and in particular the structural analysis of texts, do not postulate any theory of a double meaning and keep exclusively to the internal structures of the text in question. Within an historical perspective, it is no longer a question of asking about the meaning to which we are referred by a multiplicity of signs, which may or may not be textual. As Roland Barthes has pointed out, "the disintegration of the sign seems to be the great preoccupation of modern thinkers." Saussure insisted that meaning arises from the articulation of signs in signifying systems. We are consequently no longer concerned with the question of a continuity of meaning beyond the textual or historical distance. What concerns us now is the production of meaning and its functioning within a closed text that is organized as a significant system. The question that we now ask, in other words, is: How does the text function in order to produce certain effects of meaning? The concept of "production" has, in other words, replaced that of "understanding," just as that of "trace" or "archive" has replaced that of "sign."

If we leave the sphere of linguistics in order to explicitate the ideology that accompanies it, we find ourselves confronted with a radical protest against the hermeneutical theory insofar as it postulates a continuity of meaning and the primacy of the subject who decodes the intelligibility of a unique and always identical adventure beyond the materiality of textual or historical contexts. Structuralism does not define itself as a philosophical system, but, insofar as it represents an original system of thought, it regards itself as separate from a philosophical humanism that stresses the primacy of the subject. "The most important event of truth that has occurred in our own times is the removal of man from the center in relation to all forms of false central subjectivity."[3] This antihumanistic ideology can be found in the neo-Marxism of L. Althusser, the neo-Freudianism of J. Lacan, the neo-positivism of C. Lévi-Strauss and the archaeology of knowledge of M. Foucault.

In any case, from the point of view of modern linguistic analysis, man as the subject of language disappears in favor of a silent region, namely that of structures and that of scattered signs which do not send us back to an all-embracing significance of man and the world. We have to study the language itself as a system of signs and not as a sign or the expression of a thought. The words used have a meaning in relation to the other words in the sentence, but not in relation to an external reality. The lateral game of the signifiers has to be taken seriously without postulating an ultimate signified. We may say, then, that language as a word, a manifestation of meaning and the event of an encounter is absorbed by language as a system. "It speaks before I speak," as Lacan observed in a frequently cited sentence.

As J.-P. Osier has shown, hermeneutics were not put on trial only in the last few years. The new ways of reading the text of the Bible have all taken into account the change of ground brought about by Marx and Spinoza before him. We have to make a choice—between operating in the tradition of Spinoza or in that of Feuerbach, who did not leave the traditional field of hermeneutics when he adopted an atheistic way of interpreting Christianity. It has always been a question of decoding an intelligible essence hidden beneath cultural changes and especially that of the advent of contemporary atheism. "The exemplary change brought about by Spinoza is a 'change of ground,' " Osier has written in this context. "Spinoza did not go behind the scenes to the place occupied by the prompter—he went elsewhere to a completely different theatre. That 'elsewhere' cannot be found at the level of the religious text, whether it is literal or symbolic. It is a knowledge of the second kind, which, more geometrico, proceeds by definition deductively, that is, by causal explanation, since defining and developing the necessary cause are one and the same thing, at least at the level of science. The product of this change is a consideration of religion or its manifestation in a text as constituting an effect."⁴

The same author continues a little further on: "Spinoza has been followed by others insofar as he inaugurated a theory of reading as a condition governing the possibility of any such reading. For him the text was an effect and also the meaning of the text. Knowing what one is reading is to produce the theoretical concept of the mechanisms providing a certain text or a certain meaning, counter-meaning or non-meaning. In other words, Spinoza subjected all 'understanding' or recollection of meaning to a preliminary scrutiny by a theory of knowledge of the 'effects-understanding' or 'recollection.' He reduced hermeneutics to the level of 'hermeneutical effect,' thus depriving the latter of any privilege of knowledge."⁵

We must now turn to the task of explicitating the consequences of structural analysis, especially insofar as they are concerned with questioning a certain type of traditional biblical exegesis.

(1) If we are to take really seriously the Copernican revolution brought about in linguistics since the time of Saussure, we are bound to call into question the idea of the truth of the text or that of a literal meaning that has to be discovered. This was, after all, implicitly postulated by the historico-critical method of exegesis. "If each element of language as a constitutive unit cannot be distinguished from others by what it represents or designates, the meaning will not be constituted by the extrinsic relationship of the sign with the reality, in other words, by the ticket that the word, for example, puts on the thing. It will be produced by the internal constitutive relationship that this word has with all the other words in the vocabulary."⁶ Language, then, should not be seen as a substantialist conception according to which it is a receptacle containing signs through which the reader has to decode a meaning. It should rather be understood as a totalization of differences producing meaning by oppositions. There is, in other words, no meaning already present in the text that simply has to be reconstructed. The meaning does not exist in advance of the text or underneath the text, with the result that reading a text is not decoding a prior meaning, but producing meaning by letting oneself be regulated by a chain of signifiers. A. Delzant said in this context: "Meaning can only be a regulated circulation of signifiers or a differential game of oppositions in which both a textual author and a textual reader play a part."⁷

It is obvious that there is a great deal of difference between this theory of reading a text and the positivism that is latent in a certain kind of traditional exegesis in which the content of the text itself is identified with truth. Exegetes employing the latter method have often been able to exert a kind of terrorism, acting as though the authentic interpretation of Christianity today depended entirely on the literal meaning of the texts brought up to date by exegesis. A structural reading of a biblical text, on the other hand, may be quite liberating insofar as it resists the temptation to force us to repeat a meaning that is already present in the text and becomes a pre-text for a multiplicity of readings and for communication with others. "I do not have any truth of the text. It displaces and changes me. I experience exile or ecstasy because of the text, but do not speak of what the text says."[8] The idea of "permission" is important in this context, that is, what the text does or does not permit insofar as it is not identified with a fullness of truth that is at once translucent. It would not be wrong to say the same of the presence of Christ as the event on which the present history of Christians is based. "A kenosis of the present gives rise to pluriform and communal writing."[9]

(2) Another result of a structural reading of the Bible, as distinguished from the interpretative approach of hermeneutics, is that it is clearly useless to go back, on the basis of the text as a differential game of signifiers, to the author's intention and even to an ultimate signified. If the meaning is an effect of signifiers within the closed system of the text, then it is clearly an illusion to try to come near to the intention of an author in some socio-cultural context and through some literary form. In that case too I am completely at variance with the aims of the type of exegesis based on the historico-critical method. The priority given to the synchronic point of view tends to make us give a relative value to the idea of an author in the sense of an intention or a voice situated behind the text. As I have already said with regard to structuralism in general, man as a subject and a signifying intentionality is set aside. "Man appears not as a subject giving meaning, but as the place of production and manifestation of meaning."[10] Considering the text as a textual object calls into question the ideology of an origin to be sought in an author who is the proprietor of the meaning and that of a finality on the part of a reader who has to appropriate the meaning. All ideas of author, message and recipient have therefore to be put between brackets and we have simply to remain within the immanence of the text and mark out the laws by which it functions.

The structural analysis of texts as applied to a reading of the Bible also calls into question at an even deeper level the fundamental presupposition of a hermeneutical approach, namely that we are referred back to an ultimate signified and therefore to a divine author. We are still at the level of the game of signifiers, and in this case it is the distinction between the signifier and the signified that becomes irrelevant. The basic hermeneutical principle that there is a double meaning, an original meaning through the means of a first meaning, has therefore to be abandoned.

According to the traditional notion of hermeneutics, the signifying material of a symbol always goes back to an ultimate signified. This is what P. Ricoeur means when he says that the symbol makes us think. If, however, we follow a structural approach, we are bound to confuse the symbolic order with the functioning of the imaginary representation that claims to give itself reality on the basis of and in an image. If we are in fact to have access to a real symbolic order, we must call the priority of the signified into question. The symbol does not refer us back to a fullness of meaning. It does not make us think, but it does permit the coming of the subject and encounter with others. "The symbol takes us back to society, to the covenant that it implies and to the communication that forms part of its fabric."[11] Since, then, a hermeneutical reading of the symbol presupposes the priority of the signified, it is not wrong to say that "the signified is always in the position of the signifier"[12] in the symbolic order. What is more, God cannot be identified with the ultimate signified and must be regarded as a signifier, sending us back to other lateral signifiers.

(3) A third point that is well worth stressing because it has many important consequences for our praxis of Scripture is the closed nature of the texts. This priority given to the synchronic point of view is a direct challenge to the implicit presupposition of all hermeneutical understanding, that is, that tradition is the necessary sphere of our understanding of the past. Unlike the historical method, which tries to understand a text on the basis of its development and its actualizing rereadings within tradition, it is necessary, when the hermeneutical method is used, to remain within the text and to produce its meaning by being guided by the differential game of signifiers. In the traditional form of hermeneutics, especially since Gadamer, far from being an obstacle, historical distance is the most reliable way of understanding the past. It has become the place of an irreducible gap, a radical "dissemination," as Derrida would call it.

In any attempt to interpret Christianity in terms of tradition, priority has to be given, then, to breaks in continuity, differences in likeness and changes in identity. The text of Scripture not only gives rise to a multiplicity of interpretations, but also acts as a pretext for new interpretations which each time create a difference. It is futile to postulate a single and definitive meaning in Scripture that can simply be taken up and repeated throughout the centuries. "The meaning is not already present, nor is it in the access to meaning. It is in the excess of meaning that is given gratuitously from the moment that one renounces its presence and its possession. The work of the meaning of a text is that renunciation, the journey toward the promised land, the way and the method."[13]

If, then, it is necessary to renounce the presence of a continuity of meaning persisting beyond the distances in culture and breaks in history, it is equally necessary to reject the claim that it is possible to retranslate the same meaning into different languages. To do that would be to cling to an inadequate notion of language and to insist on an illusory difference between the signifiers and the signified. We cannot claim to say the same thing using different words. Words only have meaning in relation to other words according to lateral relationships, and this differential game changes according to whether it functions in a different textual or historical context. We are always referred back to language as a closed system. If the rules of the game are changed, the production of meaning is altered. Meaning does not exist prior to the system of signifiers that constitute it, nor does it transcend that system.

Within this synchronic perspective, we are, it may be supposed, led to a radically new praxis of Scripture. The well-known problem that has always troubled the Christian consciousness, that is, how to reconcile creative newness with faithfulness, arises here in a very acute form. And since there is no truth in Scripture that can provide us with a certain criterion by which the Christian message can be interpreted for today, it is not difficult to understand the special use that is made of going back to the signifying praxis of Christians or orthopraxis. [14]

Hermeneutics and Grammatology

I have tried to show how the new theories of reading and especially the structural analysis of texts directly challenge hermeneutics as a process of interpretation that is tied to a double meaning, as access to meaning through the means of a meaning. This renews our praxis of Scripture. In exegesis, however, structural analysis can be treated as a method that completes the historico-critical method. The two methods are not necessarily absolutely incompatible. This is not, however, the case with ideologies underlying these two methods, which present us with a radical incompatibility and even a struggle to the death. Derrida has given the most extreme form to this putting on trial of hermeneutics as a thought-process. According to him, there is no possible compromise between what he calls "grammatology or hermeneutics." He regards the crisis in hermeneutics as the crisis of the whole of Western thinking. At the same time, the thought-process known as "grammatology" is the most radical protest against all theology based on hermeneutics. "The encounter between hermeneutics and grammatology has necessarily to take the form of a struggle to the death, a confrontation that straightaway excludes any possibility of reconciliation or mediation." [15]

(1) According to an initial approach, the opposition between hermeneutics and grammatology can be traced back to the opposition between writing and the word, but this can only be done so long as one does not

remain at the purely linguistic level. In giving priority to writing, grammatology aims to be a radical deconstruction of metaphysics insofar as it is in the line of logocentrism. The priority that is given to the voice, the *phone*, is a metaphysical priority. It is inseparable from a metaphysic of the presence that presupposes a fullness of meaning, a transcendental signified existing prior to any signifier. Writing is simply the expression of the event of language by which man makes the world present to himself.

(2) The aim of grammatology is to take the deconstruction of metaphysics as onto-theology that was initiated by Heidegger to its ultimate conclusion. This means that the thinking involved in the hermeneutical theory is inescapably dominated by onto-theology as thinking about Being as presence, identity, belonging or origin. Derrida is more radical than Heidegger in seeking to go beyond this onto-theology and move toward an idea of *differance*. "Whereas *differance* takes us back in the last resort to the concepts of production and economy, marking an irreducible predominance of spatiality, hermeneutics continue to be dominated by the meaning that is manifested."[16] It is also possible to object that Gadamer's hermeneutics form part of the thought-process initiated by Heidegger, but Derrida is of the opinion that not only Gadamer, but also Heidegger himself did not take the implications of the historical destiny of the idea of being and the closed nature of metaphysics to their ultimate conclusion.

(3) In his conviction that structuralism is still dominated by metaphysics because it gives too high a priority to phonetics, Derrida provides the latter with its theoretical justification by defining language as a system of signs or a "formal game of differences." Grammatology has to be seen as a destruction of the sign in favor of the trace that points to the game of differences. "The trace," he has said, "is the absolute origin of meaning in general and this amounts to saying once again that there is no absolute origin of meaning in general."[15] As we have already seen, it is the relationship between the signifier and the signified, the presupposition of all hermeneutics, that breaks down here. Meaning can only come from the opposition between signifiers. We should therefore not hesitate to say that every signified is already in the position of a signifier. "That the signified is originally and essentially (and not simply for a finite and created spirit) a trace and that it is always already in the position of the signifier—that is the apparently innocent proposition in which the metaphysics of the logos, the presence and the consciousness has to reflect writing as its death and its resource."[18] If we think language as an organization of the signified-signifier type, we shall give priority to the signified as the fullness of meaning and we shall not avoid logocentrism as the destiny of Western thought. "Each time that we affirm that the signified cannot be reduced to the signifier we give the meaning of being as identity, belonging and origin."[19]

We still have to discover whether the hermeneutical tradition is as fatally linked as Derrida believes it to be to the destiny of metaphyics as onto-theology. It is certainly true to say that a necessary presupposition of hermeneutics is a philosophy of meaning. Derrida's radical thought-process undoubtedly leads to the collapse of all philosophy of meaning, whether in the classical, metaphysical form or in the more recent form given to it by Husserl or Heidegger.[20]

By way of a conclusion to this all too brief summary of the irreducible conflict between these two thought-processes, grammatology on the one hand and hermeneutics on the other, it is worth stressing how destructive Derrida's idea of difference is bound to be for any theological plan. What we have here is not simply a conflict of method in our approach to the text of the Bible. It is much more than this. It is in fact the problem of truth and therefore also the problem of theological understanding as such.

This can perhaps be illustrated by comparing the modernist crisis with the crisis in hermeneutics, while making it clear at once that the very foundations of theological discourse are even more radically challenged by hermeneutics than they were by modernism.

The modernist crisis came about because reconciliation between the new scientific praxis of history and a theological understanding of Christian dogma seemed impossible. The present crisis in hermeneutics is a symptom of the even wider gulf between a theological understanding of the Christian mystery and an approach to the Christian fact made on the basis of the praxis of the humane and historical sciences. Our present situation only points even more clearly to the epistemological gap that was already present at the time of the modernist crisis between "scientific understanding," "speculative reason" and "theologal experience." We have already seen how important the concept of "production" is both from the linguistic point of view and from that of ideological structuralism. It points to a situation and a praxis that are totally different from those of modernism. We continue to study the socio-cultural, psychological and economic "conditions of production" of the religious object, but, as a reality and as a truth and a meaning to be decoded, that religious object itself disappears in the course of our study. "In modernism, it was the specifically Christian factor, the 'Ephapax,' that disappeared, being replaced by an experience that could not in itself be expressed and was supra-historical. In the crisis of hermeneutics, on the other hand, it is the entire religious object that has been displaced. At a time when analysis no longer has the truth of the discourse or of the religious symbol in view, but is concerned with the mechanisms governing their production—mechanisms that, according to the scientific praxis that has been chosen, form part of a sociological, psychological or other system—the religious symbol or phenomenon can no

longer continue to be a special object. It is rather reduced to a single point
in the relational field which from now on will have other points of reference."[21]

2. THE PRESENT CHANGE OF EMPHASIS IN HERMENEUTICS

The Destiny of Theological Hermeneutics

I have tried in the preceding section to reconstruct certain aspects of
the crisis in hermeneutics. In its most radical form, that of Derrida's grammatology, the challenge to the way of thinking that is an essential aspect
of hermeneutics has led to serious questions being asked about whether a
theological discourse is even possible. Is the crisis in hermeneutics, then,
not the crisis of theology itself? As I have already said, the crisis in hermeneutics is not simply a crisis of language—it is a crisis of thought. That
is why I cannot see at present how it may be possible to negotiate any kind
of compromise between grammatology and theology. We are, in other
words, confronted with an alternative that prevents any attempt at reconciliation.

We have therefore to resign ourselves to living in the discomfort of a
crisis, all the consequences of which have not yet been assessed. I do not
think, however, that all theological hermeneutics are doomed to failure,
if only because theological hermeneutics cannot be reduced to general
hermeneutics. I am not thinking in particular here of the fact that putting
onto-theology on trial may make every hermeneutical plan definitively
null and void. That trial is not of recent date and, since the time of Heidegger, theologians practicing hermeneutics have rightly tried to take seriously the consequences of the deconstruction of metaphysics by being
increasingly careful not to confuse the theological emphases derived from
the Western onto-theological tradition with those coming from the Judaeo-
Christian tradition.

I am well aware of the enormous benefits that our praxis of Scripture
can derive from a structural analysis of the texts. The ascetic aspect of
structural analysis undoubtedly has the great merit of protecting us from
indulging in subjective, psychological and apologetical fantasy in our interpretation of the texts. That is a temptation to which traditional Christian
exegetes have all too often given way. At the same time, however, I can
hardly see how the theologian can simply go no further than the linguistic
point of view in his understanding of language. As we have seen, the linguist sees language exclusively as a differential system of signs and not as

the word, as signifying intentionality and as a message addressed to a recipient. It could be said that the linguist abstracts from the phenomenological function of language as mediation. That mediation is, however, the real event of the word: I—thou—and that of which they are speaking. Whoever says "message" says someone who speaks or writes and someone who listens or reads.

In other words, the theologian cannot avoid considering language from the semantic rather than from the purely linguistic point of view. Language does not depend exclusively on structural analysis. It also depends on a phenomenology in which the signifying intentionality takes priority in the discourse. Following the linguistics of Saussure, a distinction has to be made between the linguistics of "language" and those of the "discourse." In the case of the first, the basic unit is the sign, whereas in the case of the second it is the sentence. Another thing is to regard the word as a "difference" in a system of oppositions and yet another thing is to regard it as a function in the sentence as a signifying unit of the discourse.

It is also in my opinion necessary to add that the theologian cannot be satisfied with a purely phenomenological approach to language. A hermeneutical theology that does not try to link its historical destiny with that of onto-theology is distinctive in that it has absorbed the lesson of Heidegger when he spoke of language as a modality of being, that is, as ontophany. Before being a word addressed to someone, language is a saying, that is, it is a word as a manifestation of being. We have therefore first of all to listen to the saying of language before exercising our responsibility as speaking subjects.[22]

I am tempted to think that this ontological level of saying as a manifestation of being is the necessary presupposition for all hermeneutics of the language of revelation. Because I am already able to discern the manifestation of being in all language and especially poetic language, I am also able to receive the Word of God as an "unheard of" manifestation of being. Christian hermeneutics have the task of looking for the meaning of key-words in the language of revelation in the light of the word "God," which says much more than the word "being," especially if it is seen in its special relationship with the symbolism of the cross.

In any case, I cannot see how it is possible to remain at the level of a structural analysis in order to reveal the meaning of the key-words in the language of the Bible. I regard the Christian reading of Scripture as hermeneutical at all times, at least in the sense in which we interpret the text within the same tradition as that in which it was originally written. There can be many possible interpretations in the light of different historical situations, but the living tradition, the subject of which is the interpreting community of believers, circumscribes a hermeneutical field which excludes the possibility of deviant or wrong interpretations. This means that we cannot abandon the diachronic for the synchronic point of view in order to reach an absolutely closed system in the text and a radical discontinuity. Insofar as the founding event—Jesus Christ—took place in the past, it "permits" a certain continuity of meaning that is inseparable from the historical tradition of those who live in its spirit.

The Change in Hermeneutics According to Paul Ricoeur

Having made these preliminary remarks, I feel free to affirm the destiny of hermeneutics as having changed since the development of structuralism as a method of reading texts and as an ideology. In its least radical form, the crisis in hermeneutics is at the very least a crisis in a romantic and psychologically orientated form of hermeneutics. The present change in hermeneutics is part of the whole process of modern thought in its most significant aspects and in what may be termed its "decentralization of man" in respect of an erroneous kind of subjectivity or a "dispossession of consciousness." Those for whom the word "hermeneutics" has become taboo ought to think again and not be too hasty in their criticism of the hermeneutical method, especially when they do this, as they almost always do, on the basis of the primacy of either the metaphysical or the transcendental subject.

Paul Ricoeur has given a great deal of thought to this change in hermeneutics, according to which almost exclusive importance is attached to the textual object and little attention is paid to the aspect of the subjective appropriation of the text. That is why I have decided to refer to his more recent writings on hermeneutics in an attempt to review briefly some of the more significant aspects of the change that is still taking place.[23]

(1) Going Beyond the Opposition Between "Explaining" and "Understanding"

If we are to understand the most recent position of hermeneutics, it is necessary to stand at some distance from the romantic and psychologically orientated type of hermeneutics which, following Schleiermacher and Dilthey (and even Gadamer), gave priority to the idea of affinity and connaturality between the reader of a text and its author and also from structuralism, which above all has the objectivization of the text in mind, whatever its bearing of a message for someone may be.

It was the aim of romantic hermeneutics with regard to a specific text to "understand its author better than he understood himself." As Ricoeur has pointed out, "the object of hermeneutics is constantly taken away from the text, its meaning and its reference and applied to the living experience that is expressed in it."[24] Ricoeur himself, on the other hand, tried to absorb the lesson of Heidegger when he removed "historical understanding" from the sphere of psychology and situated it in the world. Existential understanding does not have an act of noetic knowledge in mind, but points to a "being able to be." My "situation" with regard to the world exists before my knowledge of the world as an object. Understanding a text is therefore a question of developing the possibility of being indicated by the text. Ricoeur has no intention of linking the destiny of hermeneutics to the "purely psychological notion of transference into another and developing the text, not in the direction of the author, but in the direction of an immanent meaning and the kind of world that the text reveals and discovers."[25] In this, his aim is paradoxically very close to the one of those basic demands made by structuralists when they aim to promote a type of reading that refuses to come close to an intended saying on the part of the author in order to keep to the objectivity of the text and discover the conditions under which it was produced. As Gadamer would say, being face to face with the reader involves not the author, but the thing of the text.

Ricoeur, in other words, is trying to go beyond the dilemma between being at a distance linked to the objectivity of the text and being close or belonging linked to a historical understanding. That is why he tries to avoid the alternative that is present in the title of Gadamer's great work, *Truth and Method*—that is, on the one hand, understanding linked to belonging and, on the other, a method that draws attention to the idea of distance implied in the concern for objectivity in the human sciences. Despite the use of the conjunction "and" to join the two terms, it is possible to think that Gadamer's title expresses an alternative and that he is in fact abandoning an epistemological theory of interpretation in favor of hermeneutics in the ontological sense.

Ricoeur makes a desperate attempt to reconcile the two. On the one hand, he admits that structuralism is right when he agrees to follow the long route of exegetical methods in order to establish the objectivity of the text. On the other hand, however, he rejects deconstruction in the sense in which it is practiced by the structuralists. He does not in fact reject hermeneutical understanding, which is, in the last resort, a search for truth. He does, however, regard the text as the work that mediates the truth that is to be understood. To express this more precisely, it is the idea of the "world of the text" (which is in Ricoeur's terminology the equivalent of Gadamer's "thing of the text") that enables it to mediate the relationship between distance and belonging. For him, it is the paradigm of standing at a distance in communication. "The objectivization of the discourse in the work and the structural character of the composition, to which should be added the distance brought about by the writing, obliges us to call radically into question the opposition inherited from Dilthey between 'understanding' and 'explaining.' " A little later he goes on to say: "A new period in hermeneutics has been initiated by the success of structural analysis and explanation has become the necessary way to understanding."

(2) The Mediation of the Text

In Ricoeur's theory, the notion of the "world of the text" comes directly from his understanding of language as a dialectic of the event and of meaning to which he frequently returned, especially in his dialogue with structuralism.[27] It is inseparable from the epistemological decision of giving priority to the discourse in its difference from language in order to re-emphasize the Saussurian distinction between language as "language" and language as "word."

The event of the word only exists at the level of the discourse, which in fact takes us back to a speaker and a recipient and is itself always a message about something. So, whereas structural analysis remains within the immanence of the text as a differential game of signifiers which does not take us back to a referent, the discourse in Ricoeur's view brings about a "world." It is moreover going beyond the fleeting event of the word in its lasting significance that makes the discourse original. This transcendence, which is still no more than latent at the level of the living word, becomes manifest when the discourse becomes writing and especially when that writing takes the form of a real work of literature. The work guarantees the practical function of mediation between the word and the meaning. It is the special character of style to incorporate the fleeting intentionality of the author into the work. The text thus acquires a life of its own that is not dependent on the author's intention. It can be read in a different context from the one in which it was produced and it can also lead to many readings. It is, then, the phenomenon of writing that calls for objectivization and therefore standing at a distance as a condition of all understanding. By means of this notion of the "world of the text," Ricoeur dissociates himself from the hermeneutical method, which is, in the opinion of those who practice it, able to derive an objective meaning from the text by discovering what the author intended to say. At the same time, he also dissociates himself from the structuralists, who believe that the meaning that has to be understood is to be found only in the structures of the text and mechanics of its functioning.

The text preserves its claim to say something about reality. It expresses a "world." Ricoeur says in fact: "What has to be interpreted in a text is a proposition of world, that is, of a world of the kind that I can inhabit in order to project into it one of my most distinctive possibilities. . . . That is what I call the world of the text, the world that is peculiar to that one text."[28] The alternative of hermeneutics polarized on an understanding of the author's intention and a structural method polarized on an explanation of the structure of the text has to be rejected. According to Ricoeur, "either the author's intention or the structure of the text—this is an empty alternative. Reference to the text—what I call the thing of the text or the world of the text—is, after all, neither one nor the other. Intention and structure point to the meaning, whereas the world of the text points to the reference of the discourse—not what is said, but that about which it is said. The thing of the text is the object of hermeneutics and that thing of the text is the world that the text develops ahead of itself."[29]

This idea of "developing the world ahead of the text" only has meaning in reference to the poetic language to which Ricoeur gives priority over the purely descriptive function of everyday language. Poetic discourse—which should not be confused with poetry as distinct from prose—has a revelatory function in the non-religious sense. "I am deeply convinced," Ricoeur has said, "that only poetic language can point to a belonging to an order of things that exists prior to our ability to place these things over and against ourselves like objects facing a subject."[30] The perceptive reader will not fail to observe the Heideggerian flavor of this comment. In fact, Ricoeur's insistence on the poetic aspect of language is reminiscent of Heidegger, for whom language was a saying of the being of the world before it was an instrument of interhuman communication. Ricoeur has always claimed to reflect about language as going beyond the point of view of the linguist and the phenomenologist and terminating in an ontology of language. In his excellent essay on "the hermeneutics of the idea of revelation," he describes the task confronting any theologian attempting to elaborate a theology of the Word of God since as the long journey of the "claim of the saying by being."[31]

(3) The Reader's Appropriation of the Text and His Understanding of Himself

I have insisted on the objectivization of the text, autonomy with regard to the author and his task of mediation with regard to understanding. I have now to draw a number of conclusions concerning the subjective appropriation of the text by the reader.

This theme of appropriation occurs again and again in hermeneutics. It is a justifiable criticism of Bultmann's existential hermeneutics to say that he abandoned the objectivity of the text in favor of an understanding of the historicity of personal decision. His hermeneutics are for this reason vehemently attacked by contemporary advocates of structuralist theories of reading. These concentrate on the 'language' aspect of language, whereas Bultmann was preoccupied with language as an "event of the word." As we have already seen, it was Ricoeur's intention—an intention that would have been impossible without the advent of structuralism—to overcome the opposition between standing at a distance and understanding, or rather to make that distance the way to understanding. For Ricoeur, then, it was no longer a question of understanding the text by making oneself contemporary with the author's intention. Whereas in his earlier works (especially, for example, in his preface to the French edition of Bultmann's *Jesus*) Ricoeur had still spoken of the objectivity of meaning as though there were a question of appropriating a "truth behind the text," he makes increasing use of his concept of the "world of the text" in his later writings. A characteristic statement is: "What I finally come to appropriate is a proposition of the world. This is not behind the text, as a hidden intention might be, but in front, as what is developed, discovered and revealed by the work. Understanding is therefore understanding oneself before the text."[32]

This radical break with romantic hermeneutics in the light of the primacy of subjectivity is consistent in Ricoeur's work with his constant concern, expressed in his *Symbolique du mal* and his writings since then, to denounce the "constitutional weakness of the Cartesian cogito." Just as he has increasingly dissociated himself from the speculative tradition and from onto-theology, so too is he more and more anxious to protest against the illusions of man's immediate consciousness of himself. Man can only understand himself, Ricoeur insists, by agreeing to follow the long and devious route marked by the various signs of humanity that have been left in the objectivizations of culture. The "world of the text" before which man receives a much greater self is closely correlative with a dispossession of consciousness. That is also why, on the basis of his philosophical hermeneutics, Ricoeur is able to accept not only the Marxist and Freudian criticisms of the illusions of consciousness, but also Habermas' criticism of ideologies.

Ricoeur, then, no longer claims that human consciousness is founded on itself and that it is at the origin of meaning and has returned to language in its most authentic form. But the more seriously the objectivity of the text has been taken by Ricoeur under the influence of structural analysis, the more firmly he has continued to oppose structuralism in its claim to abandon the reference of the text in favor of the only meaning of the text as a game of relationships played exclusively within the text. "The hermeneutical argument, which is diametrically opposed to the structuralist argument—but not to the method and the research of structuralism—is that the difference between the word and writing cannot do away with the fundamental function of the discourse (which includes two variants: oral and written). The discourse consists of someone saying something to someone about something. About something: that is the inalienable referential function of the discourse."[33]

3. THE THEOLOGICAL IMPLICATIONS
OF THE PRESENT CHANGE IN HERMENEUTICS

Despite the radical challenge to hermeneutics that has come from the method of structural analysis and even more from the ideology of structuralism, I am convinced that hermeneutical theology still has a future and I have given my reasons for this belief. I do not think that it will continue to be fatally and necessarily associated with the destiny of metaphysics, but believe, on the contrary, that the present crisis in metaphysics as thinking about the identity and the philosophies of the subject as the consciousness' founding of itself provides hermeneutics with new and unexpected opportunities.

This rejection of the twofold absolute of onto-theological speculation and transcendental reflection invites us to take the modality that is peculiar to language as original language really seriously. That is the important lesson in general hermeneutics provided by Paul Ricoeur that I have tried to summarize by outlining its more significant demands. It will, however, be quite clear that the change that has taken place would have been impossible without the crisis in thinking in the light of the primacy of the subject and the logos. The destiny of hermeneutic theology, then, will inevitably be conditioned by modern thought as thinking about difference and change. It must find its way forward on the basis of a twofold rejection: it must abandon romantic hermeneutics which postulates an ideal harmony between the contemporary reader and the author writing in the past, and it must also leave behind historicism which, in its modern form, continues to identify the data of the past with the truth.

In this third section, all that I can really do is to point to some of the theological implications of the present change in hermeneutics. Ideally, it would be better, of course, to show how theology might be able to accept some of the demands made by structuralism without losing its own identity.

The Object of Theology as a Textual Object

On the basis of the dialectics of explanation and understanding that is peculiar to the hermeneutical process as opposed to the psychologically orientated form of hermeneutics, it is essential, as we have already seen, not to underestimate the importance of the objectivization of the text and overemphasize the existential decision made in the presence of the text. The object of theology is not an original word which is full of meaning and of which the text is no more than an echo, nor is it a historical event in its factual existence. It is rather a text as an act of historical interpretation and as a new structuralization of the world. Writing "does not contain a 'Word' offered for reinterpretation, but systems of interpretation that 'make word.' "[34]

The notion of the "world of the text" allows us to accept a structural reading when this no longer looks for a meaning or a truth existing behind the text (for this, see biblical fundamentalism). At the same time, however, we still insist on a hermeneutic understanding because the text takes us back to something other than itself, that is, to a kind of world that has a revelatory aspect for me. Theology is always hermeneutics insofar as it lives from a previous existence, that is, the history of Christianity. At the same time, however, it is always in a state of becoming because it cannot identify the truth of Christianity either with a past period in tradition—not even with the New Testament corpus—or with the present situation of faith. There is a basic homology between the biblical statements and their socio-cultural context and then the discourse of faith which has to be held today in its relationship with our present cultural situation.

The problem of hermeneutical theology since the crisis in hermeneutics that I have outlined above can be summarized as the need to reconcile an "historical priority" with a "theological primacy." (I am indebted to Pierre Gisel for this formula and would refer the reader to his essay on Ernst Käsemann's theological program.) That form of hermeneutics has finally abandoned historicism. Those theologians who practice it still take a founding historical event as their point of departure, but they subject that event to a theological reading. For that reason, they are not necessarily condemned, as those who are unconditionally committed to structuralism like to think, to a theology of the metaphysical type that is preoccupied with the problem of origin. History that does not live from an origin is not recognized and an origin that is not expressed from within history and as an interpretation of that history is also not recognized.[35] The *intellectus fidei* of theology will inevitably have the structure of a "hermeneutical understanding" insofar as the theologian treats the history of Christianity as a text and at the same time treats the text as a history—the history of interpretations. The task ahead is in fact to work out a new form of theological epistemology that will be in accordance with the demands made by the "genealogical" model that can be found in Nietzsche.

There are critical consequences for theology as a result of the importance attached to the text and the "world of the text" in the sense outlined above. I would like to point to some of them here.

(1) The immediate object of theology is not a set of propositions that I have to try to understand, but the whole body of texts included within the hermeneutical sphere that is made open to us by revelation. The *intellectus fidei*, then, is not an act of speculative reason that operates according to the pattern of subject and object. It can in fact be assimilated to a "hermeneutical understanding" as I have already indicated in Chapter I.

(2) In their attempts to name God, theologians have to respect the original structure of the language of revelation and not reduce it immediately to a propositional content. For example, the structure of the confession of faith is closely linked to the structure of the language in which it is expressed. That is why I cannot treat the different forms of the confession of faith of the God of Israel (narrative, prophetic, legislative, Wisdom and other writings) simply as literary genres. God is named polyphonically[36] and I can work out a diversified theology of the naming of God only by following the particular characteristic that is peculiar to each biblical statement (which is inseparable from its act of being stated).

(3) A hermeneutical theology that keeps to the "thing" of the text instead of looking for the meaning that the sacred author, who himself takes us back to the divine author, intended to convey inevitably leads us to question a kind of theology of revelation that is in practice identified with inspiration, understood in the sense of an "insufflation" of meaning by a divine author. The idea of a voice behind the voice or of a writing underneath the dictation is suggested to us by the modality of prophetic revelation itself. It is, however, important to take the other original forms of revelation in the biblical corpus seriously. Those texts are "revelation" for us because they develop a "new being" before us and not primarily because they are thought to have been written subject to the dictation of God.[37]

(4) As opposed to the quite imaginative idea of inspiration as a (divine) voice behind the voice, greater emphasis has to be given to the link between inspiration and the faith of the community confessing that faith. If we are to throw light on the problem of inspiration in general, our point of departure has to be the link between Scripture and the early Church. According to Karl Rahner, we can continue to speak of God as the "author of Scripture" in the sense that he is the author of the faith of the early Church, the one who gathered together that community whose faith was expressed and objectivized in Scripture.[38]

The present change in hermeneutics can help us, then, to renew the theology of revelation. The biblical text is a religious revelation for us because in itself it has a revelatory dimension in its textual making, just as every poetic text that goes beyond the purely descriptive function of everyday language has a revelatory dimension. Confronted with that "new being" developed by the text, man himself is able to receive a "new being," that is, a widening of his purely natural self. This actualization of a possibility that is peculiar to man can be verified in the case of every poetic text. In the case of the biblical text, however, an appropriation of the text coincides not only with a new understanding of self, but also with a new possibility of existence and with the will to make a new world exist. In other words, there can be no revelation in the full sense of the word without personal conversion and the inauguration of a new ethical and social praxis.

Tradition and Production: Theology as Genealogy

A hermeneutical theology that accepts as its central category the "world of the text" will not dispense with tradition as a history of interpretations of the text. As I have already pointed out, Christian theology has always lived on the basis of a precedent. If, however, care is taken not to identify the scriptural text with the original truth or Scripture with the Gospel (in the Lutheran sense), a notion of tradition that is less static will emerge. Tradition is not just the transmission of a datum that is valid for all time. An application or an appropriation of the "world of the text" will lead not only to new productions in the order of language, but also to new practices.

Traditional hermeneutics have always postulated a pre-established harmony, a founding identity and a "merging of spheres." The new form of hermeneutics is, insofar as it takes the textual materiality of the founding text and its radical historicity seriously, above all a creative form. Using it, I have to agree to live subject to the rule of difference. If I take the text in its autonomy as an original work, I do not have to make myself contemporary with the intended saying of an author writing in the past, nor do I have to accept an obvious transcendence present in the text. The condition governing my taking over the text creatively is its closed nature. "The text is not so much a second testimony of a radical (and prior) origin as a coming at a definite time and place of a specific configuration and a structuralization of the world."[39]

Theology lives of necessity from an origin—the event of Jesus Christ as a founding event. But, as a testimony to that event, the New Testament is not a text that immediately surrenders its full and definitive meaning to us. We regard that text as an "act of interpretation," and the distance that separates us from it, far from being an obstacle, is the very condition for us today of a new act of interpretation. There is an analogy between the New Testament and the function that it exercised in the early Church on the one hand and the production of a new text today and the function that it exercises in contemporary society on the other. "The task of theology today is less an understanding of a Word spoken at another time than a 'new production' of a text, a praxis or an institution. . . ."[40] We can therefore better understand the dialectic of continuity and rupture that is constitutive in the Christian tradition. "When we turn to the origin, we are not returning to what it was and to the concrete world in which it came about. This is because what we find there is an act that has to be taken up again in a way that is always creative and not simply repeated literally."[41]

We therefore dissociate ourselves from a form of hermeneutics that claims to reconstitute the original meaning of a past event by making itself contemporary with it or by re-expressing an identical meaning in a plurality of languages. Practicing hermeneutics therefore is creating new historical figures of Christianity at different times and places. This hermeneutical praxis is correlative with a notion of truth that is not identified with an original fullness of being or with an historical figure. Truth has rather to be seen in the perspective of becoming. It is a permanent coming. That is the meaning of biblical truth as a reality of the eschatological order.

Christianity is tradition because it lives from a first origin that is given. At the same time, however, it is also of necessity always a production, because that origin can only be re-expressed historically and by creative interpretation. Theology has justifiably been compared with genealogy in the sense in which Nietzsche used this term, because its task is always to express origin and history at the same time. I shall have more to say about this question in the following chapter.

Hermeneutics and Political Theology

I have continued to insist on the challenge that structuralism represents for hermeneutics, both as a method and as an ideology. But, in a discussion of the crisis in hermeneutics, it is well worth remembering that hermeneutics have also been subject to criticism from various kinds of political theology. It would not be entirely wrong to describe the tendency of Protestant theology for more than twenty years now as a movement from theologies of the word to theologies of history and political theologies. The first are often criticized for being no more than a new theoretical interpretation of Christianity and for not leading to an effective change in the world and history under the impulse of the coming of the kingdom of God. There have, on the other hand, been successful attempts to prove that the antithesis between theology of the word and theology of history is a false one. It is, however, interesting to show how the new direction followed by hermeneutics as centered on the "world of the text" does not allow us to keep to a merely textual interpretation in the order of language, but inevitably leads us to a practical reinterpretation, in other words, to an action.

It is worth recalling at this point what I said, following Ricoeur, about the poetic aspect of the language of the Bible. As a form of poetry, biblical language is not simply a celebration of the name of God. It is also a re-creation of a new world. The object of a hermeneutical understanding of the language of the Bible is therefore the new world to which we are taken by the text. That understanding is brought about, as we have seen, by a new understanding of oneself before the text. That understanding of one-self before the text is, however, not a question of handing oneself over to a purely intellectual understanding of the text. It is rather realizing a new possibility of existence and making a new world exist. Hermeneutical understanding therefore results in social and political praxis. Ricoeur himself has said, for example: "I believe that hermeneutics that have the 'world of the text' as their central category do not run the risk of giving priority to the relationship in dialogue between the author and the reader of the text or to the personal decision made in the presence of the text. The scope of the world of the text calls for equal scope in application, and the latter will take the form of political praxis and of thought and language."[42]

There can be no hermeneutical theology, then, without praxis. What really distinguishes theology of this kind from an ideology is that it leads us to signifying praxis. One of the most striking features of the new hermeneutical theory that gives such emphasis to understanding the text of the New Testament as an act of interpretation on the part of the early Christian community is the conviction that, in the act of interpretation to-day, an interpretation of the language of faith cannot be separated from an interpretation of Christian existence. Theology based on hermeneutics does not simply repeat an original truth. It rather "makes" truth in the Johannine sense. In this creative hermeneutical theology, praxis is not just the field in which a Christian truth that has already been constituted once and for all time is applied. The signifying praxis of Christians intervenes as a constitutive element in the coming of the truth.

The language of theology is not, of course, a poetic language like that of the Bible. It is a speculative language lacking a revelatory dimension simply because of the structure of that language. Theology can, however, be compared with "poetry" in that it is the theory of an action. Theology always tells the truth that is entrusted to it in an historical difference. That new historical situation leads it to an act of interpretation which is the permanent establishment of a poem of faith that is as much in the order of confession as it is in that of praxis.

CONCLUSION

In this chapter I have tried to take very seriously the protest made against hermeneutics by many contemporary thinkers whose aim is to end the tyranny of the logos. I have not, however, come to accept the failure of all forms of hermeneutical theology, although I am sure that we have to be very alert to the consequences of the change that has inevitably taken place in hermeneutics as a result of the challenge of structuralism.

It is probable that I shall be criticized for having undertaken what seems very much like a recuperative operation. My only reply to those critics is at the same time my conclusion to this essay. It is that we cannot afford to ignore the destiny of general hermeneutics, nor can we make the future of theology as a whole subordinate to the destiny of hermeneutics. Christian theology cannot in fact be reduced to every other hermeneutical experience. It aims to be the theory of an absolutely original experience. How, then, are we to describe that original hermeneutical experience? I would say that theology is overcome by the "thing" of the text, that is, a change that makes all discourse about objectivization fail, as soon as it becomes the praxis of a text and aims to theorize about the praxis brought about by that text.

I would also repeat here a recent statement made by Gadamer: "There is no hermeneutical theory that does not depend on hermeneutical praxis."[43] It is precisely that dependence that constitutes what he calls the "hermeneutical situation." Well, perhaps I should say that, before trying to settle the dispute between structuralism and hermeneutics and deciding between them on a theoretical basis, we should perhaps reflect a little more about the "hermeneutical situation" of Christian theology.

Chapter III

DOGMATICS OR HERMENEUTICS?

It was not so very long ago that the conflict between dogmatic theologians and exegetes was being debated. Is there a debate now about the conflict between dogmatic and hermeneutic theologians? If there is, it would not be very sensible, because hermeneutics have not really become a new discipline within theological studies. The whole of dogmatic theology tends rather to think of itself as hermeneutics of the Word of God. It cannot be denied, however, that the words "dogmatics" and "hermeneutics" have, in the concrete practice of theologians, come to denote two very different tendencies. We should perhaps even speak of two paradigms of theological study. It would not be wrong to say that they are separated by an epistemological revolution.

As a systematic presentation of Christian truths, dogmatic theology is still a legitimate study of contemporary importance. But the word "dogmatic" tends to point to what may be called a "dogmatist" approach to theology. By this I mean that it claims to present the truths of faith in an authoritarian way as guarantees given exclusively by the authority of the Church's magisterium or by the Bible. There is no concern to verify critically the truth to which the Church bears witness. If this is an accurate description of dogmatic theology, then it is condemned to endless repetition, insofar as it is exclusively preoccupied with a scrupulous transmission of the *tradita*. At the same time, it is not at all concerned with what is implied in the *traditio* as an act of transmission. A "hermeneutical" theology, on the other hand, calls to mind a thought-process which, because of its living relationship with the past and the present, runs the risk of interpreting Christianity in a new way for today. This hermeneutical process in theology leads us to a non-authoritarian conception of authority, a non-traditionalist notion of tradition and a pluriform understanding of Christian truth.

Catholics witnessed a dogmatic inflation of theology within the Church until Vatican II. Would it not also be true to say that, since that time, there has been a hermeneutical inflation in the Church? It is well worth asking this question, especially because the recent protest against hermeneutics as a method of reading that has been made by structuralists has done nothing to rectify this profound change in direction on the part of modern theology. Contrary to what was taught in the earlier form of epistemology, the spheres of truth and meaning do not necessarily overlap and serious questions are being asked whether theology can still make affirmations and decisions in the order of truth. Should the theologian perhaps not confine himself exclusively to the task of revealing meaning—or rather the many different meanings of the various languages of faith? Has the field of Christian theological research not been given over to the conflicts between various interpretations and have not hermeneutics too often become identified with a miraculous way of harmonizing the different statements made by Scripture and dogma and resolving the very obvious discontinuities in the dogmatic and theological tradition?

I am of the opinion that the best way of replying to these objections is to consider the causes of this movement from dogmatics to hermeneutics. I shall also try to show in this chapter how a modern understanding of theology as hermeneutics can in fact help us to draw attention to the originality of Christian truth.

In Part 1, I shall therefore attempt to describe the movement from the dogmatic to the hermeneutical model of theological writing. In Part 2, I shall examine the historical and theological aspects of that change. Finally, in Part 3, I shall consider the status of Christian truth within a hermeneutical theology.

1. THE MOVEMENT FROM THE DOGMATIC
TO THE HERMENEUTICAL MODEL

Theology can be described as a phenomenon of writing. In fact, like any other form of writing, it is always a question of "rewriting." At each period of its history, theology has had the task of making the already constituted language of revelation more intelligible and more speaking. That language is both special and normative for the whole faith of the Church. We cannot, however, be satisfied simply to repeat it passively. It has to be made again and again present in a living way in the light of each new historical situation and in dialogue with the new methods of each culture. Theology is therefore a "rewriting" on the basis of previous writings, and those earlier writings are not only the source writing of the Old and New Testaments, but also later writings brought about under the inspiration of that source throughout the whole life of the Church.

Ever since its origins, Christian theology has made use of various models of writing. The Fathers of the Church used allegory in their scriptural exegesis. The medieval theologians fashioned a model of scientific theological language in the Aristotelian sense. The Reformers gave priority to commentaries on Scripture, in opposition to the dialectical methods of scholasticism. What is of greater interest to us here, however, is the dogmatic model that dominated the whole of Catholic theology from the Council of Trent to Vatican II.

I do not intend to spend very long describing this dogmatic model of theology. A very good account of it can be found, for example, in Marc Michel's little book on "new ways" in theology.[1] Here I shall simply draw attention to a few salient facts.

There were three stages in the pattern of teaching based on the dogmatic model of theology found in the classical handbooks that were used in seminaries in the past. The first stage consisted of stating a given thesis of faith. The second stage was an explanation of that thesis, in which the official decisions of the Church's magisterium were recalled and especially those of the Council of Trent. The third step was the proof. This consisted of quotations from Scripture, the Church Fathers and certain theologians. This pattern often concluded with a rejection of opposing theses, especially those of the Reformation.

What is particularly worth noting in this context is the point of departure taken in this theological endeavor: the initial thesis. This acted as the first principle and was always the teaching of the magisterium. It therefore played the part of an exclusive hermeneutical principle. It is also clear that a selection was made from earlier writings: the New Testament, patristic texts and various theological treatises from the past. This means, of course, that there was also exclusion: adverse opinions were excluded.

Dogmatic theology can therefore be defined as a faithful commentary on dogma, that is, what the Church has always understood and taught. Scripture is used only as a proof of what has already been established by other means. In the writings of Thomas Aquinas, propositions that are external to faith—those of the councils, theologians and bishops—are only true insofar as they express divine truth in the free event of God's revelation. This means that propositions of faith, from which theological reasoning proceeds, function on the basis of the evidence of the first principles and their truth depends exclusively on the authority of the Church's magisterium.[2] What we have here is clearly an authoritarian system in which the authority of the magisterium has in practice replaced the authority of Scripture. If this is borne in mind it is not difficult to understand how one of the greatest concerns of this "authoritarian" type of theology has always been to show that there is a continuous development between Scripture, the Fathers and the current teaching of the magisterium. It is the same apologetical concern that gave rise to the well-known theories of the homogeneous development of dogma.[3]

Others have already noted, in connection with this "dogmatic" model of theology, the importance of the hierarchy as an institution in the production of truth, theology faithfully reflecting the institutional Church. The latter is understood on the basis of a distinction (that was not made at the time of classical mediaeval theology) between the teaching and the taught Church. Clearly, then, theology can only carry out its task within a social framework. The question that arises at once, however, is whether the only task of theology is to reproduce the official teaching of the hierarchy as the authority responsible for orthodoxy in the Church by making that teaching legitimate or whether it is called to exercise another task—namely a critical and even prophetic function with regard to those invested with the power to define and interpret faith.

The great danger confronting theology based on the "dogmatic" model is that its attitude toward the truth of the Christian message will be determined by its attitude toward the institution of the hierarchy. There is, in other words, a danger that theology may be degraded to the level of an ideology that is at the service of the dominant power in the Church. As happens in the case of every religious society, the hierarchical authority is often tempted to ask theology to reproduce the discourse that legitimizes the monopoly that it enjoys as the only authentic interpreter by suppressing any discourses that introduce innovations as marginal or as deviations.[4]

It is clear that such a close dependence on the institution of the Church on the part of theology will inevitably lead to a special kind of relationship between the Church and society in general. The Church will, in other words, have an essentially defensive attitude toward society. The most obvious recent example of this is the anathema of modern ideas expressed in the Syllabus of Pius IX.[5] The best possible attitude that can emerge when Catholic dogma is challenged by the findings of the natural sciences and history is apologetical. We may conclude this brief survey of the "dogmatic" model of theology, which is usually known by the name of "Counter-Reformation theology," by saying that it persisted until the eve of Vatican II.

For at least two decades now, this system of dogmatic theology, which can be characterized as a closed and authoritarian system, has been gradually broken down and replaced. On the basis of a number of historical and cultural determining factors, which I shall be discussing later on, the "dogmatic" model of writing theology has given way to a model of writing that has come to be known as "hermeneutical." When it is claimed that contemporary theology sees itself as a form of hermeneutics, this does not mean that it has become a-dogmatic. What it above all means is that it takes the historicity of all truth, including revealed truth, and that of man as the interpreting subject seriously and that it tries to actualize the contemporary meaning of the Christian message for today. As I have already insisted earlier in this book and in other writings on the hermeneutical character of all Christian theology,[6] I shall do no more here than simply summarize, in a number of statements, the most typical aspects of this "hermeneutical" model of theological writing.

(1) The point of departure of theology as hermeneutics is not a collection of unchanging propositions of faith, but the plurality of writings included within the hermeneutical field made open by the event of Jesus Christ. The first of these writings is, as committed to writing by the witness borne to the event of Jesus Christ, itself an act of interpretation made by the first Christian community. On the basis of a new historical situation, that first writing gave rise to new writings, which were also acts of interpretation bearing witness, under the impulse of the Spirit, to the fundamental experience of the Christian community and to a new historical experience of the Church. As hermeneutics, then, theology is always a rewriting in the light of previous writings. It can be defined as a new act of interpretation of the event of Jesus Christ on the basis of a critical correlation between the fundamental Christian experience to which tradition bears witness and contemporary human experience.[7]

(2) The *intellectus fidei* of theology as hermeneutics is not an act of speculative reason in the classical metaphysical sense. It can be identified with an historical understanding in which an understanding of the past is inseparable from an interpretation of self and a creative actualization orientated toward the future. Theological writing of the "hermeneutical" kind, then, is a form of anamnesis in that it is always preceded by the founding event. At the same time, it is also a form of prophecy in that it can only actualize that founding event as a contemporary event by producing a new text and new historical figures. Theology as a constitutive aspect of tradition is therefore of necessity a form of creative faithfulness.

(3) Contrary to what is taught in the classical method of dogmatic theology, theology that is based on the hermeneutical model is not content simply to draw attention to and explain the unchanging dogmas of Catholic faith by showing how they are in accordance with Scripture, the Church Fathers and the theological tradition. It tries rather to reveal the contemporary significance of the Word of God, whether that is present in a scriptural, a dogmatic or a theological form, in the light of the Church's and man's historical experiences today. That is why it does not take into account a fundamental difference between so-called positive theology, which tends to make a historical inventory of the "datum of faith," and so-

called speculative theology, which gives a rational explanation of that datum. It is always concerned with "textual objects" and tries to decode their meaning for today. From this point of departure, it undertakes a new writing.

Hermeneutical theology is stimulated by a dynamic and lasting reciprocal relationship between Scripture and tradition, which continue to be the special place of all theological study. It also tries to understand the Christian message in a new way by respecting the hermeneutical circle between Scripture and dogma. Both of these bear witness to the fullness of the Word of God, although Scripture remains the ultimate authority (the *norma normans non normata*) in respect of the new writings to which it gives rise in the Church. The dogmatic form of theology that resulted from the Counter-Reformation read Scripture above all on the basis of the later explanations evolved in the dogmatic tradition. Theology based on the "hermeneutical" model is not afraid of being submitted to a reinterpretation of dogmatic statements made in the light of a better knowledge of the historical situation within which they were originally formulated and of our present reading of Scripture, that is, a reading that takes into consideration the irrefutable results of modern exegesis.

2. THE HISTORICAL AND THEOLOGICAL ASPECTS
OF THE DISAPPEARANCE OF THE DOGMATIC MODEL

It would be easy to write a detailed and highly critical historical account of all the factors leading to the decline of the "dogmatic" model of theological writing and its replacement by the "hermeneutical" model. I do not intend to do this. In this section, I shall simply consider some of the most essential factors, making a distinction between three kinds—historical, epistemological and psychological—but in each case concentrating on the theological aspect of the change that has taken place. What is in fact involved is a certain understanding of truth. Far from compromising the future of dogmatic theology as a systematic exposition of Christian truths, the hermeneutical orientation in contemporary theology in fact has as its aim an improved knowledge of the special form of originality found in theological truth. That is what has to be demonstrated here.

A. The Breakdown of the Single Ideology
of the Dogmatic System

Catholic theology, as a closed and authoritarian system, was first shaken when historical methods of research came to be used within the sphere of faith and the Church. It was this that brought about the modernist crisis at the turn of the century. The hierarchy failed to recognize the relevance of the questions asked by the modernists, but the movement undoubtedly made the first major breach in the hitherto impregnable defenses of the dogmatic theologians.[8]

What has been called the system of "double truth" was developed at that time. There was, in other words, the truth of the exegetes and the historians concerning the origins of Christianity on the one hand and that of the dogmatic theologians on the other. It is, of course, true that the truth of Christianity cannot be identified with a reconstitution of historical facts—historicism was guilty of this error. It is, however, equally true that the division between dogmatic pronouncements and their scriptural and historical foundations that is found in a certain kind of scholastic theology is also unacceptable—and some forms of theological rationalism have been guilty of this error.

At the beginning of what is usually known as the modern era, the Church thought of itself as an exclusive society based on the model of a single ideology. A monolithic type of dogmatic theology was quite consistent with its defensive attitude toward modern society. At the same time, it rejected the ideological and cultural pluralism that existed outside its frontiers in the liberal Western societies and condemned all doctrinal pluralism within its own frontiers, defining increasingly strict rules of orthodoxy. All professors of theology in the Catholic Church were obliged to teach what is known as Thomism. This continued until the Second Vatican Council, with the result that the question of theological pluralism did not even arise within Catholicism.

Theology based on the "dogmatic" model, especially in the form of scholastic theology that has been described as "baroque," was imprisoned in the problem of eighteenth century rationalism and, as we have already seen, there was in it an irresistible tendency to construct a system in which the authority of the Church's magisterium acquired an authority that was in practice greater that that of Scripture itself. For the first time in the history of theology, in reaction to the Reformers' insistence on the primacy of Scripture, the Bible lost its place as the source of revelation and ceased to be the first form of faith in the Judaeo-Christian revelation. In its rationalist form, then, scholastic theology tended to become a system of propositions capable of deducing all the aspects of the content of faith from credible principles. What seems to me to be a factor of decisive importance in the debate "dogmatics or hermeneutics" is that the essence of this theological construction is not the truth of what has to be believed, but the certainty that God has said this or that—a certainty that has been given a guarantee by the magisterium.[9]

Since Vatican II, the Church has been increasingly in dialogue with the world, which is characterized by a great plurality of options in favor of one or other system of values or ideology. It is challenged by an historical situation in which Christians are much more radically conscious of the relative nature of Western civilization and even of Christianity itself as an historical religion. This has inevitably resulted in a deep transformation of theological studies and methods.

In the first place, theologians have to take an insurmountable philosophical pluralism into consideration. This means that no one philosophical "system" can claim to cover all the sources of human experience. In addition to this, philosophers are no longer the only persons in dialogue with theologians, and the latter can also no longer study the Christian datum without reference to the results of the various humane sciences of religion. The way of doing theology is also constantly called into question by the new rational processes used in those humane sciences. This means that new places of theological production are always being developed, and these include not only new areas of knowledge within the framework of contemporary Western culture, but also methods used by other non-Western cultures.[10]

The ancient building of scholastic theology that claimed to be the one structure of teaching for the whole of the Church is collapsing. It is being replaced by theology of the hermeneutical type, which is of necessity pluriform insofar as it aims to be inseparably hermeneutical with regard not only to the Word of God, but also to the historical experience of mankind. On the basis of the circle between reading in faith the founding texts that bear witness to the original Christian existence on the one hand and Christian existence today on the other, a new interpretation of the Christian message may come about. That contemporary Christian experience, however, is conditioned culturally, socially and politically according to the historical situation that is peculiar to each church. This has resulted in a theological pluralism that is, as Karl Rahner has often pointed out, "qualitatively new."[11] This pluralism, it should be noted, is not the same as the plurality of "theological schools" that existed in one and the same sphere of culture and civilization at an earlier period of European history.

We are now approaching the end of the twentieth century and know that theological pluralism has become the historical destiny of the Western Church.[12] It is also clear that the future of Christianity is not to be found principally in the West. There are, for example, the Latin American theologies of liberation and several African and Asian theologies that are making hesitant beginnings. Many Christians are depressed and believe that we are moving toward a dangerous relativism and that the unity of faith is seriously threatened. I do not share their conviction and think that this pluralism of theologies and even of confessions of faith should be seen as the expression of and the need for real catholicity in the Church. Theology is clearly required to rethink the status of Christian truth as something that cannot be identified with a dogmatic knowledge that has been constituted once and for all time.

B. A New Theological Epistemology

The movement from a theology based on the "dogmatic" model to one based on the "hermeneutical" model raises the formidable problem of the status of truth in theology. In this section, I shall do no more than provide a few landmarks in a territory that has still not been completely cleared of undergrowth.

The Challenge to Truth as Adaequatio

I will not use the analytical theories of logical neo-positivism as my point of departure here.[13] It is possible to make a distinction between various theories within this area. There are, for example, the criteriological theories, which ask the question: What are the criteria that enable us to identify a true statement? And there are the verificatory theories, that ask: What are the procedures for verifying whether a statement is true or false? I would say that what underlies these theories is the problem of the statement and its foundation.

Within the context of our own European theology, however, I think that Heidegger provides a better point of departure than neo-positivism, because he questions precisely the link between the problem of truth and the statement and tries to deconstruct that link either by throwing light on a more original sphere (an existential sphere in his earlier writings) or by going back to an original history of truth and being (in his later writings).[14]

Historical "understanding," in the sense in which Heidegger understood this, is of decisive importance in our theological understanding of the statements of faith.[15] It invites us above all to question our habit of judging (as *adaequatio rei et intellectus*) the exclusive place of theological truth. Heidegger wanted to go beyond the individualistic and romantic hermeneutics of Dilthey and did so by showing that it was necessary to understand our existence itself as a perpetual projection of ourselves and grasp it moreover as a comprehensive interpretation. In his later writings, Heidegger insisted on the fact that this interpretative mode of existence was a gift of language and through it also a gift of history and being itself. Language interprets us and truth comes to us in it.

Following Heidegger, Gadamer has made tradition the place of interpretation. This is no more than the product of the difference between two historical limits that are already signifying through themselves: the past and the present. A knowledge of the past is therefore not simply an arbitrary reconstruction. It is rather a grasp of what seizes hold of us. Today, under the impact of the humane sciences and structuralism, the new theory of hermeneutics is much more alert to the social, psychological and linguistic conditions governing understanding and takes the objectivity of the text in its conditions of production much more seriously. In this way, it is quite close to the process of "explanation" that distinguishes the natural sciences. As we have seen in the previous chapter, however, in the case of an author such as Paul Ricoeur hermeneutics do not abandon the task of understanding the text and therefore do not cease to look for the truth. I have already quoted Ricoeur as saying: "A new period in hermeneutics has been initiated by the success of structural analysis and explanation has become the necessary way to understanding."[16]

A hermeneutical understanding of truth following Heidegger invites us to stand at a distance both from the metaphysical notion of truth that was characteristic of the classical form of dogmatic theology and from the idea of truth presupposed by historicism. What these two notions, both of which ultimately inherit the rationalist problem of the Enlightenment, have in common is the idea of *adaequatio* or correspondence between a subject and an object on the basis of an immediate relationship with the origin, according to which the latter is identified with a fullness of being in metaphysical thinking or with an historical fact in the past in historicism.

The metaphysical knowledge of truth that has commonly been used in dogmatic theology fails to understand the radical historicity of all truth, including that of revealed truth. Tradition is therefore seen as a treasure or deposit containing a number of intangible truths that have simply to be handed on. Historicism, on the other hand, implicitly presupposes that the truth of Christianity is to be found in a biblical text that can be reconstituted in accordance with scientific methods. Whether it is dealing with texts or with facts, historicism believes that it is possible to establish an immediate relationship with an origin that it identifies with the truth. All the efforts made by Karl Barth, Rudolf Bultmann and dialectic theologians generally have been directed toward leaving the dead-end into which historicism had run and replacing the historical limit understood as the origin by a theological one.

One author who has reacted against Bultmann is Ernst Käsemann, who has given almost exclusive emphasis to the historical factor, while at the same time taking care to maintain the theological pertinence of the historical Jesus.[17] Insofar as the latter gave rise to a plurality of testimonies, the truth of Christianity cannot be identified with the historical figure of Jesus. Gadamer has tried to overcome the Kantian rupture between facts and meaning, whereas Käsemann attempts to go beyond the antithesis between an extrinsically orientated theology and historicism. It is possible to say that the most fruitful research that is being done at present in the field of fundamental theology is concerned with the relationships between truth and history. Those engaged in this work have dissociated themselves from a metaphysical relationship with truth which is always dominated by the logic of metaphysics and an immediate coincidence with the origin and which rules out all discontinuity, difference or plurality. The task is seen as establishing a relationship between history and truth that is completely open to be marked by discontinuity, difference and change. This has led these theologians to think of tradition not as reproducing a dead past, but as producing something that is always new. Pierre Gisel, who has commented on the work of Käsemann, has suggested that this new form of epistemology should be called a "genealogy" in the Nietzschean sense.

A Genealogical Relationship with the Truth

I will take the following quotation from Gisel's book on Käsemann's theology as my point of departure: "All discourse goes back to an act of interpretation, an evaluation of the world and a unique entry into humanity. That has been the sense in which the term genealogy has been used since Nietzsche. Going beyond the alternative of historicism and metaphysics, the terms origin and history are pronounced together, because we have no knowledge of history which does not live from an origin and which is not expressed from within history and as an interpretation of that history."[18] A genealogical relationship between the past and the present has therefore to be established. The significance of the origin can only be expressed in the present will to accept the past as the origin. Calling theology "genealogy" in fact amounts to saying that it is thoroughly historical and that it is in the act of interpreting Christianity in the present that it can also express the meaning of the origins of Christianity.

For Nietzsche, gaining access to the truth was always a painful act of childbirth that transcended illusion. He puts us on our guard against the illusions of speculative dogmatism and historicism. In this, he initiated our modern critical attitude, which is not simply epistemological, in the Kantian sense, but "genealogical." The subtle mechanisms at the origin of our certainties have to be dismantled and we have to ask ourselves where they come from. Above all the illusion that consists of identifying the origin with a fullness of meaning has to be demystified, since that origin only expresses its meaning in the present.

The "hammer of genealogical analysis" does not necessarily condemn us, however, to silence or to a superficial reflection of an indefinite number of interpretations. The genealogical relationship between the past and the present is the place where truth is produced, and theology as an historical discourse should learn from this method.[19] It is in the very act of expressing the present world that theology is able to express the meaning of the origins of Christianity. In other words, theological statements about Christianity are inseparable from a present act of stating made in the present situation of the Church. The true Christian tradition is always a creative interpretation resulting from a living confrontation between the past discourse of the first Christian community and the present discourse of the Church aware of its concrete praxis.

In describing Scripture, I have insisted on the idea of "bearing witness," but it is important to remember that, as a testimony to the event of Jesus Christ, the New Testament is not a text that yields its full and definitive meaning to us straightaway. It has to be understood as an "act of interpretation" for us today. According to Pierre Gisel, it is important to draw all the conclusions from the analogy between the New Testament on the one hand and, on the other, the function that it fulfilled in the early Church, the production of a new text today and the function that it fulfils now in society and culture. The task of theology as a hermeneutical writing is to create new interpretations of Christianity and further signifying Christian practices at the service of the concrete situation in which the Church is placed at a given time and place. This way of understanding and doing theology is obviously correlative with a conception of truth that is not, as we have already seen, identified with a fullness of being at the origin or with a particular historical figure. The truth is rather subject to a permanent coming. That is the meaning of biblical truth as an eschatological reality.[20]

The Pathology of Dogmatic Truth

I have tried to throw light above on some of the historical and epistemological factors that have contributed to the disappearance of the "dogmatic" model of theological writing. I would now like briefly to consider some of the psychological factors. In entitling this section the "pathology of truth," what I have in mind is the disorder to which dogmatic theology is prone when it turns to dogmatism.

Moral theology can easily lead to legalism. In the same way, dogmatic theology can tend toward dogmatism. Why is that? We are better informed nowadays about the unconscious sources that can lead religion along the road to dogmatism. There is always a temptation in religion—it may be doctrinal, ritual or institutional—to give a hypostatic reality to for-tuitous forms and to bestow the seal of eternity on certain historical fig-ures. This would even seem to be the habitual strategy of the religious authorities when the "traditional" forms of religion are challenged by new human states of consciousness. Without going as far as some have done and speaking of the "fascist" nature of all language, I would certainly agree that there is a violence in the discourse about truth, which is, of its very nature, a discourse concerned with totalization which tries to make itself master of the past and the future and tends to become totalitarian.[21]

The Church's dogmatic discourse has not avoided this temptation, es-pecially when it has made use of the methods of speculative knowledge. We may well ask whether the secret mainspring of onto-theological think-ing that underlies all dogmatic discourses is not in fact a nostalgia for an origin that is identified with the fullness of being and truth. The world is defined by contingency and man by lack. This leads to making the idea of God the metaphysical place which totalizes all the meanings of the world, reconciles all conflicts and does away with all differences. The God of the speculative plan is no more than a projection of a megalomania of desire on the part of man who does not accept his finite nature. In fact, as A. Vergote has rightly stressed, "God, if he is really God, can only enter the kingdom of truth as a signifier who makes the field in which it is manifested open. He cannot enter as a factor inhibiting the power of significance in an ultimate response. If he has meaning, that must be insofar as he rep-resents a super-power to give meaning."[22]

There is, then, an intimate connection between the desire for abso-lute knowledge that is inherent in the metaphysical way of thinking and the tendency on the part of Christian theologians to dogmatize. Certainly from the eighteenth century onward, the notion of truth that has been em-ployed in theology as the scientific study of faith has been that of the logic of propositions based on the principle of non-contradiction. The word "dogma," which normally goes back to the event of divine truth occurring in history, in fact became synonymous with an infallible truth guaranteed by the Church's magisterium. At a later period, when the dogma of papal infallibility was proclaimed, that pronouncement could quite correctly be described as the ideology that characterized that historical figure of Chris-tianity, namely intransigent Catholicism. It would not be wrong to regard this increasing subjection to infallibility as the characteristic expression of the pathology of Catholic truth.[23] In that perspective, does not Christian faith, as a clinging to a truth that "comes" quite gratuitously, become un-consciously merged into the age-old need that man experiences for infal-lible certainty in his existence? If we are to expose the hidden roots of dogmatism and fundamentalism, we have to analyze the psychological component parts of the religious consciousness. I would conclude this section by asking whether the intolerance shown by some Christians toward theological pluralism and any attempt to reformulate Christian faith does not perhaps point to a fundamental insecurity with regard to any apparent violation of a closed system of unchanging dogmatic truths.

3. THE TRUTH OF THEOLOGY
AS AN INTERPRETATIVE LANGUAGE

All that I am trying to do in this chapter is to show that, so long as it is not functioning in accordance with the "dogmatic" model, theology does not cease to serve the truth. I would even go so far as to claim that, insofar as it is understood as a form of hermeneutics, it has even greater respect for the originality of the truth that is entrusted to us in the Christian revelation. I would like to develop this idea in this final part of the chapter.

Theology can be defined as an attempt to make the already constituted language of revelation more intelligible and meaningful for contemporary man. That language is already an interpretative language and, as a new interpretative language, theology relies on it to develop the meanings of the Christian mystery that are valuable in the present for the Church and society. Theology, then, is the way to a truth that is more full and at the same time also a way without an end. Theological language is inevitably interpretative insofar as it has the reality of the mystery of God in view on the basis of inadequate signifiers. The distinctive feature of speculative theology is that it transgresses the first signifiers of the language of revelation because of the new signifiers that are offered to it by a particular state of philosophical and scientific culture.[24] The distinctive mistake made by dogmatism, on the other hand, is that it reduces the signifiers of revelation to their conceptual expressions. Hermeneutical theology does not cease to exercise a rigorous logic with regard to the truths of faith, but it is conscious of the constitutive limitations of its own language with regard to an ideal of conceptual systematization.

Theological language has its own criteria of truth. By definition, those criteria cannot be empirical because the object of theology is an invisible reality. The point of departure of theology is, however, an historical objectivity, namely the founding events of Christianity. That is why one of the distinctively theological criteria of verification is the practice of comparing new expressions of faith with the earliest language of revelation concerned with those founding events and with the various interpretative languages found in tradition.[25]

As a new writing based on constant confrontation with previous writ-

ings, theology is measured by the same nature of truth for which it is responsible. We have therefore to attempt to describe the distinctive
features of that truth for which theology has to answer. I will consider three
of those aspects here.

A. The Truth of Theology Is in the Order of Testimony

Theological knowledge does not have a complex of conceptual truths
as its object. That object is in fact a mystery, the act by which God made
himself known to men. Jesus is, in his act of self-revelation, the unsur-
passable and unique witness of that divine truth. His testimony has been
expressed in statements about faith which have formed the work of countless theologians. Those statements can, however, never be separated from
the event of their proclamation. Christian truth, then, is a truth which only
comes in the ever present event of its proclamation and which is entirely
directed toward a fullness of manifestation of an eschatological order.
Truth in the biblical sense has rightly been compared with the essence of
truth as understood by Heidegger,[26] who has spoken of an original truth
which is situated on this side of judgment and is no more than an opening
out of meaning. This means that all truth is correlative with a non-truth
linked to a state of original obscurity. The truth with which theology is
concerned is always conscious of its original state of obscurity and can
never be reduced to the situation of those objective truths that are the
object of theoretical knowledge.

This means that there can be no theological knowledge of the truth of
faith without an active participation in the truth of God as an act of coming.
The language of theology may even be a speculative language. It still continues to be a language of commitment, however, or a self-implicative language. It can be traced back to a testimony because it is not concerned
with verifiable truths and the believing subject is totally implicated in his
act of proclamation. The truth with which the theologian is concerned,
then, is a celebrated and confessed truth. It can be compared with the
truths of practical reason in the Kantian sense. Those truths lack the objective evidence of scientific or philosophical truths. They are not arbitrary, however, because they are in accordance with man's necessary ends.
They are, in other words, necessary on the basis of internal evidence.[27]
Theology is therefore preceded by a truth that is known to it by testimony,
ex auditu, and to which it in turn bears witness. It recognizes that it is
bound by a truth which it does not have freely at its disposal. However
speculative it may be, the language of theology must remain conscious of
this initial passivity. It would not be wrong to say that theological language
as a celebration of the truth that came in Jesus Christ has not only a dox-

ological aspect, but also a practical dimension in that it bears witness to a truth that continues to come into the heart of the world and tends to be embodied in new historical figures. So, even if, as a speculative language, it lacks the evocative and suggestive quality of the language of the Bible, it still continues to be a poetic language at a very radical level and in the sense that it is the theory of an action. It is therefore bound to result in new and meaningful practices in the Church and society. In that sense, theology normally has a social and political responsibility.[28] It has the function of judging the practices of the world.

B. The Truth of Theology Is Radically Historical

When I say that Christian truth as reflected in theology has from the very beginning been in the order of testimony—a testimony that became a writing, in this case Scripture—what I mean is that it lacks the immediacy of the truth that came in Jesus Christ. The word testimony—or witness—implies a distance, a human density or an interpretation. The same can be said of all the new testimonies that constitute the theologies that have evolved throughout the history of the Church. It is clear that theology cannot expect to have immediate access to the truth, as though the latter were identical with the Word of God in its pure state or with the historical event that took place at the beginning. As hermeneutics, theology can only reach the truth of the statements of faith in an historical perspective.

Claiming that the truths of faith have an absolute value, dogmatic theologians have often made the mistake of forgetting that our possession of those truths is always historical and therefore relative. Statements of faith are as true today as they were yesterday, but man's correct understanding of them depends on his power of signification at a given historical moment. The truth of such a statement is also determined by the historical situation of question and answer that was at the origin of the formulation of the statement.

Theological knowledge as an interpretative knowledge shares in the radical historicity of that situation of question and answer. Whether the statement is an article of faith or a definition of dogma, our correct understanding of it presupposes the creation of the correct "hermeneutical situation" that is determined by the game of question and answer.[29] It is clear, for example, that a dogmatic definition is an answer that cannot be understood without reference to the historical question that gave rise to it. There are no affirmations of dogma in the pure state which do not refer to a concrete situation in the Church—usually a situation of crisis—and which are not marked by the system of representations valid at the period. Thanks to the work of theologians throughout history, it is possible for the theologian to understand the permanent content of truth in a given dog-matic definition and its function as an answer to a particular error. That definition of dogma would not be wrong or no longer valid in a different situation in the Church. It can, however, take on a meaning that is new with regard to the original meaning that was the meaning that it had in the presence of an emergency in the Church. It can also have a different func-tion in the general economy of faith, insofar as the truth of faith on which it insisted was the object not of a protest, but of a peaceful possession.

All this should help us to understand the connection between a her-meneutical theology and truth. That connection has to be seen in the light of the mutual relationship on which I have already insisted several times: that between the founding event and the situation in which the Christian community is placed today. We have to move away from the illusion of a truth to which we must adhere or a truth in the sense of *adaequatio* that presupposes an unchanging object and a constant knowing subject. Since God has made himself known to men, the interpretative aspect of the Christian community forms an integral part of the content of the truth of faith. Christian truth is therefore not an unvarying datum that is handed on from century to century in the form of a fixed deposit. It is rather a permanent coming that is exposed to the risk of history and the interpre-tative freedom of the Church under the impulse of the Spirit.

It is simply not enough to go on speaking in connection with faith about a connection between an unchanging datum and a variable cultural register. We have to be on our guard against the illusion of unvarying se-mantics that claim to subsist beyond all the contingencies of expression.[30] To persist in this illusion would be to have a purely vehicular and instru-mental understanding of language. We have rather to speak of a connec-tion of connections. According to the different historical situations in the Church, there is a production of a new connection between the Christian message and the newness of the semantic connection. It is the theologian's responsibility to make manifest the discontinuous continuity of the Chris-tian tradition which is always creating new historical figures in response to the permanent coming of the original truth that was revealed in Jesus Christ.

C. The Truth of Theology as an Expression of the Consensus of the Church

On the basis of our considerations so far, it would seem that Christian experience of the truth cannot be identified with a purely speculative knowledge. The truth of faith is a way that has to be followed, a permanent coming and a journey made together with others. It can be traced back to a testimony and it is always embodied in and at grips with the concrete situation in the world and the Church, even though it cannot be dissociated from the places of its coming.

Should we, then, speak of a pluriform truth in theology and are we in that case not exposed to the risk of an indefinite number of interpretations? This question, of course, summarizes the objections raised by all those who cannot accept the disappearance of dogmatic theology in favor of hermeneutics in theology. Is it possible, then, to escape from this painful dilemma between a monolithic dogmatism and an arbitrary choice between many different interpretations?

My reply to this question is that it is true on the one hand that there can never be one single interpretation because there must always be several possible ways of reading the same text and the truth of a text cannot be sacralized and on the other hand that there can also never be an infinite number of interpretations. This possibility of interpreting a text in a number, but not in an indefinite number of ways is present within a hermeneneutical field that is determined by a community of interpretation.[31] Progress in the truth comes about through a mutual recognition on the part of several subjects bearing witness to a truth that is always inaccessible. In this question, the theologian can learn a great deal from J. Habermas' consensus theory, according to which truth is the result of an intersubjective process of consensus. It is not, according to Habermas, a question of arriving at all costs at a consensus, but one of achieving a consensus without violence, that is, reaching an ideal situation in which communication is not disturbed by power or violence. Truth does not therefore go back to an immediate knowledge, but to a process of intersubjective argument.

For the theologian, the hermeneutic field—the sphere of truth—is the Church as the adequate subject of faith. Paul VI's statement that "faith is not pluriform" is undoubtedly correct, but I would add that it is essential to understand what faith is. If we think of faith according to its expression in a language (and it never exists in the pure state, that is, outside a state of embodiment) we could also speak of a pluriform unity of faith in time and space. If, then, we are to overcome a possible conflict between the demands for unity and the rights of a legitimate pluralism in our interpretative knowledge of the truth, we have always to return to the experience of the whole of the Church, in other words, to what is usually known as the *consensus fidelium*. There is what might be called a flair that was deeply rooted in the fundamental experience of the early Christian community and has continued to be present in all the subsequent experiences of the Church. Despite all the breaks that have occurred throughout history, the identity of the "I" of the Church has always been guaranteed by the lasting gift of the Spirit of truth (Jn 14:26) together with the identity of the experience of the believing community, which is expressed not only in confessions of faith, but also in the liturgical prayer of the Church and the service of the Gospel of the beatitudes.

I know, of course, that it is far too general to base a decision about what is true and what is false in theology on a claim that the Church is a hermeneutical place. We are always being required to provide infallible criteria. I have, however, already tried to set aside the illusion that we have a static infallible criterion at our disposal, either in the sense of scriptural or dogmatic statements or in that of an infallible magisterial decision. Here I would simply add that we have to look for the norm of theological judgment that is in conformity with the truth that is entrusted to us in the Christian revelation in the reciprocal correlation between the fundamental experience of the New Testament and the collective experience of the Church as marked by man's new states of consciousness.

What form should theology take, then? Should it be dogmatics or hermeneutics? The question appears to be ingenuous enough, but it is in fact treacherous, because it has to do with the status of truth in theology. As we approach the end of this chapter, three possible conclusions can, I think, be drawn.

(1) Theology understood as hermeneutics is not a-dogmatic. By this I mean that, although it challenges the dogmatism of a certain type of scholastic theology, it does not claim to call into question the legitimacy of dogmatic theology as a rigorous statement of the truths of faith. The myth that there is a universally valid theology has to be rejected, but each individual theology is therefore called to be even more radically Christian. In other words, each theology has to reveal the "yes" and the "no" of the Gospel and work toward a pronouncement of judgment on the world.

(2) Theology as hermeneutics should help us to respect the original nature of the truth of the Christian revelation, which is in the order of testimony and which is always coming in the present situation of the Church. It invites us above all not to reduce the signifiers of revelation to their conceptual expressions and not to identify theological with speculative reason.

(3) Finally, hermeneutical theology is in accordance with an historical situation in which the Church has the task of defending the truth entrusted to it in revelation, and that defense is not directly linked with the existence of an authoritarian dogmatic theology that claims to be universal. We are therefore invited to go beyond dogmatism and its breakdown and reconsider what a pluriform unity of Christian truth in which the unanimity of faith is not compromised might be.

Chapter IV

THE THEOLOGIAN'S
HERMENEUTICAL FREEDOM

The theologian is responsible before God and his fellow men for the Word of God and has to carry out that responsibility within the Church as a community called together and instituted by the same Word of God. In this chapter I shall be considering the theologian's special function in the present changed circumstances of the Church under the pontificate of John Paul II, but before doing that I would like to make two preliminary remarks.

(1) Since the Word of God has been established once and for all time in Jesus Christ, the theological act is subject to an irreducible tension between the faith that has been handed down historically by the first witnesses and the need that is always experienced anew to understand and actualize that faith for today. Theology is, in other words, always both anamnesis and prophecy. The theologian, then, has to be modestly but unremittingly responsible for the universal hope that has risen up in the world with the coming of Jesus Christ. That is why he is responsible not only before the community of believers, but also before all men.

(2) All believers as a community have a responsibility for actualizing the good news of the Gospel and they have all received a certain charism of truth. The community of the Church is, however, an organic whole within which it is possible to distinguish different functions and ministries. A distinction has traditionally been made in the ministry of the apostolic faith between the pastoral magisterium of the bishops and the scientific magisterium of the theologians.

The bishop's ministry is to transmit the apostolic faith and watch over its purity and fullness. The theologian's ministry is to reflect about that faith and to elaborate it at a scientific level. He makes use of the critical instruments of history, philosophy and the humane sciences in his study of faith, which is carried out in the light of the questions that arise again and again from the historical situation in which the Church and the world are placed.

There should normally be interaction between these two functions, which may even be regarded as complementary. In fact, there is often conflict between them. This has been particularly evident in recent years.[1] It is important, however, to stand back in order to go beyond the polemics and try to understand the fundamental cause of the conflict. Has it perhaps not come about because of a different understanding of what is known as the "deposit of faith" and the "rule of faith"? And has this different understanding come about because a different conception of language and truth is presupposed each time?

1. THE SPECIAL FUNCTION OF THEOLOGY

Before going on to outline my own view of the theologian's ministry the Church, I should like to mention three inadequate conceptions of theology.

(1) In the past, theology was frequently regarded as an extension of the Church's magisterium. This attitude still persists to some extent today.[2] According to this view, the theologian's task is to hand on and explain the teaching of the magisterium, elaborating it and justifying it scientifically. Theology, in other words, has no other function than that of aiding the magisterium. This would certainly seem to be so in the case of the theology of the Roman curia, which therefore runs the constant risk of exercising an ideological function in its legitimation for believers of the positions assumed by the magisterium with regard to doctrine and discipline. This task cannot be given to the whole body of theologians in the Church because they are rooted in different local churches, each with its own problems.

(2) It is also insufficient in my view to regard theology as a systematic presentation of the experience of a particular community or a local church. Theology is always rooted in concrete praxis, but it runs the risk of becoming degraded to the level of an ideology—the ideology of one or another pressure group within the Church—if it does not remain in dialogue with other interpretations of Christianity in time and space. There is no doubt that it would be impossible to evolve a universal theology in the Church of today. Despite this, however, every theology must tend to manifest the universality of Christian faith.[3]

(3) Finally, it quite common for theologians to regard their work as translating the official teaching of the Church into a more suitably adapted language. This too reflects an incomplete understanding of theology. It is

often said that the theologian's task is to "renew the language of faith." This statement is in itself very ambiguous, since it can be understood in the sense of a mere renovation or resurfacing of the worn stonework of language. This view of theology is inadequate because it is not simply a question of providing the old and unchanging doctrinal data with fresh translations, adaptations or additions.

In the light of man's new states of consciousness, the theologian has to call fundamentally into question matters that have to do with the very heart of faith. P. Labarrière has rightly called theological research centripetal as opposed to centrifugal. Believers at the grass roots of the Church are also not mistaken—their difficulties are not simply with the language of faith, but also and above all with the content of faith. It would therefore be unjust to blame theologians for making the "simple faithful" anxious or disturbing their faith. They are rather constantly listening to believers in an attempt to analyze their unease critically and to take the risk of reinterpreting for them the language of faith.

It quite certainly betrays an inadequate grasp both of truth and of language to think that it is possible to retranslate the good old traditional truths of Christianity into a new language without needing to reinterpret the truths themselves. On the one hand, it indicates that the fundamentally historical nature of all truth, including revealed truth, has been forgotten. On the other hand, it also points to an instrumental view of language, that is, an understanding of language as no more than the neutral instrument of a thought that is omnipotent and unchanging, its immutability of meaning being guaranteed at all times despite its possibly changing verbal expressions.

I would like to suggest, as opposed to this conception of theology, which I regard as insufficient, a definition of theology as a creative reinterpretation of the Christian message.

The point of departure for all theology should, in my opinion, always be what has been called the "revealed datum" or the "deposit of faith," that is, what has been handed down since apostolic times. This deposit of faith is in fact the testimony which was brought about by the event of Jesus Christ and which has become a writing—Scripture. In other words, it is not possible to separate what is revealed in God's saving action, which takes place in the event of Jesus Christ, from the experience of faith of the early Christian community, which is always an interpretative form of knowledge. This means that the theologian is bound to work on a text which is itself an act of interpretation.

It also means that, in the early Christian community, theology, as an interpretative discourse, was contemporary with faith. Theology, in other words, is not only reflection about faith and its content taking place at a later stage—it also intervenes in the content of faith itself. This should help us to demystify the idea that the content of faith is an unvarying factor underlying many varying theological translations. Revelation and faith (which also includes dogma) are as radically historical as theology itself.

As I have already shown in Chapter II, then, the immediate object of theology is not an original word full of meaning, of which Scripture is no more than an echo, nor is it an historical event in its crude factual existence. It is rather a text as an historical act of interpretation. It is also the distance separating us from that text that is the condition of theology as a new act of interpretation for us today. There is, then, a homology or a connection of connections between the New Testament and its practical effectiveness in the early Church and also between the production of a new text today and its operational character in the contemporary life of the Church. This kind of praxis of theology as a creative taking over is correlative with a notion of the truth not as a form of knowledge, but as a gradual development tending toward a fullness in the eschatological order. The truth of the Gospel is a permanent coming measured by the distance between Christ yesterday and Christ tomorrow.

The deposit of faith on which the theologian works includes not only Scripture, but also tradition, not in the sense of a second source, but in that of Scripture as understood by the Church (see the Dogmatic Constitution on Divine Revelation, *Dei Verbum*, 6, 24). The latter is essentially the dogmatic tradition as a text produced by the Church on the basis of previous writings produced in certain particular circumstances.

As a creative taking over, theology has to expose itself to a reinterpretation of dogmatic truths in the light of our new readings of Scripture. With the help of the methods of historical criticism, it tries to distinguish between what belongs to the apostolic faith and what can be traced back to the spontaneous notions and attitudes of a given period of history. The important methodological principle that has to play a part in this is that of question and answer.[4] The answer given by a dogma as an act of consciousness on the Church's part of the content of faith at a given moment can only be understood in the light of the historical question that gave rise to it.[5]

It is, however, possible that a simple reinterpretation of the answer in a new context such as our own may not be enough. In that case, the possibility of a reformulation of the original dogma should not be ruled out. A mere repetition of dogmatic formulae may simply give rise to misunderstanding and confusion, especially if the words and philosophical concepts used in the original dogma have a different meaning today. It may therefore be necessary to accept a change in the formulation if we are to be faithful to the lasting value of an affirmation of faith. It is well known that dogmatic formulae are often the result of a particular theological construction, and for this reason it is not wrong to ask whether the magisterium can still determine faith by means of dogmatic definitions at a time when the Church has to resign itself to inevitable theological pluralism. Those in authority in the Church should consider that question very seriously, now that the Church, approaching the end of the second millennium, is confronted with the urgent task of actualizing the Christian message in cultures different from that of the West. It is clear from the history of tradition that differences in expression can in fact safeguard the unanimity of faith. In 433 A.D., for example, at the time of the act of union of Cyril of Alexandria, the difference between the Christological formulae of Alexandria and Antioch were recognized. Could what was possible at that time not be possible today?

In conclusion to this first section on the function of theology, I would say that a reinterpretation of dogma does not consist of declaring that what was true yesterday is false today, but of resituating a particular dogma within the whole of Christian faith and understanding that it can have a function today that is different from the function that it had when it was originally formulated. In that respect, it is important to take very seriously into account the principle known as the "hierarchy of truths" that was reemphasized at Vatican II.[6] With this principle in mind, it would, for example, be wrong, in dialogue with other Christian confessions, to treat the dogma of the divine motherhood of the Council of Ephesus as equal in importance to the more recent Marian dogmas, the Immaculate Conception and the Assumption.

Finally, I would stress that taking the radically historical nature of dogmatic formulae seriously is bound to help us to understand the dialectical tension between continuity and rupture that is a constitutive part of the Christian tradition. Tradition is not a purely mechanical process of reproduction. It is always a new production. Christianity is not a linear development of a history that is already contained in principle in its origin. The strong apologetical flavor of the idea of a homogeneous development is, moreover, a familiar one in theology.[7]

2. THE MEANING OF A RULE OF FAITH IN THE CHURCH

Since the beginning of the history of Christianity, there have always been many different confessions of faith. There are several theologies that cannot be reduced to a simple doctrinal unity even in the New Testament itself.[8] This plurality can be found not only in Scripture, but also during the period of the first post-apostolic expressions of faith within the Church and at the time of later dogmatic developments. It is therefore possible to speak of a continuous process of genesis in these confessions of faith, and that process is subject to the pressure of constantly new historical conditioning.

Theological pluralism is nowadays accepted in practice, if not in principle, as a result of the divisions in culture and society, and a quite legitimate pluralism of confessions of faith, as distinct from the permanent divisions in the Christian churches, has to be acknowledged, at least insofar as the various local churches are rooted in irreducible historical, cultural and socio-political experiences. It is therefore impossible not to be uneasy when the magisterium places itself too exclusively in the tradition of the Western Church. This is especially disquieting since the future of Christian faith is increasingly to be found in other continents.

This situation has led to the question of regulating faith being asked with increasing urgency. Two extreme positions have emerged in response to this question. The first consists of an insistence on the absolute claim that Christianity has universal validity. Relying on the formal authority of a central power, those who make this claim try to further uniformity of doctrine and praxis in Christianity. This universality is, however, wrongly based and abstract and its protagonists run the serious risk of promoting a verbal orthodoxy that is not related to the irreducible living experience of each believer. There is also the grave danger that the confession of faith will cease to be a spontaneous expression on the part of the people of God and become an instrument of power in the hands of members of the hierarchy.

The second extreme position with regard to a rule of faith is this. Respect for all shades of opinion and toleration of all forms of Christian praxis have led to a "dismantled" Christianity. If this extreme position is accepted, the very identity of the faith handed down to us from the apostles is in danger of being compromised and the visible social aspect of Christianity in the world is threatened.

It is clear, then, that we cannot dispense with a rule of faith, which will also have to play a part in regulating the language of faith in society. Within the Church, a certain tension will have to be accepted between the demands for authenticity in my own personal faith ("What do I care about a way of speaking that is not true for me?") on the one hand and the demands made by my communion with those who also appeal to Christ ("What do I care about a truth that separates me from my brothers?") on the other.[9]

I would now like to consider three aspects of this rule of faith in turn: first, the historical meaning of the term *regula fidei*, second, authorities of this regulation of faith within the Church, and, third, the criteria of a true rule of faith.

A. The Term *Regula Fidei*

The term "rule of truth" appears for the first time in the work of Irenaeus. During the first few centuries of the Church's life, the expression *regula fidei* did not denote an act on the part of the teaching Church in the sense of a norm that was different from the teaching received from the apostles and handed on to the Church.

Because of a historical evolution that Yves Congar has traced in his work on tradition,[10] however, a distinction came increasingly to be made between a passive tradition, that is, the content of faith, and an active tradition, that is, the magisterium that puts forward that content. In fact, the magisterium became the immediate rule of faith by virtue of its normative function. This resulted in undue emphasis being given to the power of the authority in the Church responsible for defining faith, at the expense of the sole rule of faith of the whole Church. That rule of faith is in fact not a created authority, but God himself, who is described by Thomas Aquinas as the first Truth. In identifying the rule of faith with the magisterium, what is forgotten is the truth of the Gospel as an object of faith and not simply as a body of doctrine or a thing of truth. The Gospel is above all a dynamic truth, a truth that is coming, a truth that is practiced in the Johannine sense and a truth that is aimed at but never possessed.

The inexhaustible character of the Christian message is rooted in the distance between the Word of God contained in Scripture and the Gospel as eschatological fullness. It is both a memory and a promise. From its origins, the capital of evangelical truth contained in the Church's praxis has always exceeded the explicit content of the confessions of faith. Just as the Church and the kingdom of God are not identical, so too is it wrong to identify a dogmatic confession of faith with the Word of God.

B. Authorities of the Rule of Faith

Three such authorities can be distinguished: first, the authority of the believing people of God, second, that of the body of pastors, and, third, that of the community of theologians. Interaction between all three authorities is a pre-condition for the sound functioning of the rule of faith.

(1) The Believing People of God

Indefectibility, that is, remaining permanently in the truth, was promised to the whole of the Church, the people of God, by Christ. The ministerial infallibility of the members of the hierarchy is only an expression of that indefectibility given to the whole Church.

Whatever may be the case with regard to errors, distortions and the overlapping of what can and what cannot be reformed, the Church is permanently subject to the epiclesis of the Spirit. It is therefore always necessary to take the *sensus fidei* of all believers seriously and to speak of a "self-regulation" of all the believing people of God as a living organism in search of the whole truth. As Paul says, "Test everything, hold fast to what is good" (1 Thess 5:21). These words are addressed to all Christians. The importance of this *sensus fidei* is stressed above all in the Dogmatic Constitution on the Church, *Lumen Gentium*, 2, 12, of Vatican II: "The body of the faithful as a whole, anointed as they are by the Holy One, cannot err in matters of belief. Thanks to a supernatural sense of faith which characterizes the people as a whole, it manifests this unerring quality. . . ."[11]

It is not difficult to find examples of this watchfulness in the faith of the whole people of God throughout the history of the Church. At the time of the Arian controversy, for instance, the confession of faith was preserved not by the bishops, but by the faith of the whole Christian community. Today, the active non-reception by believers at the grass roots of the Church of a teaching or a law promulgated by those officially in authority undoubtedly has the value of a sign. It is just not enough to condemn as illegal new praxis of this kind in the Church. History is full of examples of practices initially in conflict with the official teaching of the Church eventually becoming the dominant praxis in the Church and in the end receiving the official sanction of those in authority. We have therefore to trust in the evangelical vitality of the Christian people and recognize that the renewals that conform most closely to the predicament of the people of God in their exodus come from below and not from above. In the sphere of liturgy, for example, did Vatican II not sanction initiatives that had to a great extent come from the grass roots?

(2) The Body of Pastors

This is the authority for regulating faith which occurs to us most spontaneously. The body of bishops in communion with the Bishop of Rome perpetuates the mission entrusted to the apostles to hand on the message of Jesus Christ. It is therefore in a conviction of faith that we accept the distinctive part played by the pastoral magisterium of the Pope and the bishops in deciding in cases of conflict or trouble whether a new interpretation of the confession of faith or a new confession of faith is legitimate. I will do no more here than simply recall some of the most widely accepted conditions under which this magisterial regulation of faith can be properly carried out.

1. The magisterium is subject to the Word of God, that is, the testimony of Scripture reread in the faith of the Church, but taking into account the irrefutable results of critical exegesis.

2. The magisterium is at the service of the community of the Church and its testimony. This means that it may not use the confession of faith as an instrument of power. It has rather to listen to the *sensus fidei* of all Christians that is expressed in many different ways throughout the Church. In other words, the reception by the whole of the people of God of the teaching of those in authority in the hierarchy is a reliable criterion by which the credibility and persuasive force of that teaching can be verified.

3. The magisterium must—especially when it expresses itself through that authority to regulate faith known as the Congregation of Faith—express itself for the whole of the community of the Church in the name of the apostolic faith and not in the name of a particular theology, even if that is the theology of the Roman curia.

4. The magisterium has authority over the interpretation of faith suggested by theologians, but it must take the research carried out by theologians very seriously into account in its attempt to express in a scientifically responsible way the *sensus fidei* of believers and to reinterpret the confession of faith on the basis of the most radical contemporary questionings.[12]

(3) The Community of Theologians

I have already discussed the theologian's task of creative reinterpretation at some length. Here I would simply like to insist on his organic role in the complex process of the regulation of faith, in which I make a distinction between a more pastorally orientated function and a scientific function.

1. This first function carried out by theologians is to mediate between the magisterium and believers. There are two aspects to this task. On the one hand, theologians have to give considered expression to the evangelical vitality of the Christian community in solidarity with the life led and the questions asked by all men. In that way, they can help the magisterium in its task by making its members sensitive to the real needs of the believing community and changes in society. On the other hand, theologians also have to try to explain and interpret the official teaching of the Church so that it enters not just verbally, but really into the hearts and minds of believers.

2. Theologians have a right to an area of freedom in order to devote themselves to demanding and painstaking research, the only pre-condition for which is a love of the truth and the certainty that the mystery of Christ transcends all the statements that the Church can ever make about

it. They see themselves as especially responsible for the future of faith in the presence of man's critical reasoning. This means that they have to bear in mind that not only the weak, but also the strong may be scandalized, with the result that they have not only to criticize progressive heresies, but also to denounce conservative heresies. To do this within the framework of serious theological research, they are bound to reflect in their teaching and writing the distance that exists between the official teaching of the Church and the Christian confession of faith at its most authentic level.

In practice, the theologian will be critically aware in his approach to the traditional statements about faith that they contain nothing that is irreversible as far as their formulation is concerned. He will, for example, learn how to distinguish between the truth of a dogmatic formulation made in response to the historical situation in which it was produced (recognizing that this will be a case of the Church's exercise of authority at a given moment in time) and the truth of the affirmation of faith that is contained in that formulation (recognizing that this is a case of the authority of the Word of God). He needs to have, in other words, a sound spirit of criticism if he is to avoid giving the same value and the same authority to every pronouncement made by the magisterium.

This is a risky but very responsible task, and the theologian has to proceed cautiously. He also cannot be denied the right to err. He must also be able to benefit from the control exercised and the constructive criticism offered by the community of his fellow theologians before his researches are prematurely stopped by the disciplinary measures of the Roman Congregation.

C. The Question of Criteria

All that I have tried to say in this chapter points to the fact that it is not enough for the magisterium to assert its juridical authority in order to ensure a rule of faith in the Church. We have rather to think in terms of a self-regulation of faith by the whole of the Church as a living body in which each member is called to play his part. The rule of faith is in fact the object of faith, the mystery of Christ, in that it is able to give rise to historical figures that are always new in the order of the confession of faith and praxis.

In cases where there is conflict or an irreducible plurality of interpretations, however, what criterion should be used so that we can judge what is and what is not in accordance with the faith of the Church?

In the case of a new formulation of faith, it is not enough either to appeal literally to Scripture or to some kind of chemically pure unvarying factor that is regarded as the minimal content of faith in the form of a centuries-old unchanging and unchangeable pronouncement. In the light of what continues to be at the heart of Christian faith, it will always be necessary look for Jesus Christ and his life and preaching. This will always remain a valid criterion, but it is, of course, very general.

The real criterion to be applied in such a case is not a static and external, but a dynamic norm, a proportional relationship between the various ideas that form a constitutive part of the substance of Christianity and refer directly to Christ as their central point.

Finally, the whole Christian community, the Church as a community confessing faith and interpreting as it listens in constantly new ways to the Word of God, has the task of verifying and therefore of judging in cases of conflict and a plurality of interpretations. There is not an indefinite freedom of interpretation and, as a living reality, the faith of the Church has real discernment with regard to itself as a confession. It is not wrong to say that freedom of interpretation should be measured not by an intangible content expressed in propositions that have been handed down mechanically from century to century, but by the lasting relationship between man and God first established in Jesus Christ, the identity of which throughout the history of the Church has been ensured by the Holy Spirit.

If the need arises and the magisterium has to intervene, its members should act as servants of the totality of the Church's faith, that is, Catholic faith in the sense of the universality of faith in time and space. It is of primary importance always to look for what is essential in the apostolic faith. *Id quod requiritur et id quod sufficit:* this is a fundamental principle in all ecumenical striving that has to be always borne in mind in the search for a formula uniting the different Christian confessions. It should also be applied within the Catholic Church.

In the first part of this chapter, I spoke of the theologian's creative faithfulness. Theology is always tradition in the sense of having been preceded by an origin that is given, that origin being the event of Jesus Christ. No statement made by theologians can ever express the full meaning of that event. At the same time, however, theology is also always the production of a new language, since it can only continue to repeat that origin historically and in accordance with a creative interpretation.

Part II

The Interpretative Testimony
To Faith

Chapter V

THE RESURRECTION OF CHRIST AS AN INTERPRETATIVE TESTIMONY

Testimony is undoubtedly the most irreducible possibility in human discourse. It is in itself a "process of interpretation" as a creative encounter between the event and its meaning, experience and language. It is in the discourse of testimony that the inextricable bond between reality and language about which the new hermeneutics speak to us appears most clearly. An event that has not been taken possession of in a tradition of language and therefore in a succession of testimonies soon becomes an insignificant event and even ceases to be an historical event. According to Enrico Castelli, "a fact does not testify if it is not interpreted."

Testimony as an original possibility of human discourse testifies both to the irreducibility of historical events to crude facts and to the irreducibility of the word to language as a system. Testimony is always a word event. It is the "saying" of someone to someone. Reflection about testimony forces us to go beyond the positivism of words as a positivism of facts, since testimony is situated precisely at the nodal point of the living articulation of the word and the event. And in the presence of a structuralism that aimed to remain in the "positivism of signs," testimony, as the original possibility of human discourse, is the most suitable means enabling us to sense the mystery of language as a development of the "saying" by a free decision.

Testimony always takes us back to the freedom of the witness, to his signifying intentionality and therefore to a recipient. As soon as man no longer inhabits language as a sign of being and of God, the word becomes more urgent than ever as a testimony, that is, as a calling to account of man's conscience. This testimony challenges all Caesarisms, beginning with the "Caesarism of science." Electronic brains are more capable than the human memory and can always supply us with increasingly certain and increasingly abundant information. On the other hand, however, they can

79

never bear witness or testify. And since, in the opinion of some thinkers, we shall have increasingly to abandon as lost a certain normativity both in the order of objective knowledge and in the ethical order, it is quite possible that testimony—especially when it is the expression of a human community—may become the source of a new objectivity, going beyond the typically modern dilemma of an "alienating objectivity" or an "inconsistent subjectivity."

These few words about testimony as the original possibility of human discourse invite us to reflect about the structure of testimony, insofar as it goes back indissociably to personal faith and knowledge. Testimony is inseparably an historical attestation and a "word event." I would like to demonstrate this in connection with testimony to the resurrection of Christ. What we have here is certainly a limit case, but it is also a privileged case to seize hold of the interpreting activity at work in the testimony. Doing the hermeneutics of testimony is doing the interpretation of the interpretation in action. And it is in connection with the testimony borne to the founding events of Christianity that we are best able to see the limits of historical positivism as psychological hermeneutics.

Before studying the relationships between experience and language as constitutive elements in the testimony to the resurrection, however, I would like to consider the lesson that can be learned from a study of the origins of the word "witness."

1. AT THE ORIGIN OF THE WORD "WITNESS"

A. "Witness" in Ordinary Language

It is important to bear in mind that the word "witness" (*martus*) was first used in legal language. The witness in a trial is the one who can give information at first hand about the events in which he has been involved or in which he has been personally present. His testimony is therefore based on an immediate experience. The ear- and eye-witness is the only witness who is worthy of our faith.

There is, however, in classical Greek another use of the word "witness" and its derivatives[1] which can be traced back not to the juridical, but to the ethical sphere. The witness in this case is not the one who testifies to real events on the basis of an immediate experience. He is the one who makes himself the spokesman of a personal opinion or of truths of which he is personally convinced. In other words, his testimony is no longer the expression of a knowledge based on experience. It is rather the expression of a faith.

Despite this divergence of meaning (testimony about events—testimony borne to a truth), there is a very deep relationship justifying this change of position in the objective order of the process to the sphere of ethics, that is, an intimate and unimpeachable conviction as the source of the testimony and the involvement of the witness in his word. The one who testifies to a truth does not testify in the name of the compelling evidence of an empirical fact. He does speak, however, in the name of an inner certainty which has for him the force of evidence. Testimony is, then, the public expression of an inner unimpeachable word. That is why the one who testifies to a truth in the order of values and human action is ready to sacrifice the freedom to live to the freedom to speak. Current language knows instinctively that one does not testify to scientific truths. One only testifies to truths or values for which one is ready to die. It is in this that the difference between the part played by the informer and that played by the witness is visible. Computers can supply language with information, but they can never supply the word of the witness.

The originality of testimony bearing on value-judgments would suggest to us that it cannot be reduced to pure subjective testimony in opposition to objective testimony alone, that which bears on verifiable events or situations. The freedom of the witness is always involved, but he does not testify to the point of death in order to provide information about a simple personal conviction—that would be either obstinacy or fanaticism. He testifies in order to celebrate an objective order of truth.

We begin here to sense the original epistemological status of testimony, when it is the testimony of a "believer." It has a mixed status which is both objectively insufficient and subjectively sufficient and which can be compared with the mixed status of the postulates of practical reason in Kant. In the order of theoretical knowledge, faith-belief has the fragility of the probable. In the practical order, however, reasonable faith corresponds to the objective order of the necessary ends of human action. If the truth respected by testimony goes back to the sphere of necessary ends in the order of action, it will be understood that testimony cannot be reduced to the arbitrary nature of a subjectivity. It is the expression of a certain normativity—that of practical truths which escape the possession of purely theoretical knowledge. We may say that the territory of testimony corresponds to Kant's question: "What am I permitted to hope?"

Despite the force of conviction that is common to the two types of testimony, testimony, understood as the testimony of faith-belief in the order of value, will tend increasingly, in ordinary language, to lose its state of being rooted in the first sense of the word "witness," the one that it has in juridical language. More precisely, in the language of the New Testament, the two meanings of the word "witness" that have so far been distinguished will find themselves associated in an original way—both the eye-witness of events in a process and the witness in the order of values. It will be a question of the testimony of a "believer." Here, however, "believer" does not go back to philosophical faith, but to the positive faith that is founded on an historical revelation.

B. "Witness" in the Language of the New Testament

It is above all in St. Luke that the word "witness" points in an indissociable way to the one who was the witness of the historical events in the life of Jesus and in particular his resurrection and to the one who testifies to those events in faith.[2] Although the idea of witness is connected in St. Luke with testimony borne to historical events, it is wider than this in that it is always a testimony of believers. The resurrection is a real event, but it is not situated at the same level as the other events in the historical life of Jesus. It cannot be attested simply on the basis of the testimony of eye-witnesses. It has to be united in faith and it is then that it becomes the object of testimony.

It is very remarkable that in the theology of Luke only the Twelve are witnesses to the resurrection (Acts 1:22; 2:32; 4:33; 10:40), whereas there were many more eye-witnesses of the appearances. The testimony of the resurrection is limited to the little circle of the twelve, since "knowing" the resurrection is knowing in faith. Bearing testimony to the resurrection does not consist in transmitting neutral information about an historical event. It is identifying and therefore interpreting in faith that event as the saving event par excellence. And if the quality of apostles is limited to the group of the twelve, that is because the testimony of the resurrection is the object of the apostolic ministry. The apostolic testimony not only requires that the witness should be a direct witness who is worthy of faith, but also that he should adhere in faith to the Gospel as the message of salvation. That apostolic testimony will be the source of all the other testimonies in the Church. Christian consciousness of the resurrection will always be an apostolic knowledge "built upon the foundation of the apostles" (Eph 2:20), that is, a participation in the knowledge of the apostles.

In St. John, the verb "to testify" or "to bear witness to" (*martirein*) retains its early meaning, that of legal language, and that is why it is necessary for the witness to have seen and heard (Jn 1:34/; 3:11–12; 19:34; 1 Jn 1:2; 4:14) that to which he testifies.[3] The Johannine writings, however, again and again go beyond this first meaning in an original conception of testimony in which the "knowledge" of the witness comes from faith in the testimony of Jesus and not from a tangible experience. Jesus alone is the faithful witness par excellence (Rev 1:5; 3:14) and he can also be a truthful witness because he is the one who knows (5:32). He bears witness to what he has seen and heard with the Father (3:11, 32). And if, from then onward, men are able to transmit the testimony that they have received, it is because they too know in faith.

According to the Johannine understanding, there is no testimony without eye-testimony, but the eye-witnesses testify definitively to the "things of heaven." This is because their testimony can only be received in faith that does not judge "according to the flesh" (8:15). Because testimony bears on a revelation, the only guarantee of the authenticity of that testimony is the authority of the witness. Jesus claims the testimony of the Father and the disciples claim the testimony of Jesus. Whereas in St. Luke the authenticity of the testimony is based on a guarantee of historical order—that of the witnesses of the resurrection—in St. John the testimony goes back to the witness himself and his truthfulness. The testimony bearing on revelation has to be accepted because the witnesses are worthy of faith and only faith provides that certainty. The Johannine theology of testimony does not, it is true, break the link between faith and history, but it does not try to accredit faith in the mystery of the incarnate Word to the historical testimony borne to the event of the resurrection. Is it not above all anxious to show that faith can only be really founded on the "revelation of the Father" and not on "flesh and blood"? It is also the Fourth Gospel especially which gives priority to faith without seeing with regard to the faith of Thomas who wanted to see in order to believe (Jn 20:29).

With these brief comments on the meaning of the word "witness" in mind, I would confirm that the meaning of "witness" in juridical language, that is, in the language that attests the existence of an empirical fact, tends to move further and further away—at least in ordinary language—from the meaning of "witness" in the language of ethics or religion. Our brief examination of the vocabulary of the New Testament, however, has shown that the two meanings of the word "witness" are inextricably associated with each other in the language of Christianity.

I would now like to study the testimony of the resurrection as the expression of a unique experience in which the attestation of an event cannot be dissociated from a believing reinterpretation. This will not simply be a question of re-editing a typically apologetical debate about the relationships between historical certainty and supernatural faith in the act of faith. What I am concerned with here is to reflect about testimony as an exemplary case of the encounter between reality and language. The resurrection of Christ is both a real event that in fact occurred and an event of the language of faith, a word event. It cannot be reduced to any other historical event, but it can help us to situate what is at stake in the structure of every testimony when it bears on an historical event. Testifying is making the immediate experience of an event "come to word." This is not the same as a simple repetition. It is rather always an original "reproduction" of the event.

2. EXPERIENCE AND LANGUAGE

IN THE TESTIMONY OF THE RESURRECTION

A. *The Languages of Paschal Faith*

The best way to discern the elements involved in the structure of the testimony borne to the resurrection of Christ would undoubtedly be to make a rigorous analysis of the language of the New Testament relating to the risen Jesus. This task has, however, already been carried out by other scholars.[4] In this chapter, I shall simply bring together the conclusions that are most directly concerned with my own subject matter.

If we consider all the texts in the New Testament that refer to the resurrection, we can distinguish certain types of language. Alongside the language of testimony or of confession of faith, there are narrative accounts, liturgical accounts and theological interpretations. We can, however, confine ourselves to two fundamental literary genres—testimony and narration. Examples of these are Paul's testimony in his First Letter to the Corinthians and the Gospel accounts referring to the discovery of the empty tomb and the appearances.[5]

In the First Letter to the Corinthians, Paul makes himself the spokesman for the tradition concerning the appearances: "He appeared to Cephas, then to the twelve. Then he appeared to more than five hundred brethren at one time, most of whom are still alive, though some have fallen asleep. Then he appeared to James, then to all the apostles. Last of all, as to one untimely born, he appeared also to me" (1 Cor 15:5–8). This objective account of the appearances, however, forms part of a discourse that goes back to the genre of testimony. The appearances are the object of the creed that he is transmitting to the Corinthians. This can be seen, for example, in verse 11: "So we preach and so you believed" and in verses 14–17: "We are even found to be misrepresenting (= false witnesses to) God . . . if Christ has not been raised." Similarly, the a-personal Gospel accounts referring to the appearances are also an expression of an immediate personal experience and of a believing reinterpretation of that experience. "According to the evolution of the discourses in the New Testament, the appearance could not for a long time have been the object of an autobiographical account. It was at a very early stage integrated into the a-personal account."[6]

It is therefore not difficult to see that it would be wrong to insist on the distinction between "testimonies" and "narrations" in the statements made in the New Testament about the resurrection of Christ. What is more interesting in our present context is to note that there is, in the structure of every discourse about the resurrection of Jesus, a relationship of the type of that between the preacher and the believer. In other words, the witness is always implicated in his account, and the person addressed, that is, the one in whom it is aimed to arouse faith, is always envisaged. This is clear in the discourses of Peter and Paul that are reported to us in the Acts of the Apostles. It can, however, also be detected in the narrative discourse of the prologue to those Acts (Acts 1:1–3).

Our anxiety, then, to rediscover the historicity of the resurrection on the basis of the most descriptive and the most narrative texts in the New Testament should not make us forget that those accounts are the object of a preaching addressed to Jews and Greeks. They are the Gospel proposed to faith. To take up a distinction that is familiar to linguists, they are not constative, but performative statements. And, in the case of such brief and early confessions of faith as "The Lord has risen indeed!" (Lk 24:34), these "proclaim faith rather than state it."[7] In other words, "they are not to be regarded as descriptive. They do not provide information. They rather mediate an adherence to God and to Jesus Christ."[8] With the help of Austin's analyses, J. Delorme has studied the "illocutionary" force of the Greek verbs used by Paul to proclaim paschal faith.[9] It emerges from his study that what we have here is a type of discourse in which Paul is entirely involved in his word and in which the interlocutor is invited to make a personal decision. Language is not the neutral instrument communicating information. Even if it makes use of the register of the account, Paul's discourse on the risen Christ is not presented as a constative statement. It is closer to a performative statement.

It has to be added that it is the same power of God that is manifested in the resurrection of Christ which is manifested in the preaching of the apostles. The latter is a "demonstration of the Spirit and power" (1 Cor 2:4). Testimony itself is therefore a "word event" in continuity with the event of the resurrection at the origin of testimony. The two "events" are manifestations of God's power, and it is still God's power that is at work in the believer's adherence to the testimony borne by the apostle. Whether it is a question of the testimony of the first witnesses, the apostolic preaching or the confession of faith made by believers, we are in the presence of different expressions of a single shared experience in which an historical attestation, faith and the power of the Spirit are indissociably implicated.

An analysis of the language of the resurrection is therefore instructive with regard to the nature of the testimony borne to the risen Christ and the very nature of the event of the resurrection. It is not a question of an empirical report or account of events of the kind that could be made by a witness at a trial. At the origin of the testimony, there is an experience of something new, an event which is external to the witness and which he did not initiate. The best way of doing justice to the texts is to speak of "objective vision": "To them (the apostles) he presented himself alive after his passion by many proofs, appearing to them during forty days and speaking of the kingdom of God" (Acts 1:3). This original experience is, however, enclosed within an experience of faith which recognizes the risen Lord in the Jesus who "presented himself alive." That is why the testimony, as an affirmation of the event, is immediately transformed into a "confession of faith," the aim of which is to arouse faith in the one to whom it is addressed.

A study of the texts would therefore suggest that the empirical dimension of the event to which testimony is borne is simply one component part of an event that transcends the order of ordinary historical events.[10] In other words, the resurrection of Christ is something other than a crude fact. It is an interpreted event that can only be reached on the basis of the language of paschal faith. The real event that in fact happened is always refracted in a "word event."

I would now like to show how the plurality of the languages of paschal faith can help us to define more precisely the original relationship between historical experience and language in the testimony of the resurrection.

B. Historical Experience and Language

It is recognized in the new hermeneutics that two gulfs have to be bridged. There is, in other words, not only a distance between the past of the text and the present of our own culture, but also a distance between the text and the events to which it refers. In other words, Scripture is not so much a datum directly inspired by God as a testimony with a meaning that has to be deciphered by resituating it within a tradition. Protestant theologians have therefore been led to question the "autonomous" authority of Scripture. As Pannenberg has pointed out, "For Luther, the literal meaning of Scripture was still identical with its historical content. For us, on the other hand, the two are different. We can no longer equate the image of Jesus and its history as given by the various New Testament authors with the real origin of the events."[11]

We cannot, then, equate the various testimonies of paschal faith with the real origin of the events. And, as we have already seen, those testimonies are not so much of the order of discourse as of the order of proclamation. They are a speaking rather than a spoken or written word. They testify to real events—the appearances. But those events are not reported as crude facts. They are interpreted events. This is already true of history in general, in which I cannot dissociate its practice, its interpreting activity, from its object, the events related. Making history is always "producing" the same events differently.[12] "History never becomes a whole on the basis of crude facts. As a history of men, it is always mixed with understanding, hope and memory. The transformation of that understanding itself unites the events of history. History and understanding cannot be dissociated in the early data of a history."[13]

The indissociable link between historical experience and the language of interpretation becomes even more striking if we consider the historical testimonies that are available to us in the case of something that happened during the "fifty days" between the death of Christ and the birth of the Church. I have been saying for a long time that, if it is true that the resurrection of Christ is a real and new event with regard to the cross of Jesus, this does not prevent it from being an event that cannot be reduced to the crude facts of universal history, those which go back to historical inquiry. It is in fact the very act which is not accessible to direct witnesses and by which God glorified Jesus of Nazareth who was placed in the tomb. I have, however, also been saying that the transcendent event of the resurrection also has an historical dimension, the concrete traces that it left in the history of men, namely the appearances, the empty tomb and the paschal preaching of the apostles. When it reaches this point, theological reflection about the resurrection, which has all too frequently been preoccupied with the task of establishing the historicity of the appearances, often behaves as though it were possible to rediscover the "historical facts" outside the believing interpretation of the first witnesses. The appearances are inseparably both real events and "language events."

It is possible to speak of the appearances as historical signs of the resurrection. But this means that they are precisely signs and not demonstrative proofs. As Thomas Aquinas said, *non sunt probationes, sed signa.* Insofar as they have an empirical dimension, the appearances are the object of sensual experience. But insofar as they are signs of something else, they leave the witness entirely free. "They are an appeal made to faith and not to empirical confirmations."[14]

As far as the relationship between historical experience and the language of faith is concerned, the most suggestive lesson that can be learned from recent exegetical studies is that we should be sensitive to the diversity of languages that try to express the mystery of the resurrection. We are in the presence of a unique experience, and the plurality of vocabularies betrays the inexpressible character of the experience. There is no paschal faith without witnesses, and so there is none without language. But paschal faith cannot be reduced to one of its languages.

Among the different languages of the paschal mystery, it is the very early formula "God raised Jesus from the dead" which made itself so strongly felt in the traditional language of the Church. Despite its imperfections, the language of the resurrection continues to have privileged status. It is what X. Léon-Dufour has called the "language of reference," against which every interpretation ought to measure itself.[15] At the same time, the other languages of the New Testament ought not to be neglected, including those of life and exaltation, which have the function of correcting and completing the vocabulary of the resurrection.

Writing for the Greeks, who were hostile to the idea of resurrection, Luke and Paul gave priority to the vocabulary of life. They also tried to affirm both the reality and the newness of the life of the risen Lord (speaking of "eternal" life in the case of Christ or describing him as "the firstborn from the dead"). But whether it is a question of the language of the resurrection or that of life, there is a serious danger of remaining with an imaginary representation of Jesus' return to his previous life. That is why the vocabulary of exaltation has the function of emphasizing the eschatological character of Christ's resurrection. This new interpretation of the reality of the resurrection can help us to become aware of the distance between the miracle of the resurrection as exaltation to God's right hand and entering into glory. We are in that case invited to go beyond all the traps laid by the imagination and think of another life and another body beyond life here below on earth. Paschal faith is able to confess quite simply: "Jesus is Lord." It says in a different way everything that is contained in the primitive formula: "God raised Jesus from the dead."

This plurality of paschal expressions confirms what I have said about the structure of testimony as an historical experience and as a language event. There would be no testimony of the resurrection without experience of a real phenomenon. But that "historical" experience is surrounded by an experience of faith that is expressed in many different ways, since the experience itself goes beyond the possible means of expression available to one language.

The hermeneutical freedom of the expressions of paschal faith testifies to the trans-historical dimension of the resurrection. Just as the resurrection, as an eschatological event, cannot be reduced to its purely historical component part, so too is the testimony of the resurrection a movement toward the word of an experience in which interpretative faith is more important than an empirical confirmation. Thus, when we say that our faith in the resurrection of Christ is based on the historical testimony of the apostles, who were witnesses of the appearances, it is less concerned with the character of the facts reported as events than with the person of the risen Jesus who is revealed via those facts. We only know those facts via the testimony of men who were themselves believers, "witnesses chosen (previously appointed) by God" (Acts 10:41). In other words, faith bears within itself its own testimony, even though it is founded on a testimony that goes back to an historical inquiry.

An examination of the various languages of paschal faith has therefore enabled me to emphasize the inseparable bond between experience and interpretation in testimony. But it is putting it mildly to say that experience and interpretation do not have to be dissociated from each other and that testimony is a reflection of a unique experience in which the event and meaning are mingled. The inaugurating aspect of testimony has to be emphasized much more in respect of the event itself, which, by becoming a "word event," is given to a new existence. In contrast to what would be thought in a narrow historical positivism, it is when we leave empirical history that we in fact rediscover real human history as tradition.

C. Testimony as a "Word Event"

If Bultmann's well-known statement "Jesus is raised in the kerygma" implies a denial of the historicity of the resurrection, it is an unacceptable formula. If, on the other hand, it tries to make us grasp hold of the fact that the resurrection of Jesus entered into history not simply through the appearances as empirical facts, but in and via the testimony of faith borne by the apostles, then what Bultmann says has a very deep meaning. There is a carrying out of the resurrection in the kerygma itself. Every historical event has the ability to give rise to a word or a testimony, and it is when the real event has become a "word event" that it really belongs to the human history that has never ceased to actualize its meaning.

It is more true of the event of Jesus Christ than of any other event that "the historicity of an event depends less on its 'factual' density, its crude materiality, than on its ability to enter into a discourse in which a human community can recognize (and also reconsider and remake) its own history."[16] A fact or an experience which does not give rise to testimony is without interest or even non-existent. History only collects events that have been named, interpreted and resituated by a word in a tradition, that is to say, in a network of meanings. "The word by which I make a given situation come to language is in fact the human inauguration of the event and, in that sense, its constitution, whatever its consistency and its reality may otherwise be."[17]

Testifying, then, is making an event that has really happened come to the word. It is not simply relating an event, but giving that event a new existence. It is not in fact possible to dissociate the event from the new meaning that it assumes in testimony. Testimony is par excellence a "word event," and that is why I said at the very beginning of this chapter that, as a possibility of human discourse, testimony is the best way of making manifest the irreducibility of the Word to language as a system. As Paul Ricoeur has shown in his study, "Evénement et sens," it is in the linguistics of the Word that the living articulation of the event and of meaning is verified.[18] Testimony goes back to the linguistics of discourse or of the message, not to the linguistics of the language or of the code.

It is, however, writing which makes very clearly manifest what takes place already in testimony as an immediate word about the event. There is a going beyond the event as fleeting in its meaning as lasting. By becoming writing or Scripture, the first testimony of the apostles came to belong in a lasting way to human history and disclosed possibilities of actualization that were quite new both in the order of meaning and in that of action. As Ricoeur has said, "the career of the text escapes from the finite sphere of the author's experience. What the text says is now more important than what the author intended to say and all exegesis develops its procedures within the framework of a meaning that has broken its links with the psychology of its author."[19]

This separation of meaning from the factual event takes place already in testimony as a proclamation of the event. In the case of the resurrection, this means that we can only reach the resurrection of Christ in testimonies about it, that is, in confessions of faith. In other words, we reach it not in its spatio-temporal dimensions, but insofar as it has become a "language event." One of the examples of the establishing character of paschal language is its eschatological perspective—the apostles identified the risen Christ as the eschatological Savior and Judge.[20] Human testimony is different from a photograph or a short-hand summary of what has happened. By making the event come to the word, testimony recreates it and gives it a new existence. From then onward, the event, as something proclaimed, has its own life, although it is not possible to dissociate it in its facticity from its possession by the witness.

What I have said above applies to every event that has been given the dignity of an "historical fact" in the complex whole that constitutes an historical account. It is true to say that the historian "produces" the facts. In the case of the resurrection, however, the event to which testimony is borne has not been given a new existence simply by virtue of the interpretative freedom of the witness. His confession and therefore his interpretation are the work of faith and the Spirit of God. As we have already seen, it is the same power of God that is at work in the resurrection of Christ as an historical event and also at work in the testimony borne to the event, that is, in the resurrection that is confessed, the resurrection that has become a "word event." It is therefore not enough to say that we cannot reach the resurrection outside the testimonies of believers about it. It is necessary to say that the proper place of the resurrection is not so much history in its empirical data as the language of paschal faith as the language of the first Christian community.

Only those who do not know anything about the way in which reality and language are interwoven can conclude that the resurrection of Christ is no longer the product of the faith of the first witnesses. It is rather because the resurrection escapes from the facticity of a physical prodigy of which the witnesses are reputed to have handed a conscientious report on to us and because it has become the "saying" of an entire believing community that it has acquired real historicity. The testimonies of the resurrection go back to the historical event which gave rise to them, but they go back to that event in a way which cannot be dissociated from the tradition of a community confessing faith of which they are the historical traces. It is because we belong to the same tradition of faith that we can rediscover the person of the risen Christ via these different testimonies.

To conclude this chapter, I would like very briefly to situate the testimony borne to the resurrection by believers today and to do this from the vantage point of the relationship between experience and language.

3. THE TESTIMONY OF BELIEVERS TODAY

Testimony is always an interpretation of a particular experience. In considering the apostolic testimony of the resurrection, I drew attention to the constant interaction between an unexpected experience, the fact of the appearances and a faith aroused by the words of Jesus, through knowledge of Scripture and the eschatological promises. The entire import of my investigation has been to show that it is not easy to dissociate experience from language in testimony. Experience is identified in a certain language which is already an interpretation of "what happened." That is why testimony is different from a mere verbal translation of a living experience. It recreates in a sense the experience to which one intends to bear witness. What, then, is the situation today with regard to our testimony as an original encounter between an experience and a language? We shall see that it will be necessary to stress both the newness and the continuity of our own situation with regard to that of the apostles.

1. The apostolic testimony is a testimony in faith, but it is also a testimony borne at first hand and without intermediaries. The apostles were direct witnesses of what Jesus said or did from the time of his baptism by

John the Baptist until his ascension. They were in a very special way the eye-witnesses of his death and resurrection (Acts 1:22). And it is because they saw that they "could not but speak" (Acts 4:20). This knowledge "according to the flesh" was the special privilege of the apostles, and that privilege, their apostolic charism, is not transferable. Believers who have come after them have always been and will always be, from that point of view, witnesses by proxy, since they have not seen what the apostles saw. They simply know that the apostles saw it and their own testimony can only be a handing on of what they have received. They therefore only deserve to be called witnesses in their turn strictly insofar as their words are in continuity with the testimony of those first and unique witnesses, the apostles.

2. Having said this, it is also important to stress what has been central throughout the whole of my investigation in this chapter, namely that the testimony of the apostles is not simply an account of events, but a "word event" as the inseparable consequence of the experience of a phenomenon and a believing interpretation. The apostles were not neutral witnesses, but believers. Seen from the point of view of the relationship between faith in the mystery of the glorified Christ and the historical signs which accredit that faith, the faith of the apostles is not different from our own. They were eye-witnesses of the appearances, but their recognition of Christ as the glorified Lord was the work of the Spirit. In other words, their seeing was not constitutive of their faith. The same applies to us. Our knowledge, which is founded on the historical testimony of those who saw, that is, the apostles, is not constitutive of our faith in the risen Christ.

So, whether it is a question of the apostles' faith or of our own, that faith itself bears its own testimony, whether it is based on historical signs, the fact of the appearances in the case of the apostles or the historical reality of their testimony in our case. As I pointed out above, it is the same power of God which is manifested through the resurrection of Christ and which is at work in the preaching of the apostles and the testimony of believers today. Because of the inner testimony of the Spirit, every believer is established in contemporaneity with what happened during the "fifty days" of which Scripture speaks. The faith of the apostles is concerned not with the facticity of the events according to their dimension as phenomena, but with those events as signs of the eschatological salvation that came in Jesus Christ. In the same way, our faith is concerned not with the materiality of the Gospel accounts as reports of "what happened," but with the apostolic testimony as the good news of the salvation that has come in Christ. The believer who relies on that apostolic testimony has decided in favor of the testimony of Jesus and in this way himself becomes a witness. Even though he has not known Jesus "according to the flesh," he is nonetheless an "eye" witness in the sense of St. John. He in fact testifies to what has become evidence for him.[21]

At the origin of the testimony borne today to the resurrection, there is, as there was in the case of the apostles' testimony, an indissociable link between a personal experience and an interpretation in faith. There is a personal encounter with Jesus of Nazareth through the historical testimonies contained in the Gospel, through the ecclesial signs of his presence and through the signs of his love. He is, then, recognized and identified as the risen Christ in the light both of faith and of the living tradition of the Church. And that recognition leads me to proclaim the good news of salvation, in other words, the presence here and now of the risen Christ: "I believed and so I spoke" (2 Cor 4:13). The testimony of believers in the Church is based both on the founding events of the Christian community and on the apostolic testimonies bearing on those events. Our interpretation in faith of those events today takes place within the tradition that was constitutive of those testimonies.

3. The testimony of the believer today, then, is not simply the expression of a personal experience. It takes place within a living tradition of interpretation, that of the Church as a community confessing faith through the centuries. It is not, however, a testimony in the strict sense without a new act of interpretation and therefore without a certain degree of inventiveness of language. I have already pointed to that search at the level of the apostolic testimonies for a new language capable of testifying to an altogether too rich experience. Exposed to the objections raised by the Corinthians, St. Paul did not simply repeat the early formulas that he had received, but went further, speaking, for example, about the body of Christ raised like a "celestial body" which comes from on high. There is no testimony without a mediation of my own existence and so there is no testimony without a will on my part to appropriate the content of paschal faith into my own language. That is the only means at our disposal by which we can retranslate the paschal message into a language that can arouse our contemporaries to faith. The language of the resurrection will always continue to be the "language of reference" because it has been the language of the Church for centuries. Since the apostolic age, however, it has always needed to be completed and reinterpreted by other languages, and this need is more urgent today than perhaps at any other time, in a situation in which we have to testify to the risen Christ in a post-Christian world that is remote from the language of the Bible.

It is not possible for me to say here how the testimony to paschal faith can be translated into a contemporary language without betraying the meaning that it has always had in the tradition of the Church. All that I can do is to point out that the testimony borne to the resurrection of the Lord has never been reducible to the experience that a believer may have of it. It is a living testimony only if it expresses the way in which I have verified in my own existence the presence and the energy of the risen Christ. But testimony borne to the resurrection must also be the expression of the faith and unity of the Church. Rereading and reinterpreting the formulae of paschal faith always takes place within a community of interpretation in continuity with the first community of faith from which the apostolic testimonies came.

At the conclusion of this investigation into the testimony of the resurrection as an experience and as language, it is at least possible to say that the only language that may be both adequate to the experience of the first witnesses and in conformity with the expectations of people today is the language of hope. This means that testifying to the contemporary relevance of the paschal mystery cannot simply consist of repeating the old confession of faith of the first Christians: "Christ is risen!" It is bringing about in the lives of individuals, in society and in history significant anticipations of the future promised in Jesus Christ.

I said at the beginning of this chapter that testimony borne to the values of human existence corresponds to the question: "What am I permitted to hope?" This means that all testimony is a practical interpretation of a glimpsed future. It would seem, then, that all human testimony points obscurely to the truth of paschal testimony. In the desert of languages that are closed and without words, it is the task of human testimony to keep history open to something that is always new and unforeseeable.

Chapter VI

THE ATHEISTIC HERMENEUTICS
OF THE TITLE "THE SON OF MAN"
IN ERNST BLOCH

Ludwig Feuerbach's *The Essence of Christianity* has often been described as an example of "atheistic hermeneutics" of Christianity. In contrast to the theological hermeneutics that I have attempted to outline in the rest of this book, I would like in this chapter to deal with a particularly significant example of modern atheistic hermeneutics. For this purpose, I have chosen to examine Ernst Bloch's interpretation of the title "the Son of Man" in his *Atheismus im Christentum*.

Bloch's exegesis of the title "the Son of Man" can be found in Chapter V of his book, which he has entitled "Aut Caesar aut Christus."[1] This chapter follows a chapter (IV) devoted to the exodus in the representation of Yahweh. Chapter IV is, in other words, devoted to what Bloch calls "detheocratization." He extends this theme by showing how the title "the Son of Man," that is, the union of man with God, denotes the end-point of the messianic theme of the exodus that runs through the whole of the Bible. The exodus of the Jews becomes the exodus of God himself and the figure of the Son of Man brings that exodus, in other words, God's going out of himself, to its conclusion.

Before considering Bloch's exegesis in Chapter V of his book, however, I shall try to summarize the characteristic originality of his hermeneutical program.

1. In the first place, it is an atheistic form of hermeneutics placed at the service of a radical secularization. Unlike Feuerbach, however, Bloch does not try to restore to man what has been attributed in an illusory manner to God. He aims rather to keep God as a concrete utopia in the movement of man's transcendence of himself. No attempt is made by Bloch, in other words, to change theology into anthropology. Man does not take the place of God. He is only a real possibility to come.

2. Bloch's hermeneutics are subversive. What is meant by this is that, in contrast to the dialectics of "religion and politics," Bloch does not attempt to reduce religion to politics, but rather aims to criticize religion by means of religion itself. His hermeneutics subvert religion insofar as they secularize it. This secularization, however, in fact has the aim of revealing the irreducible dimension of religion. Far from putting an end to religion, Bloch's work upholds the practical power of religion as the dialectics of hope. In that sense, it is more correct to speak of a criticism of the politico-religious element by religion than it is to speak of a reduction of religion to politics. In any case, it would seem that, for Bloch, religion constitutes an irreducible factor that cannot be gone beyond, as it can in the case of Hegel, in the concept.

3. Bloch's hermeneutics can be defined more accurately as a program of detheocratization than as one of demythologization. Like all hermeneutics, Bloch's look for what is clear and manifest under what is hidden and obscure. The opaqueness of Scripture, however, is not simply the result of its mythological clothing and the historical distance separating us from it. It also reflects the opaqueness of the present condition of man. It is also and above all the result of the process of theocratization which is inherent in Scripture itself and will be until the second coming of Christ. Bloch therefore devotes himself to a rereading of the text of the Bible in the light of a detheocratized exodus and the promise of a new earth inaugurated by Christ. He clears a path for himself through the opaqueness of the text with the aim of restoring the revolt that is present in the text, a revolt that has been obscured not only by successive rereadings of the Gospel by the Church, but also by the process of putting the message of Christ into writing.

It is therefore legitimate to speak of a subversive use of traditional hermeneutics and to speak of that use in two senses. On the one hand, instead of looking for a divine sense beyond the literal sense, Bloch looks for a secular sense, that is, a human reality or man as a real possibility. In this regard, he is faithful to the Marxist utopia of the human that is expressed both by the naturalization of man and by the humanization of nature.[2] On the other hand, he attempts to restore the movement of subversion which is contained within Scripture, but which is always being concealed or mitigated in Scripture itself by the theocratic logic of domination.

What I have said above may lead us to a better understanding of Bloch's now famous paradoxical statement: "Only a real Christian can be a good atheist and only a real atheist can be a good Christian." Bloch is saying that only a real Christian can be a good atheist because it is the Christian who takes the movement of detheocratization to its conclusion.

He is also saying that only a real atheist can be a good Christian because it is the atheist who is working for the coming of the kingdom that has already been inaugurated by Christ, in other words, the kingdom of man.

Bloch's exegesis of the title "the Son of Man" is very difficult to summarize. It is a text that is full of movement forward and backward and full of digressions, and the breathless character of the author's writing echoes the menacing nature of the text on which he is commenting. At the risk of simplifying, I think that it is possible to reduce Bloch's exegesis of the title "the Son of Man" to three basic themes, although it has to be borne in mind that they are inseparable.

1. THE INVESTING OF YAHWEH
BY JESUS OR THE EXODUS THEME

It would seem that Bloch's exegesis of the texts of the New Testament is dominated by two ideas. On the one hand, Jesus as the Son of Man is the sign of the coming of God in man. This is the theme of the exodus, the religious utopia par excellence and the opening onto the unknown.

On the other hand, Jesus is also the sign of man's incompleteness. In other words, the God of present man is the *homo absconditus* of the future (historical ontology). It is not a question of ending with a humanization of God that is a mere secularization in the sense of Feuerbach or a prometheism. It is rather a question of dialectically transforming Christianity as a cultic religion into a utopian religion in which God is the reality of the hidden man who can only be realized and revealed by a transformation of the present reality. In doing this, Bloch as an exegete is simply aiming to be faithful to the eschatological dimension of the New Testament.

The theme of the investing of Yahweh by Jesus returns again and again. The coming of Jesus coincided with the end of Israel's politico-religious theocratism. It was this subversion of theocratism that led to Jesus' death. In fact, however, the coming of the Son of Man was fully in the line of Jewish eschatological messianism. The exodus of the Jews became the exodus of God himself. Jesus went to the end of the religion of the God of the exodus. As Bloch himself says, "That Messiah, the Son of Man, did not pass himself off as the one who was struggling with a quite romantic zeal to uphold or to restore the kingdom of David as it had been with its Lord God. No, he affirmed at every point that he was the exodus, a new exodus, thoroughly eschatological and revolutionary, the coming of God in man" (p. 171).

Bloch goes counter to the view most widely held concerning Jesus' transcendent messianism and believes that he was quite conscious that he was the Messiah whom the Jews expected, that is, "a Messiah who would fulfill the promise of a political and religious salvation by putting an end to concrete misery and by initiating an era of concrete happiness" (p. 164). This insistence on the political realism of Jesus' messianism is, Bloch believes, the only possible way of being faithful to its eschatological dimension. In his opinion, liberal and anti-Semitic theologians such as Renan, Wellhausen and Harnack betrayed the eschatology of the New Testament in the emphasis that they placed on the expectation of an inner and purely ethical kingdom. Bloch insists that "from its very beginning, the authenticity of the Gospel implied its real and revolutionary meaning" (p. 165).

In support of his thesis, Bloch interprets certain classical texts in the New Testament in a very personal way. In the account of the temptations of Jesus in the desert in Chapter IV, for example, he believes that Jesus undoubtedly felt that he was succumbing to the devil by calling himself "the Son of Man." In the same way, the need for the messianic secret in St. Mark cannot, in Bloch's opinion, be understood if Jesus had not wanted to be the Messiah whom the Jews expected. In that case, he would simply have been described as a good man, a pastor, and at the most a successor to the early prophets. Jesus' cry during his agony on the cross: "My God, my God, why have you forsaken me?" was, moreover, according to Bloch, not a cry of despair resulting from a feeling of having been abandoned by God. It was rather an expression of the anguish suffered by someone who was conscious that the work that he had been doing would not be fulfilled. It was the only moment when, in respect of the assurance that he had of being the one who was opening the way to Zion that was nearest at hand, faith failed him (p. 163).

When Jesus said that his yoke was easy and his burden light, this was not a reference to the crucifixion. It was rather a proclamation of the enthronement of the Messiah-King. Finally, the good news of the Gospel is also a proclamation of social and political happiness that nothing can extinguish (p. 164). The text that follows these statements provides a very clear summary of Bloch's practical hermeneutics placed at the service of secularization. The author writes: "Subjectively, Jesus regarded himself unreservedly as the Messiah of whom tradition had spoken. Objectively, he was the one who had hardly at all thought of seeking refuge in an interiority which did not make itself manifest or of coming to the fore in the expectation of a transcendent kingdom of heaven. On the contrary, salvation for him was Canaan. It was the fulfillment of what had been prophesied to his ancestors, but without its fragility, its triviality and its failures. It was a Canaan realized quintessentially. . . . There had already been quite enough interiority in the expectation of the Messiah and more than enough heaven in faith in the hereafter. It was the earth that needed the Savior and the Gospel" (p. 164).

As we shall see later on, the title "the Son of Man," which is Jesus' own creation and not that of his disciples, stresses both the political realism of Jesus' messianism and the end of theocratism. Bloch's principal thesis in the chapter that we have been considering is in fact to say that the title "the Son of Man" is eschatological, whereas the later title of Kyrios Christos only goes back to cult.

In attributing the title "the Son of Man" to himself, Jesus proclaimed the name of an exodus which had until that time been unknown to the Jews and which was concerned with all the representations of God in use by those who were in a position of religious power. He put an end to the false hypostasis of a Creator God. "As for the Gospel according to St. John," Bloch writes, "if he makes eschatology retreat behind his own protological treatment, it is only in order to make this logos the alpha of another world than the already given one of creation and in order to make it come into being with Christ at the end as a prologue to a new world. The real Creator is Christ the Logos, bringing about a new creature . . ."(p. 202).

For Bloch, the mysterious title "the Son of Man" is the cipher of de-theocratization. It points to a reinvesting in a *humanum* that is still enigmatical of all the treasures that had been confiscated by the hypostasis of a heavenly Father. The biblical formula *Deus homo factus est* is the ultimate expression of the biblical exodus that is an "exodus out of Yahweh. It is no longer necessary to speak of antitheocratism. We now have to speak of a-theocratism or even of a 'complete Christocentrism' " (see Section 31). Bloch sees in John 17 the key to the *homoousia*, that is, not the divinity of Christ, but his equality with God. The ancient "day of Yahweh," which was to come at the end of time, is presented in the Fourth Gospel as a parousia of Christ, the Son of Man existing without Yahweh, A-Kyrios and A-Theos at the same time. Bloch believes that he has in this way laid the exegetical foundation of the radical atheism that he professed in his earlier book, *Das Prinzip Hoffnung:* "The truth of the ideal of God is nothing but the utopia of the kingdom, and this correctly presupposes that no God dwells in heaven, since none is found there and has never been found there" (*Das Prinzip Hoffnung,* 1959, p. 1514, cited on p. 204).

In support of his thesis, Bloch devotes himself to a careful rereading of the trial of Jesus. The high priests' condemnation of Jesus was not, he concludes, because he committed blasphemy by claiming to be the Messiah, that is, the Son of God, but because he threatened the entire clerical theocracy and the whole of institutional religion as it had been set up since the time of Ezra and Nehemiah. Jesus was regarded as dangerous because his kingdom, that of the Son of Man, was so different from the theocratic kingdom of Yahweh. He was crucified because he had appeared as subversive, inasmuch as he was "the exemplary figure of a different world, one without oppression and without a Lord God" (p. 170).

2. THE COMING OF THE KINGDOM
OF GOD AS AN EARTHLY KINGDOM

All that Bloch suggests is in reaction to an interpretation of Christianity conceived as the vanishing point of a consoling flight. He therefore interprets Christianity as a perspective that is open to what has not yet been accomplished and is new.

In the light of his exegesis of the mysterious title "the Son of Man," it is possible to summarize his interpretation of the texts of the New Testament concerning the kingdom in the following way:

1. What takes first place in the Gospel is not love, but the proclamation of the kingdom.

2. The kingdom of God is not an inner kingdom or a kingdom in the hereafter, but the coming of a kingdom of freedom on earth.

3. The kingdom of God is realized on earth, but, as an eschatological kingdom, it has not yet been given. It is realized only in a germinal state.

A. The Kingdom of God and Not Love Is Primordial

Bloch insists on the chiliastic immediacy of the reference to the kingdom of heaven. It is essential in his opinion to interpret the ethical significance of the kingdom on the basis of its eschatological expectation and not vice versa. The words of Jesus are full of apocalyptic expectation, and it was later Christianity which, partly under the influence of Paul, deprived the Gospel message of its subversive aspect. The words of Mark: "The time is fulfilled and the kingdom of God is at hand" show that Jesus never gave his mission a meaning that was mitigated or exterior to the world.

Jesus' preaching is harsher than that of the prophets who had appeared before him. Jesus violently rejected those who were lukewarm. Bloch cites with some satisfaction his words in Matthew 10:34: "I have not come to bring peace (on earth), but a sword" and those in John 12:48: "He who rejects me and does not receive my sayings has a judge. The word that I have spoken will be his judge on the last day."

How, then, should all Jesus' words in the Sermon on the Mount about non-violence and loving one's enemies be interpreted? Bloch interprets them always in the light of the imminence of the kingdom that is coming and within an apocalyptic context. I will do no more here than simply cite a text that is especially clear in this respect. Bloch writes: "The old, all too old earth is in the grip of the kairos of this urgency and that is why it would seem that the kingdom that is so near at hand no longer calls for the slightest violence. The Jesus of the Sermon on the Mount is totally in this spirit, since behind each one of the beatitudes to the glory of non-violence he reveals a glimpse (Mt 5:3–10) of the imminence that is that of the kingdom of heaven. This means that it is not or it is not only a popular reward, but that the 'for' that precedes and establishes 'theirs is the kingdom of heaven' means at a deeper level that any violence or any attempt to drive the merchants from a temple—which will in any case be destroyed—is declared to be superfluous at a time of which the time has finally come. It is true that a violent revolution which exalts the humble and puts down the mighty is brought about totally within the nature in an apocalyptic Jesus, and this replaces to some extent a revolt brought about by men themselves, by the superior weapon of a cosmic catastrophe" (pp. 168–169).

The proclamation of the kingdom, then, has priority over the ethical content of Jesus' message. Bloch does not, for this reason, deny that love is at the center of that message, but he believes that it should be interpreted in the light of an imminent coming. And this is precisely what has not been done, he claims, in the history of Christianity, which has made the message of Christ harmless and has fostered an attitude of resignation with regard to injustice. Love in the sense of agape is a love of one's fellow men which is entirely without precedent. It overthrows all forms of aggression. Bloch insists, however, that it is only found in Jesus' preaching in the light of a coming that is already imminent.

B. The Coming of a Kingdom of Freedom on Earth

On the basis of the thesis of "the Son of Man" who invests Yahweh, I have already indicated Bloch's insistence on the carnal and political realism of the kingdom proclaimed by Jesus. It is also interesting to examine Bloch's exegesis of the texts of the New Testament that point in the direction of an inner kingdom or a kingdom that is "not of this world." He is in fact convinced that these texts have been excessively exploited in a spiritualistic sense for two thousand years with the aim of showing how harmless Christianity really is.

In Luke 17:21, for example, Jesus never meant the words "The kingdom of God is in the midst of you," which is the exact translation, to be understood in the sense of interiority as "The Kingdom of God is within you." He was in fact addressing not his disciples, but the Pharisees and therefore replying to the trap set in their question about the moment of the coming of the kingdom. His reply, then, means: "The kingdom is equally imminent in space. It is here in the community of those who recognize it" (p. 166).

In the same way, Jesus' famous reply to Pilate: "My kingdom is not of this world" does not have the meaning that Christianity has for so long wanted to give to it. Bloch thinks that this statement, attributed by St. John to Jesus in the presence of Pilate, is not historical and that John was influenced here by Paul. He was conscious of the distress suffered by the first Christian communities and was providing them with the a way of escaping from their difficulties with the Roman authorities. The theme is, in Bloch's opinion, judiciary and apologetic. "It is contrary to the courage and even to the dignity of Christ that he should have said these defeatist words in the presence of Pilate, that he should have presented himself to his Roman judge as a dreamer and as eccentric and that he should have provided the Romans with the spectacle of a harmless and almost comic personality" (p. 167). To this, Bloch adds that this Johannine passage did not save a single Christian from Nero's persecution, but rather served as an apology to the masters of the world. It served to deprive the earthly aspirations of Christianity of all their strength.

The opposition between this world and the other world, then, has a different meaning from that given to it by twenty centuries of Christian spirituality. The original meaning stressed an eschatological tension between this world, in other words the present aeon, and the other world, in other words, "the future and better aeon, that of a future age of the world in opposition to the existing world."

Bloch obviously knows the logion in Matthew 22:21: "Render to Caesar the things that are Caesar's and to God the things that are God's," but refuses to interpret it as a moral lesson about disinterestedness with regard to the world. It has, in his opinion, above all an eschatological meaning. It is precisely because the kingdom is so imminent that Caesar can be treated with such indifference. Unlike Luther, who was able to construct his doctrine of the two kingdoms on the basis of this text, Bloch believes that it has no dualistic meaning. He rejects the idea of a double accountability, which in any case leads to the worst kinds of compromise.

The following text summarizes very clearly Bloch's conception of the attitude with regard to the world that emerges from the Gospel: "The imperial world is insignificant, and despite its splendor it is as dull as spending a night in an inn when it is necessary to leave the next morning at dawn. For Jesus, what counts is above all this authentically chiliastic counsel: to distribute one's goods among the poor and to avoid, not only subjectively, but also objectively, the interests assembled around Caesar—interests that are contemptible and condemned in the short term. In this perspective, the Gospel has no social teaching, but it is also not essentially moral. It is rather a Gospel of eschatological redemption" (p. 172).

C. The Kingdom of God Is Only Realized in a Germinal State

To understand what is meant by this statement it is necessary to comment on Section 29, which is quite difficult. Bloch gives this section the title: "Even the greatness of the Son of Man disappears. The Kingdom is 'little.' " He is opposed both to the pagan and anthropomorphic myth of *makanthropos* man as the incarnation of the future kingdom and to the Hegelian theme of a reconciliation between the absolute Spirit and man as a finite spirit.

It is possible to say that, according to Bloch, the kingdom coincides with the restless activity that is present in every man. As the Son of Man, Jesus is the historical figure of this openness. But it is an openness onto the unknown—the *anthropos agnotos*. "It is the unknown, the nearness of the unknown that is lacking in all the classical or neo-classical religious manifestations of anthropomorphism. They lack the open aspect of the *anthropos agnostos*" (p. 192).

What Bloch criticizes in Hegelian humanism is that Hegel traces the divine back to a human measure. If it is true that being in itself is saved from religious alienation, then it reifies itself in history. Hegel's *humanum* disappears in the state. Going beyond atheistic humanism, Bloch fundamentally aims to keep God as the concrete utopia of man's becoming man, a becoming that is never either completed or manifested. The distinctive contribution made by Christianity is summed up in the figure of the Son of Man. There is a kingdom without God and without transcendence, but the Son of Man points to the act in which all reification of man is transcended.

I would like to quote the following text of Bloch because it shows clearly what separates his religious atheism from the platitude of atheistic humanism. "Classical humanism fails to go as far, even in the sphere of religion," Bloch writes, "as Job and as the idea of the Son of Man. It also does not go as far as discovering that man can be better, that he can be, even more than his God, the center of all things. A religion in which the Son of Man is no more than beauty and moderation in fact always means, as it does in Hegel, 'consciousness of man's reconciliation with God.' A religion in which the kingdom is in a state of fermentation can never trace the divine back to human dimensions. It does not tend toward an equilibrium of reconciliation. On the contrary, the Son of Man and his kingdom are human without having been already given" (pp. 192–193).

This is clear confirmation of the fact that the figure of "the Son of Man" is a very important key to our understanding of Bloch's atheistic hermeneutics of Christianity. It is not simply a question of being satisfied with the overthrow of theology by atheistic humanism. It is rather a question of maintaining within an atheistic form, in the image of the Son of Man, what is covered by the God of the exodus. The God of modern man who is open to new possibilities is the *homo absconditus* who has not yet been revealed. "The image of the Son of Man," Bloch insists, "is one of the most incomplete of all images. It does not yet contain within itself the solution to its own mystery" (p. 193).

So, after the disappearance of the theocratic God of the Old Testament, the mystery still remains. But that mystery is nothing but the enigma of the man of whom the Son of Man is the historical figure. And that enigma of the man coincides with the coming of the kingdom. The Messiah as the Son of Man does not complete history, but he certainly opens it. He is the cipher of not-yet-being as an historical possibility.[3]

3. THE DIALECTICAL OVERTHROWING OF THE
CULTIC TITLE "THE SON OF GOD" BY THE
ESCHATOLOGICAL TITLE
"THE SON OF MAN"

Following Bousset, Bloch thinks that it is possible to make a complete break between the eschatological title "the Son of Man," which, he believes, is a creation that is peculiar to Jesus and was in constant use in the early Palestinian community, and the titles Kyrios and "the Son of God." In his opinion, the latter tended gradually to replace the former in Hellenistic Christianity, in which an attempt was made to establish a cult of Christ based on the model of a new deity.

The cultic title Kyrios, which, like the title Pancrator, always had a tendency to return to its original pagan meaning, also tended to lead to the gradual disappearance of the title "the Son of Man," although it continued, from the time of the early Church until that of Thomas Münzer, to be used on the side of the poor and those who were in revolt. As Bloch says, "Only what was, in the future, characteristic of the authority of the institutional Church belonged and continued to belong to the title Kyrios, but not what, in the spirit of the early community and the Son of Man, was valid only in the future, that is, the coming of the 'better aeon,' that which constituted from then onward the stumbling block for Christianity of its image of the Lord Jesus, which it tried again and again to cause hypocritically to disappear" (p. 199).

Bloch has not failed to note that this hypothesis concerning the purely Palestinian origin of the title "the Son of Man" is contradicted in the Gospel of John, which, although it was much later, uses this title in a special sense. He does not, however, try to explain this. In Section 31, which is entitled "A Complete Christocentrism," he is rightly conscious of this as a confirmation of the fundamental anti-theocraticism of Jesus' message. It is, in his opinion, John's Gospel which clearly reveals to us Jesus' *homoousia*, that is, his equality with God. If the same Gospel appears to contain a theodicy, in other words, if Jesus ascribes to the Father certain qualities that belong only to him, this is in fact a purely external impression. Jesus in fact only says of him, of his first coming as the Logos, that he is the light and the life. All the verses (in John 15–17) about the world that has known neither the Father nor the Son are concerned with a God who is still unknown not only to the pagans, but also the Jews themselves.

It is at least possible to accept that the title Kyrios, which forms part of the post-paschal preaching, should be directly linked to the resurrection of Christ. For Bloch, however, the resurrection is simply the product of the imagination of the disciples, who could not recover from the experience of Jesus' death. It is Paul, who was above all responsible for the myth of the death and resurrection of Christ, who makes us go back to the earliest naturalistic pagan mysteries. According to Bloch, the idea of voluntary sacrifice is Paul's creation. It is dialectically related to the resurrection, and it was necessary for the missionary preaching that was addressed to the pagans. If Jesus was in fact the Messiah who was expected, this was not in spite of, but precisely because of the crucifixion. It was therefore not by investing the earlier theocratism of Yahweh that the Son of Man revealed himself as the Messiah. It was rather by dying on the cross at Golgotha. Bloch rejects the relationship between the Messiah and the figure of the Suffering Servant in Deutero-Isaiah, which seems to have been made for Jesus. He believes that the prophecy in Isaiah 53 refers to Israel and not to the Messiah himself.

It was, then, the apostle to the pagans, with his responsible attitude, who made a connection between the pagan myth of the death of the god who dies and rises again each year and the juridical logic of the debt to be paid to the god Moloch by the blood of an innocent victim. From the point of view of apologetics, it was necessary to clear God the Father of the charge of having handed over his innocent Son. If Jesus voluntarily sacrificed himself in order to pay that debt, this was because of man's guilt. This idea is not, however, entirely Paul's own. As Bloch points out, "it is deeply rooted in a soil that is not only soaked in blood, but also very old. It comes from the ancient idea of human sacrifice that had for a long time been avoided, an idea that had existed even before Moloch. This means that it is revealed as essentially opposed to Christianity" (p. 209).

Bloch is conscious of a deep relationship from the time of St. Paul until that of Luther, between the theme of the claimed patience of the cross and that of the unconditional obedience to authority which serves the interests of those who hold power in the churches. Thanks to the myth of the sacrificed lamb, "the subversion that is present in the Bible is definitively broken" (p. 211). Once again, then, we are confronted with the principal objective of Bloch's hermeneutics. This is to restore, in contrast to the patience of the crucified Christ, the ferment of revolution and the anger and spirit of revolt that are present in the New Testament.

If, however, we are to be quite just to Bloch and assess his position correctly, we have to recognize that it is true that, although, in his opinion, hope in the resurrection has never helped a single oppressed person to overcome his misery, he nonetheless regards Paul as "a tribune of humanity insofar as he protested against the most pitiless of anti-utopias harbored by this heteronomous world that confronts us—death" (p. 212).

4. THE VALUE OF EXEGESIS OF THE TITLE "THE SON OF MAN" ACCORDING TO BLOCH

I have tried to show how Bloch's exegesis of the title "the Son of Man" illustrates perfectly the movement of his hermeneutics as a program of detheocratization. It would undoubtedly be interesting to compare his atheistic hermeneutics with the results of contemporary scientific exegesis. His book *Atheismus im Christentum* dates back to 1968 and he is familiar with the work done by such great modern exegetes as Schweizer, Bultmann, von Rad, Käsemann, Jeremias, Stauffer and Wellhausen. It is worth noting, however, that he himself gives priority in the matter of Christian origins to such authors as Bousset and Bauer, whose conclusions have now been to a great extent superseded.

If I were to make a serious comparison between his work and that of contemporary exegetes, I would have to write a separate article. Here I shall have to be satisfied with four brief comments, based principally on the conclusions drawn by Jeremias in his theology of the New Testament.[4]

1. The title "the Son of Man" occurs eighty-three times in the Gospels—sixty-nine times in the synoptics and thirteen times in the Gospel of John. It is beyond dispute—and here we have to admit that Bloch is quite right—that the application of the title "the Son of Man" to Christ comes

from an ancient tradition of Palestinian origin. Even though it can also be found in Iranian antiquity, the New Testament "Son of Man" is a resumption of the Son of the first heavenly man in Daniel 7 that is found in late post-exilic Judaism. It is a fact that the Greek Church avoided the title "the Son of Man." The title is also not encountered in any formula of faith in primitive Christianity.

St. Paul must have known the expression "the Son of Man," even though he never uses it. It is even possible to think that his typology "Adam-Christ," which is totally unknown both in early Judaism and in pre-Christian Hellenism, was inspired by the application of the title "the Son of Man" to Christ. He undoubtedly avoided the title in his preaching to the Gentiles in order to prevent the danger that Christians of Greek birth would interpret it wrongly, regarding it as a sign of descent.

2. Contemporary exegetes have become increasingly unanimous in accepting that the title goes back to Jesus himself. Here too we have to admit that Bloch is quite right. An indication of this is provided by the fact that Jesus always speaks of himself as "the Son of Man" in the third person. This would not be meaningful if the title had been a creation of the disciples. They took it as a matter of course that Jesus identified himself with the Son of Man. It has also been pointed out by exegetes that the resurrection and the parousia are not mentioned together in any of the logia concerning the Son of Man. The distinction between the resurrection and the parousia was in fact made in post-paschal Christology. This absence of any distinction between the resurrection and the parousia, then, points to a pre-paschal use of the formula "the Son of Man."

It may seem surprising that the first community of Christians never used the formula in their creeds even though they handed it on in the *verba Christi* and even in the synoptic tradition. This, however, at least proves that the title was sacred insofar as it went back to Jesus himself and no one was allowed to do away with it.[5]

3. It would appear to be firmly established today that the origin of the idea of the title "the Son of Man" should not be sought in the myths of primordial man that abounded in Mesopotamia, Persia and India and in the teaching of the gnostics. The idea of "the Son of Man" goes back to the apocalyptic tradition of early Judaism and in particular to Daniel 7:1–14.

The radical opposition that Bloch has insisted exists between the eschatological title "the Son of Man" and the cultic title "the Son of God" is, however, exegetically untenable. The most ancient testimonies concerning the coming of the Son of Man and his manifestation tend to show that this took place in the form of a raising up toward God. The titles "the Son of God" and Kyrios are therefore perfectly suited to the epiphany of the Son of Man on the last day. In other words, even if the idea of the glorification of the Son of Man may have evolved in the light of the paschal experience, it can nonetheless already be found in a germinal state in the revelation of the Son of Man according to Daniel 7. The expected Messiah therefore has the dignity and the attributes of a king. Contrary to what Bloch affirms, then, this messianic expectation has nothing to do with the nationalistic hopes of Israel. Two kinds of messianic hope were present in Israel. These were, first, the national hope that there would be a warrior hero of the race of David, and, second, the hope of a *bar 'enasha*, the Son of Man who would be the "light of the nations." In claiming explicitly for himself the expectation of the *bar 'enasha*, Jesus was rejecting the other hope of a political Messiah. The title "the Son of Man" expressed precisely the universality of his power and the fact that he was the Savior of the whole world[6] (see Mt 25:31–46). What is more, the fact that Jesus always spoke of himself as the Son of Man in the third person suggests that he made a distinction between his present state and his state of exaltation when he was to be raised to the rank of "the Son of Man."

4. As we have already seen above, Bloch regards the idea of voluntary sacrifice as a later creation by Paul. It would, however, seem to be beyond all doubt that Jesus foresaw and proclaimed his passion and death (see, for example, the three prophecies of the passion in Mark 8:31; 9:31; 10:33) and that he himself also made the comparison between the Son of Man and the Suffering Servant of Isaiah 53. In the famous text of Mark 10:45 (cf. Lk 22:24–27): "The Son of Man came not to be served but to serve and to give his life as a ransom for many," it is clear at least that Jesus presents himself as a model of service from the point of view of the sacrifice of his life and with reference to Isaiah 53. Whether or not this verse is authentic, it cannot be disputed that it comes, in the case of Mark, from an ancient Palestinian tradition in which the idea of the expiatory power of death was current. It therefore cannot be a later dogmatic creation of St. Paul. If Jesus was conscious of having been sent from God and if he expected to be violently put to death, it is quite normal that he should have interpreted his own death in terms of service and expiation and that he should also have found the meaning of that death in the preaching of Isaiah 53.

CONCLUSION

1. Bloch's atheistic hermeneutics of the New Testament challenge in a very stimulating way a certain debased understanding of Christianity, according to which the teaching of Jesus is no more than a harmless message or a kind of popular Platonism. He has certainly helped Christian theologians to rediscover the eschatological dimension of Christianity and to

dissociate God from the biblical tradition of the God of theism.[7] We no longer have to think of God as conceived as a hypostasis of the eternal present, but can say that the future is the ontological determination that is most suited to him. From the point of view of the Bible, God's being is identical with his kingdom. It is only in the fulfillment of his kingdom that he is God, and that fulfillment of God's kingdom is determined by the future. In other words, we have gone beyond the question of the *Ens perfectissimum*, which has been replaced by the more utopian problem of the end. In this sense, it is true to say that "only an atheist can be a good Christian."

2. The Son of Man is the cipher of the incompleteness of man tending toward an unknown realization of himself. Finally, the kingdom of God is nothing but the gradual coming of an earthly kingdom as the kingdom of freedom that coincides with a humanization of nature and a naturalization of man. The question that remains is: How are we to recognize the foundation of the irreducibility of the Novum with regard to everything that has been and is? If the future is already given in the potentialities and the latencies of the processes of nature or even in the hopes and desires of man, then it is no longer the New in its irreducibility and its unavailability. In other words, if we are to find the foundation of the ontological primacy of the future with regard to all reality, do we not have to postulate the "exteriority" of what we designate biblically as the kingdom of God?

3. Bloch subverts the hypostasis of the God who has been and is by the figure of the Son of Man. Is he, however, doing any more than simply putting a new hypostasis in its place—a hypostasis of the future? In other words, is the God "ahead" a real alternative for the God "beyond"? For Bloch, God is the expression of man's hope that is never fulfilled, and he rightly criticizes Christianity for aiming to supply a response to this expectation and to fill in the ontological hollow which defines man, on the basis of killing hope by faith.

Would it, however, not be true to say that this preoccupation with fulfillment does not come from Bloch's conception of the future in the Greek sense, as the dialectical opposite of the past, whereas the future in the biblical sense should be conceived as a coming, an advent or a parousia?[8] The God who is coming as the God of the promise makes a break in the immanence of nature and history, but he does not do away with hope, but rather provides a foundation for it. Bloch professes atheism with regard to a God given a hypostatic reality for the love of God and his kingdom, God being nothing but the reality of man hidden as the utopia of present man. His atheistic hermeneutics of religion consist of a preservation of God as the factor of transcendentality by suppressing God as transcendence. But whether we regard history as a degradation with regard to an origin or as an accession that is never completed to an origin that has not yet been realized, we still remain within the circle of immanence or of totality. Can there in fact ever be any outcome other than a Novum that is the exteriority of an Other providing in me the foundation of an infinite responsibility (see Levinas)?

The originality of Bloch's hermeneutics consists of a criticism of religion and a criticism by religion placed at the service of secularization. He aims to subvert Christianity as a cultic religion by means of messianism. But has he not in fact succeeded in subverting Jewish messianism itself by replacing the dialectics of a promise and its fulfillment with the dialectics of a totality that is always aimed at but is always incomplete?

Chapter VII

FROM THE GOD OF THEISM
TO THE CRUCIFIED GOD

Nowadays either God is unknown—it is no longer historically possible for anyone in any circumstances to ask the question of God—or else he is too well known. By this I mean that the divine names of classical theism have become hackneyed and this has led many believers to remain silent about God.

Many people, both unbelievers and even believers, have either a negative experience of the absence of God or a painful one of the contrast between the injustice of the world and the existence of a God who is both Omnipotence and Love. Despite this, however, it remains true that a confession of God cannot be restricted to a mere repetition of words.

What we have to do is to go off to reconquer the lost name of God. We cannot plead that we respect the inexpressible name of God so much that we can cease to invoke it and name him. How, if we can no longer name God, can we make sure of his presence in our midst? If, however, we are to do that, it is not enough simply to transmit a confession that has been received via revelation. God also receives his baptismal name from man according to the period of history in question. [1]

The naming of God is a creative task. We have to go on taking the risk of naming God in order to make him appear always new, living and actual. He has a history in human consciousness, and the history of the divine names is a history of the images of God. It would not be difficult to show that those images have been produced in connection with clearly determined interests. But the theologian's task is to examine critically the various images of God and to look for the names that are the least unsuitable—those that express, in other words, what God has said about himself and man's historical situation in his presence.

Our task, then, is to discover whether we are still able to express God, to name the one personal God, both in the presence of modern atheistic

111

criticism and in that of the hidden immanentism of the contemporary religious renewal. When we consider the urgency of this task, our Christian
ecumenical endeavor seems very restricted. There is good reason therefore to bear in mind that at least three great monotheistic world religions
are mutually complementary as far as the future of the naming of God is
concerned. Those three great religions that can be traced back to Abraham
can learn from one another how not to invoke the name of God in vain.

The rest of this chapter will take the following form. First I shall try
to evaluate the recent situation in theology. This can be summarized as a
situation of contestation, that is, of a philosophical and a political protest
against the God of theism. Then, taking into account recent thinking tending in the direction of a "Christical theism," I shall attempt to say what are
the special names of God that are in accordance with the expectations of
contemporary man.

1. THE SITUATION OF THE
DISCOURSE ABOUT GOD TODAY

Within Christianity, the theology of the divine names is essentially
dependent on the part played by Jesus in defining the special image of
God. It is possible to say that this theology is drawn in two directions. The
first is that in which God is seen to be continuity with the Absolute Being
of philosophy and the great religions. In the second direction, he is seen
above all on the basis of his manifestation in Jesus of Nazareth. In fact, it
is almost possible to speak of a struggle between God and Jesus.[2]

It has been the historical destiny of Christianity to be exposed to this
twofold temptation. On the one hand, it has to sacrifice the irreducible
identity of the God of Jesus, in which case that identity is compromised.
On the other hand, it has to take the manifestation of God in Jesus so seriously that the status of God's personal transcendence is made uncertain
and dialogue with the other great monotheistic religions becomes problematical. This dilemma, which has always confronted Christianity, is in
fact a false one. It is, however, not enough to demonstrate it theoretically
in order to eliminate this duality of interests and this hesitation or lame-
ness, to which both the praxis and the language of Christians bear witness.

In this respect, the movement known as the "death of God" theology
reveals very clearly this opposition between God and Jesus. The positive
result of this theological movement was paradoxically that it was at the beginning of a third direction that pointed beyond metaphysical theism and
beyond Jesuanism. Christian theology has in fact experienced a remarkable Christological renewal which is attempting to achieve a reconciliation

between the demands made by a Trinitarian theology and a theology of the cross.[3]

The secular and the "death of God" theologies were the result of a twofold contestation—a protest against the God of metaphysics and a protest against the social function of God. It is important to look more closely at this contestation. It coincides with a criticism of a number of the images of God and therefore of some of the divine names that are not the exclusive property of the God of Christians. The imperialism of the figure of Jesus in many Christian circles can be interpreted as a reaction against a time when theism was dominant. In other words, it is a reaction against a period in which God was regarded as "quasi-evident" and thought to have a face that was very little different from the face that he might have assumed in the common form of belief in God.

A. The Protest Against the God of Metaphysics

This protest can be understood in the light of the change that has taken place in our cultural situation, in other words, in the light of our new image of man and the world, and on the basis of the crisis that has occurred in the philosophical language applied to God.

The Change in our Image of Man and the World

The traditional language applied to God, that is, the language of theism, was linked to a view of the world as a stable and hierarchically ordered cosmos that was dependent on a God who was the first cause and the absolute foundation. Man was integrated into his place in this hierarchically ordered universe.

Our present image of the world is no longer one of a cosmos that has been determined once and for all time. We see the world as defined above all as history, as a becoming or as the unlimited territory of human activity. It goes back in the first place to man's transforming freedom and not to a transcendent principle as the explanatory cause of the world. The dominant image is therefore not one of an omnipotent and unchangeable God who predetermines the progress of the world. It is rather the image of a history which man produces and for which he is responsible. It is not difficult to see how important this replacement of nature by history is in the question of the naming of God.

This idea of man's becoming himself can, it would seem, hardly be reconciled with the conception of a God who is omnipotent and provident. Insofar as man was seen as not having become himself and as alienating his own substance in the Absolute, then God still had a certain number of functions to carry out in his life and in the world. Now, however, we have to accept that in the modern world God's status is one of increasing uselessness—he recedes as man's power is extended.[4]

Our modern view of man invites us therefore to abandon the image of a God who is provident and who intervenes miraculously in his creation in order to touch it up or who acts directly in the course of history in order to bring about some fortunate or unfortunate event as a reward or a punishment for men's actions. It is precisely because we want to go beyond this image of God as the supreme utility of man that contemporary theology has followed Karl Barth in emphasizing the distance between the God of religion and the God of faith.

The God of religion or the cosmic God of nature is a God who corresponds too well to man's needs. He is in accordance with a state of childhood in mankind. He is the God who is the hypothesis of work, the God who gives meaning, the God who consoles us and gives us a good conscience and the God who protects us and guarantees our human activities.

The God of Abraham, Isaac and Jacob, that is, the God of history, is the quite other God who creates the question of salvation in us and whose reply goes far beyond our expectations. He is a God for whom we are looking for himself. He is not a God who is "available" and who adapts himself to our needs. We are in search of a name by which we can invoke God as the mystery of gratuity.

The Crisis of the Philosophical Language About God

Our image of man and the world has changed too much, then, for us to be able to be satisfied with an image of God that is tied to a different cultural state. In fact, some divine names no longer have a place in contemporary man's spontaneous religious consciousness.

If, however, we are to go to the root cause of the difficulties of traditional theological language, we have to mention the crisis in the philosophical language about God. Or, to express this more precisely, we have to speak about the crisis in the metaphysical foundations of theology.

Metaphysical thought has received a series of fatal blows since the time of Kant, and the way of understanding has been denounced as a transcendental illusion. We have had access to God only as a postulate of practical reason, in other words, at the level of ethical demands.

This important event continued for a long time to be obscured in Catholic theological circles, partly because of the recent renewal of Thomism. Now, however, the success of "Jesus centrism" has come at a time when the idea of the omnipotent and unchangeable God of metaphysical theism has been profoundly shaken. At the same time, Protestant theologians have for a long time been trying to construct a discourse about God since Kant.[5]

Thanks to Heidegger and his criticism of onto-theology, we are more aware of the death of the God of metaphysics as forming part of the destiny of metaphysics since its origin. It is in fact the same movement of metaphysics which makes God the absolute Foundation of being and which kills him. In this inverse theology, which is in fact atheistic humanism, man has replaced God as the supreme being and, in Nietzsche, we end with the murder of God by the will of power.[6]

One of the positive results of the present crisis of metaphysics is the inauguration of a new "historical" period for Christian theology, a period in which it is no longer possible to confuse the "theological" factor that comes from God with the "theological" factor that is ontological.[7] Christian theology is therefore invited to dare to be itself and not to sacrifice its own names of God that have been entrusted to it in divine revelation to the imperatives of a metaphysical theism. As one author has recently shown with considerable force, the conceptual God of onto-theology could only be an idol, in other words, a placing of the divine at man's disposal in a face that is called God and therefore a failure to recognize his absolute distance.[8]

It is possible to find endless fault with the historical bond that has been established between Greek thought and the Judaeo-Christian revelation, but it cannot be denied that the idea of a supreme being which finds its most perfect expression in the figure of the *causa sui* belongs to the very essence of metaphysics. "That is why the supreme being and, with it, an onto-theological construction continues to be present even when God, as Christian, has disappeared," J.-L. Marion has said. He goes on: "The *causa sui* only has theological validity when it is in control of the divine function and uses it, while at the same time venerating it. The characters of the idol apply equally to a 'God' who serves as a foundation, but himself receives a foundation, to a 'God' who supremely proclaims the Being of beings in general and in that sense traces them back to a faithful image of that through which they are and of which they are and to a 'God' who only continues to be at a distance from the common ontology within a settlement (*Austrag*) which protects us from a fundamental familiarity. That 'God,' who has been produced by and for onto-theology, is orientated toward the latter as the idol is toward the city (insofar as the political game of the idol cannot be traced back to onto-theology). There is, however, one difference and that is that the idol here continues to be conceptual. Not only does it not, like the icon, send us back to the invisible—it also does not even provide any face with which the divine can look at us and give himself to be looked at."[9]

It will, of course, be quite correctly pointed out here that the metaphysical theology of the greatest Christian authors (such as Thomas Aquinas) has been able to avoid having the God of revelation compromised by the onto-theological idol. But even if it is true that Thomas had a very keen perception of the conceptual beyondness and irreducible otherness of the God who was identified with absolute being, it is still not easy to affirm that he avoided the destiny of Western metaphysics or at least that he avoided the movement of metaphysics as an attempt to explain reality on the basis of a supreme foundation.

As I have already suggested elsewhere,[10] Thomas' theory of the divine names (his famous Quaestio 13) may continue to be a model of theological epistemology, but it clearly reveals the limitations of theology as a rigorous science of God. We are in fact witnessing a rigorous reduction of the biblical attributes of God, especially when they are expressed in the form of verbs of action, to the pure actuality of being. This leads to formidable difficulties as soon as we have to take God's "historical" actions (creation, the incarnation and deification) seriously. If, moreover, we make a distinction between "proper names" and "metaphorical names," we run the risk of letting the suggestive power of the great biblical symbols be lost, since these are reduced to the level of metaphors with a simple teaching function.

In any case, this theology of the divine names explicitates the consequences of Thomas' bold option to interpret the God of revelation in terms of being and to identify him with the Foundation of beings. In its desire to explain, theology as a science provides an explanation of the God of Abraham, Isaac and Jacob on the basis of something that precedes this, a human experience of the divine reality, in other words, the idea of God conceived as the absolute Being. The hermeneutical criterion by which we can know what name, whether it is biblical or not, is most suitable for God is its convertibility with God conceived as the First Being. What is certain is that the God of revelation is not different from the God of creation, who can be interpreted as the God who is the Foundation of onto-theology. But a Christian theology of the divine names also has to show us that the holiness and love revealed in Jesus Christ add something specific to the transcendental properties of being transposed into God.

It is important to bear this criticism of the God of onto-theology in mind if we are to understand the crisis of theism in contemporary theology. In the concrete, it has coincided with the trial of objectivizing theology and with the success of the various existential theologies. We can, however, more easily understand nowadays that this second tendency, which refuses to call God anything other than an inexpressible "Thou," may itself be the expression of a certain triumph of man's subjectivity and therefore of a certain humanization of God. At a time when theological existentialism (of the kind, for example, carried out by Bultmann) does not venture to objectivize God in order to safeguard his inexpressible character, is it not reducing God to the meaning that he has for man?[11] It would then be the destiny of Christian theology to verify Feuerbach's prophetic words: "God is a word, the only meaning of which is man." And in contrast to certain rather scanty interpretations of Nietzschean atheism, it is possible to understand the cry: "God is dead!" as a refusal to accept the metaphysical idol God. For Nietzsche, the death of God was the death of the moral and ideal God, the death of a concept of God that humanizes him and does not respect the necessary distance between man and God.

B. The Protest Against the Social Function of God

The causes of the protest against the God of theism are not exclusively philosophical. There are also social and political causes. However different their orientations may be, the secular theological movements known as the "death of God" theologies are in agreement with each other in their rejection of the God of metaphysics and their adherence to Jesus. The omnipotent and unchangeable God, the metaphysical God and even the symbol of the fatherhood of God all seem to be the ideological guarantee of a conservative social order to which the whole contemporary movement of emancipation is opposed. It would seem that the names traditionally given to God—omnipotence, unchangeability, eternity and so on—legitimate and sacralize a type of Church institution which bore witness to the metaphysical order of the world and effectively exercised power over civil societies.

The Marxist critique of ideologies has given us a clearer understanding today of the ideological function that can be exercised at a given moment in history by theology. There is no innocent theological discourse. It is not necessary to be a Marxist in order to take seriously the idea that the history of the images of God and therefore the divine names is connected with the history of the production, in other words, the development of the material basis of a society.[12] There is a lasting correlation between the conditions of historical existence of a society and the representations that it makes of itself. This "world-view" does not simply reflect socio-economic structures. It has a function to justify and legitimate a group (the dominant class) within society. And that is precisely the moment when the "world-view" degenerates to the level of an ideology.[13]

Theology degenerates into ideology every time that it becomes a system of social justification and legitimation and tries to impose, in the name of "faithfulness to the Gospel," one or other social or political option, when it is in fact defending the interests of the dominant group either within the society of the Church or within the society to which the Church is tied.

Who would be able to deny that, throughout the course of its long history, the Christian discourse about God has not tried to justify the prevailing social injustice and to provide men with the illusion of a recompense for the injustice to which they have been subjected? One of the most important social functions of theism has always been to explain the inequalities of powers and privileges existing in society. This essential function of theology, carried out in the perspective of metaphysical theism, was, according to the new liberation theologians for example, to justify the existing social order and to maintain whatever institutional order was in force.[14]

In the modern age, this discourse about God as a justification of social inequalities has lost its validity. For a great number of men, submission to the paternal will of God, hope mediated by the presence of Christ and expectation of an eschaton brought about by God are all incapable of alleviating man's suffering. Man's history and activity in history have become the essential instruments by which he has to try to integrate suffering and evil.

We are, then, invited to develop a post-Marxist discourse about God, in other words, a discourse that avoids the Marxist critique of religion as ideology. It cannot be disputed that a certain type of traditional theology was able to serve as an ideological guarantee with regard to one or other state of society. Nowadays, several recent theologies (under the influence of existentialism, personalism or the transcendental method) have dealt at too great length with the social dimension of Christianity as an accidental aspect. It is the special characteristic of the new political theologies or theologies of liberation to take seriously the historical effectiveness of Christianity and to provide an image of God as the Lord of history who is not in competition with man's transforming activity.[15] The discourse about God cannot serve to sacralize or maintain a deterministic and fatalistic view of history which might involve a theoretical and practical acceptance of its deficiencies and contradictions.

2. IN SEARCH OF THE PROPER NAME OF GOD

In the preceding section, I have tried to take stock of the crisis in the traditional discourse about God, considering it, first, in the perspective of the crisis in metaphysics, understood as onto-theology, and, second, in that of the protest against the social function that the God of theism has exercised for too long in the West.

We have become increasingly conscious today of the inadequacy of simply replacing the theism of the earlier theology by a "Jesus centrism," since this leads inevitably to a dead-end with regard to the future of Christianity. Simply saying "yes" to Jesus and "no" to God has become fashionable among certain Christians, but it compromises the universality of Christianity. It also makes dialogue with the great non-Christian religions much more difficult and is discouraging to those agnostics who are looking for God.

Contrary to what is often said or written nowadays, it is not God himself who gives rise to difficulties for many believers today. It is rather the scandalously historical character of Christianity—the fact that God has linked his fate to that of a first century Jew. The idol God of conceptual thinking has to be rejected. But to replace God by Jesus is to make Jesus himself an idol.

We have rather to be faithful to the movement of the New Testament, in which it is clearly impossible to know Jesus outside his relationship with the Father, just as it is also impossible to know God outside Jesus. One of the essential functions of Jesus' ministry was to liberate men from false images of God so that they could learn again what was the true name of God.[16]

Christ is not simply the model of human existence. He is not simply the one who defines a new type of existence with others. He is the one who reveals God. His life was at the same time inseparably an "orthopraxis," that is, a praxis led in conformity with the kingdom of God and a "celebration" of God's sovereignty.[17] Jesus liberates us from an oppressive image of God, but does so in order to reveal to us the true meaning of God's fatherhood and sovereignty.

It was because he identified himself with God's cause, which is also man's cause, that he was rejected by men. It is in his agony that he yields his secret to us—his special union with God. It is also in the resurrection that God's lasting commitment to Jesus is manifested. It is therefore in the mystery of the cross and the resurrection that the special relationship between the Father and the Son is revealed. The question of the God of Jesus as the Trinitarian mystery is therefore already postulated.

Since the crisis of metaphysical theism, the Christian theology of the mystery of God has been confronted with a new task. It is invited to take even more seriously the originality of the God of Jesus. It has become important to elaborate what might be called a "Christical theism." It is not sufficient simply to repeat materially the biblical datum without reworking it to some extent speculatively. If we want to name God in such a way that he will have some resonance in our own culture, theology can no more fail to express the demands of faith and reason today than it did in the past. In the past, speculative theologians had great difficulties with the God of the Bible. Now, it is the rational discourse of natural theology that gives rise to difficulties. We have to keep in mind the particular aim of speculative theology, while at the same time having recourse to other conceptual methods. Here, I would like to suggest only two areas of research which may possibly help us to think of the true name of the God of Jesus.

A. Christ as Universal Concrete

From the point of view of theological reason, it is a question of in-augurating a movement of thought which appropriates the truth revealed on the basis of its proper place instead of trying to take into account the hidden name of God on the basis of a previous foundation, whether that is God conceived as the absolute Being or whether it is man in his under-standing of himself. It is a question of taking not rational man with his will to representation in the presence of God, but rather man defined as re-ceptivity and openness as our point of departure. In that case, God himself should rather be conceived as an Event and as Coming, as an Appeal that is always new and as an unconditional Demand.[18]

In the same way, there is also a proper place in which the truth of being is revealed, just as there is a proper place in which the original truth of God can be appropriated. That place is Christ in his nearness to the Father. Thus, going beyond the cosmological and the anthropological re-duction of Christianity, the only way is a "theological theology" which takes as its point of departure the confession "God is love" as revealed in the event of Jesus Christ. In the incarnate Word, truth has opened the way which leads to it: "I am the way and the truth and the life."[19]

In our wish to name God today, we are exposed to a twofold danger. On the one hand, we can continue with our metaphysical conception of a God beyond this world and outside reality. That God is remote from hu-man experience. On the other hand, we can, in our desire to come closer to man, no longer take the risk of speaking about God. In that case, all that we shall retain of Christianity is its ethical dimension of serving men. And if we still speak about God, it will simply be an anthropological discourse, in other words, a discourse that is indirectly about man.

In fact, only a Christological realism will allow us to ward off both the danger of metaphysical thought, that is, speaking about a God outside real-ity, and the temptation of modern anthropocentrism, that is, a breaking up of God in the reality of a world that has come of age.[20]

Confronted with the atheistic criticism of a God beyond this world and the criticism of religion as an alienation of man, an attempt has to be made to reconcile the reality of God with the reality of man by trying to think of Christ as "universal concrete." If we go to the limit of the realism of the incarnation as God's becoming man and as man's becoming God, we can understand how the reality of God discloses itself as the reality of man and vice versa. Since God became man in Jesus Christ, God and reality have been mysteriously combined, without being identified, in the being of Christ. The alienation is situated in responding to God without being responsible for reality, since it is impossible to be responsible for reality in depth without responding to God.

God has revealed his proper name to us in Christ. But the accomplishment of his revelation in Christ is a word that is too full for it to be satisfactorily conceptualized. Unlike the conceptual idols of theism, Christ is the icon of the invisible God, making him present at the very moment at which it respects his distance. Christ as the icon of God can be understood as the concrete trace of the difference between the irreducible mystery of God and his presence among men. Christ as universal concrete is the place where the difference between the veiled and the unveiled God, between revelation as universal meaning and as a particular historical event and between God and man is mysteriously expressed.

It is possible to say that a theological discourse can only avoid falling into idolatry if it fails to eliminate the difference between what is given to it to think in revelation and what always remains hidden from it. All revealed truth emerges in fact from a place where what is given and what is held back continue to be indissociably united. It is at that place that the movement of negative theology and its game of affirmations and denials made in the service of the respect of the hidden God can be found.

B. A Transcendence Reconciling the Unchangeability of God and Becoming

The originality of the God of the Judaeo-Christian revelation is that he has revealed himself in history, in contingency and in the concrete. We have to try to think out the relationship between the eternal Logos and the particular event of Jesus Christ. This will always continue to be a scandal to reason. This historical revelation which brings God so close to man is also what forms the greatest difficulty for contemporary man. How can we claim that Christianity as a historical religion has a monopoly of true relationship with the Absolute? And how, above all, can we make the salvation of all men depend on that particular and contingent event that is Jesus Christ?[21]

It is not, however, by avoiding the historical particularity of Jesus Christ that we shall have some chance of ensuring his universality. He is the Absolute who has become historical. It is not possible to deduce God's becoming man from an a priori idea of God as Absolute. We have to be open to accept the scandal of the incarnation in the unconditionality of faith. If we say, following Hans Urs von Balthasar, that Jesus is the "figure" of God as absolute Love, it is inasmuch as the event of Jesus intrinsically qualifies the Being of God and therefore the proper name of God as Love.

Christian thinkers have always had difficulty in taking the historical positivity of the Christian mystery seriously. In its attempts to account for the mysteries of creation and the incarnation, in other words, the acts in which God has acted most freely, metaphysical theology has therefore always been anxious to safeguard God's transcendence, as identified with the unchangeability of the absolute Being. It has consequently insisted on the impassiveness of God, who, as a pure Act, is not affected by the contingent works of creation and the incarnation. It is therefore both possible and correct to ask whether, in this perspective, metaphysical theology can really account for the incarnation as the mystery of God's kenosis.

The rationalism of the Enlightenment in the eighteenth century did no more than simply point to this inability to think speculatively about the historical particularity of Jesus as universal concrete. We have only to think, for example, of the influence of Wolff in theology. Theologians who are attempting to think speculatively about the God of the Bible, the God of Jesus, have clearly to take into account the break introduced by Hegel into the idea of the historical.[22]

It would not be wrong to claim that Hegel helped Christian theologians to give speculative "support" to the idea of an incarnate God. He believed that true universality could only exist concretely. The universal had, in his opinion, to be incarnate, and it could only really be if it was incarnate. This is expressed in his well-known axiom: "Everything that is rational is real and everything that is real is rational." In other words, it is when the truly rational is effective that it is also fully rational.

Since Hegel, then, we are more clearly aware that the concrete, the historical, the positive and the contingent are not necessarily in conflict with intelligibility and universality. He is above all the philosopher of reconciliation. As Christian theologians, we should therefore be able to think of the proper name of the historical God without being too impressed by the "fearful ditch" between the universal and the historical of which Lessing spoke. Without seeking refuge in a pure and biblical theology, we ought to have an alternative to a natural theology that claims to be incapable of evaluating the universal concrete, in other words, of expressing historicity and intelligibility, contingency and rationality. The Christian fact makes men think. It does not insist that intelligence should be sacrificed, because it is itself speculative. The most historical religion is also the most rational.

Karl Rahner is one theologian who has tried to reconsider the mystery of the incarnation while avoiding the logic of identity of the Aristotelian-Thomistic philosophy. The transcendence of the God of Jesus is manifested in that he goes beyond the opposition that we place, in a metaphysic of being, between unchangeability and becoming. It is possible to say that God is distinctive in that he becomes different while remaining God. It is the privilege of God alone to constitute himself what differentiates him from himself.[23] With regard to the incarnation, we should not be afraid to speak of God's "becoming man." At the same time, this also throws light on the mystery of man's creation. The creation of man is only meaningful as a possibility for God to exist in another who is different from himself. In this sense, it is correct to follow Rahner and to think of anthropology as a "defective Christology."

God's plan, which is already at work in creation, is to put others in relation to himself and to associate them with the exchanges between the Father and the Son in the Spirit. Creation prepares and makes possible the incarnation as a possibility for God to exist in another who is different from himself. If we give up because of the dead-end of metaphysical theology, in other words, if we no longer make a desperate effort to reconcile the free acts of a creative and saving God with the eternal presence of the pure Act, then it is possible to say that Love leads God to annihilate himself and to do that from the moment of creation. According to Rahner's audacious statement, "God communicates himself to his creation in such a way . . . that he annihilates himself and becomes a creature."[24] We can no longer insert a break between creation and incarnation. The incarnation of the Word of God in a reality that is distinct from his own essence is the supreme act of God's creation and corresponds to an "expropriation" of God.

I have appealed to the resources of contemporary philosophy, but have not, in so doing, set aside the theological program of the great Christian tradition, that of the Fathers of the Church, when they tell us that the economy is the only place of theology, that is, of the knowledge and naming of God. The question is not: "Can we know God in Jesus Christ?" as though we already had a previous idea of God, but rather: "Who is the God whom we know in Jesus Christ?" The very word "God" can only be understood on the basis of the particularity of the history of Jesus—the God of Jesus is the God of Israel. And it is as such that Jesus is that particular man, who died and rose again, and that he is specially united with the God of Israel, whom he called his Father[25] in a union of such a kind that he is more than simply the special manifestation of God among men. He is the Son of God who is consubstantial with the Father, in the sense that was, several centuries after the event, to be defined by the Church at the Council of Chalcedon.

It is by contemplating Jesus' human relationship with the God of Israel that we can be led to discover the mystery of the divine sonship and are able to situate ourselves in the presence of God and invoke him by his name. We can, in other words, in this way know that we are "sons" and call him "Father." It is inasmuch as Jesus is that man who identified his will with that of God and made himself obedient to the point of death that he is the Son of God. It is as Son that Jesus is God himself. It is in this way that we are introduced to the intimate heart of the mystery of God as a mystery of fatherhood and sonship.

3. GOD AS GOOD NEWS FOR MAN TODAY

I have so far tried to spell out the proper name of God, but, as we cannot define God, but only name him, we have to have recourse to several names if we are to invoke him. Going beyond the false dilemma between Jesus and God, I have insisted on God's transcendence, but only after having made it clear that that transcendence was one of love and not one of the absolute Being. This means that he is essentially the mystery of communication in himself. He goes beyond the antimony of the isolated person and that of suprapersonal love. That is why we invoke him according to the symbolic expression of Father, Son and Holy Spirit.[26] The mystery of the Trinity should not be confused with tritheism. It is the way in which we confess the suprapersonal mystery of God in conformity with the practice of our relationship with the one God.

It is, however, not enough simply to repeat the official confession of the faith of the Church. We have to name God in such a way that he comes as good news in the consciousness of men. The naming of God operates in accordance with a complex dialectic. On the one hand, if we cease to name God, we can no longer ensure his presence among men. On the other hand, if we drift into an impenitent dogmatism, we shall no longer respect his distance and his presence may become unendurable. God must also be known as the Other, the one who is absent or missing, the failure or the trace.[27]

Naming God as good news for men, that is, naming him not as a repressive and judging God, but as a loving and liberating God, has been and will continue to be the historical responsibility of the three great monotheistic religions during this last quarter of the twentieth century.

It is appropriate to speak of monotheism in this context and not of theism. We are not, after all, confronted simply with atheism. As was the case long ago with biblical monotheism, we have to claim for ourselves one God in contrast with a factual polytheism. We have to confess one God as opposed to the many idols of the present time, that is, as opposed to what is experienced as an absolute, whether it is money, power, the state or individual freedom. As we have seen, Jesus himself can become an idol or a fetish.

I would like to conclude this chapter by invoking two divine names, both of which seem to me to be particularly consonant with the expectations of man today. We need to invoke God first as the "anti-destiny" and second as the one who is "in solidarity." He is both the one who is coming and the one who is with us.

A. God the Anti-Destiny

Invoking God as the anti-destiny is emphasizing the originality of the biblical God with regard to the pagan gods. Whereas the latter impose on man the burden of an insurmountable fatality, the revelation of the God of the Bible coincides with the good news of a liberation from those false fatalities.

We have to call on God and expect him as the one who defatalizes history in general and our own personal history. As we are invited to do by Marxism, we have to reject the claimed fatalities of history in the name of the creative power of human freedom. It is true, of course, that a certain God of theism seems to serve the interests of the most static forces in the world and that belief in a provident God who has foreseen everything in advance seems to contradict the idea of newness at the level of history. History is in that case no more than the unfolding of a scenario that has been written in advance.

In fact, however, if we have an understanding of the biblical God and the God of Jesus, we can claim that history does not elude God without making him a super-agent in competition with man's activity. It is not necessary to think of creation as something that has already been established in advance. We can think of it as the territory of man's possibilities, where man is co-creator in the name of God and that is the meaning of human history. God's creative plan is that man and the whole of creation should be successful. Man is the necessary agent of that success. It also has to be said that it is human freedom which is the place of divine action in this world. That is why human responsibility is so great.

Traditional theology conceived the relationships between God and history in accordance with the Greek pattern of a manifestation of the eternal present in successive events that were repeated. Nature or changing history is the manifestation of God as that eternal present. This pattern is not suitable, however, if we speak, not of the absolute Being of philosophical thought, but of the God of Jesus Christ.

According to the originality of history in the biblical sense, the real dialectic is not that of the present and the eternal, but that of the present and the future.[28] And God is not defined as the eternal present or the place of ideas and values of which the world and history are only passing manifestations. He is rather defined as the God of the future or the God of the promise. That is certainly the name of God that was revealed to Moses: not "I shall be who I have always been," but "I shall be who I shall be."

It is therefore correct to go as far as to say that there is in God more newness than unchangeability as defined once and for all time. If the real category of history is not the past, but the future, then history is an open history, a history that is orientated toward a God who is ahead and rises up from the future.[29] It is not enough to speak of God in terms of an unforeseeable future. We have to speak of the future of God himself. If we take the event of Jesus Christ seriously as God's coming in human history, then we are bound to say that the future of God and the future of man are inseparable. Just as the becoming of mankind is not yet completed, so too is it possible to say that the future of God is still open.

It seems to me in any case that naming God for contemporary man should be a way of escaping from the harsh law of the repetition of the same thing and from the oppressiveness of an inescapable destiny, of which human death is only the most tragic signifier. That is why our God is the God of hope, the God of the promise and the God who is always new and lets himself be known in unforeseeable events.

The proof par excellence that God is really a liberating God is the resurrection of Jesus. And the energy of the resurrection as anti-destiny and as a victory over death and all forms of negativity is at work in history. Faith in God coincides with the need to postulate an otherness or an "exteriority" with regard to the intolerable closedness of historical immanence. That is why we can no more be satisfied with any religion of totality, whether it is that of man, progress or the future, than we can with a pantheism. It is, moreover, this "exteriority" that forms the basis of our infinite responsibility with regard to the other, whose face is the epiphany of God (see E. Levinas).

God is therefore the one who defatalizes history. He is another name for the freedom and grace in our life. We are all subject to the law and to economic and social laws. We are all necessarily "men for death." What we have to know is whether man can be defined simply by what is "available" to him or whether he can also be defined by a mysterious openness that cannot be reduced to the social, economic and political structures that necessarily determine him. The key statement of atheistic humanism is: "God must be suppressed so that man may be." We could, however, begin to verify the urgent need for a new form of humanism that might rediscover the very old truth expressed in these statements: "God must live so that man may be," and "Tell me who your God is and I will tell you who your man is," and finally Moltmann's "God is the criticism of man."[30]

B. A God in Solidarity

The God who is coming and who is "anti-destiny" is also the God who is in solidarity—God with us. We have to show that the God of Jesus is the God who is in solidarity with us because he is the crucified God.

It is here, of course, that we encounter the fundamental objection to the existence of God—the power of evil in all its forms in the human condition. Job put God on trial and that trial has continued throughout human history to the present day. Several years ago, I read this remark, for example, in an article: "Confronted by the scandal of the suffering of the innocent man, whether he is called Job or whether he died on Calvary or in Auschwitz, simple theism becomes definitively ridiculous."[31] In his book *The Crucified God*, Moltmann wrote: "The question of the history of the world is fundamentally the question of justice. And that question leads to transcendence. The question as to whether there is a God or not is a speculative question when confronted with the cry of those who are murdered and those who have been sent to the gas chamber."[32] Later, the same author says: "The question of the existence of God in himself is trivial when confronted with the question of his justice in the world."[33]

It is when we are confronted with this painful question of evil that we become very acutely aware of the dead-end of all theodocies. Simply to profess that God is omnipotent, wise and good is not a satisfactory answer to the question of evil and injustice. We have rather to reinterpret God's omnipotence on the basis of the ultimate manifestation of the name of God in the cross of Christ. Bonhoeffer's bold attempt to do this is worth considering here. He changed the structure of Feuerbach's argument that man empties himself into an illusory absolute which is God by showing that, in the Bible, God does not become rich at man's expense. Man is not exhausted by the faith of the Bible. On the contrary, God dies so that man may live. It is religion in general that sends man back to the omnipotence of God. The Bible, on the other hand, sends him back to the weakness and suffering of God.

It is valuable to follow F. Varillon and go as far as to speak of God's humility[34] in the presence of his creation, as though he were impotent when the forces of evil are unleashed. God does not deny that evil exists, but he freely takes charge of it and puts himself in solidarity with it in Christ to abolish it. God is the anti-evil who does not let evil have the last word. But he wants to need men. As Nabert has said, "God's life is entrusted to us." This humility of God is the mark of his love and is therefore not in contradiction with his omnipotence. It is rather what Luther may have said, the special manifestation of his glory. We are therefore invited to follow Christ and share with him in God's own struggle against the power of evil. The pagan gods are "powers," whereas the God of Jesus is weak and suffering. What precedes any theology of the redemption and is made manifest to us in the blasphemous name "the crucified God" is God's solidarity with what cannot above all be justified—the innocent man who suffers.

A very pertinent note on which to conclude this reflection about the proper name of God is to recall the language of the cross (*Logos staurou*) used by St. Paul in his First Letter to the Corinthians (1:18). The apostle speaks there of the language of the cross as folly to men, but as being in fact the power and the wisdom of God.[35] There is a certain "putting to death" of the language about God that comes from the painful contrast between the absence of God and the presence of evil in the world. We have therefore to "practice" God rather than hold a discourse about him. But the man who silently serves his fellow men, doing this as a special form of the cult that we render to God, can certainly invoke him with the most suitable names. When the death of Christ condemns all carnal discourse about a God who is all too familiar, it at the same time enables us to use words "according to the Spirit" about the one God who is both the threefold holy God and the God who is very near to us.

Chapter VIII

"FATHER" AS THE PROPER NAME OF GOD

The famous contrast between the God of the philosophers and the God of Abraham, Isaac and Jacob has become almost trivial. The process by which Christianity became Hellenized did not begin recently. Since the time of Heidegger, who denounced the mutual contamination that had taken place in the onto-theological discourse between the concept of being and the concept of God, Christian theology has been confronted with a new situation.

We can no longer simply perpetuate the debate about the conflict between natural theology and dialectical theology. The whole landscape has changed, both in philosophy and in theology. We have to recognize that the crisis in metaphysics has not necessarily led to logical positivism. An author such as E. Levinas, for example, has suggested an alternative to the exclusive domination of the Greek logos by looking for a "space of transcendence" in the ethical relationship with the other. What is more, the crisis in metaphysical theology has not necessarily resulted in a biblical fundamentalism. With regard to the crisis in theism, contemporary theology is characterized by a "concentration on Christology," but this does not mean that it neglects to reflect about God's being. On the contrary, it tries to reconsider it by drawing attention to the indissociable link between the theology of the Trinity and the cross of Jesus.

Traditional theology set itself the task of reconciling the God of the philosophers and the God of the Bible. It too often did this at the risk of compromising the originality of the God who revealed himself in Jesus Christ. On the other hand, however, it is also true that it is not possible to dissociate the God of reason completely from the God of faith. (This is what dialectical theology following the tradition of Pascal and Kierkegaard tried to do.)

The God who reveals himself in history is also the foundation of the whole of created being. He is not another God from the God who is reached by reason, even though he is a God who is different. Certain au-

129

thors, such as Hans Küng, have suggested that the God of the philosophers should be raised to the level of and discontinued in the God of the Bible.[1] But how should we understand this? However serious the denial contained in this dialectical assumption may be, does it not also point to a consent to a "reconciliation" that is full of ambiguities?

I prefer the resolute path followed by E. Jüngel, who believes that a renunciation of the God of the philosophers will not absolve us from the need to reflect about the very being of God.[2] It is the historical task of theology to elaborate the Christian idea of God in a much more rigorous way than philosophy has worked out its idea of God. To take note of the collapse of our metaphysical knowledge of God, then, will not lead us to replace reflection about God by believing and finally by acting.

We have to reflect about what we believe on the basis of revelation. If we are to come to a true Christian concept of God, we have above all to see to what extent it is possible to reflect both about God and about what is transitory and perishable (*die Vergänglichkeit*).[3] It is precisely that from which metaphysical thinking cannot escape which cannot have a positive knowledge of what is transitory and dies.

It is above all within this cultural and theological context that the meaning of what I have to say in this chapter on God the "Father" should be understood. It would require a very long explanation if I were to deal with the problem of the application of the name of "Father" to the God of Christians as different from the God of the philosophers with the seriousness that it merits. It must be satisfied here with much less. I shall briefly outline the biblical revelation of God the Father and then go on to suggest two directions in which we can look.

In both, what has to be shown is that the name "Father" is the most proper one for manifesting the newness of the God of Jesus, not only with regard to the God of the Greeks, but also with regard to the God of the Jews. Was this not, after all, Paul's avowed intention when he made a contrast between the reasons sought by the Greeks and the signs demanded by the Jews on the one hand and the language of the cross as the ultimate word in which God made himself known on the other?

1. THE BIBLICAL REVELATION OF GOD THE FATHER

(1) It is important to point out straightaway that it would be wrong to try to find in the name "Father" the characteristic aspect of the God of Israel, as distinct from God as the Principle of Greek thought (whether this is applied to Plato's Good, Aristotle's Prime Mover or Plotinus' One). The God of Israel is certainly the personal God par excellence. He is the living

God who is both quite other and very near. What is striking, however, is the hesitation of biblical thought to designate God as Father, even though that name was not simply current, but quite commonplace in the ancient Near East.

As distinct from the pagan myths describing the genealogy of the gods, the fatherhood of God in the biblical sense is completely dissociated from the idea of begetting. (See the very specific meaning of the verb *bara'* to denote the creative act.) God is described as Father in the Bible in relation to an act of election, which cannot itself be dissociated from God's historical intervention in favor of his people. God is the father of Israel, not the father of all men.

In this connection, Jeremias has said: "The decisively new factor here is the election of Israel, as God's first-born has been made manifest in an historical action, the exodus from Egypt. Combining God's fatherhood with an historical action involves a profound revision of the concept of God as Father."[4] In the traditio-historical theology (see G. von Rad), the God of Israel is a liberating hero, one who acts, rather than a Father. This reservation on the part of the Hebrews with regard to the figure of the father and their absolutely trans-sexual conception of divine fatherhood urges me therefore to avoid filling this symbol with exclusively male characteristics. In this, I am also bearing in mind a number of very legitimate requests that are currently being made in opposition to representations of God that are too exclusively male and even paternalistic.

According to Paul Ricoeur, we have to reach "nought degree" before the figure of the father in order to venture to invoke God as "Father."[5] This is the movement that began with the Old Testament prophets (Hosea, Jeremiah and Third Isaiah). God the Father, however, is no longer simply the ancestor or the figure of the origin, but the father of a new creation, a new covenant, so it is by an indirect way of speaking that God is invoked as Father: "I thought you would call me 'my Father' and would not turn from following me" (Jer 3:19). In the prophetic writings, then, God is the Father who forgives the unfaithful acts of his people and, in order to avoid identifying the figure of the father with that of one who begets or dominates, it is completed, in Hosea, by another figure of a relative—that of the husband.

(2) In the New Testament, the word "Father" occurs as many as one hundred and seventy times on the lips of Jesus. I do not intend to consider this question, which has been studied elsewhere.[6] It is, however, worth drawing attention to the connection between Jesus' insistence on the Fatherhood of God and his preaching about the kingdom that is to come. (See especially the petitions in the Our Father.)

Jesus does not proclaim another God from the one proclaimed by the covenant, but, unlike John the Baptist, he extends the merciful Father-hood of God to include evil and godless men. God is the Father of those who have gone astray. (See the parable of the prodigal son.) There is in the New Testament a development with regard to the God of Israel insofar as God is the God of grace before being the God of the law.

Merely belonging to the chosen people is no guarantee of salvation. What counts is belonging to the kingdom that is to come. Since that king-dom has to be entered in the manner of a child, the special name by which God has to be invoked is that of Father. It is therefore on the basis of the eschatological nearness of that kingdom that all the texts in the Gospel that speak to us of the paternal providence of God, who makes his sun rise, who makes rain fall on good and evil men alike and who cares for the birds of the sky and the flowers of the fields, have to be interpreted.

This is enough to show us how great is the distance between a meta-physical conception of a provident God and the Judaeo-Christian revela-tion of God the Father. According to W. Pannenberg, it is not possible to make a contrast between the sapiential and the eschatological language of Jesus. He has said: "It is the eschatological nearness of the kingdom of God which discloses the nearness of God with regard to man and all creatures in general, thus revealing the 'natural' destiny of human existence."[7]

(3) We have already observed that there is in the prophetic books a movement from naming to invoking God as Father. This movement is completed in Jesus' characteristic prayer "Abba." As Jeremias has shown, this Aramaic term, which is not used at all in the parallel Jewish literature, expresses not only Jesus' filial obedience in his relationship with God, but also "a unique relationship with God."[8]

This unique communion between Jesus and his Father is attested by the famous logion of Matthew 11:27: "No one knows the Son except the Father and no one knows the Father except the Son." We have no reason to suspect the authenticity of this logion. If, moreover, we take into ac-count the very precise distinction made by Jesus between "my Father" and "your Father" and reserved for the disciples (Mt 5:45; 6:1; 7:11; Lk 12:32), we are justified in affirming that in Jesus God revealed himself as the Father of one unique Son.

We are therefore in the presence of a radically new stage in the rev-elation of the name of God as Father. Men are sons insofar as they share in the unique relationship between Jesus and his Father. The revelation to men of God's Fatherhood cannot be dissociated from the revelation of the unique sonship of Jesus. There is Fatherhood because there is sonship and there is sonship because there is, through the gift of the Spirit, com-munion with the one unique Son: "Because you are sons, God has sent the Spirit of his Son into our hearts, crying 'Abba! Father!' " (Gal 4:6).

2. FROM ATTRIBUTION TO INVOCATION

We have been able to detect a movement in the Bible from naming God to invoking him as Father. Similarly, it is also possible to discern how the proper name of God becomes more important than his general attribution. There is a great distance between the general attribution "El," usually translated in the Septuagint by *Theos*, and the inexpressible naming of God as YHWH.

Equipped with these signs, we can reflect about everything that separates the philosophical discourse about God from the language of religion. Metaphysical thought can attribute a certain number of names to God, but only a revelation by God himself of his proper name can enable us to invoke him by that name.

The proper name does not designate one or other property. It points to the person himself in what he has that is irreducible. The name itself does not really mean anything, but it enables me to identify myself as "I" and it also enables me to be known by others in what I have that is unique. In other words, there is no proper name outside an exchange in the form of dialogue.

As we have already seen, the divine name of Father does not belong exclusively to the Judaeo-Christian tradition, in contrast with the tetragrammaton, which is the unique privilege of Israel. It is a human representation of God (going back to what Hegel calls "naive faith"). From the very moment that we believe that God has revealed himself as Father, however, he appoints man as his interlocutor, with the power to denote by that name the inexpressible "Thou" of God.

By invoking God as "Father," we are not pointing to one or other quality in God. We are expressing symbolically the mutual recognition between man and God. We are bound, however, to go as far as to say, with A. Vergote, that the name "Father" as applied to God is something other than a symbol. A symbol always expresses an extension of meaning, in that a second meaning is envisaged on the basis of the first. "The name of God as Father, however inexhaustible its meaning may be, does not belong to this register of extended concepts. In calling God Father in the strong sense of the term, man is expressing a precise meaning which does not go back to a second meaning. The term is not based on signifying thought, but on the knowing word."[9]

The proper status of the name Father is confirmation of the fact that it belongs to the original language about God in its difference from the speculative language of attribution, whether the latter is philosophical or theological, in other words, the language which governs such statements as God is simple, perfect, good, unchanging, infinite and omnipotent.

There is a great difference between religious language, which is that of invocation, and philosophical language, which is that of attribution, which proceeds by means of intellectual composition and in which God is in the position of the subject of a number of predicates.

Reflection about the name of Father raises in an acute form the whole problem of the correlation between the personal names of the God of the Bible and the attributes of God as identified with absolute Being or the Principle. "It may be necessary to postulate as brutally as possible that Being and God are two and that idolatry threatens the greatest thinkers (not only Heidegger but also Thomas Aquinas) as soon as they come close to assimilation."[10]

It is, moreover, remarkable that the name Father cannot be found at all among the names studied in the classical treatises dealing with the divine names. In speaking of attributes in connection with God, there is always a risk of speaking of a property that he may have in common with other essences. (Karl Barth, for example, preferred to speak of perfections, since this word better emphasized the singularity of God's being.) This is also why Dionysius the Areopagite felt compelled to correct the inadequacy of the divine names by taking negation to the absolute and, by declaring ultimately that God was unnameable, to safeguard the supreme essentiality of the God who goes beyond all our concepts.

Whatever effect the correction made by the *via negationis* may have had, the movement of thought inaugurated by Pseudo-Dionysius within Christian theology was based on the power of human knowledge in its will to dispose of the divine in a concept of God as the supreme Being. When the latter assumes the figure of the *Causa sui*, we are bound to ask whether human knowledge has not completed the idolatry of God.

The replacement of metaphysical by transcendental knowledge does not radically change the hybris of human knowledge in its will to dispose of the divine. It is always the *cogito* that is at the beginning of the naming of God. God's naming of himself as Father responds in the first place to man's listening and his consenting to a name without any self-foundation of prior meaning. It is therefore legitimate to ask whether philosophical theism can claim to terminate in anything but an anonymous divine. Karl Rahner himself does not believe that metaphysical knowledge can encounter the personal God of faith. If it is possible to have a theology that will go as far as objectivizing God, it must always be on the basis of the revelatory communion that God makes of his name.

In any case, a Christian theology that takes seriously God's naming of himself as Father has to go beyond all the conceptual idols of the divine and look for what makes us think in the divine God of revelation. Our present historical situation provides us with both the opportunity and the task to assess what distinguishes the God as Father revealed in Jesus Christ from the God of onto-theology.

I would like to cite again in this context the quotation I have already made from Heidegger about that God: "Man cannot pray to that God, nor can he offer him anything, go down on his knees in respect before him, play music to him or dance for him."[12]

3. GOD THE FATHER OR THE "DIFFERENTIATED LIFE" OF GOD

A possible conclusion from the preceding argument is that fatherhood is not a philosophical concept, but is something that belongs to the order of the event and of knowledge. It is not possible to speculate about the content of divine fatherhood outside the act of proclamation by which God declares his proper identity.

I would like in this section to continue reflecting about the originality of God as the Father in his difference from the God of philosophical theism. I shall do this by showing how listening to what is to come in the revealed figure of the Father can help us to demystify the illusions of the speculative project about God as of the imaginary desire for the Absolute.

Here we are in the presence of two different registers. We know from psychoanalysis, however, how deeply rooted our vow of a fullness of meaning is in our most ancient passion of the origin. All that I shall do in what follows is to suggest how the dogma of the Trinity can send us back to a different God from the one of metaphysical thought and how the truth of the relationship of sonship between man and God is founded in it.

A Different God

Dieu différent is the title of a very good book by Christian Duquoc. In it, he writes: "What the symbol of the Trinity expresses is that the Reality of God integrates the differences evoked by the images of the Father, the Son and the Spirit and traditionally interpreted in terms of 'persons.' "[13]

The God of onto-theological knowledge is the God of identity, coincidence with himself, perfection which is not affected by any change, self-sufficiency and contemplation of himself. The life of the God who reveals himself in Jesus Christ is, however, a differentiated life. He is Father, Son and Spirit. In other words, he not only overcomes a narcissistic contemplation of himself, but also goes beyond the danger of ecstatic face to face.

The Spirit has the function of signifying and realizing the differentiated communion of God and his openness to what is not divine. Not only is God different in himself—he also brings differences about.

It is clear, then, what separates the logic of a knowledge of God based on identity from a Christian theology based on difference. In the first, God is in danger of simply duplicating man. A logical conclusion of this is atheism. In the case of the second, it is possible for God to become the openness that can set man free.

A Trinitarian theology based on difference therefore invites us to ward off the dangers of metaphysical thought when it is satisfied with representing God as the opposite of man. We are familiar with this logic of the Absolute which corresponds, moreover, to the system of projection by which man tries to escape from his finite state. According to this logic, God is the ideal of perfection, while man is defined by his shortcomings. God is eternal, whereas man is subjected to time. God is unchangeable and man is always changing. God is unvarying, but man is affected by suffering and so on. The difference between God and man, in other words, is thought out exclusively in terms of opposition.

A Christology based exclusively on the hypostatic union is of necessity held captive within this opposition as long as it fails to ask how Christ as the one who reveals the Father calls into question our *a priori* representations of God and man.

If we go to the limit of what is implied by the Trinitarian symbol, we shall cease to remain in a competitive relationship between man and God. It is precisely in the presence of God the Father that the truth of the religious relationship between man and God begins. And that relationship includes both similarity and difference.

Similarity in Difference

As we have already seen, God the Father of the biblical revelation is not simply the ancestor who sustains man's eternal nostalgia. He is the God of the promise who turns man toward a new future. The coming of God the Father in the event of a Word in which he expresses himself in the first person breaks the imaginary circle of a return to the origin. According to A. Vergote, we should not confuse "the conquest of the original with the reconquest of the origin."[14]

The God of philosophical theism, insofar as he is identified with the fullness of being and meaning, corresponds to the phantasmatic God of man's desire for the absolute. Faith in God the Father coincides with an act of mutual recognition. The price that has to be paid for this recognition, however, is the death of the paternal phantasm of God and of our megalomaniac desire to be like God.

According to Paul Ricoeur, it is a question of "passing from the phantasm to the symbol of the Father." Resolving the Oedipus crisis, moreover, has a great deal to teach us about our apprenticeship in our relationship as sons with regard to God.

If there are psychoanalytical reasons for being suspicious of the paternal image of God, it is because this may become the ideal place for the projection of man's ancient desire. The believer expects everything of God—immortality, innocence and the fulfillment of all his desires in the order of knowledge and love.

"The Freudian analysis of the Oedipus complex has shown that the son borrows from the father a life that is not the one that he effectively receives from him, but one that he would like to be able to attribute to himself."[15] Hence the desire to murder the father or else to submit to the point of death to the father's will, since these are the symmetric means by which the privileges reserved for the father can be seized. The only outcome is to renounce the infantile omnipotence of this desire, which amounts in fact to a renunciation of any attempt to identify oneself mortally with the father and an acceptance of mutual recognition. "Recognizing oneself as existing through another and accepting a word as constitutive and a law as structuring is not living subject to the imperialism of a phantasm, but living in the symbolic order structured by that word and that law."[16]

The economy of the desire manifested by the Oedipus crisis can also be found in our relationship with God. There, too, the decisive test is passing from the "paternal phantasm" of God to the reality of God the Father, who is recognized in his difference. There is a great difference here between an imaginary identification with God and an identification that accepts the game of difference and similarity. When I invoke God as Father, I recognize that I am receiving my existence from another, but at the same time I am identifying myself as a son and as a man called to work with others with the kingdom in mind.

Our "deification," then, does not take place in contradiction to our humanization. Becoming a son is learning how to respect the otherness of the one whom we call "our Father." It is therefore going to the very limit of a non-utilitarian conception of God and being taken back to our historical responsibility within the autonomy that gives us our identity as sons.

The revelation of God the Father, then, is subversive of what can only be a competitive relationship between man and God. A "master-slave" relationship is replaced by a relationship of "fatherhood and sonship." The only attitude that is a valid response to the Father's Word is that of the adopted son who experiences his similarity by accepting his difference.

Man accepts that he is not God, but he receives from God the gift of being similar to him. He has to abandon the old dream that the devil is always putting into man's mind: "You will be like gods." (This idea is the projection of an imaginary identification with God.) From that time onward, he is called to fulfill the words of Jesus: "Be perfect as your heavenly Father is perfect." (This is the reality of a communion in the Spirit which does not cancel out differences.)

CONCLUSION

My only aim in making the above all too brief remarks has been to show how the figure of God revealed as "Father" leads to a revolution in our spontaneous representations of God and the relationship between him and man. It is not sufficient to exorcise the conceptual idols of metaphysical thought. We have also to show how the different God who is revealed by the symbol of the Trinity can avoid the Freudian criticism of the "paternal phantasm" of God.

We have, however, not said everything when we have said that the condition of sonship inaugurated in Jesus Christ acts for us as a guarantee against the projection of an idealized father who can only be in competition with man. We have also to meditate about Jesus' condition as Son, in other words, about the one who, on the cross, went to the very limit of the experience of what being a son meant. I would therefore suggest that only a theology of the cross is sufficient to enable us to consider the being of the God of Jesus in his difference with the God of the philosophers. It is on this note that I would like to conclude this chapter.

The folly of the Logos of the cross (1 Cor 1:18) is the last word about the Father of Jesus. At the very moment when Jesus renounced the presence of an idealized Father in his experience of the silence and the absence of that Father, God himself manifested his solidarity with man in his suffering and death. He provided proof of his radical difference from the omnipotent and apathetic God of the philosophical tradition. By dying as the"one abandoned by God" (J. Moltmann), Jesus was taken to his true fulfillment as Son (see Heb 5:7–9).

It is in this way that the words spoken by Jesus to Philip—"He who has seen me has seen the Father" (Jn 14:9)—are given their decisive implication. Whereas the Son suffers from being abandoned by the Father, the Father also suffers from abandoning his beloved Son out of love for men.[17] God renounces his prerogatives in order to efface himself in the humanity of the one who is crucified. It is both possible and right to interpret the last word from the cross as "God's renunciation of himself" (W. Kasper).

The theology of the Trinity takes us back to a God who is different from the simple God of onto-theology. We have, however, to go to the very limit of a theology of the cross if we are to be fully conscious of the newness of God as the Father of Jesus, both with regard to the God of reason and with regard to the God of Israel, even though he is not another God.

So, going beyond both theism and atheism, we are driven to take the *theologia crucis* seriously. (This is the whole meaning of what E. Jungel is saying in *Dieu mystère du monde.*) The atheism that characterizes our modern way of thinking obliges us to work out a new Christian concept of God. As a negation of theism, this atheism is a critical aspect of Christian theology. A theology of the cross is not simply demanded by our historical situation, which is one of unbelief. It is more than that, since it alone is able to deal with the fearful question of God's justice in the world. It was the great achievement of Hegel—and, following him, Bonhoeffer—to have suggested a theological interpretation of atheism by manifesting the Christological origin of the modern discourse on the "death of God."

Chapter IX

THE BREAKDOWN OF HISTORY
AND THE LORDSHIP OF CHRIST

In what sense can we speak of a single history on the basis of Jesus as Christ and as Lord? A question of this kind takes us back to another question: Can we speak of a real intelligibility of profane history or do we have to say that it is as such without meaning and that it only has meaning in connection with the history of salvation? This subject belongs to the theology of history, but who would claim to be able to write a theology of history today?

I shall begin my discussion of this question by outlining the socio-historical context within which a Christian reflection about history can take place. I shall then go on to suggest a few elements of reflection about the relationship between the oneness of Christ and the oneness of history.

1. THE PRESENT CONTEXT OF A
CHRISTIAN REFLECTION ABOUT HISTORY

There are two aspects of this question that come at once to mind. On the one hand, there is undoubtedly a crisis of confidence in the meaning of history and, on the other, the Church is much more sharply aware of its historical responsibility with regard to the world and the future of man.

A. A Crisis of Confidence in the Meaning of History

(1) First, men and women today have the feeling that they are living in the light of a tragic and tormented history that has broken down. Irrefutable evidence of this can be found in the current skepticism with regard to all philosophies of history.

Following Hegel, philosophers have tried to make manifest the rationality that is inherent in the movement of history. They have attempted to show that history has a meaning, that it is the mediation of the becoming of man as man and therefore of his recognition by others. They have argued that it is by this mediation of history that man comes to his essential being. This meaning transcends all the various acts performed by men, just as the movement of history itself goes beyond all individual actions. In the perspective of historical materialism, it is by man's work that we pass from "pre-history" to history proper.

After the absurdity of two world wars, however, and the experience of so many forms of totalitarianism, Western thought has become more critical with regard to rational reconstructions of history. Every philosophy of history that claims to have evolved a global meaning of history seems to be doomed to failure.[1]

That is why we prefer to seek refuge in a pure analysis of the historicity of *Dasein*, in other words, of the time that measures human freedom. (See, for example, Rudolf Bultmann.) In opposition to Hegel, we believe that history is not the place where truth is necessarily and automatically unfolded. And in opposition to such thinkers as Pannenberg, we also believe that history is not the place where totality is non-problematically anticipated. An objective analysis of universal history leads rather to the recognition of the recurrent presence of a state of anomy, dispersion, disorder and breakdown.

(2) Second, it has to be admitted that Marxism itself also shares in the general crisis of ideologies. It is, of course, omnipresent as an instrument of analysis for the purpose of denouncing the defects in the status quo of our liberal societies, but the great event of the past decade, for French intellectuals at least, has been the crisis of Marxism as an ideology—because of the failure of its claim to achieve the communist ideal in history.

Whatever the situation may be with regard to the failure of Euro-communism with its claim to provide a democratic model in opposition to the Stalinist model, it would seem that some inevitable destiny leads every revolution that is inspired by Marxism to end in totalitarianism and gulags. It has also in all fairness to be said that the claims of humanism—whether in the Marxist or the bourgeois form—have been proved hollow by the tragic destiny of mankind over the past quarter of a century. Nihilism would describe this situation better than atheistic humanism.[2]

(3) Third and finally, there is the crisis in the ideology of progress. Since the beginning of the eighteenth century, this ideology of progress has been present to fill the vacuum left by the retreat of the Christian ideology. Man has come to put all his trust in the development of science and technology in his attempts to solve all mankind's problems and difficulties.

To begin with, the Church was reluctant to accept this ideology of progress, but gradually theologians began to try to reinterpret Christianity in the light of it. An obvious example is the theology of Teilhard de Chardin. That author's work tends to make the ideology of progress coincide with the recapitulation of all things in Christ.

There are also several theologies of secularization. These function as ideologies in that they try to justify by recourse to the Bible the secularization of the world, man's vocation as a demiurge with regard to creation and the idea that the transformation of the world by man works secretly for the coming of the kingdom of God. This trust in man's unlimited progress can be found in such conciliar documents as *Gaudium et Spes*.

What underlies these various ideologies of progress and secularization is ultimately faith in man. But this faith in man has been seriously shaken, and the Prometheus who was getting on so well is no longer getting on so well now. There was faith in the unlimited virtues of reason, that is to say, in the happiness and brotherhood that were founded on reason. There was also faith in the unlimited power of science and technology, but now the nuclear threat and our uncertainties regarding the consequences of genetic manipulation fill us with deep anxiety about the future of the human species. Finally, we also believed that nature could be controlled and dominated. But we have polluted nature and all that we are trying to do now is to rediscover and respect it. (The ecology movement bears witness to this.)

In a word, then, we are no longer satisfied by man, as defined only by his efficiency, profitability and quantitative progress. And millions of men and women—and especially young ones—have lost their reason for living.

B. The Church's Greater Awareness of Its Historical Responsibility with Regard to the Future of Man

This increasing awareness is based on a number of uncertainties about man's future and the dramatic situation in a world in which the gulf between the poor countries of the southern hemisphere and the rich ones of the northern hemisphere is growing greater every day.

The same growing awareness, moreover, cannot be dissociated from the historical turning point in the Church represented by Vatican II, which defined the Church's attitude toward the "Declaration of Human Rights." After more than a hundred years of tragic misunderstandings, partly the result of the "lay" context within which those human rights were made explicit in the nineteenth century, the Catholic Church has become, in the last quarter of the twentieth century, one of the major champions of those rights. Not only has it to be written: From the *Syllabus of Errors* to dialogue.[3] It has also to be said: From anathema to gathering together and the promotion of the rights of man. The latter—including the right to religious freedom—are not simply tolerated by the Church. According to Pope Paul VI's words at the 1974 Synod of Bishops, they have become a demand made by the Gospel. (See below, Chapter XIII.)

In affirming that human rights must be defended and promoted as a demand made by the Gospel, then, the Church is openly recognizing that it is impossible to separate evangelization from the promotion of man's rights within the one mission of the Church. (See Paul VI's Apostolic Exhortation, *Evangelii Nuntiandi.*)

C. A Movement Away from the Theologies of History

This new socio-historical context has led us to look again at the all too optimistic theologies of work, earthly realities and history. In this section, I shall only consider, first, the increased distance at which we stand now from the synthesis proposed by Teilhard de Chardin, second, the more balanced attitude that we have toward the political and the liberation theologies, and, third, our more critical assessment of the theology of the signs of the times.

(1) Teilhard's Evolutionistic Optimism

We are, of course, all Teilhardians insofar as we share his desire to reconcile the Church and the world and his emphasis on the unity of history, the history of salvation and history as written by men. But we are at the same time also all post-Teilhardians in that we have a much sharper awareness of the tragic aspect of history and the conflicts in the whole of human society. The evil is not simply the "blood of evolution" or the "ransom of progress" as a consequence of the incompleteness of the world.

The great limitation of Teilhard's work is that it was based on a non-dialectical view of history. In other words, Teilhard did not take into account the tragic gulf between matter and spirit. He considered evil as a means with an end in view. It is possible to say, with J.-B. Metz, that he confused teleology and eschatology. In other words, he tended to explain history on the basis of nature and he believed that it was possible to achieve a perfect reconciliation between man and nature.[4] But the substratum of human history is not nature regarded as a simple development or a kind of anonymous process. Human history is the history of man's freedom and passion.

A philosophy of history that does not take into account the suffering of men provides a non-dialectical interpretation of history, an abstract interpretation of history polarized by a mythical conception of man's emancipation, in which the conflicts and catastrophes of freedom are not taken into consideration. History tends to be identified with the history of conquerors, a history of success. In other words, it tends to be a kind of Darwinism inspired by the principle of selection.

The concrete history of man sends us back to the otherness of a liberating God who does justice to all men, both the living and the dead. It does not send us back to an evolutionary God (a Christ Omega).

(2) A More Balanced Attitude Toward the Political and the Liberation Theologies

It should not be forgotten that both the theologies of secularization and the political theologies have been sharply criticized by liberation theologians. The latter have accused their European counterparts of conformism with regard to neo-liberal societies, of going no further than an individualistic conception of freedom as emancipation and therefore of serving the interests of a certain privatization of Christianity.[5] In this way, the European political theologians have succeeded in justifying the modern world theologically as a profane world and have provided an ideological safeguard for a type of society based on technological rationality, growth at any price and work that is ultimately dehumanizing.

On the other hand, it is also important to remember that balance has been restored to political theology by Metz himself (especially in his *Faith in History and Society*) and by Moltmann (especially in *Le Dieu crucifié*).

I would like now briefly to consider some of the dangers inherent in political theology conceived as an optimistic theology of history, summarizing some of the findings of J.-B. Metz himself.[6]

(a) It guarantees a finalist view of history, that is, a view of mankind going forward unceasingly on the path to reconciliation with nature. In other words, it confuses teleology and eschatology.

(b) It is too prompt in its justification of an understanding of history as a history of conquerors, winners or successful people. It has no place for the memory of man's suffering. In other words, it is in danger of causing the Marxist theme, according to which the "evil" of the human condition has ultimately to be capable of being absorbed thanks to a number of historical causalities of the socio-economic order, to be believed in the Christian sense.

(c) Although it does not confuse the kingdom of God with political liberation, in its anxiety to react against the privatization of Christianity political theology leaves the fact that the realization of that kingdom takes place by means of a free response on the part of persons to God's call too much in the shadow. In other words, as the movement of humanization, history is not the automatic sacrament of the coming of the kingdom. Social and political liberation can only create the conditions and a space for freedom.

(d) From the point of view of the integrity of the Christian message, the various political theologies have a great deal of difficulty in providing a theological justification of the fact that the resurrection takes place by way of the passion. What we have here, in other words, is that crisis of identity in Christian theologies emphasized by Moltmann. Insofar as the Christian message is entirely adapted to the secular ideologies—either that of man's emancipation in the sense of the Enlightenment or that of revolutionary freedom in the Marxist sense—it becomes insignificant and is reduced to the level of what Metz has called "a superfluous religious paraphrase of the modern world processes."

Metz has tried to obviate the dangers facing a political theology that is concentrated on a future that has to be constructed. He has done this by stressing the importance of the idea of memory, which includes that of suffering and that of the passion of Christ. There cannot, in his view, be a view of history that effaces the memory of man's suffering. It is also the dangerous memory of Christ's passion which enables the Church to carry out its critical role with regard to society.[7]

The memory of the passion of Christ inspires us with a view of history which enables us to take seriously the divorce between man and nature and to make room for the history of man's sufferings. This history of human sufferings is not, as it might be in a Marxist perspective, a chapter in the pre-history of freedom. It is and will always be an element that is intrinsic in the history of freedom. It is even necessary to say that this memory of human suffering is one of the essential dynamic elements of history—both as a negative consciousness of a freedom that is still to come and as a stimulus to a struggle to be undertaken in the conquest of suffering. Finally, it is the God of Christ's passion who is the subject of universal history.

The memory of the passion of Christ is also a subversive and dangerous memory in that it calls into question the social and political power of the rich and those who hold power. It is not enough simply to speak about the "eschatological reserve" as the foundation of the Church's critical function with regard to society. That function has to be based on the memory of Christ's passion, which is a protest against all totalitarian systems and all ideologies that put forward a linear and one-dimensional form of human emancipation. It is opposed to any leveling down of the social and political dimension of suffering. It obliges us to take into account, in a planned society, those who have neither power nor a voice. What is more, the Christian memory of Christ's passion also has an anticipatory character. It prefigures a future which will belong to those who suffer and are without hope and those who are oppressed and regarded as useless in the world.

The Christian identity can only be understood as an act of identification with Christ crucified. "For the Christian, there is no alternative between evangelization and humanization. There is no alternative between inner conversion and changing the relationships and conditions of life."[8]

(3) A More Critical Assessment of the Theology of the Signs of the Times

Since Vatican II, we have spoken of the "signs of the times" when we have wanted to discuss phenomena which, at the human, sociological and cultural level, characterize the needs and aspirations of a period. We have also said that it is the Church's mission to discern those signs. Those signs and events have been seen as a *praeparatio evangelica* with regard to the kingdom, "stones of expectation" with regard to the ultimate fulfillment of history, which will be "God, all things to all men."[9]

Nowadays, we are on our guard against a rather naive form of optimism and tend to stress that human history is always going to remain very ambiguous. We also avoid the totally anthropomorphic view of God's activity in history that suggests that God has been more committed to some events than to others.

It has been pointed out that, in the biblical tradition, the term "signs of the times" is ambiguous.[10] On the one hand, there is the tradition of the exodus, in which the "signs and wonders" are positive omens of a salvation that will liberate men and redeem the world. On the other hand, there is also the apocalyptic tradition, in which the "signs of the end" are negative omens of the terrible end of the world. The modern "theology of the signs of the times" tends to interpret the signs of the times in an exclusively positive sense.

The true sign of the times is, of course, Christ himself. Or, rather, his coming, which coincides with the coming of the kingdom, is a factor of division, conflict and crisis. The same applies to the proclamation of the Gospel by the Church today.

Furthermore, before we see a Word of God in the "signs of the times," we have to interpret them at the human, sociological and cultural level. We have, for example, a different interpretation from that of Teilhard de Chardin of such phenomena as urbanization, socialization, planetarization and technological progress. In any case, even if we observe real progress at the level of man's consciousness or the humanization of man, we have still to establish the connection between those different phenomena and the coming of the kingdom of God.

Even if it is not the last word about the meaning of the history that is made by men, we are still able to postulate as a certain theological rule the fact that the different events of history are only "preparations" for the kingdom if they help to make human freedoms more open to the freedom of God. Finally, everything that is experienced in the field of human relationships, economics, politics, science and culture can only have ultimate meaning in the context of the relationship between man and God.[11]

2. THE ONENESS OF CHRIST AND THE ONENESS OF HISTORY

On the basis of this reconstruction of the historical and theological landscape in which we find ourselves at present, I would like to venture a few suggestions in this second section concerning the oneness of history.

It is not difficult to understand why the elaboration of a theology of history which claims straightaway to express the theological meaning of human history taken as a whole, that is, as universal history, is a very foolhardy undertaking. The most that can be done is to pose a number of questions about the relationship between human history with its own ends and salvation understood as the fulfillment and recapitulation of the whole of creation. The result will be a theology of the historical responsibility of Christians rather than a theology of history in the strict sense of the term. In that respect, such a theology of history cannot be separated from a theology of mission or "hermeneutics of sending." (See below, Chapter XIV.)

We have to try to find our way between two extremes. On the one hand, there are those who believe in absolute discontinuity. These could be called the "eschatologists." On the other hand, there are those who cling to continuity. A possible name for these is "incarnationists." Let us briefly consider each of these tendencies.

(1) K. Barth, R. Bultmann,[12] K. Lowith,[13] and above all the contemporary author H. Urs von Balthasar[14] belong to the first extreme group. All these theologians insist on an absolute discontinuity between the historical process of becoming and the coming of the kingdom of God or between profane history and the history of salvation. For them, there is no dimension in common between the unfolding of human history and the kingdom that comes from God. History undoubtedly corresponds to a divine providential plan, and it therefore has a meaning, but it is not our task to decipher that meaning.

We have to go even further and say that for Hans Urs von Balthasar— and for Louis Bouyer before him[15]—the relationship between history and the kingdom is negative. Far from being the place where God manifests himself, history is subjected to the will of man's power. Any attempt to speak of a progress of history, which by itself prepares mysteriously for the kingdom of God, is therefore to hold cheap any affirmations of revelation about the world that is subjected to the logic of evil. It is also holding cheap the cross as a judgment of that world.

What is hardly acceptable in Balthasar's work is his much too strict division between profane history and the history of salvation, resulting in an increasing secularization of the former and a greater and greater spiritualization of the latter. The history of salvation therefore becomes in his writing no more than the history of the Spirit of God in men's hearts and something that is independent of the vicissitudes of human history. The latter is simply the "external framework" within which the drama of salvation takes place and the figure of history does not even have any relationship with the eschaton. By means of a kind of "apocalyptic pleasure," it would seem that, for Balthasar, man's progress in charity is inversely proportionate to his progress in the order of historical immanence.

Speaking as Moltmann does in his *Theology of Hope*, we are bound to say that Balthasar does not understand history historically. He remains imprisoned within a Platonic perspective, according to which history is a series of changing and variable manifestations of the eternal present.

(2) The second extreme tendency is one of what I have called "evolutionistic optimism." This movement is represented today by some of Teilhard's disciples and some political theologians. These theologians insist on the continuity between man's progress that is immanent in history and the coming of the kingdom, in other words, between human progress and Christian salvation.

According to this tendency, the relationship between eschatological salvation and the construction of the future in historical time is determined in a univocal way as following a single line. It is what I have called above a teleological and non-eschatological interpretation of history and a confusion between the evolution of the natural world and the history of freedoms.[16]

The only really adequate interpretation of the meaning of history is an eschatological interpretation. This keeps history open to a future, with the result that it becomes the effective instrument of God's promises.

In other words, the relationship between the kingdom of God and human history cannot be expressed either in the form of a monism or in that of a dualism. There is no theological solution that can express this relationship in a satisfactory manner. We have to accept the need to remain in suspense according to the logion reported by Luke: "The kingdom of God is not coming with signs to be observed, nor will they say, 'Lo, here it is!' or 'There!', for behold, the kingdom of God is in the midst of you" (Lk 17:20).

At the same time, however, it is also necessary to reflect theologically about the eschatological fulfillment while taking into account two certainties that can only be reconciled in a dialectical manner. On the one hand, history in the concrete is in a sense the place where the world is transformed to the extent that it comes into contact with the mystery of God himself. On the other hand, however, the kingdom of God "guides" history and in an absolute way goes beyond all the possibilities of a fulfillment on this earth.[17]

That is why it is in my opinion better to construct a theology of Christian praxis or of the Church's sending than a theology of history in the strict sense of the term. Human history is, as I have said, always essentially ambiguous. A theology of history does not have the task of speculating about the meaning that history has in itself. Its function is rather to give it a meaning that will be at the service of the eschatological future known only to faith. It is, in other words, not only a question of interpreting, but also of transforming history.

In the following sections of this chapter, I am indebted to Moltmann (and especially to his *Theology of Hope*), to certain liberation theologians (especially G. Gutiérrez, L. Boff and J.-L. Secundo), and finally to a number of documents published by theologians in the third world.[18]

A. History Made by Men Receives Its Ultimate Meaning from the Humanization of God in Jesus Christ

No indication about the delay of the end of the world and no key for interpretating the succession of events are provided in the New Testament. With the coming of Christ, however, history entered its ultimate and decisive phase. From that time onward, it was subject to the Lordship of Christ and can no longer claim to be autonomous.

Are we therefore to conclude that there is an insurmountable dichotomy between the history of salvation and profane history? Can it be affirmed, for example, that the whole effort of profane history to move toward an increasing humanization of man and greater justice in the world corresponds to no more than a secularization of Christian hope?

Should we not rather try to show how secularization—or rather, making the world worldly—is a consequence of a preaching of the Gospel that teaches men how to regard the world and history not as a numinous presence and a blind fate, but rather as a task, as the place of our responsibility. Preaching the Gospel is in this sense the anti-destiny of history.

(1) When he became man, God came to a definitive compromise with human history. His action on history was not of the order of a miraculous act of force. He entered into history in order to bring all things to fulfillment. This fulfillment is not, however, an historical one. Death was overcome, but in hope rather than in history. This means that the New

Testament assumes the point of view of the wise men. There is no historical eschatology. This is why the New Testament makes the apocalyptic
tradition its own (Käsemann).

This rejection of an historical eschatology, in other words, of a total
liberation and reconciliation of man and nature in history itself, does not,
however, result in making all the Old Testament promises that have a
bearing on history empty. In the Old Testament, the history of salvation
is based on a temporal event of salvation: the exodus from Egypt or the
return from exile. If we recognize an evolution toward a salvation of the
heart, then salvation also certainly has a temporal connotation.

The New Testament did not do away with the Old. The New Testament authors accept the temporal, earthly and political reality of the Old
Testament. Salvation in the New Testament sense is inseparably men's
adoption as sons and the success of creation. In the sense that it is concerned with man's personal being for his eternal destiny, salvation continues to interest the whole of man and his collective destiny in history.[19] If
the Beatitudes are considered separately from their Old Testament back-
ground, there is a grave risk that they will become a form of Platonic es-
capism or an opium of the people. Finally, the real significance of the
Matthaean discourse on the eschatological judgment (Mt 25) is that it provides Jesus' disciples with the historical task of working toward the reconciliation proclaimed by the Old Testament prophets.

The New Testament, then, creates a free space. It liberates the world
from its gods and from a miraculous intervention by God. It does not reject
the dramatic dimension of history, but that dramatic dimension does not
exclude the possibility that a certain reconciliation can be achieved at the
level of history.

(2) That idea of a certain historical fulfillment of the prophetic promises has its basis in the mystery of the incarnation. God became humanized
in Jesus Christ, and the work of the Spirit of God in history consists of
making everything that the decision by which God tied himself to mankind
means appear. In other words, it devolves upon mankind to become itself,
that is, to realize its possibilities.

Christ, then, takes us back to the historical face of God and that is
nothing but man. The radical identification which Jesus makes between
himself and every man and which is sanctioned by at least two titles given
to him in the New Testament (the new Adam and the Son of Man) has not
yet made all its effects explicit. We have therefore to take God's compromise with history very seriously. Daniel's "Son of Man" came from heaven
and he had a human face, as it were on loan. Christ will also come from
heaven at the end of time. Historically, however, he came as the servant
who was a man among men and who identified himself with the poorest

and the most deprived of people. The covenant between God and man is so radical that mankind's becoming has a bearing on his mystery as man, because, identifying himself with all men, the development of man's possibilities concerns his own development.

Insofar as they proclaim a reconciliation at the level of history, the eschatological promises of the Old Testament prophets are proclaimed in a very original way. It is a question of relative liberation, because death is not overcome at the level of history. The meaning of human activity in history, however, is to unfold mankind's possibilities and to make history converge in the direction of its point of attraction. That point is the radical unity that existed in mankind at its origin, taken here at a higher level in Christ.

All the possibilities of history, then, are once again placed in the hands of the man who is the one through whom the historical task that God wants to be accomplished is carried out. True religion has not, from that time onward, consisted exclusively of cultic acts and sacrifices. It has consisted rather of bringing about a state of concrete justice.

The humanization of God makes man the real mediation of the relationship with the Absolute. The "supernatural" should not be understood as a separate entity. It is defined by a relationship—that between man and the living God. Giving food to the hungry, transforming the structures of an unjust society and working for peace—these are activities with a human content. In fact, however, they also have a "transcendent" significance, because the historical dimension of the humanization of God can be discerned objectively in them.

The humanization of God brought the "supernatural" or ultimate dimension of the human task objectively into the world. It is even possible to say that there was, from that time onward, only profane history, although since the incarnation we have known that that history is the mediation and the verification of our relationship with the Absolute. Every cultic and sacramental order becomes insignificant as soon as history is no longer regarded as a task to be carried out.[20]

B. The Church Is the Sacrament of the Presence of the Spirit of God in the Whole of Creation and the Whole of Human History

As the sacrament of salvation and as the sign of the gathering together of all men in Jesus Christ, the Church is different from mankind. It is, however, the explicit sign of a much greater mystery—that of the gratuitous presence of God in the whole of creation and the whole of history. The world and the Church are complementary expressions of the same mystery—the establishment and the recapitulation of the whole of man and the whole of creation in Christ.[21] This means that, despite the ambiguity of the motivations of human freedom, the world of creation tends by its own energy and without even knowing it to fulfill God's eternal plan.

There is a "temptation" to which Christianity is exposed and which is more subtle than the historical form known to us. That is the need to identify the Church on earth with the eschatological community of the elect in heaven. It is a temptation that consists of thinking that the only possible relationships between human history and the kingdom of God are those which of necessity take place via the Church as a visible institution.

We should, however, go beyond this narrowly ecclesiocentric attitude. We should not identify the churches of which men speak with the Church that God sees. The Church on earth is the concrete figure of the experience that men have, even without knowing it, of the history of Christ. And with regard to the much greater history of the Spirit, the Church is no more than a path and a transition toward the kingdom of God.

We also have to go beyond a too narrow and too linear conception of the history of salvation. All men receive the same fundamental vocation from the Creator and the whole of mankind is involved in a collective history which God is transforming into a history of salvation. Christ is the Word "enlightening every man coming into the world." This means that we must go beyond a purely chronological conception of the history of salvation. The first in that history is not Abraham, Moses or even Adam. In the ontological order, the first is Christ as the "new Adam." It is Christ who gives meaning not only to the post-Christian, but also to the pre-Christian religious history of mankind.

What is said of Christ as the incarnate Word has also to be said of the Spirit of the risen Christ. There is a history of the Spirit that goes beyond not only the framework of the history of Israel and that of the Church but also that of the great world religions.[22]

At least in the order of representations, we are still imprisoned within a linear conception of the history of salvation, the end-point of which is Christ, who also provides a new point of departure. Indeed, according to one Western theological form of Judaeo-Christian thinking at least, the Christian religion is no more than an extension of the Jewish religion.

A return to the non-historicist ontological conception of history of the Greek Fathers of the Church, who spoke of the economy of the mystery of God in Christ and the Spirit, would be highly desirable. This is the Pauline "mystery" which had been "hidden" and was decreed by God "before the ages" (1 Cor 2:7). And because there is no longer any descent from Abraham according to the flesh, Paul was able to tell the Athenians that the God "you worship as unknown, this I proclaim to you" (Acts 17:23).

In the light of this extension, at least two conclusions can be drawn.

(1) As an historical reality, the Church does not have any monopoly of the signs of the kingdom. Grace is offered to all men along ways that are known only to God. God is greater than the historical signs by which he has made his presence manifest.

(2) The salvation of all men, both individually and collectively, in other words, the success of the first creation, does not take place exclusively through the ministry of the Church (its preaching and its means of grace). It takes place through the work of every man, Christian and non-Christian, who is aiming at man's healing, liberation and advancement.

When it is in conformity with God's plan, the movement of profane history tends by its own energies toward a gradual liberation of man, an increasing domination of nature and a gathering together of all men within a single human family. This movement, which is peculiar to history, cannot be alien to the Church's mission, nor can it be without significance with regard to the eschatological fulfillment of history.

The history of the Spirit, then, is the sphere which embraces history as such. Subjected to the action of the Spirit, history passes into eschatology and eschatology passes into history. The Spirit can be described as the "power of the future." The future that is hoped for as a victory over death becomes in this case historical not only through the means of grace provided by the Church, but also through the energies that are peculiar to history as such. Every time there is a victory over any form of death, the energies of Christ who rose again in historical time are made actual.[23]

C. There Is a "Convergence" Between the Liberation of Men and People in History and the Coming of the Kingdom

The word "convergence" may not be the most suitable one, but it points to a mysterious link between the movement of history insofar as that is at the service of the dignity of man as the image of God and the communion of all men in God, which is a gratuitous gift given from on high by the recreative power of the risen Christ.

The order of creation and the order of salvation are not two realities in juxtaposition. They are both subject to the Lordship of Christ. Salvation is the definitive success of the first creation (see the theme of recapitulation in the Letter to the Ephesians).[24] And, as we have seen, the Church as the sacrament of salvation is the visible sign of a much greater mystery than just that of the community of the redeemed. It is the gratuitous presence of God in the whole of creation. It makes actual God's blessing of his creation in the covenant made with Noah and that made with Abraham.

So, as I pointed out at the beginning of the second part of this chapter, we have to bear in mind both that history as such is not the automatic sacrament of the kingdom of God and that the historical becoming of the world is not simply the framework or the "occasional matter" (Chenu) of the individual and collective life of grace. Insofar as it is at the service of man's advancement, it tends by its own energies to fulfill God's plan for creation. In the order of humanization, the authentic progress of collective human consciousness, peaceful relationships between men and the struggle for the human rights of the poor may form "stones of expectation," a kind of *praeparatio evangelica* with regard to the ultimate reality of man.

The third world theologians declared at the São Paulo conference in 1980 that "the fulfillment of the kingdom as God's ultimate plan for his creation is experienced in the historical processes of human liberation." Working to transform the world and to advance man is not necessarily building up the kingdom of God. Refusing to collaborate in that human plan, however, when it is in conformity with the inescapable demands made by individual and collective human life, is certainly going against God's plan.[25]

CONCLUSION

Ubi Christus, ibi Ecclesia. I would like to conclude by stressing that the true Church is not to be found only where the community is brought together to hear the Word of God and by the memorial of the body of the Lord. It is also present among the least of the brethren insofar as they are a very special presence of the Lord. The Lord's two statements—"Who listens to you listens to me" and "Who visits you has visited me"—should not be isolated from each other.

That is the whole meaning of the eschatological judgment pronounced in Matthew 25:45: "As you did it not to one of the least of these, you did it not to me." The hidden presence of the one who will judge this world in the least of the brethren is a judgment that puts the authenticity of the Church and its mission to the test.

At the conclusion of this reflection about the oneness of history at the service of the Lordship of Christ, I would like to say that it is very important to treat as a single dialectical whole that is free from inner contradiction the historical responsibility of Christianity and its absolute gratuity.

In a situation of world crisis, the Church is even more sharply aware of its responsibility with regard to the figure of man in history. But, as J.-B. Metz has so often insisted, the originality of Christian effectiveness comes from what Christianity relativizes at the very moment that it is overestimating and radicalizing the struggle for justice in the world.

The Church should in fact continue to bear witness to a hope that is beyond history. As the mystery of salvation, Christianity always goes beyond its social usefulness to man. That is why the Christian message must continue to be proclaimed on the basis of gratuity while it continues to give its radical foundation to the messianism of history. "Commemorating Jesus Christ" will always have a doxological dimension that can be justified in itself.

Part III

The Practice of Christians Reinterprets Christianity

Chapter X

THE TESTIMONY OF FAITH IN A NON-CHRISTIAN CULTURE

As soon as the words "faith" and "culture" are spoken, we think at once of a relationship of conflict. Yet Western culture is unthinkable apart from its Judaeo-Christian roots. When we speak of the West, we always have to refer to the two poles—on the one hand, Rome and the new Rome, and, on the other, Byzantium. In fact, it was in the fourth and fifth centuries that the word "West" first began to appear in documents. Was Constantinople, after all, not inseparably both Roman and Greek, Jewish and Christian?

It would not be wrong to say that Western culture was born of the synthesis between the Graeco-Roman and the Judaeo-Christian cultures. We cannot call ourselves "Westerners" outside of these two legacies. There is, on the one hand, what Renan called the Greek miracle, and there is also, on the other hand, the monotheism of the prophets of Israel. The claim to universality made by the West has its foundation in the Greek logos, the formal language of Greek philosophy and mathematics. But at the same time, we have our sense of irreversible time and a history that is moving toward an end from our Judaeo-Christian inheritance. Science and a sense of history—those are the two aspects which dominate the destiny of the West.

But, just as it is impossible to speak of a single cultural model, so too is it impossible to believe in the idea of culture itself being fixed. Culture can be defined as the complex of knowledge and technical, social and ritual patterns of behavior that characterizes a given human society. With this definition in mind, it is necessary to compare cultures with living beings who are growing and changing. Culture necessarily implies technique, art and language. How, then, is it possible to speak of Western culture in general, without at the same time speaking of the crises that it has experienced in its growth, at its turning points and above all in its modernity? If we

159

suspect that there is a conflict between Christian faith and Western culture, this is principally because we are thinking of the latter as subject to the shock of modernity.

I propose to begin this chapter by examining the nature of a critical faith subject to the shock of modernity. I shall then go on to consider the encounter between Christianity and the cultures shaped by the great non-Christian religions. Finally, I shall reflect about the conditions governing a prophetic testimony in a non-Christian culture.

1. A FAITH SUBJECTED TO CRITICAL TESTING

Faith will always take us away from the evidence of our senses, but, as a clinging to the Word of God to which Scripture testifies, it does not change with the passage of time. As a phenomenon that is also rooted in human subjectivity, however, it also has a history. As Paul Ricoeur has pointed out, the object of faith does not change, but man's "available credible" element does. The backward movement in history that is observable in certain representations of the world obliges us to make a distinction between what forms part of revelation itself and what can be traced back to the cultural vehicle of a given period in history.

Faith in God has become problematical today. It has to be able to pass the critical test that comes from the suspicion that exists at the place of traditional Christian discourse. We cannot be satisfied with a naive faith that has not come to terms with the Marxist criticism of religion as an ideology, the Nietzschean criticism of Christianity as a human illness dominated by resentment, or the Freudian criticism of an illusion of the consciousness. We have therefore rather to speak of a "second naiveté" for faith that has been through this critical test.

Rather than go over once again in detail the ground that has already been so well covered—that of the difficulties experienced in believing—I will simply discuss some of the most decisive factors that call into question the traditional language about God. At the same time, I will also try to go beyond the exclusive point of view of Western culture.

A. The Difficulties of Believing
Inherent in Our Historical Situation

The Change in Our Image of the World

The language of faith in the classical period of theology (the Middle Ages) was closely connected with a representation of the world as a world of natures that was stable and hierarchically structured according to a scale of degrees of being. Man was a certain degree of being that was perfectly integrated into and formed part of a hierarchically structured universe.

Nowadays, however, the world is defined as history, as becoming, and as the unlimited field of human action. It is traced back to man's creative freedom and not to a transcendental principle as the first explanatory cause of the world. The world has lost its enchantment and is seen as a hominized world that no longer goes back to God. This replacement of nature by history is of fundamental importance and of necessity it conditions our image of God. (See Chapter VII above.)

We are experiencing the final phase of the process of man's emancipation that began in Europe with the Enlightenment. Since the eighteenth century, what we know no longer agrees with what we believe. Man has become the measure of man, and the desacralized world can no longer be taken back to God—it can only be traced back to the power of man himself. The modern image of man is that of a being who is always creating himself and the world. This idea of man's self-genesis can hardly be reconciled with the image of an omnipotent and provident God. Insofar as man was not completely himself and insofar as he alienated his own substance in the absolute, God continued to carry out a number of functions in his life and in the world. Now, however, God seems to have become useless.

Secularization

It is not possible to speak of a crisis in our religious representations without recalling the phenomenon of secularization which has been taking place in Western civilization for some two hundred years and which has been spreading in every part of the world into which that civilization has penetrated. As I shall be dealing with this question in greater detail in the following chapter, I shall do no more here than say that secularization means that religion has receded from all the areas in which man has acquired knowledge and therefore from control in human and earthly realities and problems. The result has been that man wonders what use God can be and is at the same time afraid that religion may be opposed to his right to autonomy.

I know, of course, that secularization is a typically Western phenomenon. But however vital the non-Western cultures and religions may be, it is still possible to speak of a certain universality of the technological civilization and a certain collective imagination that engenders a secularized way of life. I know too that there is frequent reference to a "return to God" in the West (that is, in Europe and the United States). This return to God may function as a response to the disenchantment brought about by the crisis of ideologies. It may also function as a phenomenon of counter-culture in the presence of an industrial civilization that operates on the basis of profitability, anonymity and growth at all costs.

Despite this "return to God," however, we should not have any illusions about the situation of unbelief that prevails in the modern world. As far as the West (Europe and the United States) is concerned, there is a continuing decline in religious practice in almost all the Christian churches.

We can, of course, come to a more finely shaded understanding of modern man's lack of religion, but even so there can be no question of overlooking the criticism made of the illusion of religion by the whole movement of contemporary thought. In Protestant theology especially, there has often been a wrong use of the distinction between "faith" and "religion." It is, however, true that religion favors man's flight into an unreal "other" world. The God of biblical faith is not to be found where man invents gods—either fertility gods or gods of immortality—for himself, nor is he to be found in the extension of the inexpressible experiences that may be known to man. No, the God of the Bible wants to be known in a history, in other words, in incarnations. The movement is always from God to man, who responds to God's initiative. Both in the past and today, religion has always made use of the machinery to make gods that is constructed by the megalomania of man's desire or his taste for the inexpressible.

Religion represents the victory of man's desire. Faith is overcome by an encounter or presence, even when that presence comes into contact with man's spontaneity. Man quickly becomes religious, but he is slow to have faith.

Man's States of Consciousness

Speaking of the crisis of faith or the uneasiness of Christian believers, one is tempted to make a moral judgment of the situation and to attribute contemporary misfortunes, for example, to a general lowering of moral values or a lack of generosity. We have, however, to recognize that the uneasiness felt by Christians is not only the result of a feeling that there is a great difference between the Christian ideal and our contemporary way of life. It is also because we are aware that faith has become separated from modern man's states of consciousness. What is ultimately involved is the conflict between the authority of faith and that of reason in the debate about man to which I referred in Chapter I.

It is therefore not difficult to understand how discredited the characteristically moralizing way of Christian speaking has become. By this I mean that, confronted with such contemporary problems as world hunger, conflicts in society, the increase in world population and the new understanding of human sexuality, Christianity does no more than simply appeal to individual prayer and generosity. We have to accept the consequences of a normal and inevitable process of secularization. In other words, we have to take seriously a rational approach that is based on economics, international law and anthropology in general.

A critical and adult faith must meet the formidable challenge confronting Christianity in the situation of injustice in the modern world. I have already quoted, in another context, Moltmann's words: "The question of the existence of God in himself is trivial when confronted with the question of his justice in the world."[1] For millions of people, the fundamental question is not that of God, but "Who will eat?" or simply "Who is dying?" As Umberto Eco wrote, "The nearness of the Being is not the most radical relationship for the slave. The nearness of his own body and that of others comes first."[2]

If we consider mankind as a whole, according to the great collective passions distinguished by Kant, that is, possession, in other words economics, power, in other words politics, and value, in other words culture, then the situation in the modern world certainly confronts the Church with some very urgent questions. I need mention only a few of these: the population explosion, the plundering of the world's resources, the widening gap between the rich and the poor countries and the spread of nuclear weapons.

This is, of course, why the third world theologians are insisting on the necessary social and political implications of Christian faith. The Gospel is not neutral and, because of the radical evangelical nature of so many basic communities in the Church of the third world, it is possible to speak of a new spring of the Church in the last quarter of the twentieth century, insofar as it is emphatically on the side of the poor.

The painful presence of evil and injustice in the world invites us, then, seriously to doubt a naive conception of the biblical revelation, according to which that revelation has answers to all the questions that man may ask. The Book of Job bears witness to the fact that the Bible is not simply a history of the replies that God has given to the essential questions asked by man. It is also a history of the questioning of man on trial with God. That is why we cannot treat the letter of Scripture as an idol. It is rather the echo of the mysterious silence of God. God is certainly the one who gives meaning to man's existence. But it is not a light that dispels all darkness.[3]

Religious Relativism

A further obstacle to faith should also be included in this brief review of the modern man's difficulties in believing: his greater awareness of the relativity of Christianity as an historical religion. A better knowledge of the millennia preceding the coming of Christ and of the other great religious traditions of mankind has inevitably led us to question Christianity's claim to be the only true and universal religion.

How is it possible to claim that Christianity is the universal mediation of the Absolute for man? Are we not obliged to admit that all religions are valid as ways to God? And is Christianity's claim to be universal not shown to be without historical verification by a degree of failure in the Church's universal mission?

This greater awareness of the particular historical nature of Christianity should not, however, lead us to relativism and skepticism. On the contrary, it invites us to be more critically discerning of the real originality of Christianity in its difference from the other great religions, both the monotheistic religions such as Judaism and Islam and the Eastern religions such as Hinduism and Buddhism.

Only a better understanding too of the distinctive riches of each great non-Christian religion will prevent us from developing an attitude of naive Christian imperialism, as though historical Christianity had a monopoly of all positive values in the ethical, religious or spiritual order. It is one thing to accept the particular historical nature of Christianity and quite a different thing to doubt the unique mediation of Christ as the incarnation of God in history.

B. Interpretation as a Constitutive
Element of Critical Faith

I have tried to distinguish some of the essential elements in the historical situation that conditions our contemporary experience of Christian faith. If we ask ourselves about our conception of human existence as experienced today, it is possible to say that it is characterized by two central data. The first of these is man's current firm expectation of a future that will be humanly livable. The second is his anguish regarding that future, since the situation of injustice in which the great majority of men live is not only scandalous—it also permanently threatens that future. It is with these data in mind that we have to reinterpret Christianity for the present time and actualize the Christian message.

This leads us to recognize that there can be no critical faith without a "hermeneutical operation." This hermeneutical operation will begin by critically analyzing our contemporary experience. It will then try to discover the constant structures of the fundamental experience to which the New Testament and subsequent Christian tradition bear witness. Finally, it will establish a "critical correlation" between the tradition of Christian experience and our own contemporary experience.[4]

Christian Faith and Interpretative Experience[5]

I have already stressed the fundamental historicity of faith. This means that critical reflection is not simply a second stage with regard to faith and something that is reserved for an elite. Even in the New Testament, theology is contemporary with faith, in other words, faith is of necessity expressed in constant confrontation with culture. The whole of the New Testament can in fact be regarded as an act of interpretation[6] of the event of Jesus Christ carried out by the early Church. And, far from being an obstacle, the distance that separates us from the New Testament is the very condition of a new act of interpretation for us today. It is the closing of the text that is the condition of a creative taking over of the text. We have to speak of an analogy or a fundamental homology between the biblical statements and their socio-cultural environment on the one hand and, on the other, the discourse of faith that we should have today and our present social situation.

Understanding the hermeneutical demand made by every act of faith is taking seriously the historicity of the truth, even when it is a question of revealed truth, and at the same time taking seriously the historicity of man as the interpreting subject from whom every act of knowledge is inseparable from an interpretation of self and of the world. Interpretation is the demand made by faith insofar as the object of faith is not a dead, but a living truth which is always transmitted in an historical mediation and which has to be constantly actualized.

Christian faith lives of necessity from an origin. That origin is the event of Jesus Christ as a founding event. The New Testament, as the written record of the testimony borne to that event, is also already an interpretation. It is a testimony that was conditioned by the historical density of a believing community which was subjected to its own need to be legitimized and identified. As an interpretative testimony, the New Testament only yields its meaning to us when we take possession of it within the movement of an historical tradition.

Having a critical and responsible faith today means producing a new interpretation of the Christian message by taking our historical situation into account while at the same time taking our place within the same tradition that produced the original text. There is an analogy between the

New Testament and the function that it performed in the early Church on the one hand and, on the other, the production of a new text today and the function that that text fulfills in the Church and society. We should not look for the continuity that is guaranteed by the gift of the Spirit and by the faith that we experience within the community in a mechanical repetition of the same doctrinal message, but in this analogy that exists between the two acts of interpretation.

The Fundamental Christian Experience

The fundamental experience of the salvation offered by God in Jesus Christ has been given a different complexion in the synoptic Gospels, the Fourth Gospel and the Pauline epistles in the light of the questions that were being asked and the various modes of representation, of thinking and of expressing in language that were current at that time and in that sociocultural environment.

The beginning of the experience of the first Christians was constituted by the living Jesus of history, and the source, the norm and the criterion of that experience were represented by that same Jesus. A critical faith therefore has the task of reconstructing that fundamental experience by dissociating it from the representations that form part of a world of experience that has now been completed.

It is possible to trace that fundamental experience back to three essential elements:

1. Jesus proclaimed a God who wanted all men and the whole of man to be saved. In other words, the God of Jesus Christ is no other than the God to whom the various religions of mankind bear witness. And by salvation is meant not only the salvation of the living in all their physical, spiritual and social dimensions, but also the salvation of the dead.

2. Jesus' human being is defined by his relationship with the Father. Jesus, however, never dissociated his existential relationship with God as Abba from his praxis of healing, liberation and reconciliation with regard to the poor and lowly people of Israel. That is why proclaiming the good news of the Gospel is not only transmitting a message, but also making an experience of liberation manifest.

3. By the mystery of his death and resurrection, Jesus proved that human history cannot be fulfilled within a terrestrial "system" of our history. Far from being a flight into another world beyond this one, however, faith in the resurrection takes us back to our present life in this world, in order to anticipate the liberating effects of the resurrection as opposed to all forms of death.

The Two Poles of a Creative Reinterpretation of Christianity

There can be no living preaching today without a creative reinterpretation of Christianity. It is, in other words, not enough simply to "adapt" a traditional doctrine to contemporary attitudes. Our search for a new language of faith of necessity implies a reinterpretation of the content of that language. This task of reinterpretation involves a great risk and it can only be carried out by establishing a reciprocal correlation between the fundamental experience of the New Testament and the traditional faith of the Church and our contemporary human experience. I will do no more here than simply list a few of the principles that should underlie this critical task:

(a) In conformity with Vatican II, Scripture must be the "soul" and the "vital principle" of all theology. This means that even the most venerable theological hypotheses must be subjected to the irrefutable conclusions of exegesis based on historical criticism. It is not the Jesus who has been reconstructed by the science of history who is the source and the norm of Christian faith, but the living Jesus of history confessed as Christ by the first Christian community. Dogmatic theology, however, has to take into account the fact that historico-critical research is today able to manifest to us the identity that exists between the Christ confessed in faith and the man Jesus of Nazareth.

(b) Dogmatic definitions have to be reinterpreted in the light of our critical reading of Scripture and our present human experience. Our particular historical situation is in fact a constitutive element in our understanding of the Christian message. If we do not treat it as such, we are in danger of defending a purely "verbal" orthodoxy. I have discussed this question at some length in Chapter IV above.

(c) In presenting the Christian message, we have to take into account the principle put forward by Vatican II, namely that there is a "hierarchy of values." We are living at the end of the second millennium and the Church also has the urgent task of actualizing the Christian message in cultures other than that of the West.

2. THE ENCOUNTER BETWEEN CHRISTIANITY
AND THE DIVERSITY OF CULTURES

Even if we experience faith in one of the traditionally Christian countries of the West, we are all, in one way or another, concerned with the problem of the encounter between Christianity and any great non-Christian religion. This encounter cannot, however, be separated from that between two different cultures.

There cannot in fact be an encounter between two great religions in a pure form. This encounter will always also be a confrontation between two cultures. There is no such thing as a chemically pure Christian message that may already be "transmitted" into a culture and, when Christians are in a minority in a given country, they are confronted with men for whom belonging to a culture is inseparably part of belonging to the dominant religion of that culture.

What a "culture" and a "religion" have in common is the idea of "heritage." According to J. Ladrière, a culture is a state of "being rooted."[7] It is an invisible but very close link that ties a human being to his predecessors, his contemporaries and his successors. Belonging to a culture is being rooted in a particular tradition. It is being invited to live in the world in a certain language.

In this section, I shall first consider a number of aspects of the fundamental principle of the "inculturation" of Christianity. Then I shall go on to reflect about the originality of Christianity as a religion and its true universality. Finally, in the third section, I shall comment on the new demands made by bearing witness.

A. The Fundamental Principle of Inculturation[8]

At the 1977 Synod of Bishops, there was a debate about a real "incarnation of faith" in different cultures, in which it was said that "the Christian message must be rooted in human cultures and must assume and transform them . . . Christian faith must become incarnate in those cultures" (DC 74 [1977], p. 1018).

The term "inculturation" is used in French in the context of evangelization in preference to another neologism, "acculturation," because it better expresses the need for faith to germinate and grow literally *in* cultures.[9] In it, faith is compared to a seed, just as the Word of God is in the synoptic Gospels. The phrase "the incarnation of faith" similarly takes us back to the central mystery of Christianity, the incarnation of the Word of God. This means that the integrity of the Christian message is not in any way compromised when it becomes incarnate in a given culture, any more than God's becoming incarnate as man compromised his transcendence.

Whenever an attempt is made to understand the problem of the inculturation of Christianity in a foreign mentality, within which various cultural elements are inextricably mixed with religious factors, it is necessary to bear in mind on the one hand rupture or discontinuity and, on the other, creation or continuity. By discontinuity is meant that the proclamation of the Gospel coincides with the coming of new ways of thinking and imagining and new forms of human culture. By creation is meant the fact that, despite its newness, the Christian kerygma can only be heard and understood if it becomes a fact of culture, in other words, if it becomes part of the existing languages and psychologies.

The problem of inculturation has to be considered within the framework of this dialectical tension between continuity and discontinuity. The Gospel has always to be good news, but at the same time it also has to some extent to become a fact of culture. If this attempt at inculturation is not made in evangelization, there will be no evangelical event. There will only be the "false shame" of a cultural vehicle that is alien or outmoded. On the other hand, if the discourse about faith slips so easily and completely into a particular culture that it loses its own identity, there will also be no evangelical event.

The Gospel will always be a sign of contradiction. But when Christianity comes into conflict with an existing culture or with a great religion, it is important to discover whether this conflict is in the name of the Gospel itself or because of the particular culture with which it has been historically associated.

The process of evangelization follows a twofold movement. The first of these is the inculturation of Christianity and the second is the Christianization of culture. The phenomenon of Christianization is a slow and complex movement which includes a dialectical tension between assimilation and dissimilation. It operated in the encounter between early Christianity and Hellenism, and it is generally agreed that there may have been in that encounter an early assimilation which was simple and syncretist and which soon led to a movement in which Christianity was rejected and which was then followed by a second assimilation that was more critical.

As I have already said, Christianity never encounters a culture in a pure form. In Africa and Asia especially, it is always confronted with other great religious traditions. Wherever it is proclaimed, the Gospel acts as a "critical catalyst"[10] with regard to the ethical, meditative and ascetic values of those other religious traditions. At the same time, however, Christians must be prepared to question their way of living their faith if this is not to be a factor of estrangement with regard to the dominant culture of the country in which they find themselves. It is not a question of proclaiming or living a different kind of Christianity. In conformity with the Catholicity of the Church, it is rather a question of favoring the conditions which will lead to the appearance of a different historical form of Christianity.

B. The Originality of Christianity as a Religion

The encounter between Christianity and another great religion invites us to reflect about the originality of Christianity. In this respect, the relationship between Christianity in its early form and Judaism has an exemplary value for us.

The new covenant inaugurated by Christ did not lead at once to a new cult, a new priesthood and new temples. In the ethical order, the message of Christ is rather a radicalization of what was contained as an embryo in the Jewish law as a law of love. The radical newness of Christianity is summarized in the event of Jesus Christ himself with all that was new and original in his relationship with God and his fellow men in what he brought. This newness is expressed above all by the new spirit with which a whole world of thought, a vision of the world and of man, a life-style and certain ethical categories which may have been very old were assumed.

The urgent demands made by the mission to the Gentiles meant that a distinction had to be made between the contingent Jewish elements and the Gospel message itself. The Jews who had become Christ's disciples regarded it as quite normal to continue to be circumcised and not to eat certain kinds of food. This was true to the extent that, at the beginning of the life of the early Church, the new religion initiated by Christ was called quite simply the "Way" (*hodos*). It was an extension of the Jewish *halacha*, understood as a set of moral, social and religious rules. Two of Christ's sayings had to be kept: "I have come not to abolish the law and the prophets, but to fulfill them" (Mt. 5:17) and "No one puts new wine into old wineskins" (Mk 2:22 par).[11]

This co-existence of the Jewish religion and Christian practice following Christ invites us to think about the originality of Christianity as a religion. If by "religion" is meant a system of representations, a set of rites, a list of ethical precepts and a program of social practices, then one is tempted to say that Christ did not in fact found a new religion.

Christian life cannot, however, be defined *a priori*. It exists wherever the Spirit of Christ makes a new being arise both individually and collectively in man. To ask whether there is a specifically Christian character is to ask the wrong question. There is no Christian "species," only a Christian "genus" which can hardly be discerned.[12] We have simply to say that there is a Christian way of being a man, of loving, suffering and working and of being an Iraqi, an Indonesian, Turkish, African or Chinese.

Christianity has to become incarnate in mentalities in which cultural and religious elements are inextricably mixed, but this does not mean that we can speak of a double belonging—Christian and cultural. Can we, however, go so far as to speak of a double religious belonging? This question is not, after all, simply one of asking whether it is possible to be integrally both Chinese and Christian or an Arab and a Christian. It is rather whether it is possible to be both Buddhist and Christian or both a Muslim and a Christian.

This is not an absurd question. It takes us back, after all, to another more radical question, namely: What is the most important element in Christianity? Is it a set of rites, representations and practices, which are also the structural elements that are common to all religions, or is it the unforeseeable power of the Gospel?

It is not because the relationships between Christianity and the other great religions have been experienced historically in terms of exclusion that this situation has become normative for the end of the second millennium. There are in Asia numerous cases of "Christian Buddhism" and "Christian Hinduism," and these are not examples of an idle form of syncretism, but original creations of the Spirit of Jesus. It is in cases such as these that we may find verification of the fact that the relationship between early Christianity and Judaism is illuminating in our attempt to understand the encounter between contemporary Christianity and the great non-Christian religions. [13]

I refer to this risky question of a double religious belonging because I think that it is far too simple and too triumphalist to say that Christianity is a leaven that is bound to bring about an assumption and a destruction at the same time of all other religions. There is no doubt that Christianity will always be critically discerning and purifying with regard to the other religions, but, as I have already said, we must be on our guard against the illusion of believing that we can make a clear distinction between the cultural values that we should be able to keep and the religious values that we ought to reject. The Church will remain faithful to its universal vocation, not by trying to destroy the other great religions, but by maintaining a Christian presence that will be the seed and the promise of those new historical realizations that an Arab, an Indian or a Chinese Christianity will be.

In other words, Christianity is not faithful to its exodus state when it gives an absolute value to an historical realization, that is, to a particular institutional or doctrinal production as a definitive state of the Church of Christ. The Gospel has a critical function not only with regard to the other great religions, but also with regard to the Christian religion itself. In the concrete, this means that, confronted with the challenge of other cultures and other religions, the Church can only be faithful to its Catholicity if it accepts a conversion, that is, if it accepts a need to question its Western mode of expression.

C. The Particular Historical Nature of
Christianity and Its Vocation to Universality

Within the Church, there has often been a temptation to conclude that Christianity has an absolute character as an historical religion based on the absolute character of the event of Jesus Christ as the historical manifestation of the absolute nature of God. Because of the human-divine character of Christ, the historical Church has thought of itself among men and among other religions and philosophies as the bearer of absolute truth, and it has acted accordingly.

It has therefore organized its doctrinal, political and social activity within the framework of what could be called a "unitarian ideology"[14] which has been expressed in a certain triumphalism or in a oneness conceived in terms of exclusiveness or inclusiveness. The Church has seen itself as the depositary of a "truth," and that "truth" was opposed to the rest, which was seen as "error."

There has also been another tendency—to think that Christian truth is able to embrace all the values of mankind, civilization and religion that exist outside Christianity.

It would be relatively easy to show that this claim to universality has coincided with Christianity's close relationship with the privileged and dominant civilization of the West. The more firmly it is believed that the Christian religion is universal, the more strenuously Christianity is tempted to present itself with all the attributes of power and to promote a unity conceived in terms of uniformity.

I have noticed, however, that, thanks to an increased knowledge of worlds other than that of the West, we have today a much greater awareness of the particular historical nature of Christianity which does not include all the values that are made explicit in the other great religions or other spiritual philosophies. We also have a much greater awareness of a certain failure of the universal mission of Christianity. We recognize, moreover, that the Christian claim to universality goes counter to Jesus' historical practice, since, in revealing himself in Jesus, God did not give an absolute value to a particular character. On the contrary, what this meant was that no particular historical character was absolute.

This acceptance of the particular historical nature of Christianity is not in contradiction either with our faith in the universality of the mediation of Christ or with our faith in the Church's universal mission.

It is precisely as the one who is universal in the concrete, that is, who is God made man, that Jesus is universal. We believe that Christ is not one manifestation among others of the Absolute that God is. He is God himself who has become historical. But what we say about Christ as the mediation of God cannot be said about historical Christianity. And what is more, the universal mission of the Church does not depend on the absolute character of Christianity as an historical religion.[15] Christianity has no monopoly of God's saving action. Grace is offered to all men along ways that are known only to God. As an historical reality, the Church has no monopoly of the signs of the kingdom. God is greater than the historical signs by which he has manifested his presence.

I have made these distinctions and observations in an attempt to make it clear that the real universality of Christianity is not an abstract universality that tends to impose a formal uniformity on all the churches. As Pope Paul VI said, "We are pluralist precisely because we are Catholic, in other words, universal." Catholicity ought to be able to include a pluralism of confessions and practices without leading to a breakdown—Paul VI also said: "Faith is not pluralist." If we take seriously the conditions of the Church's incarnation in a given culture, the same faith ought to bring about different historical forms of Christianity.

3. THE CONDITIONS OF A PROPHETIC TESTIMONY

As we shall see later in Chapter XII, where I discuss it as a "way," Christianity is essentially a prophetic religion and Christian existence is also essentially a prophetic existence. Christianity is, in other words, a permanent "exodus." There is therefore an inner demand made of Christianity to go beyond the historical objectivizations that it is able to give itself in the order of language, in the institutional order and in the order of practices.

This is intimately connected with the idea that has dominated the whole of this book, namely, the concept of creative faithfulness that is implied in all Christian testimony insofar as that testimony is borne in history.

Here I shall simply try to reply to the question: What are the conditions of a prophetic testimony in the Church and why do we speak of a prophetic testimony?

The difficulty of communicating faith may be connected with the difference between the language of the New Testament and the dominant language of our own culture. It is also possible to say that the same difficulty of communicating faith comes from the fact that our situation is different from that of those who were contemporary with Christ or the apostles in that we cannot rely on a religious *a priori* or a messianic expectation when we address modern man.

We are, however, able to ask whether the relative failure of our testimony does not come from the fact that it is not sufficiently prophetic, that is, not sufficiently a creative word of something new.

A. Testimony as the Victory of Faith

Testimony is of necessity a victory of our faith—a faith that has been through the test of a radical challenge, that of the atheistic culture of the modern world, the situation that I have called one of post-Christian atheism. We live, in other words, in a world that has lost its naiveté.

Although faith will always be of the order of spontaneity, a faith that is responsible for itself and others must be one that has been through the test of having been criticized and has reached what I have called, following Paul Ricoeur, a "second naiveté." Faith no longer possesses culturally the character of evidence that it may have had in the Christian centuries. It is therefore possible to say, first, that the situation of unbelief forms a kind of historical destiny which is permitted by God, and, second, that this historical situation of the absence of God is of necessity bound to condition the faith of Christians and the testimony that they bear. We may, in other words, say that the absence or the silence of God is felt as deeply by Christians as it is by non-believers.

We know that it is not a question of going on a crusade against or of calling down curses on those who are without God. We have rather to share with them—even as believers—a certain historical destiny of the absence of God.[16]

If we do this, we shall be less triumphalist, more silent and more modest and we shall have a deeper understanding of the weakness of others. There is a brotherhood in weakness between believers and non-believers. That brotherhood in weakness does not necessarily imply an abandonment of faith and testimony. On the contrary, it implies an acceptance of an historical destiny. In this situation, it is possible to go back to the intuitions expressed by Bonhoeffer, who claimed that we have to live as though God did not exist and, however paradoxical this might be for the believer, to live that in the presence of God.[17] The message of faith has become normally difficult, and what is astonishing today is not unbelief, but non-unbelief.

At the same time, however, the Christian message still has a contemporary relevance, so that we may ask: "How should we communicate faith and how should we bear testimony to Jesus Christ to men who are indifferent?"

The situation is not the same as that which prevailed during the earliest period of Christian preaching, if it is true that we cannot rely on the same religious *a priori*. Man, however, continues to be man and fascinated with truth, justice, love and freedom, and we can be certain that there is in him a possible openness with regard to the Gospel. Looking at the question from the point of view of the situation of the world, I would say that, without applying a wrong form of apologetics, the Gospel has never been more actual than it is today. It will always be of the order of gratuity, but contemporary society can discover that there is a truth in the message of the beatitudes which, if it is not respected in one way or another, will lead mankind collectively to a form of suicide.

B. Testimony as a Prophetic Act

Our testimony cannot simply be a transmitting of truths or of a knowledge. It has also to be a prophetic testimony, an epiphany of God among men. In the climate of skepticism in which we find ourselves, a certain quality of faith in a man who is normal, competent and integrated into society is always a miracle that arouses astonishment and a word that causes a shock. There is always an experience at the beginning of all testimony. Before we bring a charge against the culture or the lack of religion of modern man, we should ask ourselves whether our testimony comes from such an experience. The apostles were witnesses without equal because they had been able to touch and contemplate Christ. Twenty centuries later, we are hesitant witnesses because we have not encountered the person of Jesus Christ, the face of God.

We have the historical testimony of the apostles and the signs of the presence of Jesus Christ in the Church and the world, but this is not enough. We also need the inner testimony here and now of the Holy Spirit, who bears witness in the depths of our hearts that Christ is still alive. That is the necessary experience of Christian faith and of the testimony that comes from faith. In other words, faith is an outward testimony because it is first and foremost an inner testimony of the Spirit in us.

If this testimony is a prophetic event, it will be a testimony borne to Jesus Christ, but, like all prophetic testimony, it will consist of discerning the point of view of God in the events of the world and in the lives of those to whom we are sent. This is in conformity with the economy of revelation. Our mission is to manifest the actuality and the liberating power of the word of God in a world that has become irreligious in the process of becoming adult.

C. The Testimony Must Be Historically Situated

In the prophetic tradition of the Old Testament, the prophetic testimony was always historically situated. It was never abstract, but was always rooted in history.[18] It is possible to distinguish three poles in the prophetic testimony: first, the memory of God's action, second, a discernment of the present situation, and, third, the production of a new word that comes from an historical sensitivity to the needs of men, the world and the Church.

The testimony of Christians is therefore always tied to the particular character of the situations in which the Church finds itself in the world. A word that aims to be universal has to risk being insignificant. It is, however, always a new word at the service of a new situation. Nowadays, there cannot be any testimony borne to the Gospel of Christ unless there is at the same time some discernment of man's new states of consciousness, the new questions raised by world population and those raised by the qualitatively different form of human violence in the nuclear age and by the tension between the rich countries of the North and the poor countries of the South.

What is meant by an historically situated testimony, then, is rereading the Gospel and letting it speak in the service of our present situation. I believe that the Christian tradition must always be the bearer of the future. If it is not, it is in danger of being a "letter that kills" and not a "Spirit that gives life."

D. The Prophetic Testimony Does Not Belong
Exclusively to Christians

It would not be difficult to provide a theological justification of the fact that the prophetic testimony does not belong exclusively to Christians by showing that the marks of ecclesiality are not merely marks of visible membership of the Church as the assembly of believers. There are also all those who live from the Spirit of Christ without knowing it and who are outside the frontiers of the visible Church.

In other words, Christians do not have a monopoly of the spirit of the beatitudes, nor do they even have a monopoly of the Spirit of Jesus. There can, for example, be testimonies, actions and words which come from an atheism with an ethical content.

It is not difficult to give examples of this kind of testimony, which may not be simply verbal, but is that of an existence. There are those, for instance, who are engaged in the work of Amnesty International, the dissidents living in the Eastern bloc and those who belong to movements such as "Doctors Without Frontiers" or who work voluntarily in the third world.

There are two kinds of prophetic testimony that we have to bear. On the one hand, there is that which aims to give a new sense of direction to those who live in industrial and post-industrial societies and who feel lost and are in search of new messiahs. On the other, there is the testimony that aims to put an end to the disastrous process that widens the gulf between the rich and the poor countries. This testimony does not belong exclusively to Christians, because the Spirit of Christ is always unpredictable.

E. The Criteria of the Authenticity of the Testimony

1. First of all, there is the reference to the Gospel and the practice of Jesus. In any new historical situation, Christian testimony is unpredictable and the imitation of Christ is not a purely mechanical reproduction. There is, however, a certain practice of Jesus that should inspire all testimony. No distinction is made in that practice of Jesus or Christian sense between a sense of God and a sense of man.

In Christian testimony today, there is an urgent need to find what is essential. Since Vatican II, we have been conscious of a hierarchy of truths, and the essential truth is the mystery of the death and resurrection of Jesus and the practice of Jesus in favor of men. That practice, however, becomes meaningless if it is not a practice in reference to God, the Father of Jesus.

2. It is not possible to dissociate the testimony as a statement from the act of making that statement, from the commitment of the witness himself speaking in the first person and therefore from the way in which he has himself been converted before bearing testimony as a questioning for others.

Kierkegaard said: "There is a duplication of the testimony in the life of the one bearing witness."[19] What does "duplication" mean here? It is being what one is saying. Otherwise the testimony is merely verbal. There is a difference between the word of the tutor and that of the witness. Christian testimony is always existential. As Kierkegaard said, "In Christianity, we have to speak of the imitator, not of the teacher."

To this I would add something of importance from the point of view of a theology of testimony. It is that God himself is the instance before whom one testifies. That is a sign of the gratuity of the gift that has been given to me and of the gratuity of the testimony that I bear to others. I am responsible to God and not simply to those others. I am judged by God and not primarily by the others. Because God is grace, there is always an inner word that reveals to the heart of the listener the meaning of my statement, the meaning of my word. God is therefore the instance or authority, before whom one testifies. It is in that that there is a "duplication of the testimony" as the transmission of a certain content in my life. It is at that moment that my life itself becomes a living word.

3. The word of the witness must be man's friend. Christian testimony

borne to the Gospel is always a demanding and questioning word, a word which calls man into question and judges him, but which must always be liberating and never an additional burden. In other words, good prophets are not necessarily prophets of disaster or prophets who accuse us. Good prophets are those who go ahead of the expectation of the one who conceals within himself a number of possibilities that have not yet been revealed to him—a word that creates something new.

The newness is the possibility of existing inseparably as a man and as a Christian. We have become a little tired of discussions about what is the "most Christian" or the "specifically Christian" factor. We have therefore to remember what Karl Barth said about the "originality" of Christianity, which is better than a religion—a religion of grace. What is important is the new spirit with which I assume a number of already existing values, whether I am French, American, African or Chinese.

4. Respect for the other person's freedom in bearing testimony should be the object of a reflection about the relationship between the responsibility and the urgency of the testimony and the necessity of dialogue.

Some Christians may perhaps be bitter because we have moved from mission to dialogue, but my reply to them is that we have moved from a bad form of proselytism to dialogue. Bearing true testimony does not exclude dialogue. The theoretical problem can be expressed in the following way: How am I to discharge my responsibility with regard to the Gospel and at the same time really respect the other person's freedom? It would seem that the law of dialogue is a reciprocal calling into question of the questioners in their tentative search for truth. The foundation of my testimony is the certainty of having discovered in Jesus Christ the truth about man and about history.

Gandhi once said: "How can the one who believes that he has the truth be a brother?" Is it not in fact an untenable claim to impose my truth on the other person as the only truth, when I know very well that I cling to that truth in freedom, that is, that I have chosen it from among others. That truth is therefore not imposed with the objectivity and the universality of an evident, scientific or philosophical truth.

If we are to find our way out of this theoretical dilemma of responsibility and respect for the other person, we have to reflect about the nature of faith itself and about the fact that faith is always inseparably both a gratuitous gift from God and a free act. In other words, faith is not a definitive possession, a certainty that has been acquired once and for all time. It shares in the uncertainty that characterizes my freedom, and, what is more, what has to be emphasized, especially now in our present cultural situation, is the obscure character of faith. Not only do we no longer have any certainty about our own faith—that faith is also concerned with obscure truths of which we do not have the evidence. There is, in other words, on the one hand a great discontinuity between the truths that I share with others in the sense of a certain number of pieces of evidence and, on the other, the truths which go back to the world of faith.

Looking at the question from this point of view, then, it is possible to say that faith and unbelief exist to some extent simultaneously in the believer.[20] This means that the dialogue begins in ourselves and not simply with the other, the unbeliever. We are ourselves that possible unbeliever—it is not in the first place the other person.

In all testimony, there is therefore of necessity a certain brotherhood between the believer and the unbeliever, and that brotherhood is one of a search that is never completed. At that moment, I am not simply the possessor of a definitive answer. I am also the witness of a questioning, a truth which goes beyond me and an appeal.

If I give myself seriously in my testimony to the demands made by dialogue, then I myself, my faith, will be subjected to a radical purification. I will therefore possibly discover that I have no right to the truths to which I bear testimony, because I cannot verify them in my life. Insofar as I have not been confronted with the demand of truth made by the questioner, I can deceive myself about the authenticity of my testimony. If, on the other hand, I become aware of my own lack of logic, I may possibly perceive in the other a faith that is hidden beneath his refusal to accept the Gospel.

There may therefore be in the other person a paradoxical refusal to accept faith which is in contradiction with the truth of his life, just as I am taken back to my own lack of logic, in other words, to the fact that the faith that I confess does not coincide with the faith that I live. Bearing testimony to the Gospel and bearing testimony to the truth of Christ is always bearing testimony to a truth that goes beyond me, and it is in an act of testimony that I run the risk of coming to my truth. This is clearly illustrated in Jesus' conversation with the Samaritan woman.

This can be expressed in a different way. Dialogue between two men leads to a dialogue with oneself, and that is the truth which is celebrated and to which testimony is borne in that dialogue. When it is a testimony in the presence of God and a testimony that is disinterested, it is possible that the aim of that testimony is not so much to make the other person what he has not been until now—in the sense of a conversion—as to try to make him come to himself, that is, to be revealing of his own truth or revealing of a possibility of an existence that is still hidden.

Conclusion: The Two Great Forms of Testimony in the Church

When we speak of Christian testimony, it is never an individual testimony. It is always a testimony borne in the Church, and we have to ask ourselves what "the Spirit says to the churches" (Rev 2:7).

Within the contemporary Church, there are two kinds of prophetic testimony. On the one hand, there is a socio-political tendency and, on the other, there is a mystical tendency. I will conclude this chapter by briefly considering these two closely connected tendencies.

There is, on the one hand, the prophetic testimony of Christians in Latin American and in the countries of the East who are ready to defend the Gospel to the point of sacrificing their own lives. They are also ready to defend the values implied by the Gospel and in particular the fundamental rights of man. It is true that, at the end of the twentieth century, the Church of Christ is a prophetic Church insofar as it no longer appears in many of the poor countries to be the ally of the ruling powers or as the accomplice of the status quo.

On the other hand, there are the many charismatic communities, whose members bear collective testimony to the lasting power of the Spirit. They bear testimony to the presence of the living God in the world.

It is very regrettable that these two tendencies are often mutually exclusive in contemporary Christianity. I believe that it is a sense of the living God which prevents political prophetism from becoming a purely temporal messianism. At the same time, the fruits of a concrete and realistic charity, a love of the least of our brethren, also bears testimony to the Christian authenticity of the charismatic communities.

Chapter XI

THE IDEOLOGICAL FUNCTION
OF SECULARIZATION

To devote oneself to the hermeneutics of secularization is to interpret the very complex phenomenon which has characterized the world as modern since the time of the Enlightenment, that is to say, since the movement of emancipation in Western society from subjection not only to the Church, but also to all forms of religion.

However much agreement there may be among historians specializing in the study of culture and religious sociologists, it is still very difficult to interpret this phenomenon. Some scholars have simply treated secularization and desacralization as identical. Others believe that secularization only points to the historical process of the retreat of Christianity in Western society and that it can co-exist very well with the continuation of the sacred in the modern world. These different interpretations show clearly that it is very difficult to go no further in the matter of "secularization" than the simple historical datum of the phenomenon, in other words, that a scientific approach to the question and an ideological interest are inextricably interwoven. In this chapter, I would like to verify this statement in connection with the "theology of secularization," which is both a hermeneutical study of secularization and a hermeneutical study of Christianity.

Theologies always come about as the result of an encounter between the Christian message and a new state of culture. The "theology of secularization" is an attempt to reinterpret the Christian datum in the light of the "modernity" of the world and man that is denoted by the term "secularization."

Secularization has been raised to the level of a hermeneutical criterion of Christian theology. The entire question consists in knowing whether this now very well known concept of "secularization" has not become a theological concept or even an ideological concept that has been

181

evolved to deal with the needs of a Church confronted by a new historical situation. What is in any case remarkable is that it is above all theologians who make use of this concept of "secularization" in a very special way as a sociological model for interpreting the historical reality. It is therefore not possible to study secularization hermeneutically without reflecting about the use that is made of the concept in recent Christian thought. This should help us to discover the ideological content of the concept of secularization. It also provides us with an exemplary case that will enable us to verify the ideological function of theology in a given historical context.

Since so many others have already covered this ground, I shall not reopen the discussion between theology and ideology here,[1] but will do no more than simply make a distinction between the two functions of secularization. The first is a function of justification and legitimation. This implies a need to see how the theology of secularization provides a theoretical justification both of the secularization of the world and man and of the change that is taking place within Christianity. This legitimating function can be described as reifying.

The second function of secularization goes beyond this first legitimating function. It shows that secularization may also have an exploratory and even an utopian function for the future of Christianity. In other words, a demythologization of secularization as an ideology should coincide with a deciphering of its explanatory significance with regard to the transformation of the religious dimension of man. It has in particular the merit of being able to show us how inadequate the categories "sacred" and "profane" are for the task of accounting both for the "religious" situation of contemporary man and the specifically Christian "religious" factor.

1. THE VOCABULARY OF SECULARIZATION AND THE FUNCTION OF IDEOLOGY

Before examining the ideological function of secularization, it is important to reach agreement about the meaning of the word "secularization" and about what characterizes the function of ideology.

1. According to one approach, "secularization" is the phenomenon by which the realities of man and the world tend to establish themselves in an increasing autonomy while eliminating all reference to religion. Historically, the term "secularization" has for a long time had a juridical and neutral meaning. It denoted the legal process by which Church properties and the use of certain goods belonging to the Church were transferred to state authorities.

When these transfers were effected without the Church's consent in a climate of polemics and claims, as happened, for example, in the nineteenth century, the word "secularization" was used—together with the term "laicization"—to denote in a more general way the emancipation of modern society from dependence on the Church. This process consisted of the gradual removal of great sectors of human life from the institution of the Church and their coming to belong to the rational, scientific or political order. The most decisive aspect of this process of secularization in the modern age has undoubtedly been the extension of rationality to all sectors of reality.

This is what Max Weber described as the "disenchantment" of the world. Nature no longer conceals anything sacred. It belongs to the sphere of what can be explained and objectivized and to that of what is "available." Running parallel to this process of objectivization is an increasing affirmation of the autonomy of man as the one who controls this world without mystery.

It is therefore not difficult to see how it is quite natural to move from this first meaning of "secularization" in the sense of "laicization," that is to say, liberation from the domination of the Church, to a second meaning, that of the "desacralization" of the world and of man.

There is, however, also a third stage in this semantic development of the word "secularization," in which the process of modern man's emancipation is described as a process of "atheism." All religious dependence with regard to God is described as an alienation that is incompatible with the affirmation of man's full autonomy that has finally been given back to him. It is possible to say, at least in the perspective of those forms of atheistic humanism that are derived from Feuerbach, that the historical religions have given way to the secular religion of man.

These preliminary remarks about the vocabulary in this chapter should put us on our guard against confusions that may arise in connection with the word "secularization" when it is employed in the service of the ideological interests of the one using it. It is one thing to affirm the autonomy of the temporal power when confronted with the secular domination of the Church. It is, however, quite another thing to affirm the complete desacralization of the world simply because it is "modern" or to affirm the total lack of religion of contemporary man just because he has "come of age."

In order to have a better perception of the ideological function of secularization, I shall follow Peter Berger and make a distinction between secularization in the objective sense and secularization in the subjective sense.[2] What is meant by secularization in the objective sense is the liberation of society from the Church's authority and the withdrawal of religious motivations in the different manifestations of culture. Secularization in this sense is both a socio-structural process and a phenomenon of civilization. It is also inseparable from pluralism in that religion no longer has a monopoly as a system of social legitimation and as a system of ideation or the formation of ideas.

This objective secularization of society and culture, however, also leads to a secularization in the subjective sense, that is to say, a secularization of man's consciousness. There is, in other words, a secularization in the sense of a transformation of the structures of credibility in religion. This secularization is the inevitable consequence of the pluralism that I mentioned above. The "available credible" aspect of modern man has changed insofar as the traditional contents of religious belief have come into conflict with the new states of consciousness that are connected with modernity.

This crisis of credibility is of necessity connected with social processes that can be empirically marked out. It is not, however, a crisis that simply reflects those processes, since the secularization of religious man at the subjective level follows its own laws. We have therefore to speak of a reciprocal causality between the socio-structural level of secularization and the level of man's consciousness. The doubt and skepticism that are present in the consciousness of modern man correspond to the pluralism of the systems of ideation which claim to account for this reality.

It is possible to disagree about the various historical causes of secularization. It is also possible to formulate different interpretations of the phenomenon of secularization, and it is here that powerful ideological motivations come into play. There can, however, be no disagreement about the fact that the situation that has been created for modern man is quite new. According to Berger, "For the first time, probably in the whole of history, the religious legitimations of the world have lost their credibility not only for a few intellectuals and other marginal individuals, but also for broad strata of entire societies."[3]

2. If it is true that secularization is, in Christian writing especially, not only a "model" of the sociology of knowledge, but also an ideological concept, then our point of departure must be an attempt to provide a general description of the function of ideology.

Ideology can be defined as the "theoretical crystallization of a form of wrong consciousness." Marx was the first to denounce ideology as the wrong consciousness that is brought about in alienated man, who is not able to account for it, by the socio-economic contradictions of the society in which he is living.

In the case of bourgeois society, religion and metaphysics have been the outstanding ideologies. Men need to duplicate in their imagination the real relationships that they have with each other. This "world view" does not, however, merely reflect socio-economic structures. It also has the function of justifying and legitimating a group within society, namely the dominant class. Marx' great achievement was that he analyzed the social unconsciousness and showed how every "world view" is in danger of degenerating into an ideology.

Ideology presents itself as a system of representations, ideas and values with its own firm structure, even though its effective power is to be found in its will to satisfy the interests of one particular social group. "An ideology is a complex of ideas or representations which is regarded by the subject as an interpretation of the world or of his own situation and which represents for him the absolute truth. It comes to him, however, in the form of an illusion by means of which he justifies himself, pretends to himself and escapes from himself in one way or another, but always in his own immediate interest."[4]

Because ideology serves the interests of the dominant class, it tends to justify the social status quo in order to preserve the privileges acquired by that class. It is therefore essentially conservative and quite different from a utopia, which is always trying to transform and go beyond the existing state of society. (For this, see the distinction made by Mannheim between "ideology" and "utopia.")

Despite its will to provide a totalizing and universal image of the world, ideology is therefore always partial. It makes use of the category of totality, but does not use it dialectically in order to seize hold of reality. As Karl Jaspers pointed out long ago, every ideology therefore has a tendency to be "reifying" and "anti-historical."[5]

According to the orthodox Marxist point of view, ideologies—and religion in particular—are substitutive explanations for phenomena that have not yet been understood by science. They will consequently disappear when a really scientific understanding of reality has been achieved.

Louis Althusser has, however, rejected this theory of the disappearance of ideologies. According to him, society is a complex totality with three structures or instances—an economic, a political and an ideological structure. These structures are of necessity closely interrelated. Ideology is a permanent structure which will not be eliminated by science and which has a necessary function in the whole of society.

What we can, however, do is to mark out scientifically the way in which ideology functions. It is not possible to make an abstraction of ideology in an attempt to understand economic and political phenomena. It would also be too simplistic to try to explain a superstructure as a religion merely on the basis of the state of the productive forces.

Turning now to the question of theology, we have both to refuse to reduce it to the level of an ideology and to take very seriously into account the Marxist criticism of ideologies. As an attempt to provide a theory of the Christian datum, theology is only meaningful if it remains subject to the impulse provided by faith. But faith is above all opposed to the totalizing claim of ideology. It is an appeal to go beyond an historical situation that is purely relative and beyond a theoretical justification of a particular group within society. It can be defined as a state of being open to the future and, while taking man's suffering and uncertainties very seriously, it goes deeply into his hope.

At the same time, however, a Marxist type of analysis can help us to gain a better perception of the ideological function that theology is able to carry out a given time in history. Theology degenerates to the level of ideology every time it becomes a system of social justification and legitimation and tries to legitimate some social or political option in the name of "pure faithfulness to the Gospel" while it is in fact defending the interests of the dominant class either within society or within the Church itself.

Theological discourse has its own inner harmony. It is not merely a reflection of existing social relationships. Its meaning is never exhausted in its social significance. But it is also never unrelated to the spheres of economics and politics. Who would deny that, in the course of its long history, Christian theology has not tried to justify injustice prevailing in society and to provide men with the illusion of a reward for the injustice to which they have been subjected?

2. SECULARIZATION AS THE HISTORICAL PRODUCT OF CHRISTIAN FAITH

Having explained to some extent the meaning of "secularization" and thrown some light on the function of ideology, I would now like to ask whether secularization has, for the past twenty or so years, ceased to function as an ideology within Christian theology. Is it true to say that "secularization," which is first and foremost a sociological concept, has in fact come to be used by certain theologians as a theological concept?

To begin with, when they were confronted with the large scale phenomenon of secularization, the churches took refuge in a defensive and conservative attitude. On the Protestant side, Karl Barth, for example, stressed the absolute rights of the Word of God, however secular the attitude of modern man might be, and tended to emphasize the break between God and the world. On the Catholic side, there were the condemnation of modernism and laicism and the intransigent position of the magisterium with regard to all the manifestations of the phenomenon of secularization until the very eve of Vatican II.

From the end of the Second World War onward, however, various mainly Protestant theologians tried to reinterpret Christianity in the light of secularization as an historical process. The first of these was Friedrich Gogarten, who, it could be said, used secularization as a hermeneutical criterion of Christian faith. Later theologies of secularization, like that developed by Harvey Cox, were greatly indebted to the Bonhoeffer's key intuitions on the subject of the "world come of age" and the "end of religion."

There was, in other words, a powerful current of theological thought at that time which tended to identify the modern movement of "secularization" with the historical destiny of Christianity. It found its fulfillment in such radical theologies of the "death of God" as that of Thomas Altizer.

There were no parallel Catholic theologies, at least at the beginning of this movement, which really deserve to be called "theologies of secularization." There were admittedly theologies which, as "theologies of terrestrial realities," tried to engage in dialogue with the modern world and to provide man's profane tasks with a theological justification. But the term "secularization" did not have the same fortune in Catholicism as it did in Protestant theology. All the same, these "theologies of terrestrial realities" had a considerable influence of the Pastoral Constitution on the Church in the Modern World. This document of Vatican II, *Gaudium et Spes*, in a sense ratified a new conception of dialogue between the Church and the world.

More recently, since the Council, there has been the work of those mainly Catholic theologians who have elaborated "political theologies" and "theologies of liberation." Both of these theologies deal with a far more revolutionary problem than that treated by the theologies of secularization.

I do not intend to discuss the various theologies elaborated by the theologians of secularization in detail here.[6] All that I shall do is to try to summarize the main arguments that have been put forward and then provide a theological justification of secularization. In this, I shall rely principally on the work of Gogarten and Bonhoeffer.

The term "secularization," which tries to describe an historical situation, goes back to the sociology of knowledge, but, when used by theologians of secularization, it becomes an authentically theological concept. There is a movement from a situation of fact to one of right. Although secularization is first and foremost the result of a number of socio-economic changes, it nonetheless becomes an historical product of Christian faith. There is, in other words, an interrelationship between faith and secularization. The latter is the hermeneutical criterion on the basis of which the Christian message has to be reinterpreted for today. On the other hand, it is not an empirical datum, but an ideological product. The modern phenomenon of secularization is conceived according to the much earlier movement of desacralization and de-deification as carried out by biblical faith.

I think that it is possible to distinguish three theological presuppositions that are of fundamental importance to any contemporary Christian reflection about secularization. The first of these is the originality of the God of faith with regard to the God of religion. Secularization is therefore a theological concept that helps us to describe desacralization. The second is Luther's doctrine of justification, according to which secularization describes the autonomy of reason. The third presupposition is that there is a certain interpretation of the kenosis of God, which enables us to understand by "secularization" the world as having come of age.

Unlike the cosmic God of the pagan religions, the God of Israel was not a God who responded too well to man's needs. He blessed life without sacralizing it. The revelation of God the Creator was precisely at the point of departure of a radical desacralization of the ancient world which was full of gods. What is more, the God of Israel was not a God of immortality invented by man for himself because he was confronted by the absurdity of death. Israel's problem was not that of trying to cross the terrifying abyss of death. It was that of being able to continue to celebrate the name of God after having left the land of the living. Finally, the God of Israel was not a God whose task was to preserve the harmony of the universe. He was responsible not so much for holding up the universe as for transforming it. He intervened in the history of men and tried to live among them. The God of Israel, then, was not a God of fertility, nor was he a God of immortality or of universal harmony. In other words, he was not a God in those spheres in which the divine has above all been disclosed in the history of religion.[7]

The originality of biblical faith with regard to religion is therefore that it celebrates the name of God when confronted with a world that has been given back to itself and does not become identified with the need forged by man in order to compensate for the absences in his life or to respond to the great enigmas of the universe. The essential function of religion is to overcome the anguish of human life when confronted with the insecurity of the world. According to such theologians as Karl Barth and Rudolf Bultmann, the originality of biblical faith is that it directly attacks religion understood as man's will to make himself God's master in order to soothe his anguish. At the same time as desacralizing the world, biblical faith also gives man back to himself, to his autonomy and to his power of domination over the world. There is therefore a convergence between the dynamism of biblical faith and the modern process of secularization.

It is possible to say that the whole theology of secularization has been developed within the theological sphere of the radical distinction between faith and religion as formulated theoretically by authors such as Barth and Bultmann. In that theology, religion is always identified with the search for security and therefore with a "work" of man as a sinner. Faith, on the other hand, has always been conceived as a risk, as insecurity and as man's total handing over of himself to the Word of God without human mediation.

Bonhoeffer returned again and again to the theme of the "end of religion." This theme can be regarded as the historical fulfillment of what was contained in an embryonic form in the dynamism of biblical faith. Far from regretting the inescapable process of secularization in the modern world, we should therefore be glad of it as a new opportunity for the future of Christianity. Secularization, however, is not simply an inescapable fact. It is also a duty.

Faith is not distorted by desacralization. On the contrary, the latter is a demand made by faith. The entire history of Israel can be understood as a struggle on the part of prophetism both against the permanent risk that faith will be degraded into religion and against the temptation to sacralize something else in God's name. In contrast to the pagan religions, the Old Testament provides evidence of a change in the relationship between the sacred and the profane. In it, God is not the sacred, but the Holy One, who breaks down the opposition between the sacred and the profane. Under the old covenant, the sacred, however, plays the part of a mediator between man and God. It is only with the incarnation of God in Jesus Christ that it is possible to say that the opposition between the sacred and the profane had finally and radically been transcended. What really defines the new covenant is the fact that the sacred, which had acted until then as the mediator between man and God, is entirely concentrated in the person of Jesus Christ.

For such theologians as Gogarten and Bonhoeffer, then, the historical phenomenon of secularization, understood both as a desacralization of the world and as the autonomy of human reason, is the fulfillment of what is contained in an embryonic form in the biblical revelation, that is, the de-deification of the world by God.

This constitutes a very radical change in the religious history of mankind, one that transforms man's relationship with the world. Confronted with a world that has been de-deified, man is quite free to dominate and transform it. For Gogarten, the words of St. Paul are a program of this new freedom: "All things are yours, whether . . . the world or life or death or the present or the future" (1 Cor 3:22).

This liberating truth remained hidden in historical Christianity for as long as mankind was still living in the age of religion. It is therefore the responsibility of Christian thinkers in the modern age, that is, in the age of the end of religion, to provide secularization with a theological justification. As Berger remarks, it is strange (or, rather, we have to speak of an "irony of history") that Christianity has historically been its own grave-digger.[8]

This is certainly the case if it is true that secularization is a product of faith, even though we have also noted that secularization has undermined the credibility of Christianity. Theologians like Gogarten, however, would say in answer to this that a distinction has to be made between legitimate secularization on the one hand, that is, a radical distinction must be made between God and the world, and, on the other, illegitimate secularization, that is, the fact of man's no longer being able to understand himself as a creature of God. Gogarten therefore found it necessary to speak of secularism in the second case, and he was ready to admit that secularization contains the embryo of its own perversion.

Up till now, I have insisted on the revelation of God as the Quite Other and on a distinction between faith and religion as the theological presuppositions for any theology of secularization. I would like now to show how the theologians of secularization also make use of the Lutheran doctrine of the justification of faith without works in order to legitimate a knowledge of the world as profane and the autonomy of reason with regard to faith. In the same way, the Lutheran distinction between the two kingdoms, the kingdom of God and that of the world, means that, in the kingdom of the world, God has subjected all things to the power of human reason. Luther was above all anxious to affirm the royal freedom of the Christian, who is "a free Lord of all things and who is subjected to no one." In fact, however, without knowing it, he opened the way to the modern world, that is, to a knowledge of the autonomy of the world and to a distinction between the temporal and the spiritual orders. It is precisely as such that man is, through faith, free with regard to the world, that he is, in other words, Lord of the world and responsible for it.

Gogarten identifies the concept "world" with those of "law" and "work" in the Pauline sense and in the sense in which they have been interpreted in the tradition of the Reformation.[9] Sinful man is man who trusts in himself or in practices within the world. In so doing, he is still a man of faith. The new man, however, is man who, as a free person confronting the world, only trusts in God. It would therefore seem that nothing mediates the personal encounter between man and God. As obedience to God's invitation and openness to the future, faith is the foundation of the secularity of the world and man's free responsibility with regard to history.

Christian Duquoc has expressed Gogarten's thinking in the following way: "Faith does not represent a dogmatic or metaphysical system that has to be applied in the world. The world is profane because only man creates the values that he aims to promote in that world. He does not derive the principles of this world from a heavenly reserve. Stripped of the metaphysical dimension that it received from ancient Greece, faith provides, by its openness to the future, the foundation of the secular character of the world."[10]

Secularization is therefore another name for the autonomy of reason. Gogarten insists that there is a radical break between God and man, faith and the world and revelation and history. In another respect, however, he disagrees with Barth, who was convinced that the Word of God only comes to us in the incarnation. If the world, as a secular and de-deified world, is itself a product of faith, it can become the place where God speaks to us. What characterizes the real modality of Christian faith today is that the question of God can only be asked within the sphere of the secularization of the world and the whole of human existence.

Taking the principle of the Reformation as a point of departure, then, an attempt is made to make secularization a demand of faith itself. A break is therefore made with historical Christianity, in which "mission" has for centuries been understood as an effort to "Christianize" the world. It is, however, in order to affirm more clearly the absolute purity of faith. Every attempt to mediate faith and knowledge (classical theology), faith and civilization (Christian humanism) and faith and history (political theology) ends in an illegitimate confusion and amounts to a "secularization of faith." It is possible to say that the theology of secularization that comes from the Reformation is paradoxically enough the source of a political theology that rejects every idea of causality between the historical movements of human liberation and the coming of the kingdom of God. That is why the liberation theologians have observed in the influence of the Lutheran theologians one of the reasons why the European political theologies, whether they are Catholic or Protestant in origin, are politically conservative.[11]

Another theological doctrine that has been employed to provide a justification of "secularization" is that of the kenosis of God in Jesus Christ. Secularization denotes the "coming of age" of man and the world. This intuition can be found in Bonhoeffer's work, and it has been expressed in the most radical way in Thomas Altizer's "death of God" theology.[12]

The God of religion keeps man in an infantile state. It alienates him. For Bonhoeffer, the importance of religious man is the exact correlation of the omnipotence of God. The God of Jesus Christ wants man to be an adult. The secularization of the world is a consequence of the plan of the God who allowed himself to be driven out of the world and nailed to a cross so that man might become an adult and, in the positive aspects of his life, share in the Lordship of Christ over the world.

Bonhoeffer said that this was the difference between Christianity and all other religions: "Man's religiosity takes him back in his misery to the power of God in the world—God is the *deus ex machina*. The Bible sends him back to the suffering and weakness of God—only the suffering God can help him. In this sense, it is possible to say that the evolution of the world toward adulthood of which I have spoken, making *tabula rasa* of a false image of God, liberates man so that he can look at the God of the Bible who has gained his power and his place in the world by his impotence."[13]

Bonhoeffer's achievement can be described as having overthrown the overthrowing of religion brought about by Feuerbach, who said: "To enrich God, man must become poor. To enable God to be everything, man must become nothing." Bonhoeffer overthrew this by saying that God becomes poor to enrich man. He reinterpreted the mystery of the death of Christ in the light of secularization and was aware of a convergence between the promotion of adult man liberated from religious alienation and the revelation of a weak and suffering God in Jesus Christ. It was when man experienced his power and autonomy that he was able to understand that only that weak and suffering God could help him. He had had to wait for the time of the end of religion for the illusory functions of God with regard to man to be demystified so that he could be recognized in his true transcendence. Faith is no longer mortgaged by religion as it was in previous centuries, and because of this it is now entirely a question of "interpreting biblical terms in a non-religious way," of finding a "secular discourse" about God and of making sure of a "religionless proclamation of the Gospel."

Bonhoeffer's program of a "religionless" Christianity is full of very rich intuitions and it is still within the orbit of a Christian theology. In the case of an author such as Altizer, however, the ideological significance of the concept of secularization is such that it points not simply to the weakness, but to the death of God. The good news of the Gospel is a proclamation of the death of the omnipotent and jealous God of the Old Testament, and the result is a pure Jesuology. Omnipotence is identified with evil. If God is love, he has to cease being God. He only redeems himself through his death. Historical Christianity has not grasped the full significance of the death of Jesus, but has extended the power of religion to restrain man. The age of the total secularization of the world and man inaugurates a true understanding of the Easter mystery. The death of the omnipotent God is the condition of the coming of man's true freedom and autonomy. It is in this that God reveals his love.

3. THE IDEOLOGICAL FUNCTION OF SECULARIZATION

I have briefly reviewed some of the theological arguments put forward by various theologians of secularization. In this section, I will try to show how the theology of secularization functions as an ideology and serves the interests of the Church.

In the first place, it attempts to justify and legitimate the historical withdrawal of Christianity in the modern age. Like any other ideology, the theology of secularization has failed to look for the really historical causes of secularization in the modern world. It is in the end stubbornly opposed to reality in its attempt to find at all costs a convergence between the contemporary process of secularization and the movement of desacralization initiated by biblical faith. As I pointed out at the beginning of the previous section, secularization is first and foremost a sociological concept used to denote the phenomenon by virtue of which the structures of society tend to establish themselves in an increasing autonomy with regard to every religious or Church authority. I would add here that this initially sociological concept, however, tends to become an ideological and therefore an a-historical concept.

"Secularization" is also a phenomenon of civilization. It characterizes modern society and emphasizes its difference from a sacral society that is still subject to the domination of the Church. In order to provide a theological justification for the fact that the Church has lost its position of power in modern society, this state of fact has been given an absolute value and has, as I have said, become a state of right.

It is in any case strange that the term "secularization" should have become a word with a privileged status in the Christian vocabulary. It is obvious, of course, that the structures of contemporary society—the sciences and various forms of technology, culture, philosophy and political ideologies—have become secular in the sense that they are no longer subject to any religious regulation. This does not, however, necessarily mean that the modern world is completely desacralized. Many observers have, on the contrary, testified to the persistence of religion in the contemporary world and even to a return of the sacred.[14]

Christians who sing the praises of secularization may be in danger of being behind in a revolution! And they may be in an unfavorable position to decipher the signs of a return of the sacred because they are unconsciously presupposing that the Church still has a monopoly of the sacred. They therefore think that the crisis of the churches and the crisis of the practice of faith of necessity still coincide with the irreligious character of modern man, even though that is not at all obvious. The fact that many of our contemporaries are no longer Christians does not necessarily mean that they have become irreligious or that they are no longer able to experience the sacred.

In the first place, if we are to speak of desacralization, we have to begin by agreeing about what is meant by "sacred." The decline of a sacral society that is still subject to the Church may well coincide with a return of the sacred. The sacred is in fact an historical form of the spirit. That is why we should speak not so much of a decline as of "metamorphoses" of the sacred.[15]

The sacred should not be identified with the religious objectivizations to which it has given rise in the historical religions. Experience of the sacred is quite different from an experience of God. Its object is a specific area of being that cannot be identified with God. That is why the large-scale withdrawal of the sacred as objectively sacred is not in contradiction with the permanent survival of the sacred as a subjective experience. That experience, moreover, leads to a possible reinvestment of the sacred in other objects, which are no longer of the order of nature, but are rather of the technical order. It may, on the other hand, be reinvested in new rites, myths, feasts or even gods within our secular society. What is undeniably true is that the modern sacred is always a post-Christian sacred. It is also possible to believe that this "return of the sacred," which is so widely discussed nowadays, bears witness to a void left in our modern consciousness by the Judaeo-Christian God.

Secondly, it is beyond doubt that the opposition between faith and religion, which has played such an important part in contemporary Christian thinking, both Protestant and Catholic, has a strategic significance. On the one hand, it has an apologetical value in that it makes it possible for faith to be protected from the radical challenge of religion offered by modern atheism. On the other, it provides an ideological justification of modern man's religious indifference by affirming that religion is not a necessary presupposition for faith.

In addition to this, Christian faith has never had so many opportunities truly to be itself that it can make an abstraction of every religious *a priori*. Finally, the opposition between faith and religion also provides a theological guarantee for a great deal of spiritual literature that stresses the contrast between the "fine risk of faith" and "the petit-bourgeois secularization of religion."[16]

The thesis of the end of religion and the adulthood of modern man, then, gives the impression of being a theological affirmation that is not fully in accordance with the complex situation of contemporary humanity. It is possible to ask whether what we have here is not a rather desperate attempt to justify the failure of Christian evangelization in most of the countries in the northern hemisphere.

In contradiction to what the prophets of the "death of God" in fact proclaimed, it would seem that religion is now, for the first time since Darwin, taking the lead in its dialogue with science. This would tend to prove that, in contradiction to what all the theologians of secularization have affirmed, the sacred, the mythical, the mystical and the ecstatic have not been eliminated from the human condition. Man does not, in other words, live from bread alone or from scientific knowledge.

Moreover, far from being an expression of man's misery, as Marx believed, this religious revival is a phenomenon of the rich societies of the West. It is also not a protest against misery, but a protest against the nonsense of the prosperous consumer societies that are continuing to increase their own means while at the same time suffering from an increasing absence of ends.

In the United States especially, this religious revival is a form of counter-culture. It therefore has a social and even a political significance. It is, however, interesting to note that, for many young people today, religion is the expression not of an absence, but of a creativity, a joy and a solidarity with others.

What is certain, if religion is a program of self-justification or an escape from real life into another world, is that Christian faith is bound to criticize it. It may, however, not necessarily be the expression of man's search for a false security, but rather the expression of his longing and of the transcendence of that longing in accordance with his most positive human experiences in the order of love and creativity. In that case, we are invited to go beyond a somewhat too simplistic opposition between faith and religion.

Bonhoeffer's plan of a religionless Christianity certainly tried to provide a theological justification of the process of secularization, but it risked compromising the anthropological presuppositions of Christian faith. Faith is of necessity rooted in what may be called the "original sacred" aspect of man as a mystery of openness and communion. Whatever the case may be with regard to the metamorphoses of the sacred in history, it is man who continues to be the original place of the sacred. A Christianity which has become completely secularized and which does not anticipate the obscure sense of the sacred that is present in the heart of every man is always in danger of becoming degraded to the level of an ideology and consequently of losing its power to attract those who are today in search of the sacred.

Finally, I would like to draw attention to another paradoxical aspect of the theologies of secularization. Their aim is to be progressive and to break with all theology that has been trying to legitimate the sacralizing function of the Church with regard to the structures of society. In fact, however, they serve the interests of the neo-liberal societies of the West, all of which are marked by the typically bourgeois distinction between the private and the public spheres.[17]

We have considered the important part played by the Lutheran theory of the two kingdoms in the theology of secularization. We have also seen that this theology has provided a theological justification of the gradual marginalization of the Church in society and its loss of cultural and political influence on the one hand and, on the other, the decline of the various Christian institutions. The Christian religion is now exposed to the risk of being limited to the private sphere and of no longer being able to carry out its public activity of transforming the structures of society. Consequently, at the same time as it is providing a theological guarantee for the disappearance of the Church as an institution in contemporary secular society, the theology of secularization is also tending to legitimate the humanist ethos of the liberal societies of the West. "It is a theoretical construction which has the task of upholding the consciousness of our contemporary society and its collective orientation in its autonomy and emancipation. Its character of adaptation is therefore at the same time associated with a society which is based on the private authority of the individual situated within the economic system and, moreover, in the leisure sector."[18]

At the same time as it is guaranteeing an untouchable sphere—that of faith—the theology of secularization is also in fact, however involuntarily, providing an alibi for the neo-capitalist societies in the perspective of growth at all costs with the maximum profit and the highest degree of technological rationalization. The Christian religion has a function to provide psychological soothing. It can resolve the anguish of individuals, but it cannot touch the structures of the capitalist system. Even without knowing it, it has become its accomplice.

We should not be surprised, then, if the theology of secularization is, despite its progressive appearance, challenged today by those who are furthering the cause of the "theology of revolution" or the "theology of liberation." "The theology of secularization does not repeat the Constantinian model or even adapt it, but neither does it abolish it. It is certainly in accordance with the ideological and pragmatic work of destruction undertaken by the theologies and movements that are still subject to the impulse of the post-Tridentine Church. But, in the absence of self-criticism and criticism of the conditions governing its emergence in contemporary society, the ethos expressed as a theme by the theology of secularization simply duplicates the attitude that characterizes the Constaninian model."[19]

The Latin American liberation theologians criticize the European theologies of secularization and even the political theology of J.-B. Metz for being essentially anti-revolutionary. These theologians claim that, because those theologies are influenced by the Lutheran doctrine of faith without works, they have completely relativized all the attempts at liberation that have been made in history with respect to the eschatological absolute. They regard them as abstract and neutralist theologies, which are at the most reformist and which are unable to justify a concrete political option in the name of the Gospel and of the preparation here and now for the definitive kingdom of God.

4. SECULARIZATION AND THE FUTURE OF CHRISTIANITY

The theoreticians responsible for the various theologies of secularization regarded secularization as an historical "product" of biblical faith and, in so doing, failed to recognize the originality of the modern process of secularization. They discussed it at an abstract and metaphysical level and overlooked its concrete economic, political and cultural forms. Finally, without even knowing that they were doing it, they "produced" the very ideology that the Church needed in order to justify what it was becoming, in other words, its increasing marginalization.

At the same time, the theologians of secularization provided a guarantee for the liberal societies of the West under the heading of the division between "public" and "private." Although they continued to insist on its social and political function, they curiously enough overlooked the prophetic significance of Christianity, because this was, in their opinion, also included in the historical fate of all religions, that of being an ideology that was able to justify the established society.

I suggested earlier in this chapter that the ideology of secularization does not necessarily have to be reifying and a-historical. It is true that, because it lacks a dialectical sense, it gives an absolute value to the present and does not take fully into account the complexity of the historical reality. When, however, the question of the future of Christianity is being considered in connection with the religious change that has taken place in the world, we may certainly think that secularization has a forward-looking and even a prophetic function. This is precisely what I want to consider in this final section.

It is not enough simply to challenge the theses of the secularization of the world and the irreligion of modern man because of their opportunism. We could easily revert to a wrong form of apologetics if we tried to reassure ourselves, on the basis of a number of signs (which are in any case of necessity ambiguous) that there has been a "return of the sacred." This religious revival is above all a phenomenon of a counter-culture, and it is not at all clear whether it provides Christian faith with an opportunity for the future.

In other words, would it not be making a symmetrical mistake to take the opposite course to that of the theologies of secularization in order to defend an "unsecular man"?[20] There are, on the one hand, those who speak of a radical change in the world, involving a transition from the age of religion to an irreligious and adult age of man. On the other hand, there are others who affirm that nothing has changed or rather that we cannot decipher the signs that bear witness to the persistence of religion.[21]

Confronted with these symmetrical affirmations which only partly conceal their apologetic interest, it would seem that we have at least to insist on two orders of certainty. On the one hand, we have to be aware of the historical destiny of the question of God. By this I mean that, as opposed to the "religious rule" imposed for millennia on mankind, the question of God cannot simply be taken for granted by men in the last third of the twentieth century. That question has become completely free, and it would seem that it is not possible for anyone, whoever he is, to ask it in the conditions that prevail at present in the world.

On the other hand, however, it is also not possible to ignore the suspicion that has been inflicted by the whole of modern thought on the religious illusion. We know that religion has always made use of that machinery to make gods that is composed of the megalomania of man's longing and his taste for what cannot be expressed. That is why we have to ask ourselves seriously whether we have an interest in linking the future of Christian faith to permanent revivals of the religious instinct.

It is precisely because something new has taken place in the history of mankind that we have to take the exploratory and prophetic dimensions of "secularization" very seriously. I would say at the very outset that these contrasting theses about the secularization or the resacralization of the world show how inadequate it is simply to oppose "sacred" and "profane" in an attempt to define the specific originality of the "Christian religious" factor. Then I would stress the need to detect beneath the ideology of secularization a profoundly Christian truth of which we are just beginning to become aware. That truth, which we have to decipher, is that of the worldliness of the world as a consequence of creation and the incarnation.

It may be thought that, because the "religious" and the "sacred" have been too closely identified as a consequence of an earlier identification between the "divine" and the "sacred," it has become very difficult to take the originality that is characteristic of the Christian religion in a secular world into account. The duplication of the profane world in a secular world is symmetrical with a too rigid distinction between faith and religion.[22] Whatever the case may be with regard to the interest of that theological distinction, Christian faith is certainly a variant of the religious phenomenon.

The "religious" has been so readily identified with an "ancient sacral" factor which is challenged by the modern process of secularization that this has resulted in the theologies of secularization coming to extreme conclusions, the most dire of which is the self-destruction of Christianity. The discourse about God has become, in those theologies, no more than an indirect discourse about man, and the discourse about the realities of the next world has become simply a way of understanding the realities of this world. The opposition between the sacred and the profane is able to take the economy of other religions adequately into consideration, but it fails to take into account an essential aspect, that of the historical newness of Christianity. The truth that is sought in the ideology of secularization is the fact that, since the incarnation of God in Jesus Christ, the category of the profane is unable to account for the reality of the de-deified world and that the category of the sacred is in the same way also unable to account for the theologal reality of Christian existence.

There are two possible consequences of this. The first is that we shall end with a secularization of Christianity of such a kind that it is deprived of its essential mystery in the course being reduced to a stimulating ideology for the building up of a more human world. The second, alternative consequence is that we shall dream of a resacralization of the world or at least a sacral conception of Christianity, although neither of these will be able to take the religious change that is taking place now into account. This tension between the sacred and the profane is very pernicious. It should therefore not surprise us that, because of it, Christianity has historically disappointed many people who have been in search of an authentic experience of the sacred and just as many who have interpreted the "revolutionary" aspect of the Gospel as a need to work for a new human existence.

This brings me to a final comment that calls for a consideration of the historical function of secularization for the future of Christianity. The theological concept of secularization can be and has indeed been too freely used in order to provide a justification of the Church's loss of influence in contemporary society. Despite that, however, I think that there is, hidden behind that concept, a very real and profound insight into the new structure of the world since the incarnation of God in Jesus Christ.

It is wrong to regard secularization as an historical product of Christian faith, but it is right to say that the worldliness of the world is a consequence of the incarnation. It is precisely because Christianity has not pursued the consequences of a Christological realism to their ultimate conclusion that it has not allowed the world to be completely itself and that the bad conscience of Christians has now been replaced by a boundless optimism regarding the new opportunities open to the faith of secularization.

Commenting on Bonhoeffer's Christology, A. Dumas said that we should take seriously "the polyphonic presence of Christ in the midst of reality." We have to continue to penetrate more and more deeply into the fundamental idea that God's acceptance of the world implies a positive secularity of the world. The more fully the world, history and mankind become themselves, the more fully God will be himself.

It is therefore not enough simply to speak of the world as the profane world in opposition to the sacral world of antiquity. Nor is it enough to speak of a secularized world if secularization is understood as the modern process of the autonomy of the world with regard to all religious authorities and institutions. We should, on the contrary, speak of the new reality of the world as structured by Christ.

J.-B. Metz has pointed clearly to the intuition that is concealed behind the theological concept of "secularization" in the following statement, in which he uses the term "worldliness of the world" in preference to "secularization": "The worldliness of the world always appears as not subject to and not penetrated by faith and, in that sense, as pagan and profane. The whole of the world was undoubtedly grasped by Christ, but it is not in us and in our historical situation as believers, but in God and in the 'yes' that he alone has uttered over the world, in the impenetrable mystery of his love, that the true place of convergence between faith and the world is to be found."[23]

It is because of the realism of the incarnation that we have to learn how to decipher the reality of God at the deepest level of the reality of the world. Because the unity of God and the reality of the world are fulfilled in Jesus Christ, we must learn how to ward off the danger of metaphysical and religious thought, that is, the idea of God outside the reality of the world and how to resist the temptation of modern secularization, which is the disappearance of God in the reality of a world that has "come of age."

I would like to conclude this chapter by saying that the historical meaning of "secularization" is not exhausted in its ideological function in the service of the interests of a Church at a time of crisis. It also has a utopian function with regard to the metamorphosis of the "religious" which has been brought about by Christianity, but of which it never succeeds itself in fully becoming the historical figure.[24]

Chapter XII

CHRISTIANITY AS A WAY

The theme of the "Way" naturally reminds us of Chinese Taoism and Lao-Tzu's Book of the Way and of Virtue. I do not want to try to compare Christianity as a "Way" with the Tao in this chapter, but I would like to begin by reviewing some of the thoughts that came to me quite spontaneously after reading the Tao. I have the impression that they are of a kind that will point to the originality and the complexity of any reinterpretation of Christianity based on the image of the "Way."

The Tao can in the first place be approached as a moral way or a life-style. This would lead one to compare it with Christianity as right practice or orthopraxis. In fact, however, as Claude Larre has shown in his recent commentary, the word "Tao" points to a mysterious reality with many different harmonies.[1] To simplify it in this way would be as inadequate as saying that the word "God" means the "Absolute." "Tao" also means the "Way of Heaven" and the "Way of the saints." It calls to mind the Reality within appearances and beyond knowledge and experience. In the order of human activity, the "Way" also points to mysticism, wisdom and ascesis. What strikes me particularly is that it describes an intermediary sphere between that of the truth and that of the law. The "Way" is of the order of life. That is why I have come to the conclusion that, if we wanted to find the Christian equivalent to the Tao, we would have to speak of Christianity as the kingdom of God.

It is with reference to this very full meaning of the Chinese Tao that I would like to reflect about the special use of the image "way" in the Judaeo-Christian texts. At first sight, it cannot be denied that the word "way" (*hodos*) points in the New Testament—and especially in the Acts of the Apostles—to the way *par excellence,* the manner or way of life of the disciples of Christ. This is so, for example, in the case of Acts 9:2, where we are told that "if Saul found any belonging to the Way, men or women, he might bring them bound to Jerusalem." This is the kind of language that could easily be understood by the first Christians of Jewish origin who were familiar with the Jewish halacha as a complex of rules of moral, social and religious behavior. The term *halacha* itself comes from a root meaning "to walk" or "to go."[2]

It would, however, be greatly impoverishing the theme of "Christianity as a way" if we were to understand the "way" simply as "conduct in life." The image of the way—with all the words that are associated with it and especially the idea of a "walk" or "going"—is a key that can open the door to an understanding of the most original element in Christianity as a religious system. That is why I hope, in this chapter, to try to restore that fullness of meaning contained in the Christian theme of the Way. I also believe that this will perhaps also be a way of initiating a fruitful dialogue with Chinese thought and spirituality.

I would like here to draw one provisionary conclusion and point out that the theme of the Way in Christianity calls to mind a much wider sphere than simply that of moral conduct. At the same time, however, the word "Way" is quite inadequate to express the fullness of the Christian mystery. In that respect, it is more restricted than the Chinese word Tao, for the simple reason that Christianity as a religious system gives an essential place to the idea of a personal God and to that of creation.

1. CHRISTIANITY AS THE RELIGION OF THE EXODUS[3]

A. The Exodus as a Key Symbol of the Religion of Israel

The vocabulary of the "way," like that of "going," plays an essential part in describing the religious and moral life of the Hebrew people. The exodus or going out of Egypt is the most adequate figure by which we can understand the essence of the religion of Israel as a religion of salvation, that is, as a liberating walk with and following God himself, whether the guide of the people of God is Moses or Jesus.

From the point of view of the comparative history of religions, it is interesting to note that the religion of Israel is one of the nomadic religions, as opposed to the mythical and magical religions of the countries with an agrarian civilization. Correlatively, unlike the agrarian gods, the God of Israel is a guide who is himself on the way and who walks with his people.

The conclusions that have been drawn by the theologian Jürgen Moltmann in his book *Theology of Hope*—and especially in Chapter II on "Promise and History"—are of interest here. He has shown that the religion of Israel is essentially a religion of the Promise, in which God's revelation is closely connected to the divine promise related to the future and not to God's "appearances" and to sacred places, as is the case in the epiphanic religions.

This introduces quite a different conception of history from that of the mythical religions, which are religions of the "eternal return." A truly historical experience of time, time that is defined not by a repetition of the similar, but by a tension toward a future that is still in suspense, begins with Israel. "Under the aegis of the promise, reality is understood not as a divinely stabilized cosmos, but as a history, in which it is a matter of going forward, leaving the road behind and setting off in the direction of new horizons that have not yet been perceived."[4] What is truly remarkable is that Israel continued to interpret its historical experiences, like the settlement in Canaan, the exile and its struggles with other nations, in the light of that decisive religious experience of the exodus as a walk with God through the desert.

Like Moltmann, the philosopher Ernst Bloch has been inspired by that restlessness about the present under the pressure of a promise that had still not been fulfilled, because this was something that he had observed in the whole literature of the Bible. For him too, the religion of Israel is a religion of the exodus and of hope. According to the subversive hermeneutics that he has developed in his *Atheismus im Christentum*, however, the exodus of the Jews becomes the exodus of God himself, that is to say, the coming of God in man, of whom Jesus, the Son of Man, is the figure beyond which it is impossible to go.[5]

It is quite important to refer immediately to the exodus at the very beginning of this consideration of Christianity as a way. All religions, moral codes and philosophies in fact resort to the image of the "way" when the conduct of their disciples is under discussion. It is not possible to speak of the religion of Israel and of Christianity as a "way" without interpreting them on the basis of the decisive event of the exodus. This interpretation goes further than a purely moral acceptance of the "way," since the way that has to be followed by men is inseparable from that of the Lord as their guide.

The way itself as an historical experience of the exodus is only meaningful as an eschatological prefiguration of the journey that all men have to make in pursuit of the kingdom of God. The immense adventure of the people, walking in faith "in God's footsteps," began when Abraham set off in response to God's call (Gen 12:1–5), "not knowing where he was to go" (Heb 11:8). The author of the Letter to the Hebrews continues in his magnificent language to say: "These all died in faith, not having received what was promised, but having seen it and greeted it from afar, and having acknowledged that they were strangers and exiles on the earth. For people who speak thus make it clear that they are seeking a homeland" (Heb 11:13–14).

In fact, they are not simply "seeking a homeland." They are also seeking Someone—the face of the Lord. When Abraham left Ur of the Chaldaeans, it was because he had a meeting elsewhere with the God whose call he had recognized. When Moses left Egypt, it was so that God could enter into dialogue with his people in the desert. When Ezra left Babylonia, it was because he could no longer endure not being able to contemplate the face of his God in the temple in Jerusalem.

B. The Law as Man's Way

A study of the vocabulary of the "way" in the Old Testament has revealed that the Hebrew word *derek* means both the way of God or the Lord and the way of man. May we, then, compare it with the Tao, which means both the "Way of heaven" and the "Way of the saints"?

In the concrete, the "way of the Lord" calls to mind the manner in which God himself set off at the head of his people in order to liberate them from captivity in Egypt or from their exile in Babylonia. There are countless texts in the Bible on the theme of "going" or a "journey."[6] No more than a few can be quoted here as examples. It appears, for instance, in Ps 68:7–8: "O God, when thou didst go forth before thy people, when thou didst march through the wilderness, the earth quaked . . ." and in Ps 99:7: "He spoke to them in the pillar of cloud . . ." The "pillar of cloud" that guided the Hebrews in the desert is identified with the Wisdom of God in the Book of Wisdom: "She gave to holy men the reward of their labors. She guided them along a marvelous way and became a shelter to them by day and a starry flame through the night" (Wis 10:17).

More generally, however, the word "way" points to the mysterious ways of the Lord, that is, his own manner of behaving in order to save men. So, even after they had reached the promised land, the people of Israel continued to walk "in the ways of the Lord." This had been possible since God had revealed those ways to Moses: "Yahweh works vindication and justice for all who are oppressed. He made known his ways to Moses, his acts to the people of Israel" (Ps 103:6).

The law thus became the necessary way for man because it was first and foremost God's way, in other words, the expression of God's own way of behaving. This is a very early encounter with the theme of the imitation of God. The law certainly includes many external precepts, but these are not arbitrary. Their purpose is to identify man's actions with God's. Obeying the law is acting like God, that is, loving as God loves. That is the meaning of the "circumcision of the heart" (see Dt 10:16). The whole of the Deuteronomic text is worth reading in this context: "And now, Israel, what does Yahweh your God require of you, but to fear Yahweh your God, to walk in his ways, to love him, to serve Yahweh your God with all your heart and with all your soul . . ." (Dt 10:12–19).

Under the old covenant, man was free to choose between two ways. On the one hand, there were "the paths of life" (Prov 2:19). They were straight and in perfect conformity with the law of God. The man who walked in those paths practiced justice and "walked in the way of righteousness" (Prov 8:20). He had "chosen the way of faithfulness" (Ps 119:30) and the "way of peace" (Is 59:8). On the other hand, however, there was the twisting way followed by the "wicked," which would "perish" (Ps 1:6) and "lead to death" (Prov 12:28). These two different ways are also to be found in the Gospel. On the one hand, there is the "narrow gate" and the "hard way that leads to life" and, on the other, the "wide gate" and the "easy way that leads to destruction" (Mt 7:13–14).[7]

C. Christianity as a New Exodus

It is obvious that the authors of the New Testament regarded the whole of Christ's work of redemption as the fulfillment of the mystery of salvation prefigured in the exodus. It was the realization of the new exodus proclaimed by Deutero-Isaiah after the exile in Babylonia. And when John the Baptist is identified with "the voice of one crying in the wilderness: Prepare the way of the Lord" (Mt 3:3), this is an explicit reference to the Isaian prophecies. Just as Moses was the guide of his people during the journey through the desert, so too was Jesus the new Moses calling men to follow him on the way of the cross that led to heaven.

There is an almost endless list of cases in which such images as "way," "road," "journey," "ascent" or "going up," "walking" and so on are used in the New Testament in an attempt to formulate the Christian mystery. Living as a disciple of Christ is experiencing with him and in him his passover and his exodus from this earth to the kingdom of heaven. Since Abraham "went up" to Moriah in order to sacrifice Isaac (Gen 22), it is possible to say that, in the religion of Israel as in Christianity, the idea of going, and especially that of "going up," became associated with the idea of sacrifice. That is also the sense of our modern word "pilgrimage." When Moses tried to liberate his people from their captivity in Egypt, he presented that flight as a pilgrimage and told Pharaoh: "Let us go, we pray, a three days' journey into the wilderness and sacrifice to Yahweh our God" (Ex 5:3).

Jesus' life itself should also be seen as a "road" or pilgrimage which sets off from God and returns to God. That return to God, however, coincides with Jesus' Passover, his "going up" to Jerusalem, where he was to complete his sacrifice on the cross. The proclamation of his going up to Jerusalem is made very impressive in the synoptic Gospels by being repeated three times. "And they were on the road, going up to Jerusalem, and Jesus was walking ahead of them and they were amazed and those who followed were afraid" (Mk 10:32). The way that leads to glory has of necessity to go through the cross. The sacrifices of the Old Testament gave no access to the Holy of Holies, but, through the blood of Jesus Christ, we now have access to the true sanctuary. As the author of the Letter to the Hebrews writes, "Therefore, brethren, since we have confidence to enter the sanctuary by the blood of Jesus, by the new and living way which he opened for us through the curtain, that is, through his flesh . . ." (Heb 10:19).

We should not be surprised, then, to learn that, for those who were the first to hear the apostolic preaching, the new religion inaugurated by Christ was called quite simply the "Way" (*hodos*). This name is found in the text in the Acts of the Apostles that I have cited above (Acts 9:2; see also the note in the second edition of the Jerusalem Bible), in which it refers not so much to Christians themselves as to the conduct of the community of believers as a whole. Acts 19:9 should also be quoted in this context, since it informs us about the dispute between Paul and the Jews of the synagogue at Ephesus, some of whom "were stubborn and disbelieved, speaking evil of the Way before the congregation."

We may conclude this brief survey of the theme of the exodus by saying that we may be quite certain that the image of the "way" is not just one among many others. It is a key symbol which enables us to understand Christianity above all as an Easter mystery. It is important to bear in mind here the revolutionary idea of time that was introduced by Judaeo-Christianity. In contrast to members of the ancient world, who were subjected to the law of destiny, that is, to a repetition of the same or the similar, the members of the new people of God looked forward in the paths of history to the kingdom of God that had not yet been fully revealed. What we have here, then, is a community in a state of exodus and exercising a function of anti-destiny with regard to the whole human family, subjected to the hard law of time which passes and which leads only to death.

2. CHRIST AS THE WAY
AND THE IMITATION OF CHRIST

Christ is not just the one who went up to Jerusalem in order to "depart out of this world to the Father" (Jn 13:1). He is also and above all himself the Path, the Way or the Pilgrimage. The Hebrews were those who "walked in the law of the Lord" (Ps 119:1), in order to go in the direction of life. Christ's disciples have to walk in him (Col 2:6), in order to carry out for themselves their definitive exodus to the Father. In Christ, then, the law became a living person. If we are to appreciate the originality of Christian moral teaching, we should grasp the consequences of this new reality. To do this, we should understand the extent to which the Jewish halacha was transformed by reference to the person of Jesus. This is directly related to the theme of the imitation of Christ.

A. Our Walk Following Christ

It is above all Paul who makes very special use of the verb *peripatein*, to walk, in an attempt to describe the behavior of Christians following Christ. The new law of the Christian is a walk in the Spirit. (See, for example, Gal 5:16: "Walk by the Spirit" and 2 Cor 12:18: "Did we not walk in the same Spirit?")

C. Perrot has pointed out in his study of the halacha and Christian morality that "the Christian is no longer referred back to the law. He has recourse to the community of the Spirit and to himself insofar as he is inspired by that same Spirit, since the Spirit is now at the beginning of all moral conduct."[8]

There are still, of course, "commandments of the Lord." St. Paul, for example, appeals to the authority of Scripture, the law and the prophets and he refers to certain words of the Lord. But, in the Christian halacha, the disciple is always led back to his own conscience in solidarity with a community that lives from the Spirit of the Lord. The norm of moral behavior is no longer the law or one or other word of Scripture, but the behavior of the Lord himself. Paul himself was so apparently self-sufficient that he gave scandal to certain people: "Be imitators of me, as I am of Christ" (1 Cor 11:1).

What we have here, then, is clearly a very open and dynamic morality and an obligation on the part of each Christian to produce a moral discourse that is always new, but is based on his imitation of Christ. Finally, for the Christian, the "more excellent way" (1 Cor 12:31), superior to the charisms, is the way of charity. (See Rom 14:15: "Walk in love.")

The law of love contains no precise precepts. In reply to the question "What ought I to do?" the Christian does not know in advance what to say. He has to find his own way by looking for what is the will of God when confronted with situations that are always new, and he has to be aware of what claims are made above all here and now by his service of his fellow man.

B. From Imitation to Sonship

If this necessary interiorization of the "law of Christ" (Gal 6:2) is understood as the "law of the Spirit" (Rom 8:2) or the "law of faith" (Rom 3:27) and as the law of love, there will be no danger of the imitation of Christ being understood as a flat reproduction of an past model.

Paul's ethics put us on our guard in this context against any kind of legalism or moralism. That is why I pointed out at the beginning of this chapter that the theme of "Christianity as a way" cannot be interpreted in a narrowly moralistic sense as "moral conduct in life." Luther understood perfectly the ambiguities and risks to which Christianity as a "religion of grace" was exposed in the theme of the imitation of Christ. He therefore wanted it to be permanently subject to justification by faith alone, declaring that "imitation does not make sons, but sonship makes imitators."[9]

Since then, theologians working in the tradition of the Reformation have always had reservations with regard to the idea of the imitation of Christ, and German theologians have made a distinction between two verbs: *nachahmen* (to imitate) and *nachfolgen* (to follow after). The first should be understood in the sense of a purely moral imitation and the second calls to mind the community of destiny and the intimate sharing between the Lord and his disciples. In his book, *Le Prix de la Grâce*, Dietrich Bonhoeffer stresses that *Nachfolge* (following after) is "the exact opposite of all legalism" because it is nothing but a clinging to Jesus Christ alone, in other words, it is precisely "a total break with every program, all abstraction and all legalism."[10]

Christ, then, is more than merely an exemplary figure. He is an original or founding figure. It might therefore be better to replace the theme of "imitation" by those of "participation" and "genealogy." "The similarity between Christ and the Christian is not the purely external one between a copy and the model, but an entirely internal resemblance of the kind that exists between the principle and the effect."[11]

The idea of imitation may perhaps be adequate in the perspective of a hero morality, but in Christianity imitation can only be a consequence of sonship. For the Christian, following Christ's way is leading one's life as a child of God according to the Spirit of Christ. In other words, Christ is more than a merely external model. He is an active law, bringing about in us what attracts us in him. I would suggest that Christ is not simply a master of wisdom and we are not simply disciples. Christ is the beloved Son of the Father and we are sons and co-heirs with him.

We have to resist the illusion of obsessively reproducing certain acts in the life of Jesus and must look for the audacity of the memory of Christ in the Pauline sense.[12] Paul refused to appeal to the memory of Christ according to the flesh in the Judaeo-Christian manner. It is remarkable, for example, that he never mentions in his letters any of the episodes in the "life of Jesus" and never refers to any particular statement made by the Lord, with the exception of the words about divorce (1 Cor 7:10).

Paul is, however, logical in keeping to the principle that he expresses in the following way: "From now on, therefore, we regard no one from a human point of view. Even though we once regarded Christ from a human point of view, we regard him thus no longer" (2 Cor 5:16). What does this mean? Surely it means that Christians should not cling nostalgically to the Jesus whom they knew in the past before the Easter event.

In other words, the real memory of Christ is not a reproduction of what came in Jesus of Nazareth. It is a new creation of the Spirit of the risen Christ who is still living in his Church. Understanding the imitation of Christ in the Pauline sense, then, is conceiving a following of Jesus of such a kind that Christians find the right response that the Spirit of Jesus inspires in them in the light of new historical situations. Following Jesus is "putting him on" (see Rom 13) with all the consequences and all the risks that are involved in that action. The theme of imitation is also a confirmation for us that an authentic Christology cannot be based exclusively on purely theoretical knowledge, but has to be nourished by following Jesus in practice.[13]

We may therefore conclude that the imitation of Christ in the Pauline sense means following Jesus, not by reproducing in a voluntaristic and burdensome way an external model, but by giving oneself up completely to the son's life that Christ wants to lead in each one of us.

It would, however, be a complete misunderstanding of the nature of the imitation of Christ if we were to think of being freely available to the impulse of the Spirit as a complete absence of initiative. Imitating Christ is not mechanically copying a past model, but making ourselves contemporary with the still living Christ. The Christian way leads to a creativity that cannot be foreseen in the order of Christian practice. When the words of Scripture and the life of Christ himself are involved, they can only be made contemporary for us if we interpret them creatively.

We are always preceded by the example of Christ, who continues to be the original point of reference for all Christian practice, but the transmission of that example is always historical, that is, it is always in relation to the concrete practice of men at a given moment in history. The Christian is therefore not condemned to the impossible ideal of reproducing what Christ did in the past. He is rather handed over to his own consciousness, which has been enlightened by the Spirit so that he can discover for himself what Christ would have done today.

C. Following Jesus as a Call to Freedom

My insistence on the theologal dimension of the imitation of Christ was based on a desire to draw attention to the pitfalls involved in the reproduction in the present of a past model that exempts us from the need for a creative renewal in the first person in the name of the Spirit of Jesus. This is because we no longer know Christ according to the flesh, that is, in the manner of the past.

I would like to conclude these reflections by showing that following Jesus is the adventure of my freedom as a child of God and therefore a very risky adventure. The fascination of a model that cannot be imitated is that it is a phenomenon that leads to alienation and paralysis in the despairing consciousness that can do no more than make a clumsy copy of the original. It is in fact an operation that leads ultimately to self-destruction.

Paradoxically, our real freedom would seem to coincide with the death of our wish for an imaginary identification with Christ. What we have is a fascinating image of Christ to imitate, one which is like the projection of an image of the father by the child's all powerful wish. At the same time, however, we know that it is only when we abandon a fatal identification with the father and accept a mutual recognition that the child can ever become a subject himself.

However sublime it may be, the theme of the imitation of Christ is full of pitfalls. It leads us to make a distinction between an imaginary identification with Christ and a process of identification that accepts the interplay between similarity and difference. As in every case of love which tends toward the most absolute form of identification, in other words, which is moving unwittingly in the direction of a fatal merging together, the only way to respect the otherness of the other person and to be known oneself in one's irreplaceable and true identity is to accept the instituting function of language. Language is more than simply an instrument of communication. It is the means by which we can become aware of our limitations, of being an "I" for another person and of existing on the basis of wish and another person's recognition. Clinging inflexibly to the need for identification with another person in a kind of stubborn mimesis is an indirect way of refusing to accept one's limitations. It is, in other words, remaining enclosed within one's imaginary "I" and therefore not coming to the truth of oneself as a subject who is dependent on recognition by the other person.

In the concrete, this means that there can be no question of following Jesus if we do not listen to his words, which are received as a gift and an appeal, and if we do not participate in his way, which is a path to the Father.

Jesus' words are words of sonship. In him and through him I invoke God as Father and I am recognized as a son. I can, however, never come to the end of the task of becoming a son. Becoming a son is learning to respect the otherness of the one whom we call "our Father." It is also experiencing our similarity with God by accepting our difference from him. It is therefore accepting dependence, but at the same time becoming aware of my identity as a son and being referred back to my irreplaceable historical responsibility.

Following Jesus always coincides with a call to a vocation in the Church. That vocation, however, always has a structure that is both mystical and political in the widest sense of the words.[14] On the one hand, it is mystical because I can never come to the end of the task of penetrating more and more deeply into my "becoming a son" in Jesus Christ. On the other hand, it is also political because I can never follow Jesus outside an historical and social context, within which I have to continue Christ's struggle against all forms of death.

The problem is not simply one of reducing the following of Jesus to an exclusively inner experience, nor can it be reduced to a purely ethical activity. If we are to follow Jesus, we have to tend to reproduce in our own life Jesus' way as a "path to the Father." The whole of Jesus' life must be seen as a great movement of return to the Father.

This is exactly what the author of the Letter to the Hebrews was trying to express when he put the words of Ps 40:6–8 into Jesus' mouth: " 'Sacrifices and offerings thou hast not desired, but a body hast thou prepared for me. In burnt offerings and sin offerings thou hast taken no pleasure.' Then I said, 'Lo, I have come to do thy will, O God, as it is written of me in the roll of the book' " (Heb 10:6–8).

As a man, Jesus is defined by his obedience to the Father's will. The supreme evidence of that obedience as a son is his acceptance of death. His death was not simply the consequence of his struggle for justice in solidarity with the poorest and most deprived of people. The offering of his life in fact expresses his movement of return to the Father. It is because he only existed through and for the Father that he gave his own life in exchange as a counter-gift. In an exchange of love, the counter-gift that goes as far as giving one's life is the response to a gratuitous love that precedes us. Christ's acceptance of death, then, is quite different from a heroic obedience to a commandment given by the Father. It is the perfect expression of his love and his abandonment as a Son to the Father. "Greater love has no man than this, that a man lay down his life for his friends" (Jn 15:13). Paradoxically, acceptance of death, that is, accepting what is most inhuman, is the last word of freedom.

3. CHRISTIANITY AS ORTHOPRAXIS

When we speak of Christianity as a "way," we are, I think, giving a privileged status to the "right practice" of Christianity and not to its doctrinal message or its dogmatic content. The word that has been used for some time now to describe that aspect of Christianity is "orthopraxis."

This word has one great advantage. It emphasizes the fact that there can be no Christian orthodoxy or "right belief" that is not expressed in practice. It also has one great danger. It encourages us to look too readily for a possible comparison with other religions by putting the content of Christian faith in brackets.

In this final section, I would like to do two things. First, I shall try to show how it is impossible to oppose orthodoxy and orthopraxis in Christianity. Second, I shall attempt to demonstrate that the word "orthopraxis" refers to a characteristic which is quite distinctively part of the Christian religion and which the image of the "way" particularly tries to call to mind. That is "evangelical practice."

A. The Meaning of "Doing the Truth"

Recent attempts have been made to justify the primacy of orthopraxis over orthodoxy on the basis of the Johannine formula "doing the truth" (Jn 3:21). The aim has been to provide in this way a biblical foundation for a pragmatist conception of the truth, according to which only what is operational or can be verified by action is true.

According to one contemporary but quite wrong exegesis, the formula of St. John should be understood as though it were a moral practice inspired by faith. As I. de la Potterie, however, has pointed out in a remarkable study of this question, St. John's "doing the truth" does not refer to a moral action performed by the believer as a consequence of faith. On the contrary, it refers to the very genesis of faith itself. If it did not, it would not be possible to understand the second part of the same verse in the Fourth Gospel: "He who does what is true comes to the light."

What does this "coming to the light" mean, if it does not mean "coming to faith"? For St. John, the "doing" refers not to works as distinct from faith, as it might in the case of St. Paul, but to the work itself of faith. We therefore need do no more than compare this formula with another, parallel text, John 6:28–29, according to which the Jews asked Jesus: "What must we do, to be doing the works of God?" And Jesus answered them, "This is the work of God, that you believe in him whom he has sent."

So, far from appealing to St. John in our attempt to oppose faith and praxis, we should rather say that praxis for him is above all the work of faith itself. Doing the truth is coming gradually to faith. It is therefore not difficult to see that the idea of Christianity as a "way" can be understood not simply as a number of precepts to be followed, but also and above all as the path of faith itself. It is very interesting in this context to note that, in St. John, "walking" and "believing" are equivalent. What is believing if it not "walking in the light" (Jn 12:35–36) and "walking in the truth" (2 Jn 4 and 3 Jn 3–4)?

Both St. John and St. Paul regarded the way of Christianity above all as the way of love, but they saw it always as a way of love enlightened by faith. (See especially the expression in Galatians 5:6: "Faith working through love.")

B. Christianity Is Defined First and Foremost by Evangelical Practice

Having pointed out how faulty this interpretation of the Johannine formula "doing the truth" is, I am free to say that what is hidden behind the word "orthopraxis" is a very deep truth concerning the essence of Christianity. It is true that Christianity did not succeed in the religious environment of the Graeco-Roman world within which it found itself as a religion of "truth" (*aletheia*) or a mystery religion, but it was successful as a religion of love (*agape*). What is certain is that it is not possible to oppose the practice of faith and the practice of charity. It is also beyond dispute that Christianity is defined first and foremost by a certain knowledge and by the fact that it keeps to a number of truths.

Understanding Christianity as a "way" or as "orthopraxis" is accepting, in the light of a dialectical conception of the relationships that exist between theory and praxis, that Christian activity is not the simple consequence or the mere application of a doctrinal truth that has already been constituted. It is, on the contrary, Christian practice itself that not only reveals but also creates new meanings with regard to the Christian message.

As I have already said in connection with the content of the hermeneutical problem, acting according to the Spirit of Christ is not merely suggesting new interpretations of the event of Jesus Christ—it is also producing new historical figures of Christianity in accordance with changing times and places. This conception of Christian practice cannot be separated from a notion of truth that is not identified either with the fullness of being or with an historical figure. The truth is rather subject to a process of becoming. It is a permanent becoming and a permanent coming. This is in fact the meaning of biblical truth as a reality of the eschatological order.[16]

As we have already seen above, it is not possible to oppose the practice of faith and the practice of love in St. John, who clearly teaches that faith is itself a work. In fact, however, faith is a long movement with many stages which only gradually reaches the adult state of "mature manhood, to the measure of the stature of the fullness of Christ" (Eph 4:13). There is also an instinct for truth, a faith that exists prior to the explicit faith that enables us to understand why evangelical practice is not an exclusive monopoly of those who are members of the Church and explicitly profess faith in Jesus Christ.

It is possible to be already a disciple of Jesus before knowing it and while one is still a member of a religion that is different from Christianity as an historical religion. That is why it is so difficult to define the specifically Christian character of Christianity simply by doctrinal orthodoxy or even by orthopraxis in the sense of only one right Christian way.

It is in fact impossible to define the evangelical way of life *a priori*. The new dimension of Christian behavior is not necessarily manifested by its content. It is rather a special modality of human activity in general. There is a certain manner in which we follow Jesus and practice the beatitudes rather than any particular Christian "species." The Christian response is also as impossible to predict as the Spirit of Jesus, who does not belong exclusively to Christians.

We should therefore never be surprised if we frequently receive what is clearly Gospel teaching either from atheists or from those who belong to religions that are different from Christianity. According to St. John, Jesus said to Thomas, one of the Twelve: "Blessed are those who have not seen and yet believe" (Jn 20:29). We should be glad that we can say very often today: "Blessed are those who have lived the Gospel and yet have not known it."

We should rejoice if many people are able to follow Christ on his way and carry out the *sequela Christi* before keeping to the dogmatic content of the Christian faith and even before knowing Jesus explicitly as Lord. Speaking of Christianity as a "way," then, is suggesting that it is more than a particular religion defined by dogmas, a cult and certain criteria of membership—that it is, in other words, something that belongs to every man who is walking toward the light.

CONCLUSION

To conclude these all too brief comments that I have made on Christianity as a "way," I would like to recall a very profound statement by Kierkegaard without quoting it word for word. We can never claim to "be"

Christians, he says, but we always have to be "becoming" Christians. The image of the "way," then, is similar to the New Testament images of the leaven, the grain of wheat and the seed in that it aims to remind us of the essentially dynamic reality of the kingdom of God. This surely points at least to the possibility of a comparison with the vital vocabulary of the Tao. Like the Christian kingdom of God, the Chinese Tao is at its point of departure a seed that is almost invisible. (See Chapter 67: "All say that my Way is great, but of wretched appearance . . .")

We have, then, to speak of "becoming" both in the case of individual Christian existence and in that of the Church as the people of God. We are always on the way toward a fullness that has not yet been manifested—that of the kingdom of God. In the light of that eschatological dimension, each stage on the journey in our following of Christ can only be provisional and we have to go beyond it.

This is also true of the Church of Christ as an historical figure. There is a permanent coming of the fullness of the Gospel as an eschatological reality. That is why the objectivizations of that fullness both in the order of truth and in that of love are never adequate. They always give rise to new interpretations and even to new creations with regard to the historical practice of men.

As an historical event, the event of Jesus Christ belongs definitively to the past. But Christ is still living and he still continues to carry out his Lordship over the whole of human history. Because of the permanent gift of his Spirit, there is an actualization that is always new of what was made manifest in him during his historical existence. Christianity becomes meaningless without permanent reference to the founding event of Jesus Christ himself. At the same time, it also ceases to be a way that is open to an unforeseeable future without permanent creativity, because it then becomes unfaithful to its existence as an exodus.

Following the direction of the image of the "way" in the case of Christianity is understanding that the inheritance that we have received discloses a future that we have to make. Is it presumptuous to claim that the Christian religion can only be the religion of the future if it is faithful to itself?

Chapter XIII

TOWARD A CHRISTIAN INTERPRETATION OF HUMAN RIGHTS

It is possible to say unreservedly that the Catholic Church has become the best champion of human rights in the last quarter of the present century. This has been especially so during the pontificate of John Paul II, whose encyclicals and the many interventions that he has made on his numerous journeys bear witness to his defense of man and his rights as a most important theme in his teaching. The really decisive change in the development of the Church's concern for human rights, however, was made by John XXIII and the Second Vatican Council. I will do no more in this context than simply mention the publication of the encyclical *Pacem in terris*, which begins with a real charter of human rights and duties, and the famous Declaration on Religious Freedom, *Dignitatis Humanae*, of Vatican II, which recognizes the right of every human being freely to choose his own religion.

What a long way the Church has come since Pius IX's *Syllabus of Errors* of 1864, which condemned without appeal the following proposition: "Every man is free to embrace and to profess the religion which the light of reason has led him to judge to be the true religion" (No. 15; *DS* 2915). The nineteenth century Popes continued to pronounce anathemas against modern expressions of freedom, which represented a long and burdensome struggle on the part of laymen not only against the *Ancien Régime*, but also against the Church.

J.-F. Six gave a recent book the title *From the Syllabus to Dialogue*. This is not enough. He should have entitled it *From Anathema to Coming Together and the Promotion of Human Rights*. Those rights are now not simply tolerated by the Church. They are recognized as a demand made by the Gospel. This recognition was made explicit by Pope Paul VI in 1974: "The promotion of human rights is an evangelical demand and it should have a central place in the Church's ministry."

A great deal has already been written about this change in attitude. All that I want to do in this chapter is to ask a number of questions about its theological significance. I am, however, well aware that if there is one sphere in which it is impossible to make abstract judgments in the name of theological principles, it is certainly that of human rights. It is both astonishing and scandalizing that the Church took such a long time to become conscious of the implications of its own message. On the other hand, although I do not want to make excuses for the Church, it is important to remember the frightening complexity of the socio-historical contexts in which the Church's teaching about human rights took shape.

I shall begin by indicating a few important landmarks in the very ambiguous history of human rights in the theory and practice of the Catholic Church. I shall then go on to examine the relationship between the Charter of Human Rights and the content of the biblical revelation. In considering that question, I shall also investigate whether the three great monotheistic world religions have an urgent historical responsibility with regard to the defense and promotion of human rights.

1. AN AMBIGUOUS HISTORY

Jesus' message is essentially one of the liberation of mankind. In his teaching and in the whole of his life, Jesus constantly called for the absolute dignity of man, even sinful man, in the sight of God and the equality of all men in human society. According to St. Paul, "There is neither Jew nor Greek, there is neither slave nor free, there is neither male nor female, for you are all one in Christ Jesus" (Gal 3:28).

If it is true that we have to look for a theological foundation for human rights in the biblical theme of "man as the image of God" (Gen 1:26), then we are bound to say that this teaching is made more radical in Jesus' preaching. What is at the very center of that preaching is the nearness of the kingdom of God, in other words, man's total and final salvation. "This means that God makes his rule, his 'divine right' in the world, prevail by taking man's side and taking over himself man's lost cause in order to liberate and save him."[1]

Jesus is the messianic liberator who defends all the weak, oppressed and poor members of society in the name of the rights of God. It is clear from the Gospel accounts that Jesus' commitment in favor of the poor, the marginalized, those outside the law, and the publicans and sinners scandalized the righteous. It was this same subversive attitude that led to his trial and his death on the cross. But how has this message of the liberation of man and the defense of human rights been experienced in the concrete throughout twenty centuries of Christianity?

There have been two tendencies co-existing in the Church until the present. On the one hand, it is always possible to give examples of Christian individuals, groups and movements that have continued throughout the history of Christianity to take seriously Jesus' teaching about the sacred dignity of every man. On the other hand, it is even easier to make a list of the many perversions of the early Christian teaching. There is more than sufficient evidence of this not only in the practice, but also in the theology of the Church. This points to a deep mystery that does not go back exclusively to man's weakness and sinfulness or to simple social and other changes. We have in fact to speak of a structural evolution in this case. The question that confronts us is: How is it that the Church, which should normally be the place of freedom, has so often been hostile to freedom? It is possible to simplify this process by distinguishing three periods in the Church's history.

A. The Alliance Between Church and State

It is important not to underestimate the influence of the Christian message of liberation with regard to the idea of human rights in the ancient world during the first three centuries of the Church's existence. At that time, the Church was often in conflict with the Empire in its claims and frequently defended the dignity and the equality of all men, both slaves and free men. Even though the idea of religious freedom as an inviolable right of the person had not then been made explicit, it is still possible to say that, during the first centuries of Christianity, thousands of Christians died in the defense of their religious freedom.

A new historical destiny began for Christianity at the beginning of the fourth century with the alliance between Emperor Constantine and the Church. This marked the beginning of a period of caesaropapism and of what has been called "Christianity," even though the word itself with its sociological content did not appear until the ninth century. The Edict of Milan (313) promulgated the freedom of worship, but it remained a dead letter, and Christianity, promoted as the "state religion," came under the control of the Christian emperors. There was collusion between the Church and the state, and whenever the emperors' policy was to favor the unity and expansion of the Church, the bishops found it quite natural to make use of the secular arm against heretics and schismatics.

One historian has judged this period moderately in the following way: "During the patristic period, religious freedom was characterized by the fact that it benefited the Catholic Church. The emperors regarded religious unity as indispensable for the maintenance of political unity. The bishops called for it as an essential demand made by Christian faith and they did not hesitate to ask for the help of the state."[2]

Even the great theologian St. Augustine justified recourse to force to make the stubborn Donatists submit. It was on that occasion that he interpreted the *compelle intrare* ("compel them to come in") of the parable of the wedding feast (Lk 14:23) as a justification of the use of external constraint in the service of the one saving truth. Since the truth revealed in Jesus Christ is necessary for the salvation of every man, all means applied to maintain men in that truth or to oblige them to keep to it are good.

What we see here are the first signs of that ideology of "obligatory truth" which was to have such fatal consequences throughout the rest of the history of Christianity. Insofar as the Church's cause coincided with the interests of the Christian kings and rulers, the famous axiom "Outside the Church there is no salvation" could continue to serve as an ideological guarantee and be used to justify the deaths of thousands of men.

Even greater intolerance seems to have prevailed in the Middle Ages than in the patristic period. It is true that some degree of freedom of conscience was tolerated in the case of Jews and "infidels," by which was meant Muslims. But the intolerance with regard to heretics and schismatics was absolute. From the ninth century onward, it became current practice to impose the death penalty on those who had been unfaithful to their baptismal promises, even though Augustine had, in the past, always rejected it.

In the thirteenth century, Pope Gregory IX instituted, in agreement with Emperor Frederick II, the Holy Inquisition, and it became the regular practice to punish stubborn and relapsed heretics by fire. The theologians of the period committed themselves to the task of justifying the procedures of the Inquisition. Even Thomas Aquinas, for example, wrote that heretics and apostates "must be even physically constrained to honor their promises and to keep once and for all time what they have accepted" (ST IIa, IIae, q. 10, a. 8).

To be quite fair to Thomas, however, it should be said that he fully respected man's freedom to embrace the faith of Christ, even though he refused that freedom to anyone who claimed to leave it. "Embracing the faith is a matter of the will, but remaining in the faith that has been received is a matter of necessity" (ST IIa, IIae, q. 10, a. 8, ad 3). By "necessity" here, we should not understand simply moral necessity. The use of physical violence against a heretic is justified. In other words, it is not accepted that he may have good faith. He is always guilty. If he does not repent, he should disappear by dying, to avoid the corruption of the whole body of the Church.

Intolerance of this kind scandalizes Christians in the twentieth century. It is in contradiction to the early Christian message. To understand it, however, it is necessary to reconstruct the political and sociological context of medieval Christianity, which was the ultimate consequence of collusion between civil and religious society. Confronted with the threat of Islam, there was an urgent need to maintain by every means available the social order of Christianity. Heresy was a contagious disease that threatened to infect the whole body, which was inseparably both social and ecclesial. The right of individual persons was therefore sacrificed to the health of the social and ecclesial body.

This situation of the absence of religious freedom continued until the dawn of the modern era, and the Reformation only exacerbated the ideology of the "state religion" with all the intolerance that stemmed from it. The unity of religion became for the kings and princes a decisive factor in political unity. Jews and "infidels" were still tolerated, but all means used to do away with the dissident members who compromised the unity of the body of the Church were regarded as good. It is possible to speak prematurely of some recognition of the principle of "freedom of conscience," because a man was free to choose and keep to the Christian faith, but there was no religious freedom at that time because stubborn adhesion to heresy or schism was punishable by death.

B. The Anathemas Against Liberalism

The French Revolution and the Declaration of the Rights of Man and the Citizen made on August 26, 1789 inaugurated a new period in the history of the relationships between the Catholic Church and human rights.

The Declaration recognized the natural, inalienable and sacred rights of man. Those rights are freedom, property, safety and resistance to oppression. Article 10 states: "No one must be troubled because of his opinions, even his religious opinions, provided that their manifestation does not disturb public order as established by the law," and Article 11 recognizes "the free communication of thoughts and opinions as one of man's most precious rights."

How did the Church speak and act, confronted with this first Declaration of human rights, which seemed to be so fully in accordance with the real dignity of the human person as defended by the early Christian message? Because of a tragic historical misunderstanding, the language of the Popes in the eighteenth and nineteenth centuries was that of anathemas.[3]

In his brief *Quod Aliquantum,* Paul IV pronounced an anathema against the civil constitution of the clergy who had voted on July 12, 1790. He also, however, condemned the authors of the Declaration of 1789. He asserted that the "effect" of the civil constitution was "to destroy the Catholic religion and with it the obedience due to the kings. It is with this in mind that this absolute freedom has been established as man's right in society. It is a freedom that not only ensures man's right not to be troubled about his religious opinions, but also grants him that license to think, say, write and even have printed everything in the matter of religion that might suggest the most disordered imagination. This is a monstrous right which appears at the Assembly, however, to result from the natural equality and freedom of all men."

As B. Plongeron has pointed out, there are in this text two assumptions underlying the argumentation that were made by the magisterium until the time of Vatican II. The first is that the exercise of man's fundamental right to freedom is seen as an "unbridled freedom." The second is that the Christian's struggle for freedom is only legitimate when it is conducted in the defense of religious freedom, religion here being understood as Catholic.[4] The same author continues: "In other words, as C. Wackenheim has observed, the right to religious freedom is based on man's nature as interpreted by the Church's magisterium. It is therefore in this way that a person's inalienable right is regarded as leading to the obligation to belong to the Catholic Church!"[5]

Throughout the whole of the nineteenth century, the Popes continued to fulminate against liberalism, denouncing it as the pernicious ideology of modern times.[6] In the encyclical *Mirari vos* (1832), Gregory XVI went so far as to call the claim to freedom of conscience a "delirium" and that to the freedom of the press "execrable." The same excesses are also to be found in Pius IX's encyclical *Quanta cura* (1864). In the same year, barely a century before Vatican II, the statement that I quoted at the beginning of this chapter appears among the errors condemned in the same Pope's *Syllabus of Errors:* "Every man is free to embrace and to profess the religion which the light of reason has led him to judge to be the true religion" (No. 15; *DS* 2915)

It is therefore indisputable that a recognition of the fundamental rights of the human person has been a gradual process taking place in the mind of modern man as a lay consciousness as opposed to the explicit teaching of the Catholic magisterium. It is very difficult for us to imagine today how far habits of thought and the weight of history drove the Church quite naturally to condemn liberalism in all its forms. Liberalism was in fact not at all an innocent doctrine. It was an atheistic ideology which led men to exalt the individual and to reject all authority, including that of God. It was that liberalism that was condemned by Leo XIII in his great encyclicals *Immortale Dei* (1885) and *Rerum novarum* (1891).

Despite its ambiguity, however, the nineteenth century papacy was not able to discern the aspect of truth contained in liberalism. "In order to be able to do that, it would have needed to look at the social and human reality from a different perspective, taking not the 'rights' of God as its point of departure, but those of the human person. It would, in other words, have had to undergo a Copernican revolution."[7]

The Church, then, lacked prophetic discernment in the previous century and unfortunately appeared to all men who were in pursuit of freedom as the enemy of freedom. It is, however, possible to regard this historical error on the part of the Church as a fatal consequence of a theological deviation that began as early as the ninth century and to call it the ideology of Christianity and the myth of obligatory truth. On the one hand, the fact that the order of the Church and the socio-political order were closely merged together meant that violence was regarded as justified in the service of orthodoxy and unity. On the other hand, the Church's conviction that it possessed the one truth led it to sacrifice the rights of human persons to the exclusive rights of that truth.

C. The Catholic Church's Rallying to the Cause of Human Rights

As I have already pointed out, it was necessary to wait until the Second Vatican Council before the Catholic Church officially rallied to the cause of human rights. This was stated again and again in the Pastoral Constitution on the Church in the Modern World. A striking example is: "By virtue of the Gospel committed to it, the Church proclaims the rights of man. It acknowledges and greatly esteems the dynamic movements of today by which these rights are everywhere fostered" (*Gaudium et Spes*, 41).

The Declaration on Religious Freedom, *Dignitatis Humanae*, also represents a radical review of a pernicious theory of exclusive rights of the truth that had served to justify centuries of intolerance. This document does not outline a merely negative tolerance like that found in the politico-religious theology of thesis and hypothesis evolved in the nineteenth century, when it had to be accepted that Catholicism was no longer the dominant religion in many modern states. The tolerance described in it goes further than this and is positive.

The recognition of religious freedom by Vatican II "did not intend exclusively to ensure that Christians had the possibility of opting, in the absence of all external constraint, for one or other Christian confession. Nor did it have in mind an exclusive right of choice between the different world religions. What it wanted to do was to let everyone choose," free from all external constraint, "either a religion or unbelief."[8]

Finally, there is Article 18 of the Universal Declaration of the Rights of Man adopted by the General Assembly of the United Nations on December 10, 1948. This is officially dedicated to religious freedom: "Every person has a right to freedom of thought, conscience and religion. This right implies the freedom to change his religion or his conviction alone or in common, in public or in private, by teaching, practices, worship and the accomplishment of rites."

Before *Dignitatis Humanae* was promulgated by Paul VI, John XXIII fully ratified the Charter of Human Rights of 1948 in his great encyclical *Pacem in terris*, which was his spiritual testament. Even before him, Pius XI and especially Pius XII had initiated the great change that took place in the Catholic Church in the twentieth century in favor of human rights. Not only did the Church no longer pronounce anathemas on those rights— it also recognized as one of its essential tasks in the modern world the need to work for their defense and promotion. What was new about John XXIII, compared with his predecessors, was that he addressed not only Christians, but all men directly. "Although our thoughts were guided by the light of revelation in the composition of this document, we wanted it to be inspired above all by the demands made by human nature and to be addressed to all men."

After John XXIII, Paul VI and John Paul II in turn became the champions of the cause of human rights. They have repeatedly shown how willing they were to work in close collaboration with the United Nations Organization. The clear evidence of this is their two addresses to the General Assembly of that international body.[9]

It would be possible to discuss at great length the reasons for this change in attitude on the part of the Church. There is, however, at least one immediate cause. The Church eventually took note of the development of modern democracies in the West and came to understand that the defense of human freedom was not necessarily synonymous with atheism and anti-clericalism. Another is that the Church became aware of its own intolerance when it came into contact with totalitarian ideologies such as Nazism and Stalinism. How could Catholicism claim religious freedom, after all, when confronted with such totalitarian regimes, when it denied that freedom itself to the citizens of states in which it was still the dominant religion?

Confronted with totalitarian ideologies, it could only present the inviolable dignity of the human person. It is, however, also possible to discern a theological cause here. The Church had allowed itself to be taught by mankind's states of consciousness. By this I mean that it had learned how to interpret the revelation of which it was the repository on the basis of the history of the world and the development of cultures.

2. THE CHARTER OF HUMAN RIGHTS AND BIBLICAL REVELATION

It is, then, only gradually that our consciousness has developed sufficiently for us to affirm human rights. By a tragic misunderstanding, this
increasing consciousness was not promoted by the official Church. On the
contrary, the Church did everything possible to delay its irreversible development at least for as long as it enjoyed the privilege in certain states
of being the dominant religion.

The situation is quite different today. The Church is not lamenting its
past errors, nor is it resting content, as one of the three great monotheistic
religions, in the sad history of mutual intolerance. Most Christians regard
it as preferable to question themselves about their historical responsibility
as witnesses to the one God in the world of faith.

In the second half of this chapter, then, I shall try to point to the convergence between the doctrine of human rights and the teaching of the
biblical revelation. I shall then go on to consider what contribution the
Christian churches can make to the cause of human rights in a divided
world in which a mockery is constantly made of those rights.

A. The Theological Foundation of Human Rights

As I have already said, the Church's magisterium quite recently gave
explicit approval to the Charter of Human Rights of 1948. In this context,
I mentioned in particular John XXIII's encyclical *Pacem in terris,* which
was addressed to all men and for this reason spoke in the name of the demands made by human nature and the natural law.

This foundation is, however, rather too ambiguous. Man's common
consciousness of the dignity of the human person to which the Charter of
Human Rights refers calls itself for a more radical foundation. Otherwise,
there is a danger that it will remain hanging in the air or else be wrongly
interpreted by one or other modern state. In other words, the monotheistic religions were being misguidedly neutral when they were silent
about the theological foundation of human rights under the pretext of addressing all men, whatever their religious or philosophical convictions
might be. On the contrary, it is the common responsibility of all believers
to work out an ecumenical concept of human rights.

The doctrine of human rights has been explicitly set out in the West,
but we should still try to move toward a universal concept based on international law. That was the thrust of the two international pacts relating to
economic, social and cultural rights on the one hand and to civil and political rights on the other that were adopted in 1966 by the General Assembly of the United Nations. They represented an attempt to determine

the fundamental elements constituting the basic form of human rights. Those elements, it was concluded, are freedom, equality and participation.[10]

These three elements, of course, are reminiscent of the three of the French Revolution. But the "fraternity" of the Revolution, however fundamental, appears rather as a value. It does not characterize the juridical position of the human person in society. Consequently, the concept "participation" was chosen, since it presupposes security and property as fundamental rights enabling the person to participate in social life and in the goods of society. Each particular human right, then, must be interpreted on the basis of these three fundamental elements considered as a whole in accordance with their respective relationships. It hardly needs to be stressed how important this is in the present political situation, in which the Western democracies go no further than a purely individualistic conception of the right to freedom, while in the East human rights are treated as social rights.

In any case, if it is true that the basic form of human rights can be reduced to the three elements of freedom, equality and participation, it should not be difficult to show how the doctrine of human rights and the biblical and Christian view of man converge.

The radical foundation of the inviolable dignity of the human person is laid in the Bible in the creation of man "in the image of God" (Gen 1:26). In the concrete, what this means is that it is impossible to violate man's rights without at the same time attacking God himself, in other words, without committing blasphemy. It is because man is the image of God that his life has a sacred price. In the Genesis account, the prohibition to shed blood is based explicitly on that relationship with God: "Whoever sheds the blood of man, by man shall his blood be shed, for God made man in his own image" (Gen 9:6).

This creation of man in the image of God forms the foundation of the equality that should exist between all men. We have therefore to speak of a necessary connection between monotheism and the doctrine of human rights. And in the Old Testament, God's right is at the service of man's right. It is impossible to overestimate here the importance of the theme of the "God's justice" in the Bible. Despising the poor, the oppressed, the suffering, the widows and the orphans is violating God's right. God is not only the source of all right. He is also the one who takes sides with the most deprived against the powerful.

Jesus' preaching of the kingdom of God does no more than simply take this messianic promise of liberation for all men to its ultimate conclusions. That freedom proclaimed in his message is a definitive liberation in a hereafter beyond death in which God will do justice to everyone. It is, however, also a liberation here and now on this earth in the sense of equality and fraternity between all men. The affirmation of the kingdom of God also coincides with a refusal to give an absolute value to any human power, whether it is political or that of a charismatic leader, a privileged race, a particular people or a social class.

According to the Christian message, man's inviolable dignity and the equality that should exist between all men are not based exclusively on man's likeness to God. They are also founded on the divine sonship that man has acquired in Jesus Christ and on the salvation that he has received as a promise of divine life beyond life on this earth.

In *Pacem in terris* John XXIII was so anxious to speak to all men of good will that he based his argument on a philosophy of natural law. Popes Paul VI and John Paul II, however, followed a different approach, claiming that human rights were demands made by the Gospel itself. In this, they were quite right. To defend and promote human rights is not simply an ethical demand based on human nature understood in a timeless way. On the contrary, they form an integral part of the good news of salvation in its reference to the coming kingdom of God.

It is possible to say that, going beyond the disputes between Catholics and Protestants about the question of natural law, there is a good measure of ecumenical agreement in the attempt to found the inalienable dignity of the human person both within the Church and outside it on the Pauline doctrine of justification. By his sin, man has lost his right in God's presence and has no means, even if he fulfills the Mosaic law of justifying himself before God. But sinful man does in fact receive gratuitously God's justice as his right through the mystery of the death and resurrection of his Son Jesus Christ. Through his behavior toward the "irreligious" ones, that is, those who were excluded from religious society, Jesus made it clear that all men, even sinners, preserved their dignity in God's sight and never ceased to be his loved creatures.

B. Monotheistic Faith and Human Rights

As we have already seen, the declaration of human rights was first made explicit in the context of liberalism and the humanist ideal of the eighteenth and nineteenth centuries. It was a claim of autonomy made against every form of authority, including that of God. It would not be excessive to say that this was an "ideology" of human rights that cannot be separated in the West from the ideologies of progress and secularization. And what was concealed beneath these various ideologies was faith in man. What has in fact happened in the last quarter of the present century, however, is that that faith in man has been seriously shaken. It could be said that we are in fact leaving a period of history that has been dominated by the figure of Prometheus and are now in search of other mythical figures, on the basis of which we hope to be able to interpret the destiny of man. (For this theme, see above, Chapter IX.)

Thanks to the power of science and technology, which has acted almost as a demiurge, we believed until the fairly recent past that we would reach the summit of human success. Now, however, we are more alert to the dramatic consequences of the possible exhaustion of the world's natural resources, the lasting dangers of a nuclear conflict and the risks involved in genetic manipulations that might compromise the future of the human species. Until quite recently we had plans for building up an increasingly planned and rationalized society. Now, however, we are beginning to observe the first symptoms of a rejection of industrial society. We were congratulating ourselves not so long ago on having given man back to himself by freeing him from all faith in a Creator God. Man is now the creator and manipulator, but he feels deeply troubled by the facticity of the modern world and is in search of his roots.

It is within this general context that what has been called the "return of God" has been taking place at least in the rich societies of the first world. This is a complex phenomenon that is difficult to analyze. It is possible to ask whether it is not the effect of a reaction of fear in the presence of the apocalyptic prospect of a nuclear conflict. Whatever it may be, however, it is extremely important to note that our defense of human rights is nowadays no longer connected with the atheistic movement of human emancipation of the Enlightenment. We are therefore no longer in a cultural context in which God necessarily appears as man's rival.

It is interesting to note what Jacques Julliard says in this connection in a very clear diagnosis, which I fully support: "The most important datum of the decade is the failure of the temporal religions. . . . These have rejected God, but have deified politics, conferring on it a messianic value and deriving from it human hope for their profit. . . . On the other hand, the avowedly transcendent religions are flourishing. . . . An extraordinary change is taking place in the situation . . . which is a cause of great scandal to proud Marxist thought, but a worthy and legitimate inheritance of the Enlightenment. . . . Today, it is in the name of philosophy that there is oppression and in the name of faith that there is revolt."[11]

What we are witnessing, then, is a surprising reversal of what had become the slogan of modern atheistic humanism since Feuerbach, that is, the incompatibility between God and the existence of human freedom. Whereas in the past faith in God had seemed to make all human revolt impossible, today, in the three great monotheistic religions, it is precisely faith in God which calls men to struggle and resistance in the defense of human rights.

When the ideology of progress was at the height of its success, it was believed that a denial of God was the condition for building up the world and man's struggle against the fatalities of history. Nowadays, however, it would seem that God has to come again to the rescue of men, who are beginning to doubt their ability to act as a demiurge. Belief in God, then, does not necessarily only serve the interests of conservative forces in the world. It may, on the contrary, be of service to the forces of liberation and act as the best possible guarantee for the defense and promotion of human rights.

I would like to conclude this chapter by insisting on the historical responsibility of believers whenever human rights are violated—as they are every day—by states that have nonetheless adopted the Universal Declaration of Human Rights of 1948 and the Helsinki agreements of August 1, 1975. Here I shall do no more than outline two tasks that seem to me to be particularly urgent.

1. Freedom Is Indivisible

The Christian churches have, as we have seen, moved from anathema to rallying to the cause of human rights and even to deep commitment to the task of promoting them. It is, however, not enough to call on modern states and especially communist states to respect human rights and, among them, above all the right to religious freedom as long as the Church continues to violate those rights in the case of its own members. More generally, how can a religion claim for itself a freedom on the part of states that it does not grant to its own members? Surely the very credibility of that religion is put at risk in such a case.

I have already shown how much the Catholic Church has benefited in the modern era from this gradual explicitation of the concrete demands made by the dignity of the human person that has taken place not only within but also despite the Church. In the Declaration on Religious Freedom of Vatican II, the Church ought to have been inspired to take note of this and to recognize its historical mistake in, for example, tolerating slavery and even torture for so many centuries.

To do that, however, it would have had to abandon the sacrosanct principle of continuity and non-contradiction in its magisterial pronouncements. The idea of a dogmatic development that is always homogeneous is, of course, basically apologetical. Even today, while John Paul II is constantly defending human rights in numerous addresses in season and out of season, the Catholic Church has still not drawn from the Declaration of Human Rights every possible conclusion for the rights of Christians within the Church. Dissident theologians, for example, are probably no longer obliged to submit to questioning. When their writings are put on trial, however, the procedure used within the Congregation of the Faith contradicts in several respects both the Universal Declaration of Human Rights of 1948 and the European Convention of Human Rights of 1959, which called in particular for judiciary debates to be made public.

Freedom is indivisible. A religion cannot call for religious freedom in confrontation with modern totalitarian states when it provides evidence that it is treating its own members with an intolerance that dates back to a previous period. If we confine ourselves simply to the Christian religion alone, what are we to think of those regimes which call themselves Christian, but which do not at the same time hesitate to put in prison those Christians whose only crime is to fight for justice and equality for all men?

2. The Historical Responsibility of the Three Monotheistic Religions

In the West, one great danger is of going no further than a problem of human rights seen simply from the point of view of individual freedom. As I see it, the real danger that threatens the Christian churches of the so-called first world—above all in confrontation with Soviet totalitarianism—is that they may try to provide a religious guarantee for the capitalist economic order of the West that will inevitably favor an increasing imbalance between North and South.

No religion which claims to be struggling to promote human rights can, however, remain deaf to the universal cry of the poor. For a population of some four billion people, it has been estimated that there are at present at least eight hundred million in the world suffering from malnutrition. The churches of the first world are fortunately beginning to hear the challenge of the churches of the third world.[12] The churches of the West must also be ready to be challenged by Islam, insofar as that religion takes up the cause of all the oppressed in the developing countries. I would not hesitate to say that one of the historical responsibilities of the monotheistic religions is to work toward a situation in which the rights of the individual are not dissociated from man's social rights and to contribute toward the setting up of a new world economic order.

As we have already seen, the United Nations' Universal Declaration of Human Rights of 1948 was completed on December 16, 1966 by the International Pact on Economic, Social and Cultural Rights. This was an important step, principally because it took seriously the social aspects of human rights, but it is only too well known that, in the structural situation of injustice in the world today, it is not enough simply to proclaim formal rights, such as the right of peoples to self-determination, the right to work, the right to form trade unions, the right to strike, the right to social security, the right to a suitable standard of living and the right to education. What, then, is to be done?

Going beyond the charitable aid in which the churches of the first world play a generous part, we have to act on the economic and political structures which have as one of their direct consequences the violation of human rights in the case of millions of people. It would not, however, be wrong to say that the world religions have very little chance of influencing the international economic order.

Everything, then, must begin with the work of conscientization. In this sphere, the great monotheistic religions have an urgent responsibility. They can stir the bad conscience of the leading political figures, that it is up to those who hold power in the rich countries and those who hold neo-colonial power in many of the poor countries. Surely the vocation of the great religions which claim to represent God the liberator and Creator of man in his own image is to become the spokesman of all the oppressed peoples of the world and the voice of those without a voice.

To conclude this study of the development of the Catholic Church in the matter of human rights, I would like to suggest the idea of an ecumenical apprenticeship of the concrete implications of human rights between the three great religions. Rather than continuing in a satisfied state in our history of mutual intolerance, we should learn how to decipher the signs of the times together and how to let ourselves be taught together by the Spirit who speaks to us from the history of the world and the development of human societies.

In this, we must, of course, respect the different modalities of interpretation of human rights on the basis of our own religious traditions. But we also have a duty to work toward an effective realization of that fundamental and universal form of human rights that will integrate the three essential elements of freedom, equality and participation and of which the best guarantee is faith in the one God.

The great changes that have taken place in the modern world have already led me to reflect about faith and tradition and faith and science. At the end of the twentieth century, however, the struggle conducted by all men of good will to promote human rights has invited me to think very seriously about the essential link between monotheistic faith and justice.

Chapter XIV

REINTERPRETING THE CHURCH'S MISSION

As so often happens in the history of the Church, life subject to the action of the Holy Spirit goes ahead of thought. Although there is—rightly—a good deal of talk about a "new age of the Church's mission," we still have no theology of the mission that is perfectly homogeneous with the missionary practice of the Church as it can be observed in the missionary territories. But that practice is itself a theological place, and Christian thought must take it very seriously into consideration in its efforts to renew our understanding of the mission on the basis of Scripture and the most recent documents of the magisterium. (The most important of those documents are the Decree *Ad Gentes* [AG] promulgated by Vatican II and Paul VI's Apostolic Exhortation *Evangelii Nuntiandi* [EN].)

If we are to renew the theology of the mission, we must begin by questioning ourselves about the Christological and ecclesiological foundations of the earlier theology of the mission. It would be advisable, then, to examine critically the theology of the redemption and that of the history which underlay the most lasting of the practices characterizing missionary activity. It is not possible for me even to attempt to outline such a renewed theological synthesis here, and in its absence I shall have to be content in the pages that follow to do no more than set out a few of the reflections that I have had about the orientations that are, in my view, most characteristic of the Church's missionary practice today.

1. THE VOCABULARY OF THE MISSION
AND EVANGELIZATION

1. The word "mission" means the sending of the Church to the world. The word "evangelization" means the "proclamation" (by word and example) of the good news to the nations. Keeping to the strict sense of the words, it is possible to say that the word "mission" has a wider meaning

than "evangelization." Beyond the fundamental task of evangelization, the Church's mission includes the whole of its pastoral and sacramental activity as well as its various ways of serving man in the sense of the Gospel.

2. The word "mission" is theologically very rich. It takes us back not only to the visible missions of the Son and the Spirit, but also to the intimate life of the living God. As the Decree *Ad Gentes* stressed, the Church's missionary vocation is not based exclusively on Christ's positive mandate. It is also founded on the initial sending of the Father. The Church, then, is missionary from its origin and by its very nature. Its mission has to be understood within a dynamic movement that is much wider—that of the Father's love for the world.[1]

3. The use of the word "mission" to denote the evangelizing activity of the Church goes back no earlier than the seventeenth century. This means that it tends to denote the missionary activity that is reserved for a body of "specialist" priests or religious who are sent into distant pagan countries. This coincides with the creation of the Roman Congregation *De Propaganda Fidei* (1622).[2] The privilege of evangelizing the newly discovered countries or those still to be discovered thus became the exclusive monopoly of the Roman See.

4. The Second Vatican Council witnessed the great change that had taken place in the Church's missionary consciousness since the end of the Second World War.[3] This change can be summarized as follows. On the one hand, it was the whole Church that was now concerned with the mission. In 1965, the Council's Decree *Ad Gentes* declared that all the bishops and, with them, all the local churches were "collegially" responsible for the evangelization of the world. (In 1967, this development was taken a step further, when the Congregation for the Propagation of the Faith became the Congregation for the Evangelization of the Peoples.)

On the other hand, the Church was declared to be in a state of mission everywhere, that is to say, not only in the so-called "missionary" countries, but also in the countries of the Christian world. The "space of mission" was defined, then, less by territory than by the "world" to which the Church had been sent and, as a pagan world, that world was to be found not only in a nation or a social and cultural environment, but also in the heart of every man.

So, because of the territorial associations of the word "mission" and its historical link with the process of colonization, it is the word "evangelization" that tends to prevail in the Church's most recent documents. This is particularly the case with the Exhortation *Evangelii Nuntiandi*. In that document, however, it does not simply point to the proclamation of the good news. It also includes all the missionary tasks of the Church that can in any way be embraced within the service of the Gospel.

5. A very rich theology of testimony can be found in the New Testament, but there is nothing in it that could be called a "theology of the mission" in the modern sense of the word.[4] Testimony is an inner demand made by the dynamism of faith. "I believed and so I spoke" (2 Cor 4:13). Testimony consists first and foremost of the "kerygmatic" proclamation, in other words, the direct and public announcement of God's plan to save all men in Jesus.

In the Acts of the Apostles in particular, however, there is also another form of evangelization other than preaching—that of the testimony of the believer's life. It would seem that the conversion of non-Christians resulted as much from the quality of the Christians' lives as from their preaching (see Acts 5:12–16; cf. Mission and Evangelism [ME] 3, the preparatory document for the Assembly of the World Council of Churches at Vancouver, July 1983).

In the First Epistle of Peter, the axis of the testimony is not so much that of the kerygma as that of good works or, rather, that "good conduct" (*agatopoiein*) that is related to the day of the Lord's coming: "Maintain good conduct among the Gentiles, so that, in case they speak against you as wrongdoers, they may see your good deeds and glorify God on the day of visitation" (2 Pet 2:12).

Even though it is necessary to make a distinction between them, then, preaching and the testimony of Christian life were never opposed to each other. What is more, according to the most current usage, "Christian witness" tends to point both to the explicit proclamation of the Gospel and to good works done in the name of that Gospel.[5]

2. MISSION AS THE VOCATION
OF THE WHOLE CHURCH

1. "The Church is entirely missionary. The work of evangelization is a fundamental duty of the people of God" (AG 3, cited in EN 59). In the light of *Lumen Gentium*, the Church is defined not as a *societas perfecta*, but as the people of God, a community in a state of tension on an exodus toward the kingdom. This means that it has an essential relationship with the world and that the historical situation of the world profoundly conditions the Church's consciousness of its mission. No attempt to characterize the situation of the modern world can overlook the process of secularization that has accompanied technological civilization from the time that it has tended to become a world-wide phenomenon. In the same way, the growing gap between the poor countries of the southern hemisphere and the rich ones of the northern hemisphere on the one hand and, on the

other, the threat of nuclear destruction hanging over the future of mankind also have to be taken into consideration.

2. The Second Vatican Council gave great emphasis to episcopal collegiality. This allowed a clearer distinction to be made between the universal Church and the particular churches. In addition to this, as the colonial era was coming to an end, each Church became more conscious of its own responsibility. It is, in other words, no longer Rome which sends out and controls all the missions. It is rather the college of bishops united at Rome or each bishop (in Africa, Asia or elsewhere) in his own territory. Even the countries only recently evangelized have a missionary vocation and are able to send out missionaries to other churches. (This process can be observed taking place now in Africa and Asia. A church is not fully missionary if it only thinks of its mission as something internal. Every church must open itself to a mission outside itself. The time has come for us to cease speaking of the churches of Europe and the United States as "mother churches" and the younger churches of the so-called "missionary territories" as "daughter churches." All the churches are sister churches, sharing the responsibility for the evangelization of the world with each other.

3. In the present situation of the world, it is not possible to dissociate, within the Church's mission, evangelization from all the tasks carried out in the service of man's liberation and the promotion of human rights.[6] A response to the call made by the God who loves all men cannot be simply an acceptance into the Church of the greatest possible number of individuals and peoples. The Church ought not to be regarded simply as the people of those who have been brought together by the word in Jesus Christ. It should rather be seen as the sacrament of God's presence with the whole of mankind. Its mission can be summarized by saying, in the words of M.-D. Chenu, that it consists essentially of making the Gospel incarnate in time. This means that, both in our proclamation of Jesus Christ and in our going beyond explicitly proclaiming him, we have to work toward the transformation of man in the sense of the Gospel. In other words, the Church does not exist for itself. It is above all at the service of all men with the kingdom of God in view.

4. All the churches, conscious of their catholicity, are together responsible for the universal mission of the Church. Within each local Church, all members are called to evangelize by their words and actions. In union with their bishop, priests are responsible in a special way for the ministry of evangelization entrusted by Jesus Christ to his Church. Whether with or without a special ministry of this kind, however, all lay people are responsible for evangelization, although their activity can never be reduced to the carrying out of purely temporal tasks. It is, however, still true that, by virtue of their commitment to the world, they have a

special duty not only to bear testimony to Jesus Christ by the whole of their lives, but also to make the Gospel incarnate in the structures of modern society and in the new spaces of the contemporary world (EN 70).

There is ample evidence everywhere in the Church today that evangelization is connected in a very special way to the testimony borne by a Christian community. It has to be welcomed as one of the striking signs of the times that the Church is being reborn, especially in Africa and Latin America, in such basic communities.[7] This phenomenon invites us to go beyond a certain ecclesiocentrism and Christocentrism and to give much greater emphasis to the pneumatic dimension of the Church.[8]

5. Confronted with the challenges of the modern world, a divided Christianity is a permanent obstacle to the work of evangelization entrusted to the Church by Christ. According to Christ's own words, it is the sign of the unity of all Christians which is the most effective means of evangelization: "That they may all be one, even as thou, Father, art in me and I in thee, that they also may be in us, so that the world may believe that thou hast sent me" (Jn 17:21).

This unity is a very special demand made by the Church's mission in the world, and both the Catholic Church and the World Council of Churches have spoken of it again and again. Both the Third General Assembly of the Synod of Bishops and Pope Paul VI in his encyclical *Evangelii Nuntiandi* (EN 77) insisted that we should "collaborate more resolutely with our Christian brethren with whom we are not yet united by a perfect communion, by basing ourselves on baptism and the patrimony of faith that we have in common, in such a way that we shall be able from now on, in the same work of evangelization, to bear testimony together and more widely to Christ in the world."

It has also always been the aim of the World Council of Churches to promote this visible unity: "The present ecumenical movement came into being out of the conviction of the churches that the division of Christians is a scandal and impediment to the witness of the Church. There is a growing awareness among the churches today of the inextricable relationship between Christian unity and missionary calling, between ecumenism and evangelization. 'Evangelization is the test of our ecumenical vocation.' "[9]

It should be added here that that cause of Christian unity is all the more urgent as the indigenization of Christianity progresses and frequently favors a multiplication of evangelical or national churches among the peoples of Africa or Asia who have recently acquired national independence.

3. INCULTURATION AS A DEMAND OF EVANGELIZATION

(1) Incarnation and Inculturation

The future of Christianity is clearly going to lie more and more at the present time, that is, the end of the twentieth century, in continents other than Europe. That future will, moreover, also depend more and more on the ability of the Church to abandon its past practice of either ignoring the non-Western cultures or imposing on them the uniform pattern of a Christianity that is too exclusively conditioned by a Mediterranean culture and to evangelize and give life to them. We have therefore to speak in this context, in the words of the 1977 Synod of Bishops, of a true "incarnation of faith" in those cultures.

The inculturation of Christianity can be seen as a consequence of the incarnation of the Word of God in the manhood of Jesus (see above, Chapter X). This is, however, no more than an analogy, the interest of which is to insist on the fact that the Gospel has to assume different cultures without compromising its identity. The chief limitation of this comparison comes from the fact that it is difficult to say what we understand by the word "Christianity." Do we mean the original Christian message? Or do we mean the historical form of Christianity as it has developed in the Eastern or the Latin Church?

Ever since its first beginnings, Christianity has had to assume the particular form of a given culture. That is why the encounter both now and in the past between Christianity and various cultures has always taken the form of a collision between two cultures. It is entirely a question of knowing whether the "strangeness" of the Christian message comes from the paradox of the Gospel itself or from the special cultural vehicle with which it is historically associated.

(2) Inculturation and Adaptation

The inculturation of Christianity in new cultures of necessity leads to a critical distinction being made within the Church between the substantial elements of the Christian message and Christian practice and the contingent forms that Christianity has assumed at certain times in its history. At the present time, that is, the end of the twentieth century, Western Christianity is for the first time no longer the dominant historical model of Christian thinking and living. In the light of other cultures, anthropologies, attitudes, ways of thinking and spiritual traditions, the Church must recognize the legitimacy of a theological, liturgical and ethical pluralism. Far from compromising the unanimity of faith within the same Church of Jesus Christ, that pluralism is a demand made by its catholicity.

Inculturation as a demand of incarnation in a culture is different from a superficial adaptation to certain archaic elements of a given culture.[10] In certain countries in Africa or Asia that are changing rapidly and drastically, the effort made by the Church to become indigenized may favor the survival of outmoded cultural forms and a social and political irresponsibility on the part of Christians. The emergence of an African, Japanese or Chinese form of Christianity can never be the work of foreign missionaries. It will always be the creation—in the Spirit of Christ—by the local churches themselves of different historical forms of the same Christianity.

The movement of inculturation of Christianity of necessity always coincides with a certain "Christianization of one or other existing culture." This expression is, however, very ambiguous, since it calls to mind certain models of "Christianity" or "Christian humanism" that are open to criticism. It is far better to speak in this context of the critical and purifying function of the Gospel with regard to the pagan and anti-human elements of a culture. The Gospel should normally assume all the positive values of a given culture, especially if it is borne in mind that in Africa or Asia cultural values cannot be dissociated from the values of a great religious tradition.

The inculturation of Christianity is a task that has to be approached gradually and tentatively. It cannot be entrusted exclusively to theologians, moralists, historians or specialists of any kind. It has to take place in the everyday existence of the Christian community. In the many different exchanges of family and social life, Christians can show that it is possible to reconcile their Christian identity with their ethnic, cultural, linguistic and national identity.

(3) The Inter-Religious Dialogue

In its missionary task, the Church has to deal today not only with the challenge of non-Western cultures, but also with that of the great non-Christian religions. What marks the new age of mission since Vatican II as quite distinctive is both a new vision of the possibilities of salvation outside the Church and a new theological understanding of the lasting character of the great non-Christian religions within God's providential plan. Catholic theologians have abandoned the theology of the salvation of the pagan peoples based on their belonging to the visible Church as the only means of salvation. They have recently preferred to develop a theology of accomplishment, according to which Christ is at work in all religions as the final consummation of the human search for salvation.[11]

In that context, what finalizes the Church's missionary activity is less the will to convert the "other person" and more the proclamation in words and actions that the kingdom of God has come in Jesus Christ. In the mission to people belonging to other religions, the demands made by a true dialogue have to be fully respected. The conclusion should not, however, be drawn that those demands make it any less urgent to bear testimony to Jesus Christ as the source of our hope and our service of our fellow men. We can abandon the word "mission" insofar as it is too evocative of a certain form of proselytism, but we cannot simply replace the word "testimony" with the word "dialogue." In the various tasks of evangelization carried out in the service of the integral liberation of man, the Church always bears testimony to Jesus Christ as the life of the world.

That dialogue is not simply a demand that the other person's freedom should be respected in a period of history which has learned the lesson of tolerance. It is more than that. It is a demand that God's mysterious ways of acting in men's hearts should also be respected. From the very beginning of history, no man has ever been deprived of the help of God's grace. Outside the visible Church, God's Spirit is also at work in the hearts of men who are looking for salvation while remaining faithful to their own religious traditions. We have therefore to respect the spiritual destiny of every human being who is able to respond to his eternal vocation in the presence of God.

Faithfulness to one's own truth and openness to being questioned by the other person together form the condition of all authentic dialogue. That dialogue is always a risky adventure that does not set any conditions at the beginning. It may therefore lead to a "celebration of the truth" that goes beyond the partial point of view of each interlocutor. In the experience of dialogue, I may be able to discover that I cannot verify in my life the truth to which I am appealing and the other person may be led to do the truth in his life. Proselytism always consists in wanting at all costs to constrain the other to embrace my own conviction without respecting his own vocation. In the case of a true dialogue about a given religion as the one way of salvation for man, we are always "stewards" of a truth that goes beyond us.

In the present context of inter-religious dialogue, all the great world religions, partly under the historical influence of the universalist claim of Christianity, want to be regarded as "absolutes" that incorporate everything that is good, true and noble in the other religions. Hence the temptation to "syncretism," which is certainly not a merely illusory danger for Christianity.

Christianity is rather invited to manifest its universal vocation, that is to say, its catholicity, by fully accepting its special historical dimension in faithfulness to the "scandal" of God's becoming man in Jesus of Nazareth. We have to go beyond the triumphalism of a Christian universalism which may not have claimed to include all of the explicit values of the other religions, but has certainly claimed to lead them to their perfection.

In this context, we should not confuse the universality of Jesus Christ as the only mediator between God and men with the universality of the Christian religion as an historical phenomenon. The great non-Christian religions are questioning the Church of Christ and inviting it to make its own identity and the originality of the salvation of which it is the promise manifest in better and better ways. It is precisely insofar as he is Jesus of Nazareth that Christ is Lord of the world, and it is precisely insofar as it is a special message about God and man that the Gospel is good news for all men.[12]

We have therefore to bear testimony to the universality of salvation in Jesus Christ among those who belong to religions other than Christianity. At the same time, however, we have to respect the special approaches that are the consequence of the destiny of every human being to whom God's grace and Spirit may, in the situation in which he finds himself, make an appeal. Respect for persons is one of the essential demands made by evangelical love. According to the teaching of Vatican II on religious freedom, "man has the duty and therefore the right to seek the truth in matters religious . . . through the mediation of his conscience. In all his activity, a man is bound to follow his conscience faithfully. . . . It follows that he is not to be forced to act in a manner contrary to his conscience" (*Dignitatis humanae* 3).

It cannot be denied that the word "mission" has a certain triumphalist association. As I have pointed out, there has been a tendency to replace it with the word "dialogue," as though a more optimistic theology of the mediations of salvation outside the Church might lead us to regard the mission as less urgent. This attitude, however, is the result of a narrow, legalistic and ecclesiocentric conception of mission.[13] The texts of Vatican II affirm both the possibilities of salvation that are offered to men who are ignorant of the Gospel (see especially *Lumen Gentium* 16) and the need for the Church's mission. In the Decree on the Church's Missionary Activity, *Ad Gentes* 7, for example, we read: "Therefore, though God in ways known to himself can lead those inculpably ignorant of the Gospel to that faith without which it is impossible to please him (Heb 11:6), yet a necessity lies upon the Church (see 1 Cor 9:16), and at the same time a sacred duty, to preach the Gospel. Hence missionary activity today as always retains its power and necessity."

It is, then, certainly not enough to say that the mission *ad gentes* should be limited to a discernment of the implicitly Christian values contained in one or other religion or culture and consequently that it should be restricted to a respect for and a deeper understanding of those values. Testimony borne to the Gospel—by our words and actions—should normally lead to a questioning and possibly even to a conversion. That conversion, however, coincides with a new creation which, without destroying them, gives a new value to the intrinsic riches of every cultural and religious tradition. We have, in other words, to learn how to articulate the name of Christian in the plural.

The great non-Christian religions often display a new vitality when this happens. This invites us to reflect both about the place of the different religions in the one history of salvation and about the originality of Christianity as a religion. The relationship between very early Christianity and Judaism can help us to understand this situation.

The new covenant inaugurated by Christ did not lead immediately to a new form of cult, a new priesthood or new temples. In the ethical order, Christ's message was rather a radicalization of what had been contained in an embryonic form in the Jewish law as the law of love. The radical newness is summed up in the event of Jesus Christ himself with all that was new in what he brought in his relationship with God and others. The urgency of the mission to the Gentiles led to a critical distinction being made between certain elements of Judaism and the message of Christ himself. As I pointed out in Chapter X, it is possible to think that Jesus was not conscious that he was founding a new "religion" in the strict sense of the term. This is tantamount to saying that Christian existence cannot be defined *a priori*. Christianity exists wherever the Spirit of Christ makes a new being of individual and collective man arise.

(4) The Church as the Sacrament of Salvation

The co-existence of Christianity with non-Christian religions invites us to go beyond a narrow ecclesiocentrism, according to which the only meaning of the mission is to increase the number of those who are affiliated to the visible Church. It is wrong to regard the Church of which men speak and the Church which God sees as identical. All men receive the same vocation from the Creator, and the whole of mankind is involved in a collective history which God has made into a history of salvation.

Christ is the Word enlightening every man coming into this world. This means that we cannot allow our conception of the history of salvation to remain purely chronological. In the ontological order, what comes first is Christ as the "new Adam." It is he who gives meaning to the pre-Christian religious history of mankind and to its post-Christian history. (See above, Chapter X.)

What is said about Christ as the incarnate Word must also be said about the Spirit of the risen Christ. There is a history of the Spirit which cannot be contained within the framework of the history of Israel and the history of the Church or even within that of the history of the great world religions. Within the order of representations at least, we are held captive by a linear conception of the history of salvation, of which we think of Christ as the end, but at the same time as looking forward to a new departure. There is a danger that the Judaeo-Christian emphasis of a certain type of Western theology will make us think that the Christian religion is a simple expansion of the Jewish religion.

A rediscovery of the ontological rather than the historicist conception of the history of salvation which speaks of an economy of the mystery of God in Christ and in the Spirit is certainly very desirable. This would seek to penetrate the "mystery hidden for ages in God" (Eph 3:9) which aroused Paul's admiration. Because there were no longer any descendants of Abraham according to the flesh, Paul was able to speak to the Athenians about their "unknown God" and tell them: "What you worship as unknown, this I proclaim to you" (Acts 17:23). It was also when Jesus told the Samaritan woman that "salvation is from the Jews" that he was able to speak prophetically about "worshiping the Father in spirit and truth" (Jn 4:22–23), in other words, that he could prophesy the coming of the Spirit who would make all narrowly confessional cult null and void both in Jerusalem and on Mount Garizim.

This conception of the history of salvation is quite consistent with an ecclesiology which, in the tradition of Vatican II, insists that the Church is the sacrament of salvation for the nations.[14] Visibly belonging to the Church of Christ, vouched for by confessing the same creed and communion with the eucharistic body of the Lord, may be the sacrament of invisibly belonging to Christ which cannot be contained within the framework of the visible Church and which may coincide with belonging to other great non-Christian religions or even with supporting secular ideologies.

The Church's mission which extends the mission of Christ is universal. It is concerned with every man who is created in the image of God. Even the most profound awareness today of the special historical character of Christianity cannot diminish the importance of the universal mission of the Church in any way. We have, however, a better theological understanding of the fact that the universal mission of the Church does not depend on the absolute character of Christianity as an historical religion.[15] As an historical reality, the Church has no monopoly of the signs of the kingdom. Grace is offered to all men along paths known only to God himself. God is greater than all the historical signs by means of which he has manifested his presence.

242

4. THE EVANGELIZATION OF THE POOR
AS THE CRITERION OF THE AUTHENTICITY
OF THE CHURCH'S MISSION

1. The aim of the whole of the Church's mission is to "hasten the coming of the kingdom of God." One of the signs of that coming is the proclamation of the good news to the poor. Jesus proclaimed the Gospel of the kingdom to the poor and called prisoners to the freedom of the God who was coming.[16]

Luke sums up Jesus' mission in words taken from Isaiah 61:1–2: "The spirit of the Lord is upon me, because he has anointed me to preach good news to the poor. He has sent me to proclaim release to captives and recovering of sight to the blind, to set at liberty those who are oppressed, to proclaim the acceptable year of the Lord" (Lk 4:18–19).

Making use of Isaiah 35:5 and 61:1f, Matthew puts this reply to those sent by John the Baptist into the mouth of Jesus: "The blind receive their sight and the lame walk, lepers are cleansed and the deaf hear and the dead are raised up and the poor have good news preached to them. And blessed is he who takes no offense at me" (Mt 11:5f).

In the Old Testament, God's law is at the service of man's law. Despising the poor, the oppressed, the widows and orphans is violating God's law. God is not only the source of all that is right—he is also the one who opposes the powerful and stands up for the most deprived. Jesus' preaching of the kingdom of God only takes to its ultimate conclusions the messianic promise of liberation. That liberation is a definitive one which goes beyond death and in which God will do justice to all men, but it is also a liberation which begins here on this earth in the sense of establishing equality and fraternity among men.

Jesus, then, is the messianic liberator who, in the name of God's law, defends the weak, the oppressed and the poor.[17] What is more, it is clear from the accounts in the Gospels that Jesus' commitment to the "least of the brethren," those who were marginalized or outside the law and the publicans and sinners, deeply scandalized the just. It was precisely this subversive attitude that was the immediate cause of his trial and his death on the cross.

2. The Church is no longer subject to the obstacle that had existed for so long because of the historical link between missionary activity and colonial expansion. This means that it is once again free to be a witness to the hopes of the poor. It has often been said that the Church is enjoying a new springtime insofar as it opts for the poor.[18] How could it be otherwise, since the Christian churches have all finally become aware that the need to defend and promote human rights forms an integral part of their

mission? No religion that claims to struggle for human rights can remain deaf to the universal cry of the poor in our modern world, in which the gap between the rich and the poor countries is so clearly widening.

The countries of the third world, which were in the past colonized by the "Christian" countries, are now committed to the patient task of gaining their independence, their identity and their dignity. The local churches of those countries therefore cannot preach the good news of the kingdom of God that is coming without standing up for the most deprived of men and opposing the injustice of the international economic powers or the neo-colonial forces. Thanks to the testimony borne by the Christian communities, the kingdom of God is already being anticipated and made concrete in the historical liberation of men and women in those countries. That is why, as I have already observed, it is not very meaningful, in the evangelization of the masses of poor people, to try to maintain at all costs the earlier dichotomies that existed between "evangelization" and "social action."

In Latin America especially, the evangelization of the masses takes place in the perspective of a preferential option for the poor, being carried out from the level of the basic communities. Simply to speak about a mission among the poor is not enough. It has to be called "a mission of the poor for the poor." It is the poor themselves who proclaim and manifest the presence of the kingdom of God by their solidarity, their love for each other, their trusting prayer and their hope in their time of testing. It is therefore possible, in the case of Latin America as in the case of the primitive Church, to speak of a Church that is being born or reborn from the level of the poor. The Puebla conference was therefore able to speak quite legitimately of the "evangelizing potential of the poor" (No. 1147).[19]

3. The evangelization of the poor by the poor is a "sign of the times" for the universal Church. At present, the churches of the third world are challenging the churches of the first world. It is not simply that an appeal is being made to the generosity of Christians in the rich countries for their most deprived brethren. It is much more than this. It is an invitation to be converted made to the whole Church, which must always "commemorate" the identification of Jesus with the poor, the deprived and those without a voice in this world. The poor are God's privileged questioners and they are addressing God's Word to the whole Church and to all the churches.

In so doing, they are reminding the churches that the proclamation of the kingdom of God coincides with a rejection of all attempts to give an absolute value to human power, whether it is political power or the power of a privileged race, people or social class. They are in this way inviting the churches to reject all compromise with political or economic power and to be quite free in accomplishing their mission. The churches of the first world have the special task of questioning political leaders, appealing to their conscience and urging them to change the political and economic structures that result in violating the rights of millions of human beings.

4. The Church is sent to all men. Its mission is not confined simply to those who are poor in the economic sense. The concept "poor" in the Gospel points to a state of dependence. This means that poverty is, in the evangelical sense, economic, social and physical poverty as well as psychical, moral and religious poverty. It would seem that two extremes have to be avoided. On the one hand, evangelical "poverty" should not be limited to its religious sense, that is, understood simply as a state of dependence on and openness to God, and, on the other, it should not be seen exclusively as economic and physical poverty.

It certainly points to slavery and dehumanization in all its dimensions.[20] Those who live in the prosperous consumer societies of the West experience the death of God and are made spiritually dull by their environment, which is dominated by profit, sex, drugs and alcohol. They are also poor and are in need of the liberating words of the Gospel. The churches of the third world and especially those of Latin America are very conscious of this and of their missionary responsibility with regard to the people living without God in countries which were Christianized at an earlier date. (This is clear from the conference of bishops, priests and religious of eight Latin American countries, who met at Lima in February 1981 to reflect and talk about the present missionary responsibility of Latin American Christians.)

It would therefore not be wrong to say that the liberating words of the Gospel are addressed to all men, both rich and poor, who are enslaved to sin and dehumanization of any kind. This does not in any way call into question the priority of the Church's mission to the poor, that is, the oppressed, the deprived and those without a voice. Those who criticize the expression "preferential option for the poor" should not forget that it is not simply concerned with the political, social and economic situation of injustice in the contemporary world. It also has an ecclesiological basis.[21]

Ubi Christus, ibi Ecclesia. As I have attempted to show in a preceding chapter (IX), the true Church is not simply present where the community of believers is brought together to listen to the Word of God and to commemorate the Lord's Supper. It is also present in the assembly of the least of the brethren insofar as they are a special and privileged presence of Christ. The two statements made by the Lord cannot and should not be separated from each other: "He who hears you hears me" (Lk 10:16) and "He who visits you visits me" (see Mt 25:36).

Brotherhood with Christ through the Word and the sacrament should not, then, be opposed to brotherhood with him through the presence of the poor. The Church is present in a state of mission wherever Christ is waiting for it in the mystery of the deprived, the sick and the oppressed. That is the full meaning of the eschatological judgment pronounced in Matthew 25:31–46: "As you did it to one of the least of these my brethren, you did it to me." The hidden presence of the judge of this world in the "least of the brethren" is a criterion that judges the authenticity of our commitment to the mission and the evangelical quality of our communities.

More than ever before, the Church has to appear now as the universal sacrament of salvation acquired in Jesus Christ beyond the diversity of races, cultures and civilizations. The Church's universality should in no sense be abstract. On the contrary, it has to bear testimony to a completely concrete brotherhood with all men. It would not be wrong to say that the Church becomes universal insofar as it takes up the universal causes of the human community throughout the whole of the earth and insofar as it struggles today for human rights and puts itself at the service of the poor.

5. PROMOTING HUMAN RIGHTS
AS A DEMAND MADE BY THE GOSPEL

1. I have taken this title from Paul VI who, in his message in union with the fathers of the 1974 Synod of Bishops, declared that the Church "believes . . . firmly that the promotion of human rights is a demand made by the Gospel and that it must occupy a central place in its ministry" (DC 1664 [1974], p. 965). In their final declaration, the fathers stated: "Driven by the charity of Christ and illuminated by the light of the Gospel, we are confident that the Church, working more faithfully at evangelization, will proclaim man's total salvation or his complete liberation and will, from now onward, also begin to achieve it" (DC 1664 [1974], p. 964).

As I pointed out above, these texts invite us to go further than simply make a contrast between evangelization and social action in the service of man. It is quite legitimate to claim that, in the Church's more recent documents, the word "evangelization" tends to include the whole of the activity of the Church as sent to the world, from its charitable and social action to its proclamation of the Gospel within the eucharistic assembly. Even if it is clear that man's eschatological salvation should not be confused with his historical liberation, it is very remarkable that the fathers of the 1974 Synod on evangelization insisted on the "mutual relationships existing between evangelization and the integral salvation or complete liberation of men and peoples."

2. The theology of mission depends to a very great extent on a theology of salvation. What, then, we may ask, was the conception of salvation underlying the missionary activity of the sixteenth century which was based essentially on the need to "deliver souls from eternal damnation" or "to bring into the Catholic Church the greatest possible number of newly baptized souls"?

The theology of mission is also determined by a theology of history. Is it necessary, then, to identify the history of salvation with profane history or do we at least have to show that they are convergent? For more than thirty years now, theological articles have been appearing that range from an "evolutionary optimism" to an "apocalyptic pessimism." (See above, Chapter IX.) A very fair critical assessment of these various tendencies will be found in the Declaration on the Promotion of Human Rights and Christian Salvation made by the International Theological Commission (DC 1726 [1977], pp. 761–768).

I lack the space in this short penultimate chapter to show that a better understanding of Christian salvation and the history of salvation is gradually renewing the theology of mission. All I can do here is to make use of *Evangelii Nuntiandi* and the Vancouver document *Mission and Evangelism* to show how greatly our present understanding of mission has been conditioned by the Church's new consciousness of its historical responsibility with regard to the structure of our societies and the future of man. This new consciousness, moreover, cannot be separated from the historical turning point represented by Vatican II in the Church's attitude toward the Declaration of Human Rights. After more than a century of misunderstandings, partly attributable to the "laicist" context within which those rights were made explicit in the nineteenth century, the Catholic Church has become, in the last quarter of the twentieth century, the foremost champion of human rights. Human rights—including the right to religious freedom—are not simply tolerated by the Church. They have become, according to Paul VI, a "demand made by the Gospel." (See above, Chapter XIII.)

3. To affirm that defending and promoting human rights is a demand made by the Gospel is to admit that it is impossible to separate evangelization from the promotion of human rights within the one mission of the Church. In his Exhortation *Evangelii Nuntiandi*, Paul VI pointed to intimate bonds between the two and made a distinction between links of an anthropological, a theological and an evangelical order: "Links of an anthropological order because man to be evangelized is not an abstract being, but is the subject of social and economic questions. Links of a theological order because it is not possible to dissociate the plan of creation from the plan of redemption which reaches concrete situations of injustice

to be combatted and of justice to be restored. Links of that eminently evangelical order which is that of charity: how, in fact, can the new commandment be proclaimed without promoting in justice and peace the true and authentic growth of man?" (EN 31).

This can be developed a little further by reflecting about the relationships between the Church and the world. Three aspects of the question can be considered in this context:

(a) The world is more than merely the framework within which the kingdom of God is built up. It has an immanent meaning in itself.

All the wealth of meaning that is contained in the word "world" in the Fourth Gospel should be retained in this consideration of the relationships between the Church and the world. The word "world" can, for example, denote the world of sin which refuses to welcome the Word. At the same time, however, it can also mean both the first creation in the good that it contains as God's gift and mankind itself insofar as it is called to be reconciled with God.

When we speak of the relationships between the Church and the world, then, "world" is primarily understood in this third sense, that is, as the historical world called to reconciliation with God. As historical, the world as world remains ambiguous. It bears within itself the temptation to be self-sufficient. In the past, the word "world" pointed in the language of Christian spirituality above all to a negative reality. Today, however, the Church recognizes that it may denote the collective human plan (cf. the gradual explicitation of the fundamental rights of the human person), which is different from the eschatological plan to which the Church is the witness, but which is a legitimate plan that does not necessarily coincide with a plan of self-sufficiency.

(b) The building up of the world does not directly result in the kingdom of God.

The liberation of man and the promotion of human rights at the level of history are different from the communion of men with God in a transhistorical future. All relationship of cause to effect between the historical struggles for man's liberation and eschatological salvation must be excluded. Even if profane history and the history of salvation are inseparable, history itself is not the effective sacrament of the coming of the kingdom of God. As M.-D. Chenu pointed out many years ago, "grace is grace and history is not the source of salvation."[22] And, according to the International Commission of Theology, "the kingdom of God" guides "history and in an absolute manner goes beyond all the possibilities of its fulfillment on earth." That is precisely why evangelization, as the explicit proclamation of the salvation acquired in Jesus Christ, has lost none of its urgency.

(c) There is a mysterious link between the historical processes of man's liberation and the realization of the kingdom of God.

In Chapter IX, I quoted this statement made by the third world theologians at their conference in São Paulo in 1980: "The fulfillment of the kingdom as God's ultimate plan for his creation is experienced in the historical processes of human liberation" (No. 33). This takes us back to the idea of a mysterious relationship between the completion of creation by man and the fulfillment of the kingdom of God, without that relationship being expressed visibly at the level of the Church as an institution. Even if the word "convergence" is too strong, we can still speak of a certain continuity between the building up of a more human world in conformity with God's plan and the coming of the kingdom of God.

If we take the Lordship of Christ seriously, it is possible for us to say that each time that man works to heal the first creation and to liberate his fellow men, he is making the energies of the resurrection of Jesus present here and now as the victory over death and all the forces of nothingness. As the sacrament of salvation, then, the Church is the visible sign "for the nations" of a mystery that is much greater than simply the community of the redeemed. It is, in other words, the gratuitous presence of God for the whole of creation and the promise of a definitive liberation for every man.

In any case, if we are alert to that unity existing between the Church and the world in God's total plan for man, it is possible to verify the extent to which it is artificial to want at all costs to define, within the one mission of the Church, the frontiers between the so-called "spiritual" tasks of pure evangelization and the so-called "temporal" tasks of service to one's fellow men. It is, to quote M.-D. Chenu once again, a question of making the Gospel incarnate in time. It cannot, however, be made incarnate simply by bearing explicit testimony to Jesus Christ. It can only be made incarnate by transforming man and society totally in the sense of the Gospel.

CONCLUSION

To conclude these reflections about the most characteristic aspects of the Christian mission, I am bound once again to stress the urgency of that mission now, at the end of the twentieth century.

It is precisely because the Church is the witness to the living and liberating God that it is aware of its historical responsibility with regard to the future of man and always ready to work with all men of good will in the building up of a world which is less inhuman and in which the inalienable rights of every man to freedom, dignity and work are recognized.

The Church's mission, then, is of the order of testimony. It is not limited to the historical and visible bringing together of the greatest possible number of men into the visible Church, as though every man were called to form part of that visible institution in historical time. It is also because the Church is the witness to a hope beyond this world that it is at the same time the witness here on earth to the hope of the poor.

Testimony in the sense of the Gospel is always possible, then, even though the time is not always ripe for clear and explicit words to be spoken about Jesus Christ either in our secularized and pluralist Western societies or in other countries in which another great religion is the dominant religion. It continues to be the testimony borne by the life of each Christian and that borne by the lives of Christian communities. But this making the Gospel incarnate in time on the basis of our decisions and choices, our struggles and self-sacrifices and our solidarity with each other does not in any way lessen the urgency of evangelization in the sense of an explicit testimony borne to Jesus Christ. Or else, whatever the possibilities of salvation may be that are offered to all men of good will, it would be holding cheap the liberating power of the person and the words of Jesus spoken on this earth.

The Church of Christ should not simply be the witness of the demands made in the Gospel for justice. It should also be the witness to the kingdom which is to come and which coincides with the total salvation of man. Our contemporaries are in fact not only looking for justice, bread and love. They are desperately in need of meaning, and those who have responsibility for the mission of the Church should reveal to all men who are in search of reasons for living the name of their hope—Jesus Christ.

Epilogue

THE SILENCE AND PROMISES
OF FRENCH THEOLOGY

Now that I have come to the end of these essays on theological hermeneutics, I would like, by way of a conclusion, to situate my own en-
deavors within the framework of the present movement of French
theology. In the first place, this will give me the opportunity to express
my indebtedness to the many authors to whom I owe so much. At the same
time, however, it will also enable me to make clear what is at stake in a
certain style of French theology which aims to provide a better understanding of what is implied today by faith.

It is certainly very difficult to judge the present situation of theology
in France. I am myself too closely involved in the day to day tasks of theology—teaching on the one hand and working as editor of a series of theological books in a publishing house on the other—to be able to stand back
sufficiently and view that situation.

In any case, the theologian only has to leave France and take part in
international conferences to learn that one opinion is very widely shared.
It is that, since Vatican II, French theology no longer has the same international readership as it did before the Council. Many theologians deplore
the silence—or desert—of contemporary French theology. I very well remember an open letter written by Hans Küng to Yves Congar in 1970, in
which the Swiss theologian said: "Between the Second World War and
Vatican II, it was above all French theology which continued to raise its
voice in favor of a renewal of the Church and theology. Why, then, has
there been such a deep silence since the Council?"[1]

I also remember that, when the international review of theology *Concilium* was created in 1965, the only section entrusted to French theologians (who were in fact Christian Duquoc and myself) was that entitled
"spirituality." As the editor of a large series of works of theology too, I have
to admit that, although there is still a great demand for French works of

spirituality abroad, relatively few of our dogmatic or exegetical books are translated into foreign languages. (This applies especially to Germany and the United States.)

A certain amount of light and shade must, however, be added to this first very negative judgment. Some careful observers, who do not judge the value of a theology by the number of best-sellers that it produces, are able to recognize the richness of the various theological currents in France today, many of them subterranean and discreet, but letting us hope for a new spring.[2]

In the first part of this final chapter, I shall try to account for this double phenomenon: the vitality of French theology in the recent past and its apparent sterility today. In the second part, I shall provide an introduction to the most promising contemporary orientations in French theology.

1. FRENCH THEOLOGY YESTERDAY AND TODAY

A. The Vitality of French Theology Before Vatican II

The historians of the Second Vatican Council will undoubtedly say how much the Council owed to French-speaking theologians. In many respects, the Council was a point of arrival. It was a ratification of the great theological renewal that began after the Second World War and French theologians were the best workers in that field.

The "success" of French theology has its place, however, in a much wider context—that of the exuberance of French Catholicism in the immediate post-war period. France as a Republic had inherited a long tradition of anti-clericalism which could not be dissociated from the sacrosanct separation of Church and state, and the post-war religious revival was to a great extent attributable to lay people.

(a) In the first place, we have to acknowledge with gratitude as a new reality in France that, thanks largely to the writings of such great laymen as Charles Péguy, Georges Bernanos, Paul Claudel and François Mauriac, a degree of reconciliation had been achieved between religion and culture. At the same time, in the field of philosophy, a great influence, going far beyond the relatively narrow confines of neo-Thomism, was exerted by such authors as Jacques Maritain and Etienne Gilson. Finally, for many intellectuals who belonged to the scientific world, the name of Pierre Teilhard de Chardin was the symbol both of a reconciliation between science and faith and of a positive attitude on the part of the Church toward the modern world and progress.

(b) Secondly, it has to be pointed out that no one will understand the

French theology of the pre-conciliar period if he underestimates the importance both of the new spirit of Christian militancy in the world and of the militant movements of Catholic Action such as the "Young Christian Workers" (Jeunesse Ouvrière Chrétienne or J.O.C.) and the related J.A.C. and J.E.C. Awareness of the end of a Church of Christianity coincided with a magnificent missionary impulse above all among and directed towards the working class.

The little book written by the Abbés Godin and Daniel—*France, pays de mission*—became the symbol of this new era. The creation of the Mission de France by Cardinal Suhard and the experience of the worker-priests were the two most striking aspects of this new era, in which the Church was no longer enclosed within itself, but was looking urgently for dialogue with the world of unbelievers and secularization. It was also at this time that a lay Christian such as Emmanuel Mounier could, with his team of collaborators in the review *Esprit*, become the theoretician and prophet for the whole of the Church in what Marie-Dominique Chenu called "the end of the Constantinian period."

(c) Finally, this wider context within which French theology operated would be incomplete if I did not include the great figures of a spirituality that can be called a "missionary spirituality." The two most striking are, of course, Thérèse de Lisieux and Charles de Foucauld. Their "spirit" produced thousands of missionary vocations and put France into the first place among the Western countries supplying Catholic missionaries.

Having outlined, however rapidly, this wider framework, I must now try to define why French theology was so original and enjoyed such a high reputation after the Second World War. It is possible, I think, to distinguish three essential elements. They are a return to the sources, an interest in ecclesiology and a pastoral and ecumenical orientation. All three orientations can be found in the great doctrinal texts of the Second Vatican Council.

A Return to the Sources

Post-war French theology was characterized above all by a return to the sources. An attempt was made to break with the scholastic form of theology practiced in the Church since the Counter-Reformation and to rediscover some of the traditional riches that had been forgotten. It is impossible to overemphasize the enormous importance of the biblical, patristic and liturgical renewal that took place in France between 1946 and 1962.

During that period, there were, for example, numerous translations of the Bible, of which I will mention only the one published by the Editions du Cerf—the *Bible de Jérusalem*. The liturgical movement was deeply influenced by what appeared in such journals as *La Maison-Dieu* or series such as *Lex Orandi*. One of the most famous books that appeared in that collection was, for example, Louis Bouyer's *Mystère pascal*. Then there was a return to patristic sources, resulting in the famous collection *Sources chrétiennes*, which was launched by the Editions du Cerf in 1942. The volumes in this series placed the treasures of the patristic period at the disposal of a wide public. In the field of ecclesiology, Yves Congar's collection *Unam Sanctam* enabled many readers to rediscover the riches of a teaching about the Church which was not restricted to that of the Roman school and which was ecumenically very open.

It was, however, precisely this return to the sources that led to conflict between French theologians with the highest reputation and the Roman authority during the pontificate of Pius XII. What was at the time called the "new theology" was the work of the two outstanding post-war French schools of theology—the Jesuit school at Fourvière and the Dominican school of Le Saulchoir. They were in the end criticized for having introduced historical reasoning into dogmatic theology and because their theology had resulted in an historical relativism not only in the case of theological systems, but also in that of the Church's dogmatic pronouncements themselves. Let me give just four examples.

A pupil of Henri de Lubac, Fr. Bouillard, posed the question in his book *Conversion et grâce* (1942) of the historical relativity of Thomism as theology. Unlike the great commentators, Chenu reinterpreted Thomas Aquinas within the framework of a global history reconstructed in its economic, social and ideological mediations. He also rehabilitated symbolic theology, which contrasted sharply with the hitherto prevailing abstract scholastic theology.

Henri de Lubac revived the symbolic exegesis of the patristic and medieval periods and emphasized the deeply sacramental nature of the Church. Yves Congar's strenuous historical studies resulted in his being able to distance himself from the hierarchical ecclesiology of the Counter-Reformation and rediscover an earlier tradition based on Scripture, the Church Fathers and Thomas Aquinas.

Paradoxically, these four men, who were in conflict with Rome because they appealed to an earlier tradition rather than to a more recent tradition, were among the best workers in the doctrinal field of Vatican II. It was the theology of that post-war period in France, because it was more open to the economy of salvation than to an abstract theological study of the "in itself" of the Christian mysteries, that reached its fulfillment in the two great dogmatic Constitutions of Vatican II, *Lumen Gentium* on the Church and *Dei Verbum* on Revelation.

It has in fact been said that the second of these documents in particular marked the end of the Counter-Reformation. It certainly marked the end of a scholastic theology that was purely analytical and deductive. What the Second Vatican Council did was to ratify a new way of doing theology which had been striving for recognition for more than thirty years in France and which aimed to take seriously all the consequences of a conception of Christian revelation understood as the history of salvation and not as a list of revealed statements.[3]

An Interest in Ecclesiology

It is above all in the field of ecclesiology that French theology acquired an international reputation. I have, of course, just mentioned this in connection with the French theologians' "return to the sources." This ecclesiological interest cannot be separated from the vitality of French Catholicism at the time and the problems raised by the emergence of a responsible laity, the calling into question of certain forms of priestly ministry and the ecumenical dialogue. Unlike their Protestant and Catholic German counterparts, the pre-conciliar French theologians did not develop a fundamental theology or a systematic dogmatic theology. There is no equivalent of Karl Barth, Rudolf Bultmann or Karl Rahner in France, or today of Gerhard Ebeling, Jürgen Moltmann, Wolfhart Pannenberg or Ernst Jüngel. In France, it was philosophers such as La Berthonnière and Maurice Blondel who asked the kind of questions that were posed in Germany by fundamental theologians.

Before *Lumen Gentium*, the Catholic Church's ecclesiology was of a full membership type which gave a too exclusive priority to the hierarchical structure of the Church. With *Lumen Gentium*, emphasis was given to a more sacramental conception of the Church as a communio, as the entirely priestly people of God and as the historical becoming of that people of God subject to the action of the Holy Spirit. The conciliar text led to a great number of commentaries in France and Belgium.

Today, greater attention is given in France to the Eastern tradition and that has made us aware of a lack of pneumatology. We are therefore also conscious of the fact that the ecclesiology of Vatican II is too Christomonist. It would, however, be impossible to overemphasize our indebtedness, in this period of post-Tridentine theology, to the influence of such scholars as Henri de Lubac (*Corpus mysticum*), Yves Congar (*Vraie et Fausse Réforme* and *La Théologie du laicat*) and Msgr. Philipps of Louvain.

The Pastoral Orientation

Several of the French theologians were authentically seeking an international reputation. Nonetheless, they did not cut themselves off from their roots and from the most immediate pastoral problems of the Church in France. In this context, it is worth remembering the special status of French theologians, which is quite different from that of their German or Dutch colleagues, who are university teachers and paid by the state. The work of French theologians is therefore inevitably less academic and more pastoral in its orientation.

It is the same theologians who were, like Yves Congar and Marie-Dominique Chenu, the representatives of university theology who were very involved at the grass-roots level in some of the Catholic Action movements or in new initiatives of an apostolic order such as the worker-priest venture.

It should also not be forgotten that pre-conciliar French theology was deeply conditioned by the dialogue with atheism. The French theologians of that time were not simply professional practitioners striving to perfect a theological system for purely internal use within the Church. They were in dialogue with representatives of the unbelieving world, with Marxists and with existentialists (Roger Garaudy, Jean-Paul Sartre and Albert Camus, to name only three) and with lay people who were immersed in the world of unbelief.

The Church had come out of its ghetto and had discovered that it had a great deal to receive from spiritual worlds other than its own, even though they might be atheistic. In that respect, the considerable influence of Teilhard de Chardin on French theology should not be underestimated. Recognition of the world in its autonomy, a certain optimism with regard to the values of a secular culture and a more finely shaded judgment of the moral dimension of certain forms of contemporary atheism were echoed, after all, in the famous Schema XIII which resulted in the Pastoral Constitution on the Church in the Modern World, *Gaudium et Spes*, promulgated at the end of the Second Vatican Council.

B. The Apparent Sterility of French Theology Since the Council

With their colleagues in Belgium and Germany, French theologians were the pioneers of a biblical, liturgical, ecclesiological and ecumenical renewal. This intensive theological work received its ratification at Vatican II. It is beyond dispute that the dogmatic achievement of the Council was above all ecclesiological. That work was both the point of arrival and the point of departure for fundamental ecclesiological research. The areas to be covered included collegiality, the local churches, the Church's ministries, the place of the laity in the Church, the unity of Christians and so on.

It is possible, however, to say that it was the very success of French theology before Vatican II which explains why it has suffered such an eclipse since the Council. That theology was above all ecclesiological. It was elaborated at the sources of the Church's tradition. It was also developed within the faith of the Church as an institution and with the purpose of serving that Church. It was a response to the expectation of a Church that was threatened by an internal dysfunction.

The climate of the post-conciliar period was quite different. The theology of that period had to do more than simply provide a commentary on the texts of Vatican II. The conciliar texts had been innovative in the name of continuity and unanimity in the Church, but there were signs of breaks appearing in the period that followed the Council. Moving from a "hierarchology" to a Church that is the people of God discovering a new freedom is not something that takes place simply automatically.

For more than twenty years now, Christian theology has been confronted with urgent tasks which were not dealt with directly by the Council. These include, for example, the encounter between Christianity and contemporary culture, the possibility of language about God, the meaning of Christian existence in a secularized world, the renewal of the language of faith and Christian rites on the basis of non-Western cultures, and finally the relationship between the historical movements of liberation and eschatological salvation.

A recognition that the French theologians who made such an enormous contribution to the theology of Vatican II were still, in many respects, both philosophically and culturally men of the nineteenth century in no way detracts from their great merit and achievement. They developed a theology which was in conformity with the leading intuitions of Vatican II and which had a special bearing on questions relating to the Church. They were almost exclusively preoccupied with this long term "institutional" work and felt much more at a loss when there was a need to confront faith with modern thought and to renew the credibility of Christianity on the basis of the modern manner of understanding reality.

It can hardly be disputed that the climate of thought has changed radically in the Church since the Vatican Council. It is also beyond dispute that faith has been increasingly subjected to searching questions posed by a culture that has been described as "post-Christian." Why, then, have those theologians who played such an active part in Vatican II been followed by so few successors? And why has the French contribution to the international theological output been so modest?

It is not easy to give satisfactory answers to these questions. It is, however, possible to take into account a number of quite indisputable data. Some of these are sociological. Others go back to the epistemological status of theology.

(a) I would like to begin by stressing how very few men are at present engaged in theological studies in France. The dramatic decline in vocations to the priesthood and religious orders since about 1965 has forced many seminaries and theological colleges either to close or to regroup.

Before Vatican II, there was approximately one seminary per diocese.[4] Less than one-half of these remain open today and very few of them provide the full course of training in both philosophy and theology. This has resulted in many teachers having been released for the ministry and for permanent work training clergy and laity. They have therefore often been lost to theological studies and authorship.

What is more, because of the French law of 1905 separating Church and state, there are no faculties of theology in the French universities apart from Strasbourg and Metz, since Alsace and Lorraine have continued to be governed subject to the terms of the Concordat. There are several still very flourishing centers where theology is taught and which attract many clerical and lay students in Paris, Strasbourg and Lyons as well as the Sèvres Centre of the Jesuits in Paris, but the theological faculties of the other Catholic institutes in Toulouse, Lille and Angers have for some time been experiencing great difficulties in recruiting both teachers and students.

Leaving aside the theological faculties of Strasbourg University, both of which (Catholic and Protestant) are recognized by the state, all the Catholic institutes in France are also preoccupied with grave financial difficulties. They can only survive because they are subsidized by a government aid that is very uncertain in the present political and economic climate.

Because of a lack of financial resources, very few teachers of theology are able to devote themselves to full-time theological research. They are almost always overburdened with teaching or administrative duties and, unlike their German colleagues, they do not have assistants or even secretaries. They very often have to undertake other kinds of additional work in order to supplement their resources. It is quite common for theologians whose main professional task is university teaching to be asked to lead groups, give vacation courses, supervise the publication of non-scientific journals and so on. This is excellent work that perpetuates the deeply pastoral orientation of French theology, of course, but it does not lead to the production of scientific theological books.

However astonishing it may seem, the French bishops have never tried to set up a fund for helping isolated theologians to publish theses and works of theology. The uncertainty of employment in theology, the almost complete absence of grants and financial aid and, one might add, the lack of freedom in theological research in the official structures of the Church has also for some time resulted in a brain drain from pure theology into the human sciences of religion.

Finally, I am bound to add that the absence of undisputed leaders and striking works of international renown in the French theological scene should not lead us to underestimate the intense theological activity which is taking place in France today and which can no longer be situated exclusively in such classical institutions as theological faculties or seminaries.

The most interesting feature of the contemporary French theological scene is the increasing interest in theology on the part of lay men and women and the correspondingly great number of non-university centers of theology catering for them. This inevitably calls into question the value of a more or less clerical and overwhelmingly university style of theology. What seems to be required today is a more tentative type of theology that sets out to express the experience of certain basic communities or working groups. This type of theology is already appearing in print, for example, in the series *Dossiers libres* (Editions du Cerf) and in a wide variety of duplicated publications.[5]

(b) If we are really to understand its present silence, it is not enough simply to consider the sociological and demographic infrastructure underlying French theology. We have also to give our attention, more than fifteen years since the end of the Council, to a change that has taken place in theology as the result of an increasingly radical criticism of religious language and of the success of the human sciences.

It would not be wrong to say that the fifteen years since Vatican II have been marked by the deconstruction of the system of Catholic thought. That deconstruction has corresponded to a certain breakdown of the Church body itself. As a Church discourse, dogmatic theology has been increasingly called into question because it was no longer ensuring that the ecclesial body was holding together. Not only in France, but throughout the Church generally, the members of that body have in fact been becoming increasingly autonomous since the Second Vatican Council. The phenomenon has been more acute in France, however, because of the success of linguistics and the ideology of structuralism, which has led to a radical criticism of language as the language of meaning and because of the increasing success of the human sciences in general and of sociology in particular.

On the one hand, theologians have become much more critical of their own discourse. They question themselves about their conditions of production (by which I mean, of course, the socio-economic, psychological and linguistic conditions governing their productivity). On the other hand, the consequence of an absence of a consistent ideological discourse has been that theologians have become increasingly concerned with practices. And in that area they have come into conflict with various experts in the human sciences—or have collaborated with them.

In my opinion, it is this fairly recent dialogue between theologians and those who specialize in the human sciences—and in particular the human sciences of religion—which points to the new dimension in French theology and provides at least a partial explanation for the relatively low level of productivity in French theology today.[6]

In France, much more than, for example, in Germany, the totalizing perspective of dogmatic discourse has been called into question above all by the theologians themselves who are engaged in it. The earlier theological discourse has been broken down into many separate fragmentary or partial discourses. Many crucial questions of a dogmatic or moral order have been considered, but for the most part in the form of articles or essays without the classical battery of bibliographical references to works of theology and based on practices or profane scientific analyses.

There is no real lack of serious theologians in France, but they have become more modest and more silent than their great predecessors of the period before the Council. This is because they know better than anyone that the language of faith is subjected to extensive radical questioning and that Christian practices are dependent on other forms of analysis and not simply on theological judgment. At almost every congress, conference or seminar, the theologian is obliged to express countless cautious reservations when he intervenes after historians, sociologists, psychologists and linguistic experts have spoken. He knows that he cannot merely make use of the human sciences in an attempt to renew the language of faith. The dogmatic theologian above all has lost his privileged position, and it is often the exegete who has to accept the role of mediator and safeguard the principle of orthodoxy by resorting to a normative text.

I would conclude this section by saying that the absence of creativity among French theologians today is certainly to be deplored, but that it would be wrong to interpret this relative eclipse of French theology since the Second Vatican Council purely negatively. We should rather speak of a temporary silence which is the sign of a greater clarity. Despite the tentative and even stammering character of contemporary theological studies in France, we have every reason to hope that the last word has not yet been spoken. French theology is preparing itself, perhaps in a subterranean manner, to renew the challenge of the radical contestation of religious language that has followed the break with the earlier epistemological order.

2. CONTEMPORARY ORIENTATIONS IN FRENCH THEOLOGY

There are no star performers in French theology today, either individuals or schools of theology. Despite the breakdown of theological discourse, which I discussed briefly in the previous section, however, it is possible to point to a number of general tendencies that characterize French theology today. I will confine myself here to three of them. What is particularly striking is that in each of these three tendencies the dogmatic discourse is dependent on the development of French culture in general and French philosophy in particular during the past twenty years.

A. The Naming of God Beyond Atheism and Theism

As in other countries, theology in France lived for a very long time in the light of a Christological concentration and, in this light, under the influence of Karl Barth. During the post-conciliar period, however, theology has been subjected to pressure from Christians intensely engaged in political struggles and has, for this reason among others, been tempted to break the connection between Jesus and the Christ. Christology has, in other words, been in danger of becoming a mere "Jesuology" or even an atheistic Christology, as it did in the so-called "death of God" theologies.

French dogmatic theology has rediscovered "God's law."[7] It is even necessary to speak of a "return of God" in circles that are not theological. This is almost a cultural phenomenon. We have only to think, for example, of such books as *Dieu est Dieu, nom de Dieu!* by Maurice Clavel,[8] *Dieu existe, je l'ai rencontré* by André Frossard[9] and *Des choses cachées depuis la fondation du monde* by René Girard.[10] Even a "new philosopher" such as Bernard-Henri Lévy made the Old Testament idea of God the only bulwark against the tendency to give an absolute value to the totalitarian state in his *Testament de Dieu*.[11]

French dogmatic theology—both Catholic and Protestant—has shown itself to be quite radical in its search for a language about God beyond theism and atheism understood not as atheistic existentialist or Marxist humanism, but as nihilism. In that respect, French theological thinking is closer to a work such as Ernst Jüngel's *Gott als Geheimnis der Welt*[12] than to Hans Küng's still too apologetic work *Existiert Gott?*[13] If we are to understand this theological tendency, however, we must take into account a number of data that are peculiar to the French cultural scenario.

The Crisis of Metaphysical Theism

French theological thinking was openly and directly attacked by the Heideggerian criticism of onto-theology.[14] The neo-Thomism that flourished in France between the First and the Second World Wars no longer exists apart from a few isolated circles. Nothing happened in France that was parallel to what took place in Germany under the influence of Karl Rahner. In other words, no attempt was made to continue the work of Fr. Maréchal in the sense of a reconciliation between Thomistic metaphysics and the philosophy of the spirit of German idealism. With the exception of certain isolated philosophers such as Claude Bruaire and P.-J. Labarrière (see especially his book *Dieu aujourd'hui* [Paris, 1977]), there has also been no attempt in France, parallel to that made in Germany in the work of Wolfhart Pannenberg, to renew systematic theology on the basis of Hegel's dialectics.

What we have, then, in France are theological essays which try to emphasize the difference between the "theological" aspect of nature that is properly ontological and the "theological" aspect that comes properly from God as well as the difference between the God subsisting from metaphysical theism and the God of Jesus Christ. (See C. Duquoc, *Dieu différent*,[15] or the collected work edited by J. Moingt, *Dire ou taire Dieu*.[16] In the sense of a criticism of the conceptual type of theology that goes no further than the level of a representation in the pejorative sense in which this term is used by Heidegger, French theologians have received a great deal from such philosophical works as Stanislas Breton's *Du principe*[17] and Jean-Luc Marion's *L'Idole et la distance*.[18] Marion has shown that the conceptual God of onto-theology may well be nothing more than an "idol," in other words, a placing at man's disposal of the divine in a failure to recognize his absolute distance.

The Marxist Criticism of Ideology

The theologian is increasingly confronted with the question: "From what standpoint are you speaking?" French theologians have become very sensitive to the ideological function that theology can exercise at a given moment in history. They know that there is no such thing as an innocent theological discourse. It is not necessary to be a Marxist in order to take seriously the idea that the history of the images about God is connected with the economic history of human societies. It is therefore a question of knowing when theology degenerates into an ideology that is at the service of various forms of power, whether that power is within the Church or whether it takes the form of political power in the society surrounding the

Church. How is it, for example, possible to deny that a certain form of discourse about God may well function as an attempt to justify an unjust social order? The theologies of liberation have long been aware of this. Several French works also have the same tendency. (See especially C. Wackenheim's *Christianisme sans idéologie*[19] and the collected work of the Theological Faculty of Strasbourg, *Pouvoir et vérité*.[20])

The Deconstruction of Language

French dogmatic theology is still looking for the right course to follow. This is because the shaking that its philosophical presuppositions have received corresponds to the profound state of crisis in which French philosophy finds itself. I have already spoken about the criticism of onto-theology. French philosophy was dominated in the 1940's and 1950's by Jean-Paul Sartre, who was trying to reconcile phenomenology, existentialism and historical materialism. The attempts to renew dogmatic theology on the basis of existentialism and personalism proved to have no future. Sartre's philosophy was a philosophy of the subject and of creative freedom, and it was called radically into question by the French structuralism of the 1960's, the chief representatives of which are Michel Foucault, Louis Althusser, J. Lacan and Claude Lévi-Strauss.

What characterizes the cultural revolution brought about by structuralism is above all that man is no longer regarded as the subject in the classical sense of the philosophical tradition. All that is retained of man is what can be formalized. Man, as the concrete subject who becomes in history and as intentionality that is the signifier, disappears. In attacking the ideology of man as the subject of history, structuralism is also attacking both theological humanism and such forms of humanism as existentialism and Marxism, which, despite their atheism, appear as disguised forms of theology which secretly deify man.

This movement has been expressed in the most radical way by Jacques Derrida (*De la grammatologie*), whose aim is to take the deconstruction of metaphysics as onto-theology operated by Heidegger to its ultimate conclusion. He calls radically into question the relationship between the signifier and the signified which is at the beginning of every form of hermeneutics. In this way, he puts every form of the philosophy of meaning on trial—both the classical, in other words, the metaphysical form and the modern, that is, the Husserlian or even the Heideggerian form (see above, Chapter II). Derrida's radicalism calls into question all possibility of theological discourse.

Some French theologians have nonetheless taken up his challenge. One of the most notable is A. Delzant. In his book *La Communication de*

Dieu,[21] he has deliberately broken with the ontological presuppositions of traditional theology and hermeneutics, which he criticizes for their secret anthropocentrism. Taking the category "covenant" as a symbolic order as his point of departure, he has opened various ways to a new discourse about God which is based not on utilitarianism, but on gratuity.

This concludes my brief review of the most important cultural factors conditioning French theological thinking today. The obvious question that arises in this context is: What general tendencies can be found in the dogmatic theology that is appearing in France today principally in the form of articles and essays? In my opinion there are four.

1. The first is a theology that takes seriously the decline of metaphysics and does not attempt to reconstruct God conceptually, but rather lets him be the God of revelation. Rather than considering God in the discourse of representation, this form of theology tries to think of him taking the category of "coming" as its point of departure. (See A. Dumas' book, *Nommer Dieu*.[22]) It sets itself the task of meditating about the coming of a God who reveals himself in the events of history and in world events and who is manifest more in otherness than in identity and more in separation, gratuity and excess than in the immediacy of his presence. (See M. Corbin, *L'Inouï de Dieu*.[23]) The work of E. Levinas is influencing French theologians more and more in this sphere.

2. The second theological tendency is trying to reconsider the transcendence of God not as the transcendence of an absolute Being, but rather as a transcendence of Love. Following Rahner and Moltmann, the theologians of this school are attempting to go further than the classical opposition between God's unchanging nature and his becoming. Their task, as they see it, is to think again about the event of the Incarnation as an event which is universal in the concrete and goes beyond the classical conceptualization and to renew our understanding of God's concrete attributes, especially his love and his ability to suffer and to be wounded. The historical event is not reduced to its contingent factuality. As Hegel sensed, it belongs to the very emergence of truth.

3. The third form of theology goes beyond nihilism and theism in an attempt to find an answer to what cannot be justified in the contemporary world in the crucified God. In the blasphemous name of the "crucified God," what has been revealed to us before the whole theology of the redemption is God's solidarity with what above all cannot be justified—the suffering of the innocent. The French theologians who belong to this third group are making use of Bonhoeffer's key insights that it is religion in general that takes man back to God's omnipotence and the Bible that takes him back to God's weakness and suffering. The works of F. Varillon have to be quoted in this context, in particular his *L'Humilité de Dieu* and *La*

Souffrance de Dieu.[25] Jurgen Moltmann's *Le Dieu crucifié* has also had an enormous influence in France. Finally, the most original theological work to appear in French as a contribution to this "theology of the cross" has been written by Stanislas Breton and published in the series *Jésus—Jésus-Christ.*[26]

4. Finally, I would like to mention the influence that Eastern Orthodox theology has had in certain French theological circles, in which there is a great interest in the return of the Spirit and the meaning and importance of the charismatic movement for the Church. After the age of "Christological concentration" and the age of the "naming of God," we have the age of "pneumatological celebration." Is it merely by chance that the last great work by Yves Congar is dedicated to the third article, "I believe in the Holy Spirit"?[27]

B. Fundamental Theology as Hermeneutics

The cultural situation in France is, as we have seen, characterized above all by a crisis in the metaphysical foundations of thought and a similar crisis in the language of meaning. This has inevitably led to many different attempts to defend the credibility of Christianity and the conditions of validity of the discourse about God on the basis of what is known as fundamental theology.

Obviously we cannot simply be satisfied with a form of apologetics that provides only an extrinsic credibility of Christianity. We have to show on the basis of the logic of faith itself that Christianity has an abundance of meaning for human existence.

With this in mind, fundamental theology in France tries to make itself understood as hermeneutics of the Word of God. Hermeneutics here means an interpretation of the texts and the primacy of the search for meaning rather than anxiety exclusively about the objective truth.

Looking for meaning cannot, of course, mean that we end by abandoning the search for truth. The great change that has taken place in theology is that the theologian is now less preoccupied with studying objective statements outside the sphere of time in an attempt to understand them speculatively. His work is now with texts—Scripture and dogmatic and theological writings—and he studies these in their textual density in an effort to understand all their many different meanings here and now.

In France, the situation in which fundamental theology finds itself is dominated by the contestation between metaphysics based on the order of nature and a philosophy centered on the existential subject. Theologians have distanced themselves on the one hand from the classical type of theology that claimed to be able to provide a rational justification of faith on the basis of an explanation of the receptive powers possessed by man understood as a spiritual nature. On the other hand, they have also dissociated themselves both from transcendental philosophy of the kind favored by Rahner and from theological personalism. Both of these are, of course, dominated by human subjectivity.

It would seem that symbolic language is the special place for a pre-understanding of faith, whether it is concerned with human archaeology as revealed in the language of mythology or with the latent aspects of man's experience that are concealed in the language of the unconscious and brought to light by psychoanalysis. Paul Ricoeur's work in the sphere of hermeneutics[28] and Antoine Vergote's research into analytical language[29] have given a powerful impulse to French theologians in this field.

Fundamental theology has the dual task of deciphering the meanings hidden in symbolic language and of bringing to light both the continuities and the discontinuities with the great symbols of biblical language. We have, for example, only to think of such themes as the law, transgressing the law, innocence, the Father, the longing for a homeland and paradise lost. René Girard is one author who aims to persuade us that the great biblical myths are inexhaustibly rich, although, of course, we have, since Freud, been tempted to interpret our collective unconscious mind exclusively on the basis of the tragic Greek myths.

I know how difficult it is to distinguish between hermeneutics and fundamental theology, when heremeneutics have been subjected to such suspicion by structuralism. But it is all too easy to put hermeneutics on trial under the pretext that its destiny is inescapably tied to that of metaphysics. Confronted with the symbolic language of revelation, it is not possible to be satisfied with a linguistic approach. A semantic study has to be undertaken, and we have to bear in mind that all language is dependent on a phenomenology, by which an attempt is made to seize hold of the signifying intentionality that presides over the discourse. It is also necessary to add that it is not possible to dispense with a philosophy of language in which language is regarded as a manifestation of being. The ontological level of the saying as a universal manifestation of being is the necessary presupposition of a theology of the Word of God.

Finally, the structural analyses of the language lead to a change in the hermeneutics which may be of great benefit to our theological work.[30] Modern hermeneutics are reacting against the romanticism of Schleiermacher and Dilthey. They try to give priority to the objectivity of the text and not in the sense in which there is already a given and objectivized

meaning which it would suffice simply to decipher, but rather in the sense
in which there is what Paul Ricoeur would call a "world of the text" which
takes us back to an original representation of the world and of man.[31]

In the case of the biblical text, it is that new being of the text that is
creative of something new in man—of his "new being." Theological discourse understood as hermeneutics, then, does not try to explain the great
categories of revelation on the basis of concepts that are extrinsic to it. It
tries rather to achieve a demonstration of the original truth of the key symbols of the biblical universe.

C. Practice as a *Locus Theologicus*

It would be quite wrong if I were to say nothing in this attempt to
reconstitute the intellectual scenario of French theology today about the
attention that French theologians are giving to practices—both the historical practice of men in general and individual and social practices by
Christians.

As I pointed out above, this is the special place of a very fruitful dialogue between the human sciences and theology. Several important works
have already appeared in which theologians have renewed our understanding of the Christian mystery by making use of the practices and the
results of the human sciences. In this context, I am thinking especially of
Gérard Defois[32] and Jacques Audinet[33] in the field of sociology, Jacques
Pohier,[34] Denis Vasse[35] and Xavier Thévenot[36] in that of psychoanalysis,
Guy Lafon[37] and Antoine Delzant[38] in linguistics, and Louis-Marie
Chauvet[39] and Michel de Certeau[40] in the sphere of cultural anthropology.

It is also interesting to note some of the changes that have taken place
over the years, for example, in the series published by one of the leading
French publishers of religious books, Editions du Cerf. In 1972, for example, the first volumes began to appear in what was then a new series of
mainly sociological studies, *Sciences humaines et religions*. In 1974, the
already well-known liturgical series *Lex Orandi* was transformed and came
to be known as *Rites et Symboles*. Finally, in 1976, the series *Cogitatio
Fidei* was given the sub-title *Théologie et sciences religieuses*.

As I have already said, French theology has always had a strong pastoral orientation. It has always been less academic than German theology.
It is still preoccupied today with the need to bridge the gap between the
Church's theoretical pronouncements and the concrete activity of Christian practice.

The theological work of J.-P. Jossua, several of whose books have
been published by the Editions du Cerf, is a particularly good example of
this non-academic type of French theology that pays close attention to con-

crete human experience. The term "practical theology" is particularly apt when applied to the work of R. Marlé,[41] where it describes a kind of theology which not only takes practice as its *locus theologicus*, but is also prepared to be called into question by practice.

It is not so much a question of giving priority to practice in this "practical theology" or of identifying theory and practice as of maintaining a tension between the two. A theory needs to be constantly proved true or untrue by practice, and practice needs to be transcended by theory. At that level, it is possible to speak of a critical theory, and at that level too, that is, at the level of a constant confrontation between believing and doing, it is possible to speak of a critical theology. French theologians are anxious to do more than simply engage in a theological discourse that will not result in a practice.

At the same time, however, they are paying more and more attention to the historical practices of Christians. These are in fact those significant practices which create new meanings and provide new interpretations of the Christian message.

As the later history of Marxism has so clearly shown and as the representatives of the Frankfurt school have also demonstrated in their work, the attempt to identify theory and practice is an impossible ideal which is in danger of making us seek refuge in a new form of dogmatism. We have, however, not yet estimated the full extent of the consequences that a new understanding of the relationships between theory and practice may have for the way in which theology is practiced.[42]

Theology cannot afford to overlook the fact that there are other approaches to the truth apart from that of speculative knowledge in the classical sense. If it does ignore this fact, it runs the risk of being increasingly culturally marginalized. The famous dialogue with the human sciences may prove to be without a future if it is simply a question of making use of the results of the human sciences in theology. French theologians are coming to understand with increasing clarity that they have to accept that their theological rationality will be called into question by the new rationalities employed by the human sciences in their approach to the reality either of society or of the human individual. Their approach is really not that of a totalizing knowledge. It is much more the approach of an undertaking that is indissolubly both a verification and a production of rationality.

The most urgent debate is therefore of an epistemological order. What has to be acclimatized in the sphere of theology is what Michel Foucault has called "alethourgia," in other words, that interweaving of truth and action that has to be increasingly accepted as a place of mutual verification. It is possible to accept that theology should be defined as hermeneutics of the Word of God, but not possible to accept that this should be a theoretical interpretation of Scripture that abstracts from the present practice of Christians. Theology is not an absolute knowledge that exists prior to Christian praxis, that of faith and charity. The latter is the adequate place of scriptural interpretation. The concrete practice of Christians is different from the sphere in which an unchanging dogmatic theology is applied or even the simple accidental conditioning of an already constituted Christian message. In a view of faith that makes room for the permanent action of the Holy Spirit, the historical practices of Christians and of the various Christian churches have to be understood as significant practices that are at the service of a creative reinterpretation of the Christian message.

The importance given to practice as a *locus theologicus*, then, involves a real change in the way in which theological work should be understood. As a theology of praxis, theology cannot simply be satisfied with a different interpretation of the Christian message. It creates new possibilities of existence.[43] As soon as we begin to take seriously the practice that is peculiar to each church insofar as it is conditioned by an original culture and by specific historical movements, we have to abandon the illusory ideal of a universal theology that is valid for the whole of the Church. From then onward, we begin to live in a situation of insurmountable theological pluralism.

We already know how important the Latin American theologies are as theologies of liberation, but we also know that there have been African and Asian theological initiatives. Because so many students come to us from the churches in the third world, we are particularly aware of this phenomenon in Paris. We know that the future of Christian theology is not restricted to the West. We are therefore bound to question the Western ethnocentrism of our theology and to be open to new possibilities in the understanding of faith that are being revealed to us by other cultural environments. The doctoral studies of which I am in charge at the Institut catholique in Paris include, on the one hand, several seminars on the relationship between Christian theology and non-Western cultures, and, on the other, opportunities for theses to be prepared in this field of research.

I would sum up this brief outline of French theology since the Second Vatican Council by admitting that it may well seem to be modest. Not very many systematic works of international reputation have been published in French during this period. It has, however, been characterized by a close attention to the signs of the times in the cultural, social and ecclesial orders.[44] In this way, it is at the service of the universal Church and may be playing its part in preparing the way for a new theological spring on which Europe will not have a monopoly.

ABBREVIATIONS

AnBib	Analecta Biblica
ArPh	Archives de philosophie
ASRel	Archives de sociologie de religion
EThL	Ephemerides theologicae Lovanienses
ETR	Etudes théologiques et religieuses
IRM	International review of mission
LThK	Lexikon für Theologie et Kirche
LV	Lumen vitae
NRT	Nouvelle revue théologique
ParMiss	Parole et Missions
RICP	Revue de l'Institut Catholique
RMM	Revue de métaphysique et de morale
RSPhTh	Revue des sciences philosophiques et théologiques
RSR	Revue des sciences religieuses
RThL	Revue théologique de Louvain
RThPh	Revue de théologie et de philosophie
VieI	La vie intellectuelle
VS	Vie spirituelle

NOTES

Introduction

1. A summary of E. Schillebeeckx' hermeneutical method will be found in the French edition of his little book *Expérience humaine et foi en Jésus Christ* (Paris, 1981). For David Tracy, see *Blessed Rage for Order* (New York, 1975) and *The Analogical Imagination* (New York, 1981).
2. See the Bibliographical Note at the end of the book.

I. From Knowledge to Interpretation

1. For a more complete treatment of these themes, see my "Esquisse d'une théologie de la révélation," P. Ricoeur, E. Levinas et al., *La Révélation* (Brussels, 1977), pp. 171–205.
2. I would refer the reader above all to P. Ricoeur's study, "The Task of Hermeneutics," *Hermeneutics and the Human Sciences* (Cambridge/New York, 1981), pp. 43–62.
3. For this question, see especially F. Refoulé, "L'exégèse en question," *Le Supplément* 111 (Nov. 1974), pp. 391–423 and the symposium *Crise du biblisme. Chance de la Bible* (Paris, 1974).
4. Among Bultmann's writings, his *History and Eschatology* (New York, 1957) is the most important in this context. For the significance of the distinction that he makes between *Historie* and *Geschichte*, see my study "Kérygme et histoire chez Rudolf Bultmann," *RSPhTh* 49 (1965), pp. 809–839.
5. For an initial approach, see H.-G. Gadamer, *Le Problème de la conscience historique* (Louvain, 1963).
6. See especially "Hermeneutics and Universal History," *Basic Questions in Theology* Vol. I (Philadelphia, 1970), pp. 96–136.
7. J. Granier's classical *Le problème de la vérité dans la philosophie de Nietzsche* (Paris, 1966) is probably the best work to consult for this question. See also P. Gisel, "Nietzsche's Perspectivism and Theological Language," *Concilium* 145 (1981), pp. 81–88.
8. For these "authoritarian" theologies, see the chapter entitled "Dogmatic Theology in the Hermeneutic Age," *A New Age of Theology* (New York, 1974).
9. It was in the context of this distinction that Y. Congar understood the relationship between positive and speculative theology in his *La Foi et la théologie* (Paris, 1962).

10. For the origin of this tripartite division of dogmatic theology, see K. Jasper, *Renouveau de la méthode théologique* (Paris, 1968).

11. I am referring here to the use of *verstehen* by Heidegger, who saw "understanding" not as an act of noetic knowledge, but as an existential act. See his *Sein und Zeit*, Chapter 31.

12. H.-G. Gadamer, *Truth and Method* (New York, 1969).

13. For the originality of these scientific procedures and the fleeting character of a religious object as a specific object of the "religious sciences," M. de Certeau's article "La rupture instauratrice," *Esprit* (June 1971), pp. 1177–1214, can be read with profit.

14. For this dialogue, see J.-P. Deconchy's recent book, *Orthodoxie religieuse et sciences humaines* (Paris and The Hague, 1980).

II. Hermeneutics on Trial

1. I am referring here to the debate in Germany between H.-G. Gadamer and J. Habermas. An insight into it can be gained by reading the book *Hermeneutik und Ideologie-kritik* (Frankfurt, 1971).

2. See J. Greisch, K. Neufeld and C. Théobald, *La Crise contemporaine. Du modernisme à la crise des herméneutiques* (Paris, 1973), p. 144. I would also strongly recommend J. Greisch's account of the crisis in hermeneutics in the same volume, to which I am greatly indebted.

3. A. Vergote, *Interprétation du langage religieux* (Paris, 1974), p. 16.

4. J.-P. Osier, in his preface to the French translation of L. Feuerbach's *L'Essence du christianisme* (Paris, 1968), pp. 10–11.

5. *Ibid.*, p. 17.

6. L. Marin, "The Disappearance of Man in the Human Sciences— A Linguistic Model and Signifying Subject," *Concilium* 86 (1973), pp. 29–41.

7. A. Delzant, *La Communication de Dieu. Par-delà utile et inutile. Essai théologique sur l'ordre symbolique* (Paris, 1973), p. 65.

8. M. de Certeau, *Crise du biblisme, chance de la Bible* (Paris, 1973), p. 46.

9. M. de Certeau, "La rupture instauratrice," *Esprit* (June 1971), p. 1201.

10. L. Marin, *op. cit.*, p. 37.

11. G. Lafon, *Esquisses pour un christianisme* (Paris, 1979), p. 64.

12. G. Lafon, *op. cit.*, p. 68.

13. A. Delzant, *op. cit.*, p. 69.

14. For this question, see F. Refoulé's article "L'exégèse en question," *Le Supplément* 111 (1974), pp. 411–414.

15. J. Greisch, *op. cit.*, p. 157.

16. J. Greisch, *op. cit.*, pp. 165–166.

17. J. Derrida, *De la grammatologie* (Paris, 1967), p. 95.

18. J. Derrida, *op. cit.*, p. 108.

19. F. Wahl, *Qu'est-ce que le structuralism?* (Paris, 1968), p. 413.

20. For the whole of this discussion on the conflict between hermeneutics and grammatology, see J. Greisch, *Herméneutique et grammatologie* (Paris, 1977).

21. C. Théobald, "L'entrée de l'histoire dans l'univers religieux et théologique au moment du crise moderniste," *La Crise contemporaine, op. cit.*, pp. 74–75.

22. M. Heidegger's unpublished essay translated into French under the title of "Quelques indications sur des points de vue principaux du colloque théologique consacré au 'Problème d'un pensée et d'un langage non objectivisants dans la théologie d'aujourd'hui,' " *Archives de philosophie* 32 (1969), pp. 397–415, is what I have in mind here. In this context, one of his questions is particularly relevant: "Is man that being who has language in his possession? Or is it that language that 'has' man, insofar as he belongs to language, which opens the world to him and thereby at the same time his dwelling-place in the world?"—*ibid.*, p. 409.

23. I would refer the reader to the following works: "Preface to Bultmann," *Essays in Biblical Interpretation* (Philadelphia, 1980), pp. 49–72; "Toward a Hermeneutic of the Idea of Revelation," *op. cit.*, pp. 73–118; "The Task of Hermeneutics," *Hermeneutics and the Human Sciences* (Cambridge/New York, 1981), pp. 43–62; "The Hermeneutical Function of Distantiation," *op. cit.*, pp. 131–144; "Naming God," *Union Seminary Quarterly Review* xxxiv/4 (1979), pp. 215–227.

24. P. Ricoeur, *HHS*, p. 52.

25. P. Ricoeur, *ibid.*, p. 53.

26. P. Ricoeur, *ibid.*, p. 138.

27. See especially "Structure, Word, Event," *Conflict of Interpretations* (Evanston, 1974), pp. 79–96, and "Evénement et sens," E. Castelli, ed., *Révélation et Histoire* (Paris, 1971), pp. 15–34.

28. P. Ricoeur, *HHS*, p. 142.

29. P. Ricoeur, *EBI*, p. 100.

30. P. Ricoeur, *ibid.*, p. 101.

31. See *ibid.*, p. 71.

32. P. Ricoeur, *HHS*, p. 143.

33. P. Ricoeur, "Naming God," p. 217.

34. G. Crespy, "L'écriture de l'écriture," *Parole et dogmatique, hommage à Jean Bosc*, cited by P. Gisel in *Vérité et Histoire. La théologie dans la modernité, Ernst Käsemann* (Paris, 1977), p. 169.

35. See P. Gisel, *op. cit.*, p. 627.
36. P. Ricoeur, *ibid.*, p. 219.
37. P. Ricoeur, *EBI*, especially p. 93.
38. C. Geffré, "Esquisse d'une théologie de la révélation," *La Révélation, op. cit.*, pp. 185ff.
39. P. Gisel, *op. cit.*, p. 147.
40. *Ibid.*, p. 164.
41. M. Bellet, *Crise du biblisme, chance de la Bible, op. cit.*, p. 195, cited by F. Refoulé, 'L'exégèse en question', *op. cit.*, p. 413.
42. P. Ricoeur, "Naming God," p. 227.
43. H.-G. Gadamer, "Herméneutique et théologie," *RSR* 51 (1977), p. 396.

III. Dogmatics or Hermeneutics?

1. M. Michel, *Voies nouvelles pour la théologie* (Paris, 1980), especially Chapter III, "L'effacement du modèle dogmatique," pp. 55–69.
2. This difference between the theology of Thomas Aquinas and that of the Counter-Reformation has been particularly stressed by P. Eicher in his *Theologie. Eine Einführung in das Studium* (Munich, 1980), especially pp. 178–183. Y. Congar has also frequently discussed this evolution in Catholic theology that has resulted in an increasing overvaluation of the authority of the magisterium as the immediate law governing faith. See especially his "Les régulations de la foi," *Le Supplément* 133 (1980), pp. 260–281. He draws attention, for example, to the importance of the replacement at the First Vatican Council of the Thomist formula of the formal theme of faith, *Veritas prima*, by *Auctoritas Dei revelantis*, p. 268, n. 19. See also P. Eicher, *op. cit.*, p. 89.
3. For this subject, see J.-P. Jossua's clear diagnosis in his article "Immutabilité, progrès ou structurations multiples des doctrines chrétiennes," *RSPhTh* 52 (1968), pp. 173–200.
4. This "institutional game" is outlined very well in the collected work edited by M. Michel, *Pouvoir et vérité* (Paris, 1981). It is also worth consulting P. Legendre's already classical book, *L'Amour du censeur, essai sur l'ordre dogmatique* (Paris, 1974). I would also recommend two particularly suggestive sociological approaches to the subject: G. Defois, "Discours religieux et pouvoir social," *ASRel* 32 (1971), pp. 85–106 and J. Séguy, "Le conflit théologique," *Le Supplément* 133 (1980), pp. 223–242.
5. In connection with the case of atheism, P. Ladrière has shown very clearly that there was no harmonious development between Pius IX's condemnation and the opening of Vatican II, but a distinct rupture. See his

"L'esprit de mensonge dans le discours théologique," Le Supplément 139 (1981), pp. 509–529.

6. See above, Chapter I. See also my "La révélation hier et aujour-d'hui. De l'Ecriture à la prédication ou les actualisations de la Parole de Dieu," Révélation de Dieu et langage des hommes (Paris, 1962), pp. 95–121, A New Age of Theology, pp. 31–50.

7. The hermeneutical principle underlies the Christology of E. Schillbeeckx, Jesus. An Experiment in Christology (London and New York, 1979). A good summary of this author's theological method will be found in J. Doré, Expérience humaine et foi en Jésus-Christ (Paris, 1981).

8. Of the many books published on the subject of modernism, I would mention only R. Virgoulay's recent thesis, Blondel et le modernisme (Paris, 1980), which contains a very full bibliography.

9. This characteristically scholastic and rationalist conception of the work of theology has been clearly analyzed by P. Eicher, op. cit., pp. 179–180, who says that "it is not the truth of what is believed, but the certainty that God has said this or that which is the guiding principle in systematic thinking, which in turn requires, for its own security, the unshakable foundation of a theological construction" (p. 214).

10. For these new places of theology, which should not be confused with "theological places" in the usual sense of the phrase, see my conclusions to the colloquium published under the title of Le Déplacement de la théologie (Paris, 1977), pp. 171–178.

11. Karl Rahner, "Pluralism in Theology and the Oneness of the Church's Profession of Faith," Concilium 46 (1969), pp. 103–123.

12. I have tried to throw light on the historical dimension of the theological pluralism within the Church today in my essay "Pluralité des théologies et unité de la foi," Initiation pratique à la théologie (Paris, 1982), I, pp. 117–142.

13. For an introduction to these theories, see J.-F. Malherbe's very valuable work, Epistémologies anglo-saxonnes (Namur, 1981).

14. See especially O. Pöggeler, La Pensée de Martin Heidegger (Paris, 1967), pp. 124–136 and 366–382.

15. For the important part played by a hermeneutical understanding of the truth in contemporary systematic theology, see David Tracy, The Analytical Imagination. Christian Theology and the Culture of Pluralism (New York, 1981), especially Chapter III, "The Classic," pp. 99–153.

16. P. Ricoeur, "The Hermeneutical Function of Distantiation," Hermeneutics and the Human Sciences (Cambridge/New York, 1981), p. 138.

17. Pierre Gisel, in his work on Käsemann, has correctly tried to develop all the consequences of the German author's historical and theolog-

ical pertinence. See his *Vérité et histoire. La théologie dans la modernité: Ernst Käsemann* (Paris, 1977).

18. P. Gisel, *op. cit.*, p. 627.
19. For this genealogical method in Nietzsche, see J. Granier, *Nietzsche* (Paris, 1982), pp. 66–69. For the application of this method to contemporary theology, see P.-M. Beaude's interesting comments in his *L'Accomplissement des Ecritures* (Paris, 1980), pp. 292–295.
20. For this question, see I. de la Potterie's classical work, *La Vérité dans Saint Jean* (*AnBib* 73–74), 2 vols. (Rome, 1976).
21. See J. Greisch, "Le pouvoir des signes, les insignes du pouvoir," *Le Pouvoir* (Paris, 1978), pp. 175–205, especially pp. 180–181.
22. A. Vergote, *Interprétation du langage religieux* (Paris, 1974), p. 52.
23. See J. Hoffmann, "L'infaillibilité pontificale: formulation d'un dogme ou genèse d'une idéologie," *Pouvoir et vérité* (Paris, 1981), pp. 209–229.
24. For this subject, see J. Ladrière, "La théologie et le langage de l'interprétation," *RTL* 1 (1970), pp. 241–267.
25. For this study of theological criteria, see my article "Théologie" in the *Encyclopaedia Universalis* XV (Paris, 1973), pp. 1087–1091.
26. Among other works, I would mention: H. Schlier, "Méditations sur la notion johannique de vérité," *Essais sur the Nouveau Testament* (Paris, 1968), pp. 317–324; W. Kasper, *Dogme et Evangile* (Tournai, 1967), pp. 55–101; H. Ott, "Was ist systematische Theologie?" *Der spätere Heidegger und die Theologie* I (Zurich, 1964), pp. 95–133; C. Geffré, "Le problème théologique de l'objectivité de Dieu," J. Colette *et al.*, *Procès de l'objectivité de Dieu* (Paris, 1969), pp. 241–263; B. Dupuy, "L'infaillibilité selon Hans Küng," *Eglise infaillible ou intemporelle? Recherches et Débats* (Paris, 1973), pp. 33–40.
27. For the originality of the truth within the framework of a philosophy of testimony, see P. Ricoeur, "The Hermeneutics of Testimony," *Essays in Biblical Interpretation* (Philadelphia, 1980), pp. 119–154.
28. See P. Ricoeur, "Naming God," *Union Theological Seminary Quarterly* xxxiv/4 (1979), pp. 225–227. In this context, it is worth considering the ethical meaning given to transcendence by E. Levinas, who refers to Augustine's *veritas redarguens*, the "truth that accuses": "Has transcendence not a meaning which is possibly earlier than and in any case certainly different from the meaning which it derives from the ontological difference? In my responsibility for my fellow-man, it points straightaway to my neighbor or my brother. . . . No experience, appearance or knowledge can form the basis of that responsibility. It is a responsibility without guilt, but confronted with it I am exposed to an accusation that cannot be

set aside by the alibi of my otherness." See E. Levinas, "De la signifiance du sens," *Heidegger et la question de Dieu* (Paris, 1980), p. 240.

29. E. Schillebeeckx has emphasized this essential condition for a correct understanding in his article "The Problem of the Infallibility of the Church's Office—A Theological Reflection," *Concilium* 83 (1973), pp. 77–94.

30. J. Gabus has drawn attention to this danger in his *Critique du discours théologique* (Neuchâtel, 1977), p. 323.

31. See P. Ricoeur, conclusion to the colloquium *Exégèse et herméneutique* (Paris, 1971), p. 295.

IV. The Theologian's Hermeneutical Freedom

1. Recent cases of conflict include the Pohier, the Küng and the Schillebeeckx affairs. Of the countless books and articles that have appeared, I would mention only one: Y. Congar's irenical study, "Les régulations de la foi," *Le Supplément* 133 (1980), pp. 260–281.

2. I have dealt with the temptation to follow the Counter-Reformation model of dogmatic theology in the previous chapter. In his fine meditation on the "eucharistic site of theology," J.-L. Marron has not completely avoided this danger, in describing the theologian's task as a participation in the bishops's charism. See his *Dieu sans l'être* (Paris, 1982), Chap. V: "Du site eucharistique de la théologie," pp. 196–222.

3. A certain "theological provincialism" can be detected in, for example, liberation, black and feminist theology. A special number of *Concilium* will be published in 1984, probably entitled "Different Theologies, Common Responsibility: Babel or Pentecost?" in an attempt to show that theological pluralism does not necessarily have to lead to breakdown of theology. (See *Concilium* 171 [1984].)

4. For this game of question and answer, see E. Schillebeeckx, "The Problem of Ministerial Infallibility," *Concilium* 83 (1973), pp. 83–102.

5. For this question, see the way in which B. Sesboué deals with the answer provided by the Chalcedonian dogma by following Gadamer and comparing theological and juridical hermeneutics. That dogma was a decree applying the founding message of Christianity to a particular situation in the Church, Sesboué insists, and was both an act of interpretation and an act of jurisprudence. See his "Le procès contemporain de Chalcédoine," *RSR* 65/1 (1977), pp. 45–80, and his recent *Jésus-Christ dans la tradition de l'Eglise* (Paris, 1982), pp. 146–147.

6. See the commentary on this principle stated in the Decree on Ecumenism and full bibliography provided by Y. Congar, *Diversités et communion* (Paris, 1982), pp. 184–197.

7. See J.-P. Jossua, "Immutabilité," *RSPhTh* 52 (1968), n. 3.

8. E. Käsemann has shown that the different ecclesiologies of the New Testament cannot be traced back to a formal unity. See Y. Congar, *op. cit.*, pp. 19f.

9. See M. de Certeau, "Is There a Language of Unity?" *Concilium* 51 (1970), pp. 79–93.

10. See his *La Tradition et les traditions* I. *Essai historique* (Paris, 1960), pp. 233–257 and notes, pp. 279–291.

11. Of the many books and articles written on the *sensus fidelium*, I would recommend especially J.-M. R. Tillard, "Le sensus fidelium, réflexion théologique," *Foi populaire, foi savante* (Paris, 1976), pp. 9–40.

12. It is important to recognize that, until the eve of Vatican II, there was both an increasing subjection to the magisterium and some confusion between the dogmatic and the theological function in the Church. It was inevitable that, in the prevailing Counter-Reformation climate, the so-called baroque theology tended to build up a system in which the authority of the magisterium covered a wider area than that of Scripture itself. Since Vatican II, however, a clearer distinction has been made between the regulating function of the magisterium and the scientific function of theological research.

V. The Resurrection of Christ as an Interpretative Testimony

1. For the use of the word "witness" in non-biblical Greek, see Strathmann's article in Kittel, *Theological Dictionary of the New Testament* (Grand Rapids, 1967), pp. 476–481.

2. *Ibid.*, pp. 489–504.

3. For St. John, I have consulted not only Strathmann's article, but also E. Neuhäusler, "Zeugnis," *LThK*, col. 1361–1362, and N. Brox, "Témoignage," *Encyclopédie de la foi* IV (Paris, 1967), pp. 285–294.

4. I have relied here largely on two classical exegetical works in the French language: X. Léon-Dufour, *Résurrection de Jésus et message pascal* (Paris, 1971) and J. Delorme, "La résurrection de Jésus dans le langage du Nouveau Testament," *Le Langage de la foi dans l'Ecriture et dans le monde actuel* (Paris, 1971), pp. 101–182.

5. See X. Léon-Dufour, *op. cit.*, p. 258.

6. J. Delorme, *op. cit.*, p. 157.

7. *Ibid.*, p. 164.

8. *Ibid.*, p. 177.

9. *Ibid.*, p. 159f.

10. A good summary of the investigations that have been conducted into the historicity of the resurrection and of the various positions taken

with regard to this question will be found in A. Gesché, "La Résurrection de Jésus," *RTL* 21 (1971), pp. 257–306, especially pp. 265–272. For a critical assessment of the present controversy about the historicity of the resurrection of Christ, see also the recent study by P. Grelot, "La Résurrection de Jésus et l'histoire. Historicité et historialité," *Les Quatre Fleuves* 15–16 (1982), pp. 145–179.

11. W. Pannenberg, "The Crisis of the Scripture Principle," *Basic Questions in Theology*, Vol. I (Philadelphia, 1970), pp. 1–14.

12. I would refer the reader here to M. de Certeau's article with the suggestive title "Faire de l'Histoire. Problèmes de méthodes et problèmes de sens," *RSR* (1970), pp. 481–520.

13. W. Pannenberg, "Dogmatic Theses on the Doctrine of Revelation," *Revelation as History* (New York, 1968), p. 152. In an attempt to put an end to the illusion of "historical positivism," I would like to quote J. Granier's paraphrase of Nietzsche's denunciation of "positivistic realism" in his article "La pensée nietzschéenne du chaos," *RMM* (1971), p. 132: ". . . the 'spirit of heaviness' is lying in wait. And here it is questioning us in the guise of an advocate of positivistic realism. What advice is he giving us? To confine ourselves to the 'facts' by adopting an attitude of strict objectivity, so that reality will show itself as it is, without any addition of affectivity, covetousness or interest. . . . What short-sighted advice! For, Nietzsche replies, it is short-sighted to believe that it is possible to seize hold of crude facts, reality as it is, while trusting in the immediate datum. That immediate reality is an enticement! It is because our sight is too weak that we think that we have facts in front of us, whereas, if we have keen vision, we see only interpretations. The reality that we perceive is already a world that is arranged and simplified, a world with a meaning that expresses our own creative activity." For the ambiguity of the term "historical fact" and the need to go beyond the "positivism" that clings to this old problem of history, I would warmly recommend A. Vanel's "L'impact des méthodes historiques en théologie du XVIe au XXe siècle," *Le Déplacement de la théologie* (Paris, 1977), especially pp. 26ff.

14. A. Jaubert, "Christ est ressuscité," *Qui est Jésus-Christ?* (Recherches et Débats) (Paris, 1968), p. 121.

15. X. Léon-Dufour, *op. cit.*, p. 277.

16. J. Moingt, "Certitude historique et foi," *RSR* (1970), p. 572.

17. A. Gesché, *op. cit.*, p. 287.

18. See P. Ricoeur, "Evénement et sens," *Révélation et Histoire* (Colloque Castelli, 5–11 January 1971) (Paris, 1971), pp. 15–34.

19. P. Ricoeur, *op. cit.*, p. 19.

20. See A. Gesché, *op. cit.*, pp. 302–303, who correctly shows in

the third section of his article how eschatology provides us with the true place of theological intelligibility of the mystery of the resurrection.

21. I would like to quote here these very characteristic words of Hans Urs von Balthasar, *La Gloire et la Croix* (Paris, 1965), p. 170: "The fact that there is always talk of faith in the presence of the appearances of the risen Christ proves clearly that faith in the presence of the resurrection, that is, the faith of those who have not succeeded in seeing the risen Christ corporeally, but who believe in the virtue of the apostolic testimony, consists not in regarding as true a simple probability, but in the same gift of love of his own person and of his own evidence with regard to the divine Person who encloses and keeps within himself the center of gravity of all evidence."

VI. The Atheistic Hermeneutics of the Title "The Son of Man" in Ernst Bloch

1. E. Bloch, *L'Athéisme dans le christianisme* (Paris, 1978). All my quotations in this chapter are taken from this French language edition.

2. For this question, see G. Raulet, "Utopie-Discours pratique," who has edited the collected work entitled *Utopie. Marxisme selon Ernst Bloch* (Paris, 1976), in which his article appears, pp. 9–53.

3. For this, see E. Braun, "Possibilité et non-encore-être. L'ontologie traditionelle et l'ontologie du non-encore-être de Bloch," *Utopie, op. cit.*, pp. 155–169.

4. J. Jeremias, *New Testament Theology I: The Proclamation of Jesus* (New York, 1971), pp. 257–275. In addition to Jeremias, I have also consulted C. H. Dodd, *The Interpretation of the Fourth Gospel* (Cambridge, 1960); H. E. Tödt, *The Son of Man in the Synoptic Tradition* (Philadelphia, 1965); J. M. van Cangh, "Le Fils de l'homme dans la tradition synoptique," *RThL* 1 (1970), pp. 411–419.

5. J. Jeremias, *op. cit.*, p. 266.

6. *Ibid.*, p. 275.

7. C. Duquoc's contribution to this subject, "Un athéisme biblique," *LV* 156 (1982), pp. 69–81, is well worth reading.

8. See especially J. Moltmann, *Theology of Hope* (New York, 1967), and A. Dumas, "Ernst Bloch et la théologie de l'espérance de Jurgen Moltmann," *Utopie, op. cit.*, pp. 222–238.

VII. From the God of Theism to the Crucified God

1. I would like to draw attention here to André Dumas' very happy formula in his article "Dieu, pourquoi, comment?" *Bulletin du Centre protestant d'études* (June 1973), p. 17: "I would therefore say that God

is looking forward today to receiving his baptismal name from us—a name that will suit him insofar as he speaks to us and a name that has been approved by and is acceptable to both God and man."

2. See C. Duquoc, "La figure du Dieu Jésus," *LV (L)*, 128 (May–July 1976), p. 68.

3. I am thinking here especially of J. Moltmann's *The Crucified God* (New York, 1974), but I would also mention H. Urs von Balthasar, "Le mystère pascal," *Mysterium Salutis* (Paris, 1972), pp. 9–274; S. Breton, *Le Verbe et la Croix* (Paris, 1981); E. Jüngel, *Dieu mystère du monde (Cogitatio Fidei* 116 and 117) (Paris, 1983).

4. It would be interesting to trace the history of the secularization of the theological idea of creation, which tends, in the modern period, to define the essence of man who gives birth to himself. For this question, see A. Ganoczy, *Homme créateur, Dieu créateur (Cogitatio Fidei* 98) (Paris, 1970), who traces the theme of creation in Hegel, Marx, Nietzsche and Sartre. In a completely different context, that of the philosophy of A. N. Whitehead, the American "process theology" (see especially J. Cobb and S. Ogden) came about as a result of a desire to overcome the fundamental difficulties that traditional theology has for critical contemporary thought. For an introduction to this process theology in French, see A. Gounelle, "Le Dynamisme créateur de Dieu. Essai sur la théologie du Process," *ETR* (Montpellier, 1981).

5. See especially A. Dumas, "La critique de l'objectivité de Dieu dans la théologie protestant," *Nommer Dieu (Cogitatio Fidei* 100) (Paris, 1980), pp. 115–137. A carefully shaded judgment about the present contestation of the God of the onto-theological tradition will be found in P. Vignaux, "Dieu contesté, Dieu incontestable," *Les Quatre Fleuves* 6 (1976), pp. 64–77.

6. For this destiny of metaphysics as onto-theology and its consequences for Christian theology, see a number of my earlier works, especially C. Geffré, "Le problème théologique de l'objectivité de Dieu," *Procès de l'objectivité de Dieu (Cogitatio Fidei* 41) (Paris, 1969), pp. 241–263, and *ibid.*, "Sens et non-sens d'une théologie non métaphysique," *A New Age in Theology* (New York, 1974), pp. 51–62.

7. For the meaning of this distinction, see G. Granel, who has several valuable things to say in his various studies of Heidegger that have been published in his *Traditionis traditio* (Paris, 1972).

8. Here I have especially in mind a book by J.-L. Marion, the very title of which is a program in itself: *L'Idole et la distance* (Paris, 1977). For what I have to say here, see especially his Chapter 2, "Le Dieu de l'onto-théologie," pp. 27ff. In his new book, *Dieu sans l'être* (Paris, 1982), J.-L. Marion's thinking is made more radical by his attempt to set

theology free not only from the idolatry that is peculiar to metaphysics in the Heideggerian sense, but also from the idolatry that is peculiar to the idea of Being as such. God can only be thought about without idolatry on the basis of himself alone.

9. J.-L. Marion, *L'Idole et la distance, op. cit.*, pp. 34–35. This author quite naturally cites at this point Heidegger's famous text in his *Identität und Differenz:* "Man cannot pray to that God, nor can he offer him anything, go down on his knees in respect before him, play music to him or dance for him. In conformity with that, the a-theistic idea (*gottlos* in the Pauline sense), which has to abandon the God of the philosophers, the God *causa sui*, is possibly closer to the divine God. This only means, then, that this is more freely open than onto-theology would like to think." This text will be found in *Questions* I (Paris, 1968), p. 306.

10. See C. Geffré, "Dieu," *Encyclopaedia Universalis* 5 (Paris, 1969), pp. 576–580.

11. See my study above, "Le problème théologique de l'objectivité de Dieu," *op. cit.*, pp. 251–252.

12. See A. Fierro, "Histoire de Dieu," *LV (L)* 128 (May-July 1976), pp. 79–99).

13. I will refrain from listing the enormous number of books and articles on the theory of ideologies and mention simply two works in which the problem of the relationship between Christian faith and ideology is well postulated: C. Wackenheim, *Christianisme sans idéologie* (Paris, 1974) and S. Breton, *Théorie des idéologies* (Paris, 1976). See also, however, my reservations with regard to Wackenheim's approach in *Le Supplément* 116 (February 1976), pp. 125–128.

14. I would warmly recommend as an introduction to the problem that is peculiar to the theologies of liberation the special number of *Concilium* 96 (1974) on "The Mystical and Political Dimensions of Human Faith."

15. In my opinion, to regard, as H. de Lubac does, the theologies of liberation as no more than a new expression of Joachimism betrays a real misunderstanding of the ecclesiological dimension of the preferential option for the poor in the churches of the third world. See, for example, *La Postérité spirituelle de Joachim de Flore II: De Saint-Simon à nos jours* (Namur, 1981).

16. See A. Dumas, *Dieu, pourquoi, comment?* *op. cit.*, p. 16: "I have the feeling that an exclusive 'Jesus centrism' neglects this essential task of reacquiring the invented name of God in preference to the gods invented by our needs. This 'Jesus centrism' is therefore mistaken in cutting itself off from other possible gods, thus becoming itself a hermetic specialization. If Jesus has no relationship with God, why should he then

have been given the name 'Christ,' which is both his own and universal?" The following statement by G. Morel, "L'enjeu de la crise religieuse," *RSR* 63 (1975), p. 32, has the same basic meaning: "To what Christian, however, does what is the heart of Christianity, the Trinitarian God, really mean something? It is hardly possible to forget that, for Christ, life was only meaningful in relationship—a constant and intense relationship—to the Father and that, for that reason, he only gave himself as 'passing over.'"

17. I would draw attention here to this very balanced statement by E. Schillebeeckx, "The 'God of Jesus' and the 'Jesus of God,'" *Concilium* 93 (1974), pp. 110–126.

18. For an elaboration of what I have simply suggested here, I would refer the reader to my study, "Le problème théologique de l'objectivité de Dieu," *op. cit.*, pp. 255ff.

19. See Hans Urs von Balthasar, *L'Amour seul est digne de foi* (Paris, 1966).

20. What we have here is the "theology of the reality" that A. Dumas has tried to outline in his commentary on the theological work of Bonhoeffer: *Une théologie de la réalité: Dietrich Bonhoeffer* (Geneva, 1968).

21. It is precisely this kind of aporia that I have tried to deal with in my article, "La contingence historique du christianisme comme scandale de la foi," *VS* (November–December 1973), pp. 791–799.

22. See A. Gesché, "Le Dieu de la Bible et la théologie spéculative," *EThL* 51 (May 1975), pp. 5–34, especially pp. 26ff. There is also the familiar question asked by Karl Barth: "Why did Hegel not become for the Protestant world what Thomas Aquinas was for the Catholic world?" W. Pannenberg has tried to reply to this kind of question in his important study "La signification du christianisme dans la philosophie de Hegel," *ArPh* 33 (October–December 1970), pp. 775–786.

23. K. Rahner has made a bold speculative attempt to reinterpret the Chalcedonian definition. See especially his "Current Problems in Christology," *Theological Investigations I* (Baltimore, 1961), especially pp. 174–185. In that volume, he said, for example, p. 181: "God dwells 'in himself,' 'unchangeable,' when he really comes himself in what he constitutes as being at the same time both united to himself and different from himself." In a footnote, he added: "(Ontology) has to concede that God, dwelling unchangeable in himself, can exist in another and that these two statements are really and truly the fact of the same God as such." For his part, E. Jungel is conscious of the presence of the fundamental aporia of the idea of God in the modern age in the question of the relationship between God and what is perishable (*Verganglichkeit*).

He has therefore looked for a solution by going as far as possible in a reflection about the humanity of the crucified God. See his *God as the Mystery of the World, op. cit.*

24. K. Rahner, *Mission et Grâce* I (Paris, 1962), p. 76.

25. W. Pannenberg has in particular insisted on this point in his Christology. See *Jesus—God and Man* (Philadelphia, 1977).

26. See C. Duquoc, "La figure trinitaire du Dieu de Jésus," *LV(L)* 128, pp. 73ff., and *Dieu différent* (Paris, 1977).

27. I am prepared to accept responsibility for this cruel diagnosis by G. Morel, "Les vertus de la nuit," in "L'Eglise: l'épreuve du vide," *Autrement* 2 (1975), p. 83: 'Everyone will wonder whether the present reaction to atheism or agnosticism is not at least partly motivated by a certain disgust with religious positivism. The accumulation of presentations in this sphere is not unrelated to the same phenomenon in the sphere of economics. In various places, there are signs of the same need to have assurances at all costs within reach and to hold them in trust. In the case of theology, there is a noticeable contradiction existing in the same individual. On the one hand, he confesses, with reference to the philosophical discourse (which is in any case classical), that practically nothing can be known of God, while, on the other, he makes up for this wonderful poverty by a great number of concepts, already divided into four, and images. God may be complex, but he is certainly not quite as complicated as this. The Christian God has become terribly old in the West and he has not aged well."

28. J. Moltmann has stressed almost too systematically this opposition between history in the biblical sense and history in the Greek sense in his *Theology of Hope* (New York, 1967).

29. See W. Pannenberg, "The God of Hope," *Basic Questions in Theology II* (Philadelphia, 1971), pp. 234–249.

30. See J. Moltmann, *Man: Christian Anthropology in the Conflicts of the Present* (Philadelphia, 1974), p. 105.

31. P. Watte, "Job and Auschwitz," *RThL* 4 (1973), p. 189, quoted by A. Gesché, "Retrouver Dieu," *La Foi et le temps* 6 (March-April 1976), p. 139.

32. J. Moltmann, *The Crucified God*, p. 175.

33. *Ibid.*, p. 221.

34. F. Varillon, *L'Humilité de Dieu* (Paris, 1974).

35. See S. Breton, *Le Verbe et la Croix* (Paris, 1981), p. 103: "The Logos of the Cross is certainly a logos, a saying, but that saying has such a disconcerting effect on our ideas that it can only be folly. It is as folly that it is the power of God." That is, it would seem, the most likely meaning of the Pauline statement.

VIII. "Father" as the Proper Name of God

1. H. Küng, *Does God Exist?* (Garden City, 1980), p. 666.

2. "Taking leave of the 'God of the philosophers' is anything but taking leave of the obligation to think God": E. Jungel, *God as the Mystery of the World* (Grand Rapids, 1983), p. 199.

3. *Ibid.*

4. J. Jeremias, *The Prayers of Jesus* (London, 1967), p. 13.

5. See P. Ricoeur, "Fatherhood: From Phantasm to Symbol," *Conflict of Interpretations* (Evanston, 1974), p. 487.

6. Apart from the classical studies of J. Jeremias and W. Marchel (*Dieu Père dans le Nouveau Testament*, Paris, 1966), I would above all recommend the section on Jesus' experience of God the Father in E. Schillebeeckx, *Jesus: An Experiment in Christology* (New York, 1979), pp. 256–299, who also provides an abundant bibliography on this subject.

7. W. Pannenberg, *Jesus—God and Man* (Philadelphia, 1977), pp. 231–232.

8. A. Vergote, *Interprétation du langage religieux* (Paris, 1974), p. 125.

9. J. Jeremias, *Abba, Jésus et son Père* (Paris, 1972), p. 69.

10. J.-L. Marion, *L'Idole et la distance* (Paris, 1977), pp. 270–271.

11. K. Barth, *Dogmatique* II, 1, 2 (Geneva, 1957), p. 69.

12. M. Heidegger, *Identität und Differenz* (Pfullingen, 1957), p. 70. FrT: *Questions* I (Paris, 1968), p. 306.

13. C. Duquoc, *Dieu différent* (Paris, 1977), p. 119.

14. This formula will be found in A. Vergote's important study "Passion de l'origine et quete de l'originaire," which has been included in his *Interprétation du langage religieux*, *op. cit.*, p. 44.

15. J.-M. Pohier, *Au nom du Père. Recherches théologiques et psychanalytiques* (*Cogitatio Fidei* 66) (Paris, 1972), p. 105.

16. C. Duquoc, *op. cit.*, p. 102.

17. See J. Moltmann, *The Crucified God*, p. 243: "The Father handed his Son over to the cross in order to become the Father who was handed over and given," and, later on: "By abandoning the Son, the Father also abandoned himself. By handing the Son over, the Father also handed himself over, although not in the same way."

IX. The Breakdown of History and the Lordship of Christ

1. "Is it possible to speak of a 'development' without defining precisely what the invariable is 'which' develops (and which cannot be simple) and to relate it to an origin that is elusive and an end that is not given,

since we are in a history that is still continuing? To what point and to what level is it possible to postulate a single mankind that is built up in time in stages that are both successive and progressive?" These are the questions that have been asked of the plan of a universal history tending toward an interpretation of the totality of "experienced history" by A. Vanel in his "L'impact des méthodes historiques en théologie du XVIe au XXe siècle," *Le Déplacement de la théologie* (Paris, 1977), p. 36.

2. For this, see the special number of *Concilium* entitled "Humanism and Christianity," *Concilium* 86 (1973). See also C. Geffré, "La crise de l'humanisme et l'actualité d'une anthropologie chrétienne," *Humanisme et foi chrétienne (Mélanges de l'Institut catholique de Paris)* (Paris, 1976), pp. 473–482.

3. This is a reference to the title of J.-F. Six' book, *Du Syllabus au dialogue* (Paris, 1970).

4. See J.-B. Metz, *Faith in History and Society* (London and New York, 1980), p. 107: "Suffering stresses the contrast between nature and history, teleology and eschatology."

5. See especially the contributions by E. Dussel and J.-L. Secundo in the special number of *Concilium* entitled "The Mystical and Political Dimensions of Christian Faith," *Concilium* 96 (1974).

6. I would draw the reader's attention here to J.-B. Metz' article "The Future in the Memory of Suffering," *Concilium* 76 (1972), pp. 9–25 and to Chapter 6, "The Future in the Memory of Suffering," *Faith in History and Society, op. cit.*, pp. 100–118.

7. "The memory of Jesus' sufferings ought to be able to resound, in the midst of what is regarded as 'acceptable' by our society, as an evocation that is both dangerous and liberating, and the dogmas of Christology ought to be affirmed as formulae that call to mind things that are very embarrassing." See J.-B. Metz, "The Future in the Memory of Suffering," *op. cit.*, p. 18. See also Chapter V, "The Dangerous Memory of the Freedom of Jesus Christ," *Faith in History and Society, op. cit.*, pp. 88–99.

8. J. Moltmann, *The Crucified God*, p. 22.

9. M.-D. Chenu, "Les signes des temps. Réflexion théologique," *L'Eglise dans le monde de ce temps* II (Paris, 1967), pp. 205–222. See also "Les signes des temps," *NRT* 87 (1965), pp. 29–39 and "Signs of the Times," *Concilium* 25 (1967) pp. 143–152.

10. With reference to this point, see the very valid comments by J. Moltmann in *The Church in the Power of the Spirit* (New York, 1977), pp. 37–50.

11. Although I do not accept them as the last word on the theological meaning of profane history, I have drawn here to a great extent on the ideas of Fr. Valadier, who has reacted healthily to the often very facile use

of the term "signs of the times." See his "Signes des temps, signes de Dieu," *Etudes* (August-September 1971), pp. 261–279.

12. See especially his *History and Eschatology* (New York, 1957).

13. See K. Löwith, *From Hegel to Nietzsche* (New York, 1964).

14. See especially *De l'intégration. Aspects d'une théologie de l'histoire* (Paris, 1970).

15. See L. Bouyer, "Christianisme et Eschatologie," *Vie I* (October 1948), pp. 6–38 and "Où en est la théologie du corps mystique?" *RSR 22* (1948), pp. 313–333.

16. "There can be no teleological and final mediation between man and nature," J.-B. Metz has affirmed in opposition to Teilhard, *Faith in History and Society, op. cit.,* p. 107.

17. With regard to this, I am in agreement with what E. Brauns has expressed so well in these words which form the conclusion to his article "Projet et conditions d'une théologie de l'histoire," *RSR 70* (1982), pp. 321–342: "The theology of history does not aim to justify human becoming, but to put it at a distance, face to face with the eternity of God. In this way, it becomes a positive and contingent emergence of a world with regard to the otherness of God the Creator."

18. I am referring here especially to various documents published at the conclusion of a number of congresses held by the Ecumenical Association of Third World Theologians at Dar-es-Salaam (1976), Accra (1977), Colombo (1979) and São Paulo (1980).

19. "Salvation (*soteria*) should also be understood in the Old Testament sense as *šalom*. This does not mean salvation of the soul, individual deliverance from an evil world or consolation only for a consciousness put to the test. It means rather the realization of an eschatological hope of justice, man's humanization, the socialization of mankind and peace in the whole of creation." See J. Moltmann, *Theology of Hope* (New York, 1967), p. 329.

20. In my opinion, the radical foundation of the positivity of human history can be found in the mystery of the incarnation, but, as P. Gisel has shown so clearly, this presupposes a theology of creation conceived as an original break, by virtue of which history is considered not as the positivity of a reality already present, but rather as the positivity of a reality to come. See P. Gisel, *La Création* (Geneva, 1980).

21. I have drawn directly here on an early but very important article by E. Schillebeeckx, "The Church and Mankind," *Concilium 1* (1965), pp. 69–102.

22. See J. Moltmann, *The Church in the Power of the Spirit, op. cit.,* p. 33. See also K. Rahner, "Remarques sur le concept de révélation," K. Rahner and J. Ratzinger, *Révélation et Tradition* (Paris, 1972), pp. 15–36, especially pp. 24–25.

23. "The Christian expectation is directed toward no one else but the Christ who has come, but something new that has not yet happened until the present time is also expected: the fulfillment in all things of the justice promised by God, the fulfillment of the resurrection of the dead promised in his resurrection and the fulfillment of the Lordship of Christ crucified over all things promised in his exaltation and glorification." See J. Moltmann, *Theology of Hope, op. cit.*, p. 229.

24. See J.-P. Jossua, "L'enjeu de la recherche théologique actuelle sur le salut," *RSPT* 54 (1970), pp. 24–45.

25. See C. Duquoc's vigorous formula, *L'Eglise et le monde. Equipes Enseignantes* (First Term, 1964–1965), p. 81: "Affirming man is not necessarily affirming God, but denying man is certainly denying God."

X. The Testimony of Faith in a Non-Christian Culture

1. J. Moltmann, *The Crucified God*, p. 221.

2. U. Ecco, *La Structure absente* (Paris, 1972), p. 384, quoted by G. Morel, "L'enjeu de la crise religieuse," *RSR* 63 (1975), pp. 11–38.

3. See J. Moingt, "L'écho du silence," *RSR* 67 (1979), pp. 9–36.

4. For this question, see the methodological principles outlined by E. Schillebeeckx in *Expérience humaine et foi en Jésus-Christ* (Paris, 1981), especially pp. 29–64.

5. I have summarized here what I have already discussed in Part I of this book (especially Chapters I and III).

6. I have borrowed this expression from P. Gisel, *Vérité et histoire. La théologie dans la modernité. Ernst Käsemann* (Paris, 1977).

7. See J. Ladrière, *Les Enjeux de la rationalité. Le défi de la science et da la technologie aux cultures* (Paris, 1977). For the history of the concept of culture, I would recommend M. Meslin's brief study, "Culture et modernité," *RICP* 1 (1982), pp. 75–90.

8. Among the most recent works on the problem of "inculturation," I would recommend especially M. Sales, "Christianisme, culture et cultures," *Axes* XIII (1–2 January 1981), pp. 3–40.

9. For the question of vocabulary, see especially I. de la Potterie, *Culture et foi. Publication de la Commission biblique* (Turin, 1981), pp. 327–329. For the confrontation between the Bible and cultures, see also the recent work by P. Beauchamp, *Le Récit, la lettre et le corps (Cogitatio Fidei* 114) (Paris, 1982).

10. I have taken this expression from H. Küng, *On Being a Christian* (Garden City, 1976), p. 110. The same idea was used by J. Moltmann in his *The Church in the Power of the Spirit*, pp. 158ff.

11. For this question, see F. Mussner, *The Tractate on the Jews* (Philadelphia, 1984), Chapter III.

12. I have based my ideas here on Y. de Gal's stimulating suggestions in his *Questions à la théologie chrétienne* (Paris, 1975), p. 71.

13. See my article in *Concilium* 146 (1979), pp. 75–87: "Theology in the Age of China: Evangelization and Culture." See also M. Zago, "Evangelization in the Religious Situation of Asia," *Concilium* 114 (1979), pp. 72–84.

14. I have borrowed this expression from C. Duquoc, *Dieu différent* (Paris, 1977), p. 126.

15. See A. Ganoczy, "The Absolute Claim of Christianity: A Justification of Evangelization or an Obstacle to It?" *Concilium* 114 (1979), pp. 19–29.

16. See G. Morel, "Les vertus de la nuit," *Autrement* 2 (1975), pp. 79–84.

17. For this subject, see my article, "The Outlook for Christian Faith in a World of Religious Indifference," *Concilium* 165 (1983), pp. 58–70.

18. See especially P. Beauchamp's article "La prophétie d'hier," *LV(L)* 115 (1973), pp. 14–24.

19. This idea has been used again by P. Jacquemont, J.-P. Jossua and B. Quelquejeu, the authors of *Le Temps de la patience* (Paris, 1976), pp. 131–132.

20. See J.-B. Metz, "Unbelief as a Theological Problem," *Concilium* 6 (1965), pp. 59–78.

XI. The Ideological Function of Secularization

1. For this question, the reader should consult S. Breton, *Théorie des idéologies* (Paris, 1976); C. Wackenheim, *Christianisme sans idéologie* (Paris, 1974); also P. Ricoeur, "Herméneutique et critique des idéologies," in the symposium *Démythologisation et idéologie* (Paris, 1973), pp. 25–61.

2. P. Berger, *The Sacred Canopy* (Garden City, 1969), *passim*.

3. *Ibid.*, p. 124.

4. J. Gabel, "Idéologie," *Encyclopaedia Universalis* VIII (Paris, 1970), p. 719.

5. K. Jaspers, *Origine et sens de l'histoire*, cited by J. Gabel, *op. cit.*, p. 719.

6. I would mention here only the most outstanding works, which I have used in this chapter: F. Gogarten, *Despair and Hope for Our Time* (Philadelphia, 1970); D. Bonhoeffer, *Letters and Papers from Prison* (New York, 1972); Harvey Cox, *The Secular City* (New York, 1965); T. J. J. Altizer, *The Gospel of Christian Atheism* (Philadelphia, 1966). For the theo-

logies of secularization, I would strongly recommend C. Duquoc's study, *Ambigüité des théologies de la sécularisation. Essai critique* (Gembloux, 1972). The following books are also well worth consulting: L. Newbigin, *Une religion pour un monde séculier* (Tournai and Paris, 1969); R. Marlé, *La Singularité chrétienne* (Tournai and Paris, 1970); also two symposia: *Les Deux Visages de la théologie de la sécularisation* (Tournai and Paris, 1970) and E. Castelli, ed., *Herméneutique de la sécularisation* (Paris, 1976).

7. See A. Dumas, *Nommer Dieu (Cogitatio Fidei* 100) (Paris, 1980), pp. 88–89.

8. P. Berger, p. 129.

9. See *Les Deux Visages de la théologie de la sécularisation, op. cit.,* p. 32.

10. C. Duquoc reproduces Gogarten's thinking in this way in his *Ambigüité de théologies de la sécularisation,* p. 41.

11. For this question, see J.-L. Secundo, "Capitalism—Socialism: A Theological Crux," *Concilium* 96 (1974), pp. 105–123.

12. T. J. J. Altizer, *The Gospel of Christian Atheism, op. cit.*

13. D. Bonhoeffer, *Letters and Papers from Prison, op. cit.,* p. 36. It is also worth consulting the strictly theological commentary provided by E. Jüngel on these well known texts in *God as the Mystery of the World,* pp. 57–63.

14. See the symposium, *Le Retour du sacré* (Paris, 1977), with my own conclusions, pp. 129–143. In addition, I would also draw attention to two important recent works that have been brought to my notice since completing the text of the present book: J.-P. Sironneau, *Sécularisation et religions politiques* (Paris, 1982); F.-A. Isambert, *Le Sens du sacré. Fête et religion populaire* (Paris, 1982).

15. I would like to refer here to my study "Le christianisme et les métamorphoses de sacré." E. Castelli's edition of the Acts of the Roman colloquium on the subject, *Le Sacré. Etudes et recherches* (Paris, 1974). See also my contribution to the volume published in honor of Msgr. van Kamp, "Sécularisation du christianisme et retour du sacré." *Savoir, faire, espérer. Les limites de la raison* (Brussels, 1976), II, pp. 739–754.

16. See R. Bultmann, "Discours de Paul à l'Aréopage," *Le Supplément* 114 (September 1975), pp. 303–313, with a commentary by C. Geffré, "L'homme moderne face au Dieu inconnu," *ibid.,* pp. 315–321.

17. It is this criticism of freedom as the freedom of emancipation in the sense in which it is understood in neo-liberal societies that underlies the new political theology of J.-B. Metz in *Faith in History and Society, op. cit.*

18. *Les Deux Visages de la théologie de la sécularisation, op. cit.,* p. 146.

19. M. Xhaufflaire, "La théologie après la théologie de la sécularis-ation," *Les Deux Visages de la théologie de la sécularisation, op. cit.*, pp. 89–90.

20. A. M. Greeley does not avoid this danger in his book *Unsecular Man. The Persistence of Religion* (New York, 1972).

21. This is so in the case of such successful French books as those by Maurice Clavel and André Frossard.

22. My short study, "La critique de la religion chez Barth et Bon-hoeffer," *ParMiss* 31 (October 1965), pp. 567–583, can be consulted by the reader who is approaching the implications of this distinction for the first time.

23. See J.-B. Metz, *Theology of the World* (New York, 1969), p. 45.

24. I prefer to speak of a metamorphosis of the sacred and the reli-gious where R. Girard speaks of the end of the sacred inaugurated by Christianity as a non-sacrificial religion; see *Des choses cachées depuis la fondation du monde* (Paris, 1978). This is only possible because he goes no further than an altogether too universal conception of "sacrifice" and sees the only strength of the sacred in the violence of the sacrificial act. We have evidence in our own period of the persistence of a post-religious sa-cred element, which should not be confused with the "sacred" of the an-cient religions and which has not been exhausted by the religion of Jesus. Even in Western society today, we are coming increasingly to understand that atheism is not the only alternative to Christianity. There is a always a possibility of the rebirth of paganism. See M. Augé, *Le Génie du pagan-isme* (Paris, 1982).

XII. Christianity as a Way

1. Lao-Tzu, *Tao, A New Way of Thinking* (New York, 1975).

2. See C. Perrot, "Halakha juive et morale chrétienne: fonctionne-ment et référence," *Ecriture et pratique chrétienne (Lectio divina* 96) (Paris, 1978), pp. 35–51.

3. For the general theme of the exodus, see the article "Exode," *Vo-cabulaire de théologie biblique* (Paris, 2nd. ed., 1970), 423–425; J. Guillet, *Themes of the Bible* (Notre Dame, 1960); A.-M. Besnard, *Par un long chemin vers toi. Le pélerinage chrétien (Foi vivante* 184) (Paris, 1978).

4. J. Moltmann, *Theology of Hope* (New York, 1967), p. 102.

5. See above, Chapter V.

6. There are numerous references in S. Lyonnet, "Per un incontro tra Cristianesimo e Cina: Il Cristianesimo presentato come 'Via' (Tao) o come 'modo di vita' " (Florence, 1978).

7. To complete the references made in this section, see the article on "Chemin" in the *Vocabulaire de théologie biblique, op. cit.*, pp. 159–162.

8. C. Perrot., *op. cit.*, p. 48.

9. *In Ep. ad Galatas,* 1519 edition, *WA* II, p. 518, quoted by F. Refoulé, "Jésus comme référence de l'agir des chrétiens," *Ecriture et pratique chrétienne* (Paris, 1978), p. 201.

10. D. Bonhoeffer, *Le Prix de la Grâce* (Neuchâtel, 1967), pp. 25–26, quoted by F. Refoulé, *op. cit.*, p. 203.

11. F. Refoulé, *ibid.*, p. 222.

12. See C. Perrot, "L'anamnèse néo-testamentaire," *RICP* 2 (April-June 1982), pp. 21–37. For a modern rendering of the traditional theme of the "way" in Christian spirituality that keeps strictly to the original but is also poetic, I would warmly recommend the very suggestive work by M. Bellet, *La Voie* (Paris, 1982).

13. See J.-B. Metz, *Followers of Christ* (New York, 1978), pp. 39–40.

14. Following Jesus also has a socio-political aspect. It is both mystical and political. It is possible to say without hesitation that the theology of the following of Jesus is a political theology. See J.-B. Metz, *op. cit.*, p. 41.

15. I. de la Potterie, " 'Faire la vérité': devise de l'orthopraxie cu invitation à la foi?" *Le Supplément* 118 (September 1976), pp. 283–293.

16. See above, Chapter III.

XIII. Toward a Christian Interpretation of Human Rights

1. J. Blank, "The Justice of God as the Humanization of Man—The Problem of Human Rights in the New Testament," *Concilium* 124 (1979), pp. 27–38.

2. J. Leclerc, *Les Premiers Défenseurs de la liberté religieuse* I (Paris, 1969), p. 18.

3. For this subject, see B. Plongeron, "Pourquoi l'anathème catholique aux XVIIIe-XIXe siècles?" *Projet* 5 (1981), pp. 52–66.

4. See B. Plongeron, *op. cit.*, p. 56.

5. C. Wackenheim, "The Theological Meaning of the Rights of Man," *Concilium* 124 (1979), pp. 49–56.

6. See especially R. Aubert, "L'enseignement du magistère ecclésiastique au XIXe siècle," *Tolérance et communauté humaine* (Tournai and Paris, 1952), pp. 75–103. For a brief historical sketch of the modern phenomenon of religious freedom, see E. Poulat, "Liberté religieuse et dé-

veloppement historique des libertés," *La Liberté religieuse dans le judaisme, le christianisme et l'islam (Cogitatio Fidei* 110) (Paris, 1981), pp. 17–34.

7. See F. Refoulé, "L'Eglise et les libertés," *Le Supplément* 25 (1978), p. 253. For the development of the magisterium with regard to the question of human rights, a vast documentation will be found in G. Thils, *Droits de l'homme et perspectives chrétiennes* (Louvain, 1981).

8. These are Msgr. J. Willebrands' words, cited by L. de Vauchelles in his "La déclaration de Vatican II sur la liberté religieuse," *La Liberté religieuse dans le judaisme, le christianisme et l'islam (Cogitatio Fidei* 10) (Paris, 1981), p. 130.

9. A useful article to consult in this context is F. Refoulé, "Efforts Made on Behalf of Human Rights by the Supreme Authority of the Church," *Concilium* 124 (1979), pp. 77–85.

10. Here I have drawn directly on the ideas of W. Huber, "Human Rights—The Concept and Its History," *Concilium* 124 (1979), pp. 1–10.

11. J. Julliard, "Marcher sur les deux jambes," *Le Nouvel Observateur* (December 30, 1978).

12. See N. Greinacher, "The Responsibility of the Churches in the First World for Establishing Human Rights," *Concilium* 124 (1979), pp. 107–115.

XIV. Reinterpreting the Church's Mission

1. See Y. Congar, Doctrinal principles (Nos. 2 to 9) in *L'Activité missionaire de l'Eglise (décret "Ad Gentes," texte et commentaires)* (Paris, 1967), pp. 185–194.

2. For the setting up of the Congregation for the Propagation of the Faith, see B. Jacqueline, "Mission," *Dictionnaire de spiritualité* (Paris, 1979), col. 1383–1390.

3. For the importance of this change, see A.-M. Henry, "Mission," *Catholicisme* 39 (Paris, 1980), col. 328–331.

4. For this point, see P. Jacquemont, J.-P. Jossua and B. Quelquejeu, *Le Temps de la patience, op. cit.*, Chap. IV, "Proclamation ou témoignage?"

5. This extension of the word "witness" or "testimony" has been stressed in the preparatory document for the Assembly of the World Council of Churches at Vancouver (1983). It urges that the spiritual Gospel should not be separated from the material Gospel (No. 33). This document was prepared by the Council's Commission of World Mission and Evangelism (CWME) and published under the title of "Mission and Evangel-

ism. An Ecumenical Affirmation" in *IRM* 71, No. 284 (October 1982), pp. 427–451.

6. I would in this context cite this unequivocal statement made in the document "Mission and Evangelism," *op. cit.*, p. 441, n. 33: "Churches are learning afresh through the poor of the earth to overcome the old dichotomies between evangelism and social action. The 'spiritual Gospel' and 'material Gospel' were in Jesus one Gospel."

7. For a first and very valuable approach, see the special number of *Concilium:* 84 (1975).

8. I would cite here, among many other works, W. Kasper's study "Esprit-Christ-Eglise," *L'Expérience de l'Esprit (Mélanges Schillebeeckx)* (Paris, 1976), pp. 47–69.

9. "Mission and Evangelism," *op. cit.*, p. 428, n. 1.

10. For this question, see J.-M. Ela's vigorously written chapter on creating rather than inheriting the future in J.-M. Ela and R. Luneau, *Le Temps des héritiers* (Paris, 1981), Chapter V, "On n'hérite pas de l'avenir, on le crée," pp. 229–253.

11. See I. Puthiadam, "Christian Faith in a World of Religious Pluralism," *Concilium* 135 (1980), pp. 99–112.

12. C. Duquoc, "Christianity and Its Claim to Universality," *Concilium* 135 (1980) pp. 59–69.

13. C. Geffré, "Evangelization ou dialogue?" *ParMiss* 45 (1969), pp. 225–235.

14. See A.-M. Henry's pertinent comments, *op. cit.*, col. 346–347.

15. See the article quoted above by A. Ganoczy, "The Absolute Claim of Christianity: A Justification of Evangelization or an Obstacle to It?" *Concilium* 114 (1979) pp. 19–22.

16. For this biblical theme of poverty, see especially A. Gelin, *Les pauvres que Dieu aime* (Paris, 1967); J.-M.R. Tillard, *Le Salut mystère de pauvreté* (Paris, 1968). See also A. Bockmann, "What Does the New Testament Say About the Church's Attitude to the Poor?" *Concilium* 104 (1977), pp. 36–47.

17. For Jesus as the herald of God's rights, see J. Blank, "The Justice of God as the Humanization of Man—The Problem of Human Rights in the New Testament," *Concilium* 124 (1979), pp. 27–38.

18. This priority in favor of the poor is emphasized again and again in the ecumenical document "Mission and Evangelism," *op. cit.* See, for example, p. 441, n. 32: "The proclamation of the Gospel among the poor is a sign of the messianic kingdom and a priority criterion by which to judge the validity of our missionary engagement today."

19. In the final document of the Congress of Third World Theologians

at São Paulo in 1980, there are these powerful declarations: "In Latin America, evangelization led by the poor finds a special place in a concrete experience: the basic communities of the Church. The finality of evangelization is not the formation of little elitist or privileged groups in the Church. Christian communities are renewed by the movement that leads them to look for the most exploited among the most poor. The evangelization of the masses takes place in the perspective of a preferential option in favor of the poor." See *Foi et développement* 76 (April 1980), nn. 43–44. See also G. Gutiérrez, *The Power of the Poor in History* (Maryknoll, 1983).

20. See J. Moltmann, *The Church in the Power of the Spirit* (New York, 1977), p. 79.

21. This ecclesiological foundation of poverty is powerfully emphasized by J. Moltmann, p. 129: "It is not so much a question of knowing how persons or events taking place before the Church can be related to the Church, but of knowing how the Church relates to the presence of Christ in those who are 'outside,' the starving, the sick, the naked and the prisoners."

22. See M.-D. Chenu, "Les signes des temps," *NRTh* (January 1965), p. 36.

Epilogue: The Silence and Promises of French Theology

1. *La Croix* (August 7, 1970), quoted by Yves Congar, "Regards sur la théologie française d'aujourd'hui," *Savoir, faire, espérer: les limites de la raison* (Brussels, 1976), II, p. 697.

2. It is possible to refer here, for example, to the subtly shaded opinion expressed by F. Refoulé, "Orientations nouvelles de la théologie en France," *Le Supplément* 105 (May 1973), pp. 119–147.

3. This is what emerges from Henri de Lubac's commentary on the preface to and Chapter I of the Constitution on Divine Revelation, *Dei Verbum* (Paris, 1968), I, pp. 159–302.

4. See A. Rousseau and J.-P. Leconte, "The Social Conditions of Theological Activity," *Concilium* 115 (1979), pp. 12–21. See also A. Rousseau, "La formation théologique, I: Description du contexte catholique français actuel," *Initiation à la pratique de la théologie* I (Paris, 1982), pp. 329–344.

5. To be completely fair, however, it has to be admitted that such university theological reviews as *Les Quatre Fleuves* and *Communio* are not only animated, but also for the most part edited by laymen.

6. For this, see the opinion of the present secretary of the French episcopate, G. Defois, "Le pari chrétien dans l'intelligence? Une tache pour les instituts catholiques?" *Etudes* (January 1976), pp. 101–115.

7. This is the title of a book by C. Bruaire, *Le droit de Dieu* (Paris, 1974).

8. M. Clavel, *Dieu est Dieu, nom de Dieu!* (Paris, 1976).

9. A. Frossard, *Dieu existe, je l'ai rencontré* (Paris, 1975).

10. R. Girard, *Des choses cachées depuis la fondation du monde* (Paris, 1978). See also the same author's *Le Bouc émissaire* (Paris, 1982).

11. B.-H. Lévy, *Le Testament de Dieu* (Paris, 1979).

12. E. Jüngel, *God as the Mystery of the World* (Grand Rapids, 1983).

13. H. Küng, *Does God Exist?* (Garden City, 1980).

14. See above, Chapter VII.

15. C. Duquoc, *Dieu différent* (Paris, 1977). The same orientation can be found in several of the books in the series *Jésus—Jésus-Christ* edited by J. Doré and published by Desclée. This new series, which already includes seventeen titles, bears witness to the vitality of French theology as a theology which is deeply concerned with pastoral practice and the life of Christian communitites and which allows itself to be questioned both by the human sciences and by non-Christian religions.

16. "Dire ou taire Dieu. Le procès de Dieu entre paroles et silences," *RSR* (1979), with contributions by J. Moingt, S. Breton, M. de Certeau and J. Greisch especially.

17. S. Breton, *Du Principe. L'organisation contemporaine du pensable (Bibliothèque des sciences religieuses)* (Paris, 1971).

18. J.-L. Marion, *L'Idole et la distance* (Paris, 1977). See also the same author's *Dieu sans l'être* (Paris, 1982), which challenges the onto-theological tradition even more radically.

19. C. Wackenheim, *Christianisme sans idéologie* (Paris, 1974).

20. Works by C.E.R.I.T. under the direction of M. Michel, *Pouvoir et vérité (Cogitatio Fidei 108)* (Paris, 1981).

21. A. Delzant, *La Communication de Dieu. Par-delà utile et inutile. Essai théologique sur l'ordre symbolique (Cogitatio Fidei 92)* (Paris, 1978). An example of this new way of asking the question of God is G. Lafon's recent work, *Le Dieu commun* (Paris, 1982).

22. A. Dumas, *Nommer Dieu (Cogitatio Fidei 100)* (Paris, 1980).

23. M. Corbin, *L'Inoui de Dieu* (Bruges, 1980).

24. For this quest for the real name of the Christian God beyond nihilism and theism, see above, Chapter VIII, " 'Father' as the Proper Name of God."

25. F. Varillon, *L'Humilité de Dieu* (Paris, 1974); *La Souffrance de Dieu* (Paris, 1975).

26. S. Breton, *Le Verbe et la Croix (Jésus—Jésus-Christ)* (Paris, 1981).

27. Y. Congar, *I Believe in the Holy Spirit*, I, II and III (New York and London, 1983).

28. Among the many books written by P. Ricoeur, see especially *The Conflict of Interpretations* (Evanston, 1974) and *The Rule of Metaphor* (Toronto/Buffalo, 1977).

29. A. Vergote, *L'Interprétation du langage religieux* (Paris, 1974).

30. In Chapter II above, I have tried to assess the consequences for theology of this change in contemporary hermeneutics.

31. See P. Ricoeur, "Herméneutique philosophique et herméneutique biblique," *Exegesis. Problèmes de méthode et exercices de lecture (Genèse 22 et Luc 15)* (Neuchâtel, 1975), pp. 216–228.

32. G. Defois, "Révélation et société. La constitution Dei Verbum et les fonctions sociales de l'Ecriture," *RSR* (1975), pp. 457–504.

33. J. Audinet, "Théologie pratique et pratique théologique." *Le Déplacement de la théologie* (Paris, 1977), pp. 91–107.

34. J. Pohier, *Au nom du Père. Recherches théologiques et psychanalytiques* (Paris, 1972); *Quand je dis Dieu* (Paris, 1977).

35. D. Vasse, *Le Temps du désir. Essai sur le corps et la parole* (Paris, 1969).

36. X. Thévenot, *Repères éthiques* (Mulhouse, 1982); *Sexualité et vie chrétienne, point de vue catholique* (Paris, 1981).

37. G. Lafon, *Esquisses pour un christianisme* (Paris, 1979).

38. A. Delzant, *op. cit.*

39. L.-M. Chauvet, *Du symbolique au symbole. Essai sur les sacrements (Rites et symboles 9)* (Paris, 1979).

40. M. de Certeau and J.-M. Domenach, *Le Christianisme éclatée* (Paris, 1974).

41. R. Marlé, *Le projet de théologie pratique* (Paris, 1979).

42. A collected work such as *Le Déplacement de la théologie* tries to consider the consequences of this. See the conclusions drawn by C. Geffré, J. Audinet and P. Colin, *op. cit.*, pp. 169–184.

43. For this practical aspect of hermeneutics, see especially P. Gisel, *Vérité et histoire. La Théologie dans la modernité: Ernst Käsemann* (Geneva and Paris, 1977).

44. See the new publication directed by B. Lauret and F. Refoulé, *Initiation à la pratique de la théologie* I, II and III (Paris 1982–83), which contains articles by as many as sixty authors, all French-speaking. This is by far the best example to date of a specifically French style of theology, as distinct from that of theology originally published in the German or English languages.

BIBLIOGRAPHICAL NOTE

1. Chapter I resumes and completes the theme of a paper given at a conference at the Institut catholique in Paris. All the papers and lectures given at this conference have been published as *Le Déplacement de la théologie* (Paris, 1977), my paper appearing on pp. 51–64.

2. Chapter II reproduces the text of a lecture given at the C.E.R.I.T. (Centre d'études et de recherches interdisciplinaires en théologie) of the University of Strasbourg, entitled "La crise de l'herméneutique et ses conséquences pour la théologie," *RSR* 52 (1978), pp. 268–296.

3. Chapter III is the unpublished text of a lecture given within the framework of the 1982 program of the C.E.R.I.T. of Strasbourg. This program will eventually be published under the title of *La Théologie à l'épreuve de la vérité*.

4. Chapter IV resumes and completes an article originally published under the title "Liberté et responsabilité du théologien" in *Le Supplément* 133 (1980), pp. 282–293.

5. Chapter V reproduces the text of a contribution to the collected work *Le Témoignage* (a Roman colloquium edited by E. Castelli) (Paris, 1972) and published under the title *Le témoignage comme expérience et comme langage*.

6. Chapter VI reproduces the text of a contribution to the collected work *Religione e Politica* (a Roman colloquium edited by E. Castelli) (Padua, 1978).

7. Chapter VII is basically the text of an article that first appeared under the title "La crise moderne du théisme" in *Le Supplément* 122 (1977), pp. 357–379, although it has been radically changed. It was originally a lecture given at a colloquium between Jews, Christians and Muslims at the Abbey of Sénanque.

8. Chapter VIII reproduces the text of an article published in the review *Concilium: Conc(F)* 163 (1983), pp. 57–77.

9. Chapter IX resumes and completes the text of an address given at

297

a colloquium organized in May 1982 at the Institut catholique in Paris on the initiative of the Mission ouvrière. It was originally published in *RICP* 3 (1982), pp. 3–22.

10. Chapter X is a modified and completed version of a text initially published in *Le Supplément* 140 (1982), pp. 103–129. It was originally entitled "Les exigences d'une foi critique face à une culture non chrétienne" and was given as a lecture in August 1981 at Grottaferrata during the "Roman days" attended by the Dominicans working in Muslim countries.

11. Chapter XI resumes and completes the text of a contribution to a collected work, *Herméneutique de la sécularisation* (a Roman colloquium edited by E. Castelli) (Paris, 1976).

12. Chapter XII is a development of a hitherto unpublished text, the point of departure for which was a lecture given in Rome in September 1978 during the annual meeting of C.E.C.C. (Catholics in Europe concerned with China).

13. Chapter XIII resumes the unpublished text of a lecture given in May 1982 at the Third Islamic-Christian Conference at Tunis on "Islam and Christianity and Human Rights."

14. Chapter XVI resumes and completes the text of a paper written at the request of the Secretariat for Unity for the Catholic Memorandum on Mission addressed to the Central Committee with responsibility for preparing the Vancouver Conference of the World Council of Churches in July 1983.

15. The Epilogue is fundamentally the text of a lecture given in November 1981 to the Swiss Theological Society and also at Warsaw and Krakow. The original text first appeared in *RThPh* 114 (1982), pp. 227–245, *Rivista di teologia morale* 54 (1982), pp. 187–207 and the Polish journal *ZNAK* 337 (1982), pp. 1575–1593.